Basic Needlework

By the same author
Introduction to Needlework

Basic Needlework
Fifth Edition
(Metric)
by Winefride M. Bull

Formerly Head of the
Needlework Department at
Battersea College of Education
(Now Polytechnic of the South Bank)

Longman

Longman Group Limited
London
Associated companies, branches and representatives throughout the world

© Longman Group Ltd 1969, 1976, 1979
All rights reserved. No part of this publication may be reproduced, stored in a retrieval system, or transmitted in any form or by any means, electronic, mechanical, photocopying, recording, or otherwise, without the prior permission of the Copyright owner.

First published 1954
Second edition 1957
Third edition 1969
Fourth edition metric 1976
Fifth edition 1979
ISBN 0 582 33067 X

Printed in Hong Kong by
Sing Cheong Printing Co Ltd

Abbreviations

S.	selvedge or warp threads
W.	weft or woof threads
P.L.	pattern or fitting lines
R.S.	right side of garment or fabric
W.S.	wrong side of garment or fabric
C.B.	centre back
C.F.	centre front
mm	millimetre
cm	centimetre
m	metre

Reference is made to the same author's
Introduction to Needlework, Longman Group Limited.

Preface to fifth (metric) edition

When *Basic Needlework* was first published its length was restricted by a general shortage of paper. It was thought best to cover a limited number of fundamental techniques thoroughly with emphasis on quick methods, using paper patterns and sewing machines, with supporting topics.

The numbers of reprints and new editions have enabled me, encouraged by the Publishers, to make substantial alterations and additions. The book has kept pace with new developments in fibres and fabrics and their handling in needlework, the use of modern sewing machines, new and more advanced methods of work and the growing interest in pattern cutting. There have been new attitudes to clothing to be considered, changes in the kind and standard of work tackled in schools, including men's wear, the need to learn about planning and buying clothes as well as making, and of course, metrication. The title now covers a far wider field than was possible in the original book of 198 pages. Were the book, as it is now, to be presented for initial publication, it is more than probable that the Publishers would require it to be slashed by half for economic reasons!

This *fifth edition* incorporates some of the latest information on fabrics. The law on labelling the fibre content in textiles is explained, as well as the wide use of care labelling on anything made from fabrics or yarn. Extra diagrams have been put in and some old ones re-drawn. Several additional swing needle and other techniques are dealt with.

The aim now, as it was originally, is to give up-to-date information and methods with the kind of detail which makes independent work possible. With the knowledge that help is at hand, girls and boys can get on with the job without the frustration of waiting for attention in large classes. They can experience the satisfaction and pleasure which result from working it out for themselves.

I much appreciate the work of the artists, including Miss M. Moon who prepared the diagrams from my drawings.

W.M.B.

Contents

Preface

Abbreviations

Part I FOUNDATION METHODS

1 Introduction   1
Aims and scope of needlecraft

2 Equipment and fabrics   3
Equipment; tools and how to use them
Fabrics; general information; construction, finishes, qualities and uses of fabrics made from natural and man-made fibres. Treatment and handling in dressmaking

3 The use and adaptation of paper patterns   32
How to choose and understand a paper pattern
Alteration of paper patterns; how to take measurements and where to make the alterations to a pattern; adjusting length and width by tucks and insertions. Sizes and figure ranges

4 Placing patterns on fabric and cutting out   41
Preparing to cut out
The importance of graining fabrics and methods of graining; ways of folding fabric; important points to note in planning a 'lay of pattern'; how to place and pin patterns on to material
Cutting out the pattern; cutting crossway strips; ways of reducing fraying at cut edges

5 Marking pattern lines and tacking up   46
When to transfer pattern lines. Methods of transferring—dressmakers' carbon paper, tailors' tacks. Other pattern markings. Order of tacking up a garment. Round and Flat methods. Trousers

6 Sewing machines   51
Choice of a machine. Swing needle types
Setting the machine up for use—to wind the bobbin, set and thread the needle, test the stitch, alter the tensions

Directions for using machines. Learning to machine straight
Common faults. Cleaning and oiling
Machine attachments and accessories

7 Arrangement of fullness 62
How to make darts, tucks and gathers by hand and machine
Easing in fullness, pleating—treatment of seams and hems in pleats
Ways of setting in fullness. Elasticized edges

8 Seams 69
Choice of seams in regard to kind of clothing and material. Useful seams for modern fabrics and directions for making—open or plain, overlaid, french, double-stitched, piped seams
General points concerning the handling and making of seams

9 The finish of edges 88
Choice of finish—plain, strong, decorative
Hems—narrow, wide; adjusting the level of skirt hems; various finishes for skirt hems
Facings; general and special directions for straight, shaped and crossway
Binding; uses of crossway and straight; methods of fixing
Piping
Treatment of curves and angles for all finishes
Edges finished with lace

10 Openings 111
How to make them strong and flat, inconspicuous or smart. Choice of openings
Directions for making openings with a wrap—hem, faced and placket openings; openings without a wrap—faced, bound, zipped

11 Fastenings 129
Planning the kind and position
Buttonholes—worked and bound
Buttons—how to fix them
Loops
Eyelet holes, drawstrings and tie strings
Press studs, hooks, eyes and bars
Velcro

12 Stitches, plain and decorative   144
Stitches used in modern needlework and dressmaking; joining and neatening stitches—stitches for holding edges and folds in place
Foundation stitches used in embroidery and decorative stitching

13 Pressing   156
Secret of a professional finish; general points; how to use pressing equipment; pressing fabrics made from natural and man-made fibres; directions for pressing seams, darts, pleats, tucks, sleeves; how to remove shine

Charts   162
Outlines for making standard clothes
Method of estimating quantities of materials; usual choice of seams, openings and fastenings on children's and adults' clothing
Figure types and pattern sizes
Fibre content labelling of textile products

Part II CONSTRUCTING CLOTHES

14 Collars and cuffs   168
Flat and turnover collars; turn back and straight cuffs; details of making and attaching to achieve a good set

15 Sleeves   179
Sleeve styles. Making sleeves, long and short. Setting in sleeves professionally. Raglan and magyar styles. Underarm gussets

16 Waist finishes   187
Methods of finishing the waist edges of skirts and shorts with stiffened bands
Joining skirts and bodices together at the waist
Casings for elastic

17 Pockets and finishings   191
Patch, concealed, bound and welt pockets
The importance of finishing touches
Instructions for making ties, belts, belt carriers and hanging loops
Outline stitching

18	**Special dressmaking techniques**	200

Fabrics needing special treatment
Plaids, checks and stripes
Interfacings—choice, cutting and applying
Rouleau—uses, making loops
Lining—Fabrics to choose. Points in cutting, making and inserting
Lining a jacket, a dress, skirts

19	**Trousers**	221

Fabrics and styles
Measurements, pattern, cutting
Constructional details—order of making, seams, openings; method for invisible zip; waist edges; turn-ups

20	**Clothes for him**	228

Choice, fabrics, aims in making
Measurements and patterns
Quick techniques—yokes; machine-made buttonholes; fly-front opening; adhesive bonding
Fitting

21	**Pattern design, cutting and fitting**	238

The value of a knowledge of pattern making
Block patterns and their use
How to make a block pattern from trade patterns
The use of a bodice block to alter necklines, armholes; to make patterns for facings and collars
Introducing fullness into a pattern
Use of a sleeve block. Cuff patterns
Designing skirts
Fitting—preparation; main points; faults and how to make alterations; trousers; correcting after fitting

22	**Block patterns to individual measures**	263

Bodice and sleeve blocks for girls and women; alterations for children's sizes
Dress and skirt block
A knicker block for children and girls

Part III	**PLANNING AND MAINTENANCE OF CLOTHES AND HOUSEHOLD ARTICLES**	
	Fabric Care Labelling	
23	**Planning clothes**	276

Choosing clothes—how to spend and budget; colours and styles. What to wear; accessories

Clothes for children. Aims; fabrics, colours and designs
Choosing fabrics for making clothes at home. Tests.

24   **Maintenance of clothing and household articles**   292
The value of good grooming. General care of clothing.
Machine darning. Methods of repair. Use of elastic
yarn.

Index   304

Diagrams of tools for the workbox and a sewing machine
see end papers

Part I
Foundation Methods

1 Introduction

To make things is a source of enjoyment which never fails, and one which increases with experience. It is not everyone who is fond of dressmaking, but a homemaker is badly handicapped without the knowledge and practical sewing ability to look after the home and family. A girl who makes her own clothes also learns how to judge ready-made clothing and so get value for money.

For the learner, it is important to know what she hopes to achieve apart from the pleasure and satisfaction she will experience in needlecraft.

To learn needlecraft involves the following aims:

1. **To learn the correct way to use the tools needed for the craft.** Find out what tools are needed and have a look at a selection. Make your choice and learn how to use them. You would not expect to hit a tennis ball well if the racquet is wrongly held. The same principle applies to needles and scissors. Take care of the tools of the craft and practise using them as much as possible.

2. **To make clothes which are smart to look at because of colour, texture and shape, and which are practical for use.** This is more difficult because taste needs to develop through trial, error and experiment. Experience in choosing fabrics and designs has such a bearing on the final result. So improve your taste by observation of lovely clothes and craftsmanship in stores, exhibitions and dress shows. Study good fashion magazines. Be prepared to criticize your own work constructively and work for a steady improvement in skill and choice.

3. **To become sufficiently skilled to make articles which, though not necessarily perfect in workmanship, do not bear the imprint 'home-made'.** This entails some solid work in learning the craft. The learner has to study and practise methods of construction; to learn to work quickly and yet

not fall into slip-shod habits which are hard to eradicate and which prevent progress in skill. The secret of success in needlecraft lies as it does in any craft, in careful preparation and planning. A beginner cannot be expected to realise this and is often anxious to skip the preliminary work with unhappy results for the finished article. The craftswoman must be prepared to plan carefully, to think hard, and to give the proper attention to detail which good craftwork demands.

Needlecraft involves much more than learning skills. You will need to

KNOW ABOUT FABRICS
Success depends initially on the fabric chosen. The right fabric for the pattern starts you off well, but unless the fabric is suitable also for the kind of wear it will receive, time and skill used in making the article are wasted. The same applies if much time is spent on decorative work by hand or machine on fabric which will have a short life. There are a bewildering number of different fabrics but you will find that they fall into basic categories. Once you understand about them, confusion will disappear.

KNOW ABOUT BUYING AS WELL AS MAKING
Mostly it saves money to make at home but balance this against how long the job will take, the result you are likely to get, the pleasure of making and the possibly better quality of fabric you can use. Always cost the things you make and compare with similar clothes in shops. This will help develop judgment in regard to buying versus making, and to choosing clothes for good value.

USE QUICK MODERN METHODS OF WORK
Dressmaking aids can speed up construction and eliminate many hand-sewing chores. Carbon paper, crayon and thread marking gadgets are designed to save tailor tacking. Strong snap fasteners are sold which are hammered into the fabric. Button and belt making packs help with a professional finish. Modern interfacing fabrics are easy to apply and give crisp edges. Adhesive bonding webs can save sewing down hems and facings. Try them all out and assess their usefulness. A swing-needle machine on which you can neaten edges and make buttonholes is the biggest labour saver of all.

So go ahead, use brains as well as fingers and enjoy speedy and successful sewing.

2 Equipment

1. A sewing machine

Information on the choice and use of the sewing machine will be found in Chapter 6.

2. Pressing equipment

This should be at hand while needlework is being done because it will be needed constantly. The items should include the following:

AN IRON, preferably electric, or a steam iron. When the water in a steam iron is heated, steam comes from holes in the ironing plate. This saves using a damp cloth. The iron can also be used dry.

AN IRONING BOARD AND A SLEEVE BOARD. Both should be covered with flannel and have detachable calico covers, so that the flannel does not become scorched.

A WOODEN ROLLER. This should be about 5 cm in diameter, also covered with flannel and calico. It can be used for pressing seams and can make a substitute for a sleeve board. Both, however, will be found useful in the pressing equipment. Pressing pads and cushions are useful for pressing curved parts. See p. 159.

A CLOTHES BRUSH for use when pressing woollens.

DAMPING CLOTHS consisting of thin white cotton material, such as butter muslin or lawn.

3. Tools for the work box and how to use them

(Illustrated on end paper)
It is wise to buy tools of the best quality that can be afforded.

SCISSORS

1. A pair of shears for cutting out. These have one of the holes in the handle larger than the other, for convenient handling. Two or more fingers are put through the larger hole. The shears shown in the illustrations are a particularly good shape for cutting out, because in use one blade is level with the table and therefore the material is raised as little as possible during cutting.
2. A pair of scissors for trimming turnings and cutting threads will also be required, because the shears are too big to be convenient for such work. A suitable size would be 15 cm long.
3. A pair of embroidery scissors with fine, well-pointed blades.
4. Pinking shears are a good investment for neatening edges quickly.

A TAPE MEASURE

One should be chosen which is substantial and well marked on both sides. Cheap tape measures fray at the edges and become stretched.

NEEDLES

A good selection should be bought so that a needle of the correct size can be selected for the particular piece of work. The following kinds should be included:
1. Sewing needles in mixed sizes, either 'sharps' which are needles of ordinary length, or 'betweens' which are short needles and are preferred by some workers. Ball points (see p. 61) are for synthetic fabrics. The most useful sizes are 6, 7, 8 and 9. The higher numbers are finer needles.
2. Darning needles in mixed sizes. These are long needles with large eyes, and they may be bought in sizes corresponding to the sewing needles. Mixed packets are useful so that thick needles can be chosen for coarse work and fine ones for fine darning and tacking.
3. Crewel needles. These needles made specially for embroidery are of ordinary length and in the same sizes as sewing needles, but they have a large eye to take the embroidery thread.

THIMBLE

All expert craftswomen use a thimble and workers who have never been accustomed to use one will find that workmanship improves once it has become a habit to put one on for sewing. The thimble should fit comfortably and is worn on the middle finger of the hand which holds the needle. It is the side, not the top of the thimble, which supports the needle. The needle is held quite near the point so that it can be controlled in use, with the thumb below and the first finger on top.

PINS

Steel pins are the best because they are sharp and fine and do not spoil material. They are much more expensive than brass and other pins, but are worth the extra cost.

A STILETTO

A sharp instrument made of bone or steel, used for piercing holes and eyelets. A knitting needle can be used as a substitute, but as it is only slightly graduated at the point it is not as satisfactory as a well-shaped stiletto.

TAILORS' CHALK

Bought in flat pieces, white or coloured, for marking pattern lines and corrections.

DRESSMAKERS' CARBON PAPER

Used for transferring pattern markings to fabrics.

A MEASURING CARD

This can be made of stiff card, with notches cut at right angles to show required measurements, e.g. 1 cm, 3 mm. To use a measuring card for checking widths of turnings and hems is quicker than using a tape measure.

4. Haberdashery

SEWING THREADS

Reels will be bought as they are needed for use. The colour should be carefully matched and where there is difficulty in buying the exact shade, it should be remembered that a darker tone will work in more satisfactorily than a lighter one.

Cotton is sold on large and small reels in a variety of thicknesses, e.g. no. 20 is a thick thread for heavy work and fixing buttons; no. 40 is fairly coarse cotton for average household use; no. 100 is a very fine cotton for use on fine materials. Cotton can be bought with a satinised finish. Sylko types of machine twist have a very general use on all kinds of materials, because the mercerised finish has a good appearance. There are several thicknesses available and a comprehensive range of colours. Tacking cotton sold on large reels is a soft unglazed thread which is cheap to buy and easy to pull out without damaging the fabric.

Spun Terylene thread such as Trylko, Gossamer and Drima and other polyester threads are used principally on fabrics made from synthetic fibres.

Silk, for which there is little demand, is ideal on silk and woollens. The strength and elasticity of the thread give longer wear.

Heavy duty twist of various thicknesses is used for making buttonholes and for sewing on buttons on thick materials, e.g. Bold Stitch, Outline.

Mending wools, nylon mixtures and stranded cottons are bought in skeins or on cards.

FASTENINGS

An assortment of hooks and eyes, press studs and buttons will be needed. Zip fasteners will be bought as required.

BINDINGS

Bias binding consists of strips of material cut on the true cross, and with the edges folded over. This can be bought in cotton material, mercerised cotton which is soft and slightly glossy, viscose and nylon. Bias binding can be bought in approximately 5 to 8 m lengths on a card or by the metre.

Straight bindings, such as Prussian or Paris binding, are used for neatening raw edges on seams and hems.

Tape is sold in widths varying from 3 mm to 3 cm. It is made chiefly in black and white and in various qualities. The best and most durable kind is made of linen, but cotton tape is cheaper and more generally used. Tape is very strong and firm.

Other items of haberdashery, such as Velcro, skirt petersham and stiffening, will be bought as required.

5. Fabrics

Most fabrics for dress and household purposes are made from yarn. Yarn is made from fibres spun together to make threads. Thus, fabrics i.e. materials, start with fibres.

Fibres

Fibres are classified according to their sources as follows:

Natural vegetable fibres
These are taken from part of a plant, e.g. cotton fibres from the boll of cotton plants and linen fibres from the stalks of flax plants (further information, pp. 15, 16).

Natural animal fibres
Obtained from the coats of animals or are of animal origin, e.g. wool from the fleece of sheep; silk from the secretion of silk worms (further information, pp. 17, 19).

Natural fibres have to be collected, sorted and cleaned. After various processes they are spun or twisted together to make the yarn which is used in making fabric.

Man-made fibres
These are defined by the British Man-Made Fibres Federation as being 'produced entirely by the chemical treatment of certain raw materials, among them being wood-pulp, cotton linters, petroleum extracts, by-products of coal and casein'. In other words these man-made fibres can be made from vegetable, animal or mineral sources. The substances used are treated chemically so that they become liquids which can be forced at high pressure through tiny tubes in a spinneret to form fine filaments. These filaments are solidified in various ways according to the substances being used. They may be coagulated by passing them through a bath of acid, or passed through a hot air chamber to drive off solvents which have been used in the preparation of the liquid or spun into cold air so that the filaments solidify as they cool. After this the filaments are twisted together and stretched to give them strength and elasticity. The thickness of the yarn, which is dependent on the size of the holes in the spinneret and the number of filaments twisted together, is known as the denier of the yarn. A low denier indicates a light weight fine yarn, e.g. 15 denier stockings are made of a finer yarn than 30 denier. Colour is added either by adding dye to the spinning solution (spun-dyed) or by dyeing the yarn after spinning.

Man-made fibres may be classified as follows:

REGENERATED CELLULOSE FIBRES where the liquid for spinning is made from a vegetable source, e.g. wood pulp, cotton linters, which produce viscose fibres, acetate, and triacetate.

SYNTHETIC FIBRES where the substances are entirely man-made from mineral sources. Fibres are again subdivided into groups which take their name from the chemical substances and the method used in their preparation. Some of the most important are the following:

Polymide fibres to make Nylon, Celon, Bri-Nylon, Enkalon.
Polyester fibres—Terylene, Crimplene, Trevira, Lirelle.
Acrylic fibres—Acrilan. Courtelle. Orlon. Dralon.
Elastomeric or polyurethane fibres—Lycra. Spanzelle.

Yarns
Fibres, whether natural or man-made can be used for yarns in two forms, *staple* or *filament*.

Staple yarns
Staple fibre is the natural length of natural fibres, e.g. 2 cm to 5 cm cotton fibres. These are spun into yarn. Man-made filament can be cut into short lengths to make staple fibres and then spun in a similar way to natural fibres.

Filament yarns
Continuous filaments are the long smooth threads extruded through spinnerets which can be made any length desired. The only natural filament is silk. Filament yarns make finer and more lustrous yarns than threads produced by staple fibres.

When buying fabric or clothing it is a good plan to find out from which group of fibres a fabric is made. If one knows the characteristics and qualities of that group, then one can assess the use to which the fabric can be put and the care required in its use. For example, viscose fibres are weaker wet than dry, therefore great care is needed in handling viscose fabrics during laundering. Polymide fibres are very strong. Therefore, fabrics made from them can be expected to give hard wear.

Treatment in manufacture of man-made yarns
The following are some of the ways in which yarns made from man-made fibres can be treated to affect handle (the technical term for the feel of a fabric), appearance or qualities of fabric.

BULKED YARN
The yarn is blown up and fluffed so that it holds more air and becomes much softer, fluffier, warmer and more absorbent, e.g. Banlon is bulked nylon. Taslan is a process used for bulking a number of different fibres.

CRIMPED YARN

Yarn is crimped and heat set in its crimp so that it becomes stretchy and elastic. Helanca is an example of stretch yarns of crimped nylon or Terylene. Yarns may also be textured in this way by looping and curling instead of crimping.

FILAMENT SHAPE VARIATION

The tubes in the spinnerets through which the spinning liquid is forced may be varied in shape, e.g. instead of a cylindrical tubular shape it may be made triangular or trilobal with the result that yarns have edges or curves which catch and reflect the light. This results in high lustre or glitter, e.g. glitter nylon, and the effect is permanent. A trilobal shape also gives a high bulk effect as in yarns used for heavy knits.

Other terms in connection with yarns

PLY-YARNS—a number of yarns twisted together to make a thicker yarn as in knitting yarn—2 ply—4 ply.

BLENDED YARNS—two or more different kinds of fibre spun together to make one yarn, e.g. cotton and wool fibres spun together, worsted fibres and Terylene (in staple form) spun together, nylon and Tricel spun together—Tricelon.

The reasons for making blended yarns may be (1) to give a better appearance of handle—cotton/vincel blend gives a softer fabric than all cotton; (2) to improve washability—cotton and wool wash better than all wool; (3) to improve wearing qualities—wool and nylon wear better than all wool, or (4) to decrease cost—wool and acrilan is cheaper than all wool.

Making yarn into fabric

There are a number of ways of making yarn into textiles of which the main are the following:

WEAVING   KNITTING   BONDING

Weaving

Fabric is woven from two sets of yarns, the selvedge or warp which run lengthwise, and the weft or woof which are woven across them. Material is woven on a hand or machine loom, and the selvedge threads are placed in position on the loom first. The weft thread is wound on a shuttle, and it is 'thrown' across the selvedge threads passing over and under alternate threads if a plain weave is required. To simplify the work, the loom is constructed in such a way that all the selvedge threads which must have the shuttle passed under them at one passage, are raised together leaving a clear path for the shuttle.

The selvedge or warp threads are subjected to considerable strain during this process and subsequently when the woven fabric is wound on a cylinder at the front of the loom as it is finished. Stronger threads are sometimes used for the selvedge threads because of this strain they have to undergo. For this reason the selvedge way of the material is both stronger and more tightly woven than the weft. The selvedge itself is the edge at each side of the material and is more closely woven than the rest.

The weft or woof threads which are taken backwards and forwards across the selvedge threads form the width of the material, e.g. 70 cm, 90 cm approximately for single width materials, 115 cm, 140 cm, 150 cm, 180 cm for double width materials. Diagram 3. Many fabrics previously woven 90 cm wide are now being woven in widths between 107 cm and 120 cm because these are more economical for placing patterns.

There are certain basic methods of weaving on which innumerable variations are possible.

BASIC WEAVES
Plain weave
Here the weft and warp yarns (picks and ends*) pass over and under each other regularly and at right angles as in darning (see diagram 170). The more closely and tightly the threads are woven together the stronger and firmer the fabric will be. Sheeting, linen, sail cloth, cotton prints, silk, nylon, chiffon are examples of fabric woven with a plain weave.

Basket or hopsack weave is really a variation of the plain weave. Weft threads pass over and under two warp threads regularly for two rows and then the arrangement is alternated in the next two rows, so giving a chequered effect and an interesting texture to the surface. There are many variations of this weave. Diagram 1.

Twill weave
The weft thread passes over and under one, two or more

* Technical terms used in the weaving industry.

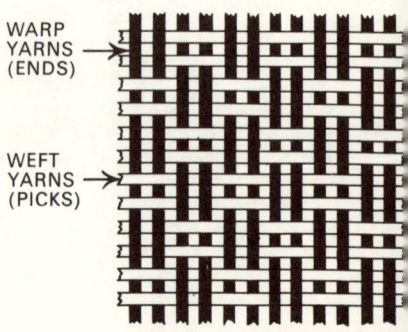

1. Basket or Hopsack weave

warp threads and each row begins the series one thread along to the right or left so that a diagonal line or wale appears on the surface. The direction of the wale is up to the right in wool fabrics and to the left in cotton and this helps in deciding the right and wrong sides of a piece of fabric. Diagram 2(i).

Twill sheeting, and denim are examples of cotton twills. Surahs are made from silk or synthetics. Cavalry twill is made from wool.

Satin weave
The weft or warp threads pass over more threads than are picked up. The resulting long threads on the surface give a smooth effect which gives lustre to the fabric, e.g. cotton sateen, cotton satin, silk satin, rayon satin. Diagram 2 (ii).

Pile weave
An extra thread is woven into the warp or weft of a plain weave background to make loops which may be left uncut, as in towelling, or cut, as in velvets, corduroys, velveteens. The closer the loops or pile the better the cloth. Pile fabrics have an 'up' and 'down' and this factor must be considered when cutting out (see p. 43), so that the pile lies in the same direction in each section.

Leno weave
The warp yarns are twisted between each set of weft yarns. Both warp and weft are woven with very few threads to the inch so that the fabric is very light and openwork. This weave is used for nets and gauzes.

MIXTURE FABRICS are those in which different kinds of yarn are *woven* together, e.g. cotton warp and wool weft, Terylene warp and linen weft.

The reasons for mixing yarns are similar to those for blending them. Note the difference between mixtures and blends — see p. 9.

To discover the selvedge and weft way of a piece of fabric:
(a) Hold a piece of straight material between thumb and first finger of each hand about 3 cm apart. Give a sharp pull along one set of threads. Repeat in the opposite direction. The sound given from the selvedge direction has a higher pitch than the sound given by the weft.
(b) If it is found difficult to distinguish the sound, hold as before and pull steadily. Note the amount of give in both

numbers show beginning series in three rows
weft passing under two warp yarns

(i). Twill weave

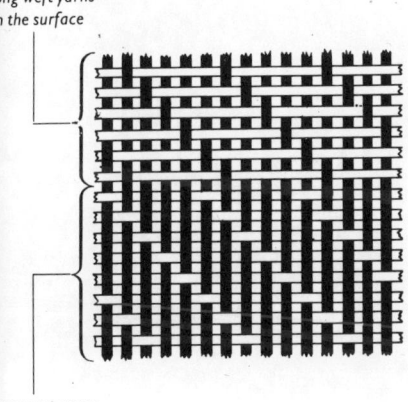

long weft yarns on the surface

long warp yarns on the surface

(ii). Satin weave—two types

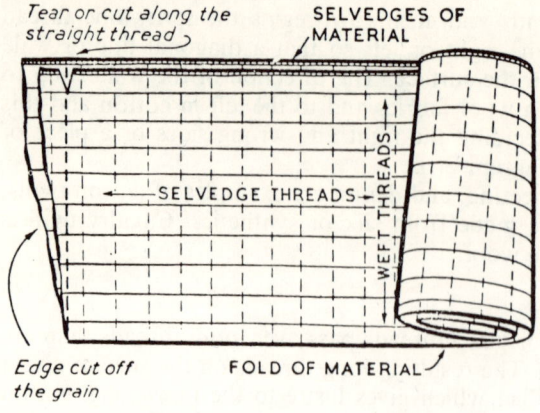

3. A length of material to show the direction of the threads and how to grain one end

directions. Because selvedge threads are more tightly woven the fabric will stretch less in this direction.

KNITTED FABRIC

There are two kinds of machine knitted fabric often made in tubular form:

WEFT or CIRCULAR KNITS where loops are formed horizontally (Diagram 170). These have good stretch in both directions. *Single knit jerseys* are soft and supple with a definite R.S. and W.S., like stocking stitch in hand knitting. *Double knits*, made on two sets of needles are firmer and the R.S. and W.S. are not so obvious.

WARP KNITS have vertical rows of chain loops stitched together. There is stretch across the fabric but only a little give vertically. On the W.S. there is a pattern of horizontal lines. Warp knits are used for tricots and lacy fabrics in lightweight yarns such as nylon, Trevira. Elastomeric fibres are incorporated into the construction of stretch knits.

Bonding

This non-woven type of fabric has some of the properties of woven cloth but is much cheaper to produce. Fibres, mostly synthetic and some with a low melting point, are spread out evenly in a web with the fibres in any direction. Heat is applied causing the fibrous mass, the fleece, to become sticky and bond. When dried, the resulting fabric has a paperlike texture. Sometimes the fleece is laid on a thin scrim backing which gives added strength and a bonding substance is applied. The chief use of non-woven bonded fabric is for interfacings, e.g. Vilene, but it has also been developed for 'paper' fabric. See p. 28.

Bonding also refers to a process used to join two layers of fabric together to give a two-sided fabric, e.g. lace bonded to an acetate lining, and for reversible cloths.

Finishes which can be applied to fabric

Fabrics may have finishes applied to them at some stage in their production which will improve their qualities in various ways. Some of the most important finishes are:

PERMANENT SHEEN gives a glossy surface which resists soiling, e.g. Everglaze. Careful washing is necessary to preserve the sheen.

EASY-CARE finishes give fabric a drip-dry quality so that no ironing, or only minimum ironing, is needed, e.g. Calpreta Care-Free—Minicare.

CREASE RESISTANCE is given by treatment with resin finishes, e.g. fabric is Tebilized. This also results in making fabric springy and more difficult to press in making up, but improves the appearance during wear.

SHRINK RESISTANT finishes control the amount of shrinkage which will occur in washing, e.g. Sanforized, Calpreta Non-Shrink, Rigmel, Dylan are all processes of shrink resistance.

WATER REPELLENT finishes make fabrics resist staining or water marking, such as on silk and velvet, e.g. Calpreta Stain Resistant. This may be durable or renewable.

WATER-PROOFING renders fabric impervious to water and is used for rainwear.

MOTH-PROOFING discourages moth from attacking fabric. A well known process which preserves woollen fabrics for life is Mitin. Washing and dry cleaning do not destroy the finish.

FLAME RESISTANT finishes prevent fabric from flaring and burning up quickly, e.g. Proban applied to cottons, Flare-free applied to nylons. An untreated cotton nightdress, e.g. of winceyette or brushed cotton can flare up and burn to cinders in 15 seconds. When treated, the burning is much slower and may give time to save terrible burns or loss of life. A law (Consumer Protection Act 1961) has been passed to make it an offence to sell ready-made children's nightwear made of untreated fabric. When night clothing, including dressing gowns is made at home for children or old people, it is *most important* to use fabric which has a flame resistant finish. Trimmings used should also have this finish. Washing of treated fabric must be such that the finish is preserved so the maker's instructions should be followed.

MILIUM FINISH is used for backing lining fabrics with a thin deposit of aluminium. This insulates against cold and is useful for lining winter coats and skirts and curtains.

PERMANENT PLEATING. Pleats are heat set and remain in after washing. Only fabrics which have been woven with a certain minimum percentage of yarn having thermoplastic properties (see p. 23) can be pleated in this way, e.g. wool and Terylene. *Durable Press* combines chemical finish and heat-setting to make edges and creases permanently sharp, e.g. Koratron finishes.

PERMANENT STIFFENING is a process which gives semi-stiffness to fabrics by bonding them with heat to an acetate fabric.

TEXTURED FINISHES. Fabrics can be given an interesting patterned surface after weaving, e.g. by *(a)* embossing—heated calendars (circular ironing machines) press a pattern into the surface; *(b)* by shrinking part of the yarns a rippled surface is achieved, as in seersucker, *(c)* by brushing to give a fluffy softness, as in brushed rayon, brushed cotton, brushed nylon.

Patterned material
There are two ways in which a pattern or design may be made on material.
1. The pattern is printed on to the fabric after it has been woven, in a way similar to the method of printing newsprint on to paper. The design is engraved on rollers which are covered with dye, and the material passes under the rollers so that the design is stamped on the fabric. Often the material has to pass under several different rollers because one part of the pattern is superimposed upon another and the design is built up of many colours. When buying printed materials it is wise to see that the pattern is printed straight with the threads of the material to avoid difficulties in cutting out. This is especially important if the design contains stripes, lines or checks. In most prints, as material patterned in this way is called, the

design shows more clearly on the right than on the wrong side of the fabric.

2. The pattern is woven into fabric by using yarns of different colours in the looms, and weaving the fabric and pattern together. There is no question in this case of the design not being true with the threads of the fabric. It is easy to distinguish by which method a piece of material has been patterned, by looking at it closely on both sides.

When buying patterned material it should be noticed if the design has an 'up and down', e.g. flowers with stalks placed in one direction only, or a very large pattern. In both cases extra material must be bought, because it will be more extravagant in cutting than a plain material or 'all over' or small design (see Chapter 4).

Fabrics made from natural vegetable fibres
The yarn for these is made from part of a plant.

COTTON
Most cotton fabrics are strong, smooth, cheap to buy, hard-wearing and with excellent washing properties. The yarn is made from the seed hairs inside the boll of the cotton plant, grown in many countries, including India, Egypt, America and the Indies.

The finest and best are Egyptian and Sea Island cottons from the West Indies. The cotton bolls are picked by hand or machine and put into ginning machines to separate the seed hairs from the seeds which are used to make cotton seed oil, an ingredient of soaps. The small fluffy ends of fibres left in the machine are called cotton linters and are used for cotton wool and making man-made fibres. The seed hairs are baled for export all over the world. In Britain, Lancashire is the centre of the cotton industry where the raw cotton is spun into yarn and woven into fine fabrics such as lawn, cambric, voile, organdie, muslin, nets and medium weight fabrics, such as calico, cotton satin, ginghams, poplin, winceyette, denim, towelling and needlecord.

Cotton fabrics are very flammable, especially if the surface is fluffy and they need special treatment when used for nightwear for children and old people (see Proban p. 13). Cotton fibres are not easily affected by alkalies, therefore fabrics made from them can stand bleaching and strong detergents in laundering. Acids tend to weaken the fibres so when used for stain removal quick neutralisation with an alkaline solution is necessary as soon as the stain disappears. The fibres are strong, even stronger when wet so that they can stand heavy washing methods without being spoilt. Cotton is a good conductor of heat so the fabric feels cool and is cool to wear. Although the fibres are absorbent closely woven fabrics are not comfortable worn next to the skin. Undergarments such as vests and pants made of knitted or cellular cotton are more absorbent because of the loose weave and also fit snugly with less bulk. Cotton knits are good for sportswear.

Cotton takes dyes and finishes well. Mercerised cotton has been treated with caustic soda to give a glossy appearance. Other finishes given are a brushed surface, shrink resistance, crease resistance, permanent glaze, permanent crispness, water repellency, easy-care, embossing and flame-proofing.

The right side of cotton is normally slightly smoother than the wrong side. The difference can be seen by placing a piece of material on the back of the hand and holding it up to the light. Most cotton fabrics are woven 90 cm wide but some are now made 115 cm wide.

Because of the hard-wearing qualities of cotton, it is widely used for household articles, underclothes and children's clothing, summer dresses, skirts, trousers, shirts, blouses, overalls and handkerchiefs.

LINEN

Generally, linen materials are very smooth fabrics which are stronger and have a better appearance than cotton. Linen yarn is made from fibres of the flax plant which is grown in France, Belgium and Ireland. The growth and manufacture of flax is expensive because much of the work in preparing the stems of the plant ready for spinning has to be done by hand which is a lengthy and costly business.

After the flax is picked the seed hairs are combed from the stalks (rippling). The seeds are used for linseed oil and the stalks are soaked in water to soften them (retting). This process was originally done in water at lake sides, now it is done mostly indoors in specially prepared tanks. After retting, the next process is scutching, when the stalks are crushed between rollers in a machine to loosen and separate the long flax fibres from the stalks. Short broken fibres are used to make tow for ropes. Flax yarn is not easily harmed by alkalies, is very strong and washes well with heavy washing methods.

Linen is a beautifully cool material because it is a very good conductor of heat and is very absorbent. Finely woven, it is suitable for baby clothes and handkerchiefs. Heavier weaves are used for household goods, table linens and towels, and dress materials. In fact, linen can be used for the same purposes as cotton where it can be afforded, because it washes and wears even better. A disadvantage to linen is that it crushes readily, but it may be made crease resistant by the application of resin finishes during manufacture.

Other finishes applied may be stain and water repellency. Linen blends very well with other fibres, e.g. with cotton or Terylene or with nylon (Nylin—a furnishing fabric containing linen and nylon).

Linen has a similar surface on both sides of the material, but the side on which it is ironed when damp will have a high gloss and the reverse side a dull finish. For some articles a high gloss is an advantage because it lasts clean longer, e.g. on table napkins, but on others some people prefer to have the dull surface which shows up the beauty of the weave, e.g. on tray cloths and mats. A needlewoman will find that linen frays more readily than cotton.

A substitute linen is made with hemp grown in the United States and with jute grown in India. The stems of these plants are prepared in a similar manner to flax, are very strong and are used ordinarily to make ropes and coarse cloths such as hessian.

Fabrics made from natural animal fibres
In these, hairs from the coats of animals are used for the yarn.

WOOL
Most materials made of wool are soft, warm, have a fluffy surface and absorb moisture easily. Woollen yarn is spun from wool shorn from the coats of sheep, goats and rabbits, many of which are reared especially for the purpose in Britain, Australia and New Zealand. Extremely soft yarns are made from camels, goats and rabbits e.g. camelhair, alpaca, vicuna, cashmere, mohair, angora.

After the fleeces are sorted according to quality and length of hairs (these qualities vary according to the breed of sheep and the position of the wool on the fleece itself) the wool is scoured to remove impurities. Then the fibres are separated by carding and straightened by combing until they form a sliver, rather like a thick soft rope. The sliver is drawn and pulled out until it is the thickness of string and is known as the roving which is wound on to bobbins ready for spinning and twisting into yarn to make:

1. Woollen fabrics such as flannel, wincey, woollen crêpes and dress woollens, tweeds and jersey cloths;
2. Worsted fabrics such as serge, gaberdine, suitings and other firm closely woven materials with a smoother surface than the soft fabrics in the previous class. Worsted fabrics also feel firmer than woollens. Special quality long fibres are selected for the yarn and the combing process is continued until the straightened fibres lie evenly together so that a comparatively smooth yarn is produced. A high twist also contributes to the characteristic appearance and handle of worsted fabrics. The worsteds are the harder wearing of the two and are used for men's and women's suits, skirts, trousers, shorts and coats.

Wool fibres have a natural crimp which gives elasticity. As a result, woollen fabrics shed creases quickly and keep their shape. The surfaces of wool fibres are covered with scales. These irregular surfaces leave spaces which hold air and since air is a bad conductor of heat, wool feels warm and woollen clothing keeps in the heat of the body. These scales are also a factor which cause wool to felt because if rubbed in washing, they can lock together and cause a matted feltlike appearance. Wool is quickly harmed by alkalies and to a lesser extent by acids; the fibres are not as strong as vegetable fibres and they shrink readily. Therefore, gentle washing methods must be used. Though simple to wash, wool is more readily spoilt by bad washing than any other fabric. Wool is not highly flammable and tends to smoulder rather than to flame. A new process is being developed which reduces flammability during the preparation of the fibres, making them flame resistant. Moths love feeding on wool especially if its soiled so that care must be taken to prevent attack unless the wool has had a moth-proofing finish. Yorkshire is the chief centre of the woollen industry in Great Britain.

Fabrics made from pure wool are more expensive than cotton or linen. Wool is often combined with other fibres to make a less expensive cloth, e.g. wool woven with cotton or viscose. Such material does not feel as soft as a cloth made entirely of wool. Fabric made from pure new wool can have the trademark *Woolmark* stamped upon it.

The right side of any fabric made from wool is fluffier than the wrong side. Woollen fabrics are generally made in a narrow single width, e.g. 70 cm or in double widths.

The comfort and warmth of wool make it suitable for

winter underclothing, baby and children's clothing and warm outer wear for people of all ages. Many household articles and furnishings too, are made from wool. Finishes can be given to wool to improve its practical use, such as shrink resistance, shower-proofing and water repellency. Many woollens are now machine washable.

SILK

The majority of silk fabrics have a beautiful soft, glossy surface, drape into lovely folds and do not crush. Silk is made from the secretion of silk worms, which hardens into a fine silky thread winding round the worm to form a case or cocoon. The cocoons are steamed to kill the grub inside and soaked in hot water to remove the gummy coating. The end of the thread on each cocoon is loosened and carefully wound off. It may be up to 600 m long. Threads from several cocoons are reeled together into yarn which is woven into fabrics of different weaves and thicknesses. Some of the fabrics produced are crêpes, jap silk, satin, foulards, brocades, chiffon, ninon, taffeta, velvet. Short threads and pieces are used as staple fibre to make spun silk. This is a cheaper silk to buy and has a less smooth surface than silk made from the long unbroken thread. Wild silk worms produce a coarser thread than the cultivated worms, resulting in material known as shantung or tussore which was originally made in China. Silk worms are reared chiefly in France, Italy, China and Japan, and these countries have become famous for silks.

Alkalies damage silk but it has some resistance to acids, e.g. silk brocade curtains are not quickly affected by acid fumes in the atmosphere but they will spoil if washed in water containing soda. Silk is also damaged by heat, so gentle washing methods must be used and a cool iron for pressing. The fibre itself is wonderfully strong and elastic and is an excellent conductor of heat which makes it warm to the touch in cold weather and cool in summer.

Silk is a very expensive material because the silk worms require great care to rear them, and the preparation of the thread for weaving is delicate work requiring highly skilled craftsmen. Silk can be used for underwear because it is fine, strong, warm, washes and wears well and absorbs perspiration readily but is too costly for most people. The lovely appearance and texture of silk make it an ideal fabric for dresses and blouses for special occasions, for scarves, ties, evening wear, and for curtains, carpets and furnishings in luxuriously furnished rooms.

Fabrics made from man-made fibres See p. 7
These are made from vegetable, animal or mineral sources.

Man-made regenerated cellulose fibres (i.e. from vegetable sources)

VISCOSE

Fibres are made by the viscose process from cellulose obtained chiefly from wood pulp. This substance is treated chemically so that it becomes a liquid which can be forced through tiny tubes at high pressure to form fine filaments. These are passed through a bath of acid to harden, stretched, twisted together and woven into fine smooth fabrics or cut into staple fibre and spun into yarn to make softer, more bulky fabrics. Viscose fibres are produced with a lustrous or a matt surface and have fair absorbency. A variety of fabrics are made from viscose yarn with surfaces which have something of the appearance of silk, e.g. crêpes, satin, shantung, taffetas, velvets, and others which have a similar appearance to wool, e.g. fibro, and yet others which are difficult to distinguish from cotton and linen. It is important to remember that these fabrics do not possess all the qualities of the vegetable and animal fibres they imitate. The fibres blend well with nylon, polyester and natural fibres.

Care is required in laundering fabrics made from viscose yarn. The fibres lose much of their strength when wet and scorch in contact with a hot iron. They need a hand-hot wash and rinse and a medium hot iron on slightly damp fabric. Viscose fabrics do not give the long service of cotton or silk, but they have a better appearance than cotton and are inexpensive to buy.

Viscose may feel cold to the touch, may crush easily, and is often a springy material for the needlewoman to handle. Fabrics fray quickly at cut edges, especially the coarser weaves.

Viscose is not the best choice for children's clothing because it does not stand up to the hard wear and washing their clothes receive. For the same reason it is not as satisfactory as other materials for household goods. The attractive appearance and texture combined with its comparatively low cost, make it a popular fabric for all types of clothing, linings, braids, ribbons, house linen and furnishings. It is particularly useful for adults' clothing.

Recent developments are enabling chemists to modify fibres to give them some of the qualities of other fibres.

Some of these modified viscose fibres are the following:

Evlan—a heavy denier crimped viscose used for carpets.

Vincel—similar in handle and appearance to fine quality cottons. It is used for knitted and woven textiles and is often blended with polyesters and natural fibres for shirts, sheetings, rainwear. It does not lose strength when wet.

Sarille—viscose with a soft wool-like handle made from crimped staple yarn. Sometimes the fabric is given a brushed surface. Sarille has good crease recovery and is used for dresses, nightwear, suits, blankets and fleece linings.

Durafil—a high strength viscose used with other fibres to improve their wearing qualities, e.g. with wool for blazers and uniforms.

Darelle—refers to viscose which has been given a flame retardent quality during manufacture of the fibres. Its main use is for toys and curtain fabrics.

ACETATE

These are made from cotton linters or wood pulp treated with chemicals to form cellulose acetate. The spinning solution is spun into warm air where the filaments solidify as the solvent evaporates. They are then stretched and slightly twisted and the yarn wound on to bobbins ready for weaving.

Fabrics produced from acetate yarn, both woven and knitted, are soft, silk-like and drape well and include satins, tricot, jersey, taffeta, brocades used for dresses, linings and soft furnishings. Many acetate fabrics are popular for lingerie because the fibres are absorbent, fairly non-static and the delicate fabrics very attractive. Although they can give good wear acetate fabrics are not as hard wearing as fabrics made from some other fibres.

Acetate fabrics melt in contact with a medium hot iron which would not harm viscose fabric. Hot water also softens acetate fabrics and they are easily damaged by acids and alkalies. Therefore, careful, gentle laundering methods are necessary (warm water, squeezing and a cool iron) to preserve the fabric and retain the attractive surface and handle. It should be ironed damp.

Dicel has special strength, colour fastness and washability and is used mainly for satins for linings. Some Dicel is made flame-resistant, e.g. Lo-flam Dicel.

Lansil and *Lancola* are made from acetate fibres.

Fabrics are also produced from acetate fibres which have had special treatment to give them certain qualities not possessed by ordinary acetate fibres of which some are as follows:

TRIACETATE

This is similar chemically to acetate and is used to make fabrics such as *Tricel, Arnel, Rhonel*. The fibres have some of the advantages of fabrics such as nylon and Terylene, though cheaper to produce. They are stronger fibres and soften at a higher temperature than ordinary acetate fibres. Tricel can be permanently pleated and made crease-resistant; it has low absorbency, it dries quickly, needs little, if any, ironing and does not attract moth. It has not the strength of nylon and since it is not much stronger than viscose or acetate, Tricel does not give hard wear. The yarns make exceptionally attractive fabrics, soft or crisp and are woven into surahs, foulards, jersey, piques, shantungs, taffetas, poplins, brocades and lightweight suitings which are used for skirts, trousers and blouses, dresses and curtains. In staple form the yarn can be used for wadding and spun into yarn for fabrics with a very soft handle used for both under and outer wear. Some Tricel fabrics are given a brushed surface. Yarns are often blended with wool, nylon, viscose, cotton or linen e.g. Tricelon, a blend with nylon.

Synthetic fibres (entirely man-made from mineral sources)

POLYMIDE FIBRES

Air, coal and water are the simple substances from which more complicated ones are obtained. These are used to form still more complicated substances called polymers, from which *polymide fibres* are made for nylon, Celon, Brinylon, Enkalon, Ultron. The polymer is formed at high temperatures, sets on cooling to a solid mass and is then cut into chips which are melted to a fluid and pumped through fine spinning jets to form filaments which harden as they cool in the air. To give them strength and elasticity they are stretched before being twisted with other filaments to make yarn for weaving and knitting.

NYLON

Nylon was the first entirely man-made fibre to be manufactured and it is used to make fabrics in many weights of outstanding strength. It is especially suitable for making fine, soft, delicate, transparent materials such as voile, organza, chiffon, seersucker, but it is used, too, for heavier weights and opaque weaves such as satins, brocades, dress crêpes, taffetas, tricots, jerseys and velvets of dress weight and for upholstery purposes. The fabrics are lustrous, drape well and rival the appearance of silk. Nylon filament yarn is also produced as staple fibre and spun in a manner similar to that used for woollen yarns. The resulting fabric is called spun nylon and in texture is comparable to woollen cloths and suitings. Nylon is also mixed with other yarns, e.g. nylon with wool, nylon with silk. This produces hardwearing cloths if the nylon is woven in both the warp and the weft. Nylon woven in one direction only may cut the weaker fibre and cause the fabric to split.

Nylon is damaged by strong acids and continuous exposure to light. Therefore, it is not suitable for curtain nets. There is a tendency for white nylon to turn a yellowish colour, but both these disadvantages have been overcome in some of the later developments in the production of nylon, e.g. *Celon, Enkalon.* Nylon yarns can be bulked, made with a permanent glitter (see p. 9) and crimped to make stretch yarns for swimsuits, trousers and upholstery covers.

Nylon yarns are light in weight and wonderfully strong, resisting both tearing and rubbing wear. Therefore they have wide and increasing use in making fabrics for clothing subjected to hard wear—shirts, underwear, overalls; for luxury wear—fine lingerie, fur fabric coats; for household goods—sheets, pillowcases, and in industry for conveyor belts, tow-ropes, tarpaulins, sacks, etc. Nylon is very elastic and has the property of being thermoplastic, enabling it to be set with heat and moisture into a shape which will be permanent. Nylon fabric can be permanently pleated and it is possible, in machinery designed for the purpose, to weld seams and buttonholes instead of stitching them. As a result of these qualities, the yarn is used for stockings, socks and other knitted garments. Too hot water for washing may set creases permanently. Hand-hot water is recommended and when light ironing is necessary, a cool iron.

Because the fibres do not absorb moisture readily, the fabric dries very quickly indeed. This fact impairs its value for garments worn next to the skin unless the yarn is 'bulked' or woven in a way to make it more absorbent. Nylon does not feel warm, and certain close, smooth weaves tend to exclude the air. This fact should be remembered when choosing nylon for underwear and for closely fitting garments, as it may prevent the free passage of air to the body and thus cause discomfort. Nylon, because it holds so little moisture, is a good insulator for electricity and therefore is inclined to retain slight charges of electricity. This is called static electricity which attracts and holds dust and dirt, making the fabric soil quickly. Courtaulds and I.C.I. have developed special nylon fibres with permanent anti-stat qualities incorporated during the manufacture of the fibres e.g. Anti-stat Celon, where clinging and crackling is much reduced. Unless the dirt is removed frequently, the nylon becomes discoloured. It has been found that certain detergents lessen the power of the fabrics to hold electrical charges and make it easier to keep garments clean and fresh. Warm or hand-hot water should be used.

Nylon resists creasing and therefore requires little or no ironing. When light ironing is necessary a cool iron must be used. Other characteristics are that it does not shrink, cannot be attacked by moth, does not rot or hold mildew, is not affected by mild bleaches, dilute acids, or solvents used in cleaning and it is not highly flammable. The price is moderate and compares with cotton and viscose.

A particular boon to the housewife is the knowledge that the life of fabrics made from polymer yarn is so long that, apart from damage caused by accidents, or faulty stitching, mending will not be needed.

The names *Bri-lon* and *Bri-nylon* are registered trade marks which show that the goods are made of British nylon. Bri-lon refers to articles made of bulked yarns and brushed fabrics and Bri-nylon to merchandise made from standard filament yarns. *Celon* is a later development of nylon. *Perlon* is the German form of nylon.

POLYESTER FIBRES
These are made from polymers based on petroleum products and spun in a similar way to nylon to make such fabrics as Terylene, Dacron, Trevira, Crimplene, and Lirelle. Polyester fibres are excellent for blending and mixing with other fibres, to improve appearance and comfort.

Terylene is the registered name given to the yarn manufactured by Imperial Chemicals Ltd. Fabrics made from it have many of the qualities of nylon but are rather softer and warmer to handle, e.g. lawn, crepon. The yarn has great tensile strength and resists abrasion; it is resilient and does not crease, but it has not the elasticity of nylon.

For this reason Terylene clothing keeps its shape well but, until recently, the yarn could not be used for stockings, although in staple form, and mixed with an elastic yarn, such as wool, it is used for socks. Now, the yarn is specially treated to give it elasticity so that it can be used alone. Like nylon, the fibre holds very little moisture, can be dried quickly, requires practically no ironing and then only with a cool iron, does not shrink and has similar powers of holding static electricity. It is unaffected by moth, mildew, acids, bleaches and most detergents and dry cleaning agents. Perspiration, too, has no harmful effects. All these qualities make Terylene valuable for clothing. Moreover, the yarn is not harmed by salt water and so it is useful for swimwear, fishing lines, sail cloth and ropes. Sunlight, through glass, does not weaken Terylene fabrics and since they drape well, can be used for curtains and furnishings. With steam and pressure, Terylene fabrics can be heat-set into creases which last through wear and washing; consequently they can be permanently pleated. Filament yarn is used for fine materials similar in type to those made from nylon yarns. Staple fibre is used to make cloths with a wool-like texture and is frequently mixed with wool and other yarns to make fabrics of various weights and textures. It is used also for filling for pillows and quilts. The price is comparable with that of nylon. For industrial purposes Terylene is widely used because of its strength and powers of resistance to chemicals.

Crimplene is a modified Terylene filament with low stretch which is used to make high bulk yarn. It is used very successfully for knitwear and double jersey because of its attractive texture and drip dry qualities. Both woven and jersey fabrics are made into fashionable dresses, coats and suits for all seasons and for children's wear. The makers recommend that Crimplene garments should be turned inside out for washing because this reduces the tendency of the fabric to 'pill' (small balls form on the surface). They should be squeezed in hand-hot water and allowed to drip dry.

Dacron is manufactured in America and Trevira in West Germany. *Lirelle*, made by Courtauld's, is popular for double knits.

ACRYLIC FIBRES

These are made from polymers based on a chemical, acrylonitrile, from which the fibre derives its name. The fibres are mostly produced in staple form and spun into yarn which is particularly light in weight, strong and resilient. Fabrics made from these yarns are warm, very soft and thick, if the yarns are high-bulked. They are particularly useful for brushed, fleecy and fur-type fabrics. *Orlon, Acrilan, Courtelle, Dralon* are all made from acrylic fibres.

Orlon is an acrylic yarn which in filament form makes sheer, cool fabrics and in staple form is crimped and spun to make warm, cosy materials for underwear, knitwear, socks, cardigans, travel coats and blankets. Although a tough fibre, it is not as strong as nylon and for this reason, and because it has some of the qualities of wool, it blends particularly well with wool—better than stronger yarns.

Orlon has great resistance to acids, gases and fumes and can be used, therefore, for protective clothing in industry and for filter cloths. It is unaffected by continuous exposure to sunlight and weathering, and is excellent for awnings, outdoor furnishings, umbrella coverings and curtains. Other qualities possessed by Orlon are that the fabrics are warm to handle, comfortable to wear, drape well, do not crease easily, wash well and do not shrink, dry quickly and need little ironing. They keep their colour well and, with heat and pressure, durable creases and pleats can be made. Moth does not attack Orlon and it is not harmed by mildew. The flammability is about the same as viscose and cotton. A cool iron must be used in pressing to prevent discoloration.

Acrilan and *Courtelle* are both made from acrylic fibres and have similar qualities though Acrilan is the stronger. The yarn of both make very light, soft, warm fabrics which give good wear, wash easily and well, if washed in warm water, dry quickly and require minimum ironing. Acrilan, particularly, is often mixed with wool, silk, cotton, viscose or nylon. The fabrics can be permanently pleated and made crease-resistant. Acrilan takes dyes readily and, mixed with wool is much used for furnishings, carpets and rugs. Both yarns are used very successfully for knitwear and for pile, fleece and fur fabrics.

Dralon—used especially for curtains and soft furnishings. The fibres take dyes particularly well.

Modified acrylic fibres are known as *Modacrylic fibres*. They are inherently flame-resistant and are therefore used for permanently flame-resistant clothing. They include:

Dynel—used particularly for pile coatings.

Teklan—used for industrial purposes, for curtains, toys, clothes and in the preparation of some simulated fur fabrics to reduce their flammability.

ELASTOFIBRES

These are fibres made from polymers based on polyurethane (elastane fibres) and polyisoprene (elastodiene fibres), which enable them to have elastic properties. Yarns made from them have more power than rubber, even when made in fine deniers. They resist the action of acids and are thus unharmed by perspiration. Elastomer yarns are used for:

Lycra, Spanzelle and Vyrene—for lightweight foundation garments with good holding power. These garments can be washed easily in hand-hot water and dry quickly. The fibres are also covered with a hard fibre such as nylon or worsted and used for knitted goods for swimsuits and for stretch suitings to make ski-pants and men's and women's suits.

Other synthetic fibres and fabrics not included in the main classifications

P.V.C.—stands for polyvinyl chloride. This is a plasticized vinyl film which is laminated to the right side of fabric to give a glossy or matt surface. The backing fabric loses its qualities of drape and absorbency because the film on top produces a paperlike texture requiring special techniques for handling and stitching.

Vinyl fabrics are waterproof unless stitching impairs this quality in making garments. In factories, edges can be welded together instead of stitching. Surfaces can be wiped clean with a damp cloth. The fabrics are popular for raincoats, aprons and hats and for bags and cases, but it should be remembered that they are very flammable. These fabrics have largely replaced plastic sheeting used for linings and toilet accessories.

Lurex—the name given to some metallic yarns. Plastic film and thin aluminium sheeting are used to produce these flat ribbon-like yarns with the appearance of gold, silver, bronze or colours with a metallic gleam. They do not tarnish, are washable and often used with other yarns for knitted goods and woven fabrics for evening wear.

Glass fibres—These fibres are produced from spun glass and fabrics made from them are strong, do not burn and have good insulating powers. Acid, rot and moths have no effect on glass fabrics and they are non-absorbent. Their use is mainly for industrial purposes and for curtaining. Fabrics wash easily but should be washed alone in case particles of the fibres adhere to other fabrics. Gentle methods should be used for frequent washing and the fabrics drip dried. They dry quickly.

Foam-backed fabrics—A spongelike foam is laminated or fixed with adhesives to the wrong side of woven or knitted cloth. This results in fabrics which have bulk with very light weight, are pliable, and give good heat insulation so that clothing made from them is warm and comfortable. Foam-backed fabrics are washable if the cloth itself is washable, otherwise they can be dry cleaned. Garments keep their shape and do not crease. Foam-backed fabrics, also called laminates, are popular for sportswear and rain wear.

A later development is to bond a lining fabric to the foam so that the foam is sandwiched between the main fabric and the lining. This simplifies construction of garments and is excellent for curtains as it enables a thin fabric to be given a luxurious bulky texture and good drape and saves the work and cost of a separate lining.

NON-WOVEN FRABRICS

These are made by bonding processes using short, waste fibres, mostly synthetics. Cheap, low-grade fabrics are produced, useful for interlinings and disposable goods. Three main methods of production are used:

Adhesive bonding – see Bonding p. 12.

Stitch bonding where, after adhesive bonding, the fleece is chain stitched with nylon thread at spaced intervals throughout its length to give some strength, e.g. for curtain linings.

Needle punching. Here the fleece is laid on a backing and barbed needles (many thousands of them fixed to boards in machinery) are pushed through the fleece and backing, forcing some fibres through the backing. Soft, thick fabrics result such as waddings and underfelts. For greater strength the fleece is adhesive bonded as well, e.g. for floor coverings.

Paper fabrics have been developed from bonding processes to make disposable and protective wear – cleaning cloths, towels, panties, nappies, sheets, pillow cases, aprons, caps and overalls.

Choice of fabrics for dressmaking – see p. 286.

Treatment of fabrics in dressmaking

All fabrics used by a dressmaker present certain problems in handling and making up. Factors which must be considered include the kind of fabric, texture, thickness, elasticity and, of course, any design whether self-patterned, printed or woven. These qualities must be considered when choosing styles, planning layouts and cutting out. They affect each stage in construction—type of seams, edge finishes and so on. Very early in the planning a dressmaker must decide on the following:

Thread to use for stitching.
Size of needle for machining and hand sewing finishes.
Size of machine stitches.
Any special handling the fabric will need because of its qualities.

Selecting threads and needles
In all cases one should aim to use the finest sewing thread and needles practicable, particularly on fabrics made from man-made and synthetic fibres. A fine thread 'beds into' the fabric better than a thick one (a No. 50 Sylko is better generally than a No. 40) and a fine needle is less damaging to the fabric. Ball point needles are useful (see p. 61). It is essential to use threads made from synthetic fibre yarn on synthetic fibre fabrics because these sewing threads are both fine and strong. If other threads (Sylko, silk) are used the stitching will wear out long before the fabric. Also the quick drying qualities of the fabric will be reduced because the stitching thread will hold moisture.

In order to make the correct choice of needle size it is necessary to understand the sizing of needles, which is as follows:

	Hand sewing needles	*Machine needles*	
		British	Continental
Fine needles	9–11	9	70
Average needles	7–8	11	80
Thick needles	6–7	14–16	90

For hand sewing needles are chosen according to the thickness of the fabric—the needle should not bend as it is pushed through.

For machine sewing it is best to experiment on a spare piece of material. As a general guide:

FINE FABRICS (e.g. lawn, lace, chiffon, foulard, nets, nylons) require fine needles.

MEDIUM WEIGHT FABRICS (e.g. piqué, poplin, linen, textured fabrics, brushed fabrics, suitings, woollens) require average needles.

HEAVY FABRICS (e.g. sail-cloth, heavy tweeds and coatings) require thick needles.

Selecting size of stitch

The size of stitch (or number of stitches to one inch of stitching) is determined by the kind of fabric. On the whole fine fabrics require small stitches, thicker fabrics a larger stitch. The following is a guide but it must be remembered that an average sized stitch will look different on various thicknesses of material. Therefore it is necessary to experiment with size and tension to obtain the best stitch for strength and appearance.

Small stitches   approximately 10 stitches to 2 cm
Average stitches   ,,   8   ,,   ,, ,,
Large stitches   ,,   6   ,,   ,, ,,

Special points in handling and treatment

VISCOSE, ACETATES AND TRIACETATES

Those fabrics which have a cotton or linen 'look' may be stitched with mercerised cotton threads.

Those fabrics which have a silk 'look' may be stitched with pure silk, or if this is too expensive, a fine mercerised cotton thread. Fine needles are required and an average sized stitch on the machine. Ball point needles are a help.

Many of the fabrics in this group have a tendency to slippage. This means that yarns tend to shift at points where there is extra friction or strain, e.g. seams on tight-fitting parts of clothing. Edges often fray badly and allowance must be made for this (see under Synthetic Fibre fabrics below). Silklike fabrics (and silk also) are slippery to handle and must be placed (and kept) very straight and flat on the table while pinning on patterns and cutting out.

SYNTHETIC FIBRE FABRICS

The qualities of these fabrics must be appreciated in the choice of styles and materials. Gossamer fabrics can be chosen for hardwearing clothing, and details of style which ordinarily required time and care in laundering, e.g. frilling and pleating, become a practical choice. Furthermore, the fabrics being so light and resilient, garments can be packed and stored in a very small space. Inexperienced home dressmakers will be advised to choose styles with a minimum of seaming and to avoid much decoration in the form of machining, e.g. tucking, rows of stitching. Haberdashery and trimmings should be made of the same kind of yarn as the fabric whenever possible.

Special treatment is needed when making up the fabrics. It will be found that materials will not tear easily to straighten them and very sharp scissors must be used for cutting.

If fabrics fray badly ample turnings must be allowed; fells of french and double-stitched seams should be no less than 6 mm; turnings of open seams no less than 1 cm to 1.5 cm when finished, and raw edges exposed to rubbing wear must be neatened, e.g. overcast by hand or machine or edge-stitched. Brushed fabrics, e.g. brushed Courtelle, often do not fray at all and in these cases seam turnings do not require neatening. To prevent edges rolling a row of machining may be stitched in the single material 3 mm from the cut edge of each turning. Alternatively, and where the style permits, such fabrics look well and seam turnings are kept flat, with machining 6 mm on either side of an open seam working from the right side. Or, if both turnings are pressed to one side, one row of machining may be done through the turnings 6 mm from the seam line. See footnote to p. 81.

Because of the yarn of which fabrics in this group are made, fine ball point needles are best for sewing and for the machine. Fabrics must be stitched with a looser tension than usual and it may be necessary to alter both needle and bobbin tensions. Slow, steady movement of the machine needle produces better results than speedy work. A Teflon presser foot is an advantage in stitching these fabrics. For further information on the treatment, handling and pressing of fabrics see pp. 157 and 200.

Tests for sewing qualities p. 290

3 Use and adaptation of paper patterns

Patterns made by well-known and reliable firms are well worth their cost, because the success of an article depends primarily on the pattern, which can be used again on future occasions. Sizes and figure ranges, see pp. 40, 165.

How to choose a paper pattern

SELECT DESIGNS which are simple in line, avoiding those which have many seams or drapery which would need a skilled hand to make up successfully. Some patterns are designed especially for beginners and are advertised as being easy to make. These are always a safe choice.

BUY THE CORRECT SIZE, choosing a larger rather than a smaller size if the exact size required falls between the stock measurements. Patterns for full length garments such as dresses are sold in bust sizes, but before buying, study the other figure measures which are given on the envelope. It may be wiser to buy a pattern a bust size larger than necessary, for instance, in order to have the correct hip measure, because it is easier to reduce a pattern than to enlarge it. In the case just quoted, if the pattern fits at the hips, only a slight reduction may be needed at the bust. Skirts are chosen by waist, pants by waist or hip measure. See p. 165.

How to understand the pattern symbols

These are also called construction marks. Their meaning will be shown on the instruction sheet given with the pattern. In general the following ways of marking are used (Diagram 4):

Pattern lines (also called *stitching* or *fitting* or *seam* lines) are those lines on which the sections are to be joined together. They are marked with *broken lines*. On some patterns a machine presser foot indicates the line. Sometimes arrow heads are marked along the line at intervals to indicate the direction in which the seam should be stitched.

USE AND ADAPTION OF PAPER PATTERNS 33

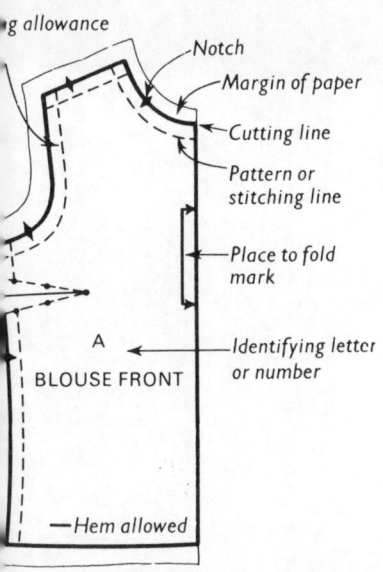

Section of a pattern to illustrate markings or symbols

Cutting lines are those on which the fabric is to be cut and are usually 1.5 cm away from the stitching lines. They are marked with *heavy black lines or double lines*. Tiny scissors may indicate the line.

On some patterns a margin of paper is allowed outside the cutting lines which falls away as the fabric is cut out.

Edges which represent a fold have no turning allowance and must be placed against a fold of fabric, as on the centre front and back of a plain blouse. They are marked with a **solid line with arrow heads** pointing towards the edge, or instructions are printed along the edge.

Straight grain indicators show how to place the pattern in the correct direction. Marked with **double headed arrows** (see Diagram 11).

Notches (also called balance points) show where to join the sections together. They are black *triangular shapes* marked in groups of one, two or three, often numbered for matching and should be cut outside the turning allowance (see p. 47).

Dots, spots, circles show such *constructional details* as where openings end, buttonholes begin, top of sleeve joins shoulder seam (see Diagram 122).

Solid lines indicate *style details* such as pleats, buttonholes, pocket positions and hem lines.

Double lines show where to adjust length. This is not standard on all makes of pattern, but the position for alteration is always clearly indicated.

How to prepare a pattern for use

1. Study the pattern envelope and decide which style is to be made if several variations are given.
2. Identify each pattern piece with those shown by diagrams on the envelope or instruction sheet.
3. Put away all the sections which are not required for the style to be made.
   Occasionally patterns may not have a turning allowance provided, so that the edge of the paper represents the pattern line. Some edges have no turning allowance because they represent a fold, e.g. the centre front and back of a plain bodice.
4. Study the significance of every mark on the pattern.

How to alter paper patterns

When an article of clothing is being made to fit a person who is not stock size, the pattern will have to be altered to individual measures. For this purpose, measures must be taken from the figure. It is a help in measuring accurately to tie a piece of string round the waist and another piece round the widest part of the hips of the figure to be measured. This means the widest part of the seat and not round the hip bones. Measures should be taken over a thin garment such as a slip or thin dress, and the model should be encouraged to relax and stand naturally. The following is a full list of measures such as would be necessary for a dress or blouse and skirt. In many cases, of course, they will not all be needed. For trousers, p. 222.

Measures required	How to take them from the figure (Diagram 5)
1. NAPE TO WAIST	Stand behind the figure. Measure from the most prominent bone in the nape of the neck down the centre back to the waist.
2. FULL LENGTH	Hold the tape at the waist and continue measuring to the full length required.
3. BUST	Place the tape measure round the fullest part of the bust. Raise the tape slightly at the back and keep two fingers inside the tape to prevent measuring too closely.
4. WAIST	Measure closely, not tightly, at waist level.
5. HIPS	Measure round the widest part of the hips (which averages 20 cm below the waist level) with two fingers inside the tape.
6. WIDTH OF BACK	Measure across the shoulder blades half-way down between the shoulder and underarm. Disregard any seams of the garment being worn and measure across the back only, taking care that the measurement is not extended on to the arms.

7. WIDTH OF CHEST — Stand squarely in front of the figure and measure across the chest half-way down between the shoulder and underarm. Observe the same care as with the width of back measure to see that the measurement is not taken too wide.

SLEEVE
8. *Inside arm length* — Instruct the model to raise the right arm slightly. Measure from where the arm joins the body, along the front of the arm in line with the thumb, to the wrist.

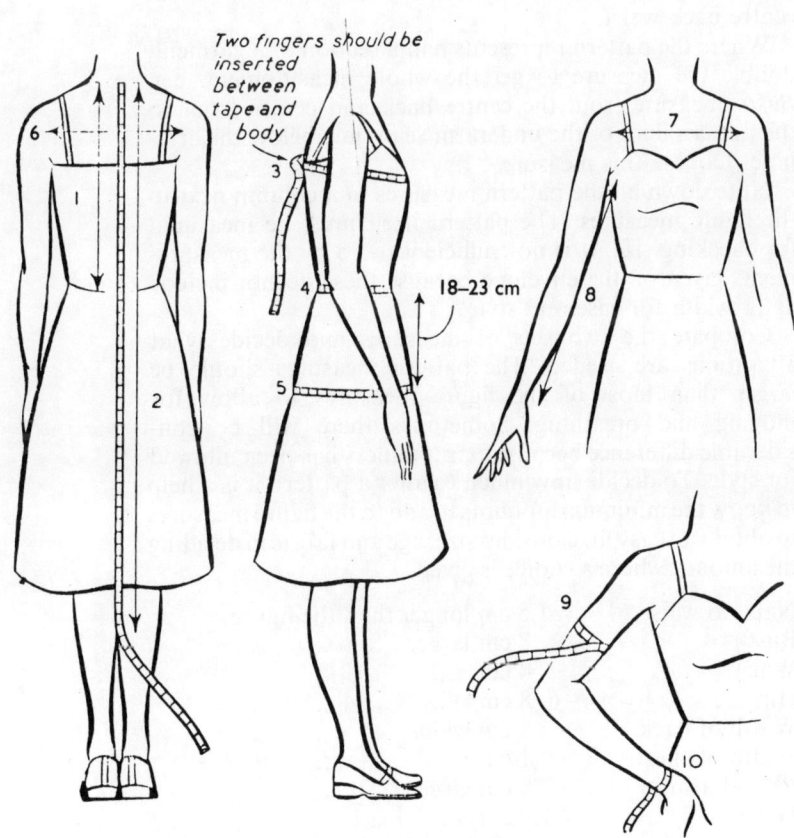

5. The way to measure the figure

9. *Round arm*   Take the measurement round the thickest part of the arm between shoulder and elbow, with the arm bent.

10. *Wrist*   Measure closely round the wrist.

MEASUREMENTS FOR MEN: see p. 230.

When the measurements required have been carefully taken and a clear list made, the corresponding measures must be taken from the pattern in order to compare them and judge the fit of the pattern.

How to measure a pattern

Measure between the pattern lines exclusive of turning allowances, e.g. *Nape to waist*—measure from the pattern line at the centre back neck down to the pattern line at centre back waist.

Where the pattern represents half a section of a garment, double the measure to get the whole measurement, e.g. *Bust*—measure from the centre back and centre front to the pattern lines of the underarm seam just below the armhole. Double this measure.

Note down all the pattern measures in a column next to the figure measures. The pattern itself must be measured for checking size. It is not sufficient to go by the measurements given on the envelope because these do not include extra width for ease and style.

Compare the two sets of measures and decide what alterations are needed. The pattern measures should be larger than most of the figure measures to allow for moving and breathing. Sometimes there will be considerable difference because extra fullness has been allowed for style. To decide how much to alter a pattern it is a help to know the minimum amounts to add to the figure measures to obtain an easy fit. Consider size, age and fabric in deciding the amount where a choice is given.

Nape to waist	1–1.5 cm longer than the figure
Bust	8 cm larger ,, ,, ,,
Waist	2–4 cm ,, ,, ,, ,,
Hips	6–8 cm ,, ,, ,, ,,
Width of back	1 cm wider ,, ,, ,,
Width of chest	1 cm ,, ,, ,, ,,
Round arm	8 cm larger ,, ,, ,,
Wrist	1.5 cm ,, ,, ,, ,,

(The sleeve length remains the same as the arm measure.)

USE AND ADAPTION OF PAPER PATTERNS

Where to alter a pattern
When it has been decided how much to alter the pattern, the next thing to do is to make alterations on the pattern. This can be done in one or other of two places.

1. AT THE EDGES
Alter at the edges of a pattern when the alterations to be made are very slight, such as adding or reducing 3 to 6 mm at the edges. Larger amounts than this would upset the proportion and shape of the pattern. Alterations should be made only at those edges where they are needed, e.g. if the measurement of the bust is 82 cm and the pattern measures 88cm, an extra 2 cm will be required. This will be obtained by adding 0.5 cm at the underarm seam of both the back bodice pattern and the front bodice pattern. Other edges of the pattern will remain unaltered unless some other adjustment is found necessary.

Because the edges of the pattern are designed to fit together, one alteration usually necessitates another in order that the pieces will join up properly. In the example just given, the additional width in the bodice will make the armhole larger. Therefore the sleeve seams must be let out too, so that the sleeve will fit the armhole.

2. THROUGH THE BODY
Alter through the body of a pattern by making tucks in the pattern to make it smaller, or by cutting it and inserting a strip of paper to make it larger. This method is used when the alterations are considerable because by it the shape of the pattern will not be spoilt e.g. to remove 10 cm from the hem edge of a skirt to make it shorter will generally reduce the width of the skirt, but a 5 cm tuck well above the hem edge will make the skirt the length required, without changing the width.

(a) Position of alterations on patterns. Diagrams 6 (i) (ii) (iii) (iv)
Alterations to width of patterns should be made in line with the straight grain indicators.
Alterations to length of patterns should be made at right angles to straight grain indicators.
In both cases the alterations should be made in such a position that the shape of the pattern is not affected and so that drastic change of style lines is not made necessary. The following list gives the best places to make alterations.

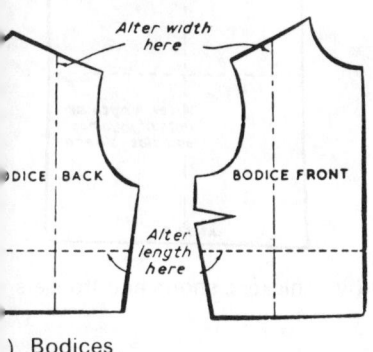

Where to alter the pattern

) Bodices

FOUNDATION METHODS

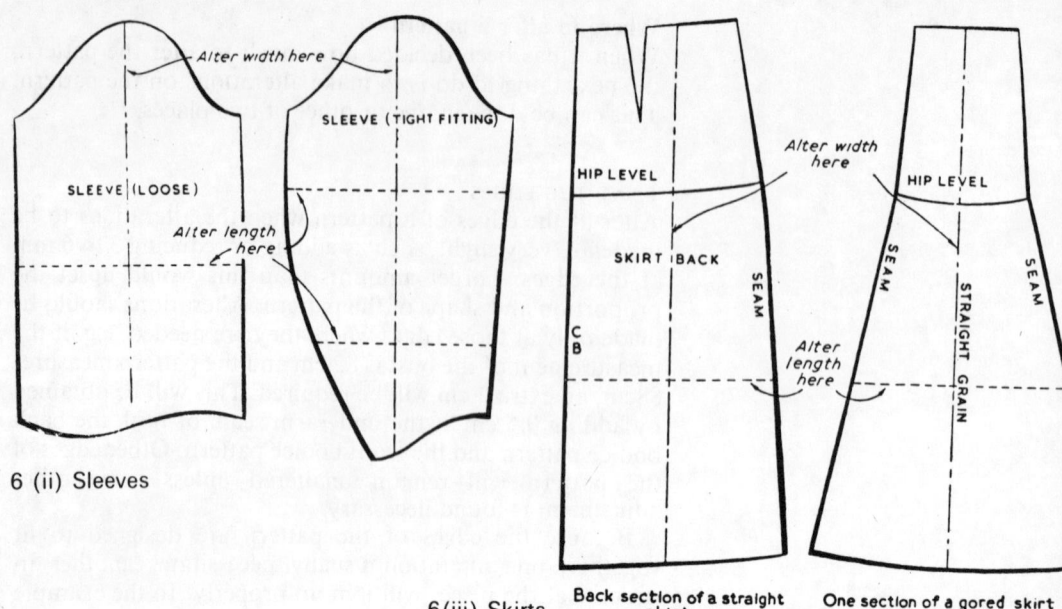

6 (ii) Sleeves

6(iii) Skirts — Back section of a straight skirt — One section of a gored skirt

6 (iv) Knickers, shorts and trousers

	To alter length	To alter width
Bodice	Between the underarm and waist line	Halfway along the shoulder to waist line, level with straight grain.
Sleeve Plain loose style	Between the underarm and wrist level at right angles to the straight grain	Through the centre of the sleeve from the crown to the wrist, level with the straight grain
Close fitting style	Alter both above and below the elbow, so that the elbow shaping is not affected	
Skirt	Between hip and hem level at right angles to the straight grain, so that the fit at the waist is not altered	Through the centre of each pattern piece in line with the straight grain

USE AND ADAPTION OF PAPER PATTERNS

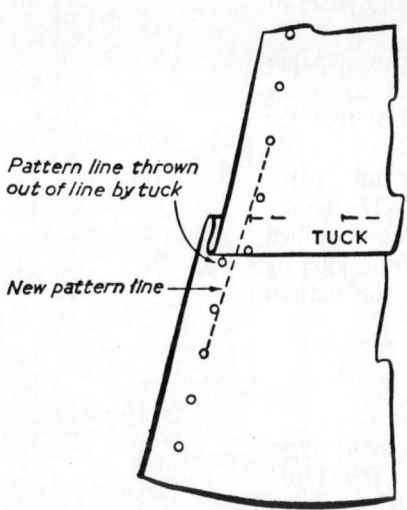

7 (i) Section of a pattern showing how to adjust the pattern line after an alteration has been made

7 (ii) To adjust a pattern line after the pattern has been widened

Knickers *Shorts* *Pyjamas* *Trousers*	Between the waist line and the fork at right angles to the straight grain, and between the fork and leg edge to alter the leg length	Through the middle of the pattern from the waistline to the leg edge, level with the straight grain

(b) Tuck a pattern to make it shorter or narrower
1. Draw a line across the pattern where the tuck is to be made.
2. Fold the pattern on this line and pin in a tuck, making the width half the amount to be reduced, e.g. a 2 cm tuck reduces the size 4 cm.
3. Flatten the tuck and re-shape the pattern line at the side where it will be thrown out of line by the alteration. Do this by placing a ruler to the pattern line a short distance equally above and below the alteration. Draw a straight line across the alteration. Diagram 7 (i).

(c) Insert a strip of paper to make a pattern longer or wider
1. Draw a line across the pattern where the insertion is to be made. Mark a short line to cross it at right angles to act as a balance point.

2. Cut through the pattern on the long line and paste or pin one cut edge on to a strip of paper.
3. Fix the other piece of pattern on to the strip of paper making the space between the two cut edges equal the amount required to be inserted. Be sure, also, that the balance lines are opposite each other.
4. Re-shape the pattern line at the edge. Diagram 7 (ii)

When a pattern has to be altered extensively, it may happen that all these methods which have been described will be used on the various pieces of the pattern, altering both at the edges and through the body of the pattern pieces.

Pattern sizes and figure ranges

Patterns are sold in ranges to suit different figure types e.g. Misses', Women's, Half-size, Junior Petite, Teen Girls, Teen Boys. Each size is known by a number which, in up to date patterns, corresponds with the sizes of the ready made garments. One can buy, for example, a pattern in bust size 87 cm to suit an average figure (Misses', Size 12) or for short figure (Junior Petite, Size 11). It will save alterations if the correct figure type is chosen (see p. 165).

The value of pinning the pattern pieces together

When the pattern has been altered so that the measurements are correct for the figure, pin up the pattern on the pattern lines. Fix the bodice pieces to the skirt, but pin up the sleeve separately. Try the pattern on over a slip, and notice particularly the position of yokes and pockets to see if they suit the figure. The fit cannot be judged in paper, but the previous measuring and alterations will have already assured this.

The chief purpose of pinning up a pattern is to face all the problems of putting the pieces together before the material is cut out and the pattern removed, e.g. just where to fold the bodice for a central opening. Details of construction are much easier to work out at this stage on the paper pattern.

4 Placing patterns on fabric and cutting out

To prepare for cutting out

When a pattern is ready to place on material, the worker can prepare for cutting out. A plentiful supply of good pins, a tape measure, and cutting out shears are, with the fabric, the only other requirements.

1. Grain the fabric

Do this by making it quite straight across the weft threads at one end of the material. There are two ways of graining material:

(a) Snip the material across the selvedge about 1 cm away from one end and tear it smartly across the weft. This has sometimes already been done in the shop by the salesman. Some material will not tear well; the threads strain near the torn edge. In these cases use the following method:

(b) Loosen a thread with a pin and pull it across the weft of the material. It is not necessary to pull the thread right out as long as the path of the thread can be seen to serve as a guide to cut along the straight grain.

To grain the material is one of the secrets of success in cutting out because it makes certain that the threads in each section of the garment are perfectly true and at right angles to each other. Diagram 3.

2. Fold the fabric

For accuracy and quickness it is best to cut out on double material whenever possible. It also makes sure that a pair of any section is cut, e.g. sleeves. Material should be folded evenly and economically and it should lie quite flat on the table. Even though material has been correctly grained, it sometimes happens that the material cannot be folded correctly and also lie flat. This is because the threads of the material have become stretched and pushed out of line during the finishing or baling of the cloth. It is a simple matter to pull them back into shape again by pulling the material across the grain throughout its length until it can be folded flat. Diagram 8 shows the

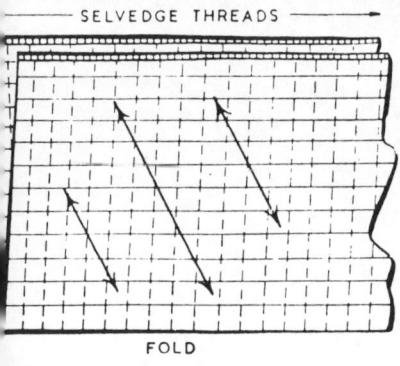

How to pull fabric which will fold flat after graining

42 FOUNDATION METHODS

direction in which to pull to remedy this fault.

The method of folding the material will depend on the size of the pattern pieces and the width of the material. The following are the most general ways of folding:

(a) Fold the material exactly in half with the fold along the selvedge threads. This is a very usual method when double

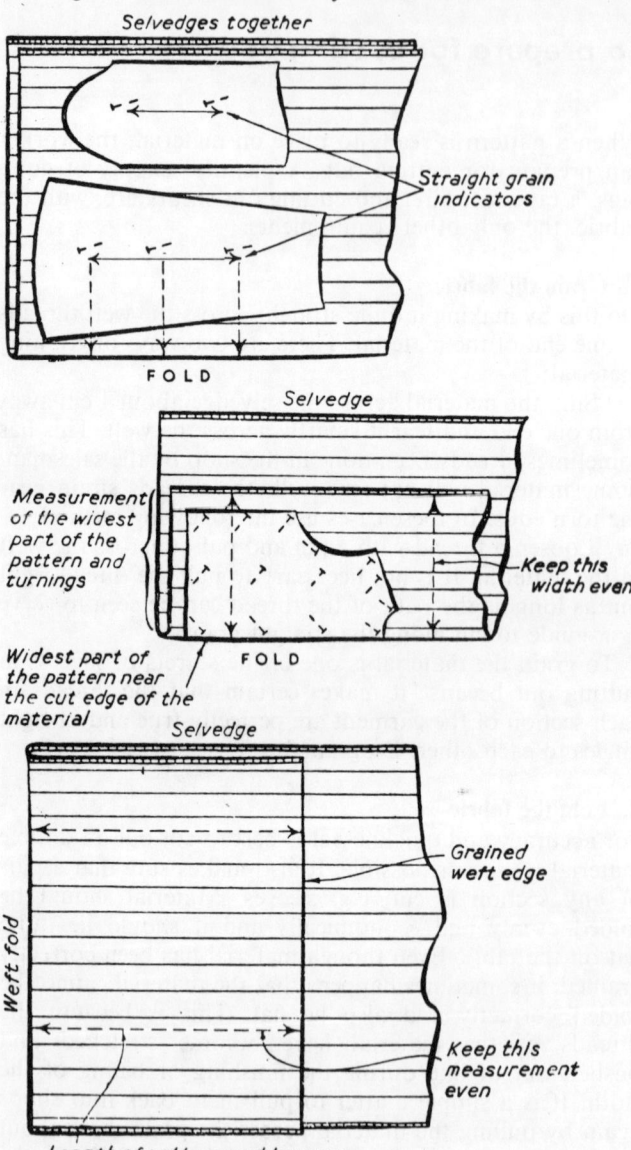

9 (i). To fold material (Method A)

9 (ii). How to fold material (Method B) and pin on a pattern

9 (iii). To fold material (Method C)

width cloth is used. The selvedges and raw edges should be pinned together. Diagram 9 (i) Method A.

(b) Fold the material with the selvedge partly across the width of the material. The amount folded over must be equal to the widest part of the pattern with extra for turnings. Keep the distance even between the fold and the selvedge and keep the weft edges together. A single layer of material extends beyond the double part, which often has to be refolded after the rest of the pattern is cut out. Sometimes this is used for sections which have to be cut from single material, e.g. belt or crossway strips. This is the most common way of folding single width material. Diagram 9 (ii) Method B.

(c) Fold the material over from the cut or torn edge so that the fold is along the weft. Measure an even distance between the fold and the grained edge and keep the selvedges together. This method is used for large pieces of pattern which take up more than half a width of material and do not require to be placed to a folded edge, e.g. shorts, skirt gores. The amount to fold over will in this case depend on the length of the pattern, plus turning allowances. Diagram (iii) Method C.

Fold patterned, checked or striped material so that the design will be suitably placed on the article and symmetrical on each side of a central line.

Finally, smooth the material straight on the table, keeping it level with the edges of the table. This applies particularly to rayons and silks which slip out of position easily.

3. Lay the pattern on fabric considering the following points

(a) Notice if the material has a pattern with an 'up and down' or a pile, in which case the pattern must be placed in such a way that the design or pile falls in the same direction in each piece of pattern. Further information, see p. 202.

(b) Plan a rough layout of the pattern before beginning to pin carefully to see how the pieces are going to fit on to the material.

(c) Follow the cutting diagram given with paper patterns as far as possible.

(d) Where the layout is planned independently of an instruction sheet, place on the largest pattern pieces first and put the widest end of the pattern nearest to the cut edge. This leaves a larger and more useful area in the

centre of the material. It will be found that smaller pieces of pattern can be fitted in more economically when the larger pieces have been placed. Diagram 9 (ii).

(e) Place the pattern so that the straight selvedge threads run *down* bodices, skirts, sleeves and frills, and *across* yokes, bands, belts, collars and cuffs. By this means the stronger set of threads takes the weight of the material and the extra strain on tight fitting parts of clothing.

(f) Place any edge on a paper pattern which represents a fold, right up to the fold of the material.

(g) When a pattern section has straight grain indications marked upon it, pin this line down first on to the material, keeping it an even distance from the fold or selvedge. Diagram 9 (i).

(h) It is best to allow a wider seam allowance than given on the pattern (an extra 6 mm to 1 cm) if the garment is to be fitted.

4. Pin the pattern on the fabric

Make sure that it is quite flat and secure. Too many pins cockle the material and mark it unnecessarily; too few will not keep it steady.

Pin first the pattern edge which is to be placed to a fold. Smooth away from these pins and pin through the centre of the pattern working in rows towards the edges. Where there is no folded edge, pin the straight grain indication line and smooth away on each side. Diagrams 9 (i), (ii). Practise the knack of putting in pins without slipping the other hand beneath the work, as this disturbs the material.

5. Cut out the pattern

Give a careful check to the layout to make sure it is correct, then:

(a) Cut along the cutting line indicated on the paper pattern or at an even distance from the pattern line, in which case the turning allowances can be marked with tailors' chalk or pencil dots as a guide for cutting.

(b) Steady the pattern by keeping the left hand spread out flat on the pattern.

(c) Cut, using the cutting shears, with long even strokes right down to the point each time. This will prevent jagged edges in cutting. Watch the point of the scissors while cutting and it will be easier to cut an even turning. Cut notches outwards, see p. 47.

Leave the pattern pinned on to the material until all markings have been transferred and the garment or article

PLACING PATTERNS ON MATERIAL AND CUTTING OUT   45

is ready to be tacked up.

6. To cut crossway strips Diagrams 10 (i), (ii), (iii)*
Frequently, the 'overs' of material are needed for crossway strips for various purposes. Cut these in the following way:

(a) Fold the material across so that the selvedge threads are in line with the weft threads. It is not necessary to know which are the selvedge and which the weft as long as the two opposite sets of straight threads are in line. The resulting fold is on the true cross. Any other fold or cut, other than with the straight threads, is on the bias. It is wasteful and unprofessional to cut a square from the fabric before folding it.

(b) Pin the material together a few inches away from the fold.

(c) Place the fold near, and level with, the edge of the table. Lay the left hand on the material behind the fold to steady it, and cut along the fold drawing the shears towards you. The cut edges are 'true cross' edges from which strips can be cut.

(d) To cut the crossway strips, measure the width of the strip required from the cut edge, measuring at right angles to the edge. Mark the width lightly with tailors' chalk or with pencil dots but not with pins because they make it difficult to cut the strips. Cut along the marked line.

(e) Cut along the marked line.

FRAYING EDGES

Certain materials fray quickly at cut edges and unless they are going to be handled quickly and expertly in making-up, it is wise to treat them so that ravelling is checked, otherwise the seam allowances are likely to fray out. Use one of the following methods to minimise fraying:

1. Cut out with pinking shears instead of cutting shears.
2. After pattern-marking, remove the pattern from the material; open the material out and machine close to the raw edge all round each section of the article or garment. This is also very good machine practice and in some cases partly neatens seam edges as well.
3. Work large overcasting stitches over the edge. This method is suitable for small articles.

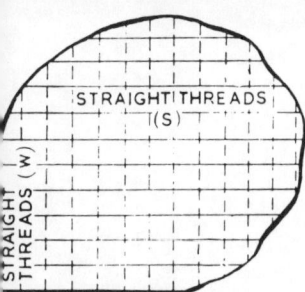

(i). A piece of material from which to cut crossway strips

(ii). Material folded on the cross showing weft threads in line with selvedge threads along this true cross fold

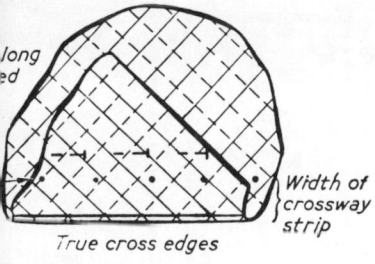

(iii). Material cut on the cross for cutting crossway strips

True cross edges / Width of crossway strip

---

* The use of pins to aid in making a correct fold is given in *Introduction to Needlework*, p. 138.

5 Marking pattern lines and tacking up

The first question to arise after the cutting out is completed is whether pattern lines are to be transferred on to the material. There are many circumstances when this need not be done as long as turning allowances have been evenly cut.

PATTERN LINES NEED NOT BE TRANSFERRED when loosely fitting articles and garments are being made; e.g. underclothes, children's clothing, overalls and household articles.

PATTERN LINES SHOULD BE CLEARLY MARKED on the material
(a) in good dressmaking, when a garment is going to be carefully fitted. It simplifies alterations to have the original pattern lines marked,
(b) when seam allowances are cut at varying widths to allow extra for fitting or with uneven widths because of shortage of material. Obviously the pattern lines would be lost unless they are transferred on to the material.

Methods of transferring pattern lines to material

1. Dressmakers' carbon paper
This paper with waxed surfaces can be bought in white and various colours. A colour should be chosen to tone with the fabric but with sufficient contrast to show up. The method is not successful on all fabrics, e.g. thick woollens or those with a nap, so it is best to experiment first to discover the most suitable colour to use and the amount of pressure needed to transfer the markings with a tracing wheel or blunt instrument such as an *empty* biro pen or a knitting needle.

Protect the table surface with cardboard.

Place a cut-out section with pattern pinned to it, on the cardboard and take out pins from the area to be marked.

The markings *must be transferred to the wrong side* of the fabric and these directions refer to fabric which has

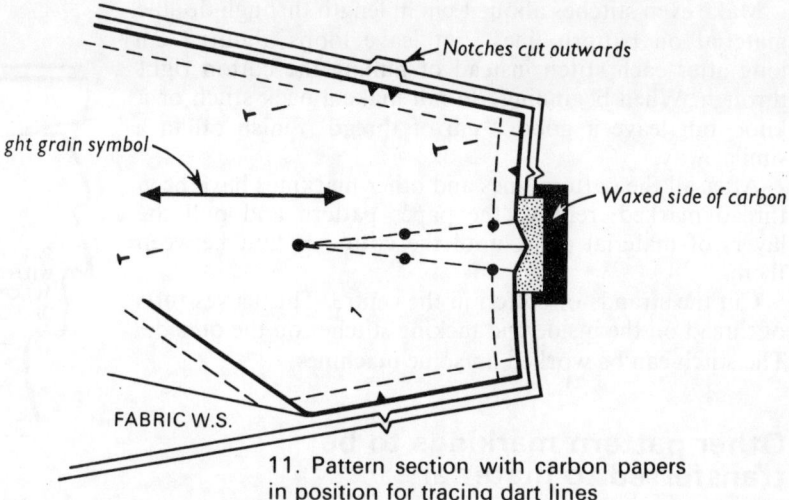

11. Pattern section with carbon papers in position for tracing dart lines

been folded for cutting with W.S. outwards. Put two strips of carbon paper with waxed surfaces against the W.S. of the fabric, one under the pattern and one on the table so that both carbons are under the lines to be marked. Diagram 11.

Now trace over the lines on the pattern (seam lines, buttonhole marks, dart lines, pockets lines, etc.). A ruler can be used along straight lines. Do not use a tracing wheel on fabrics which would be injured by the metal points, e.g. fabrics with a silky texture.

Take out pins from a further section and slip the carbon papers along to continue transferring the markings.

2. Tailors' tacks

This is a quick way of marking pattern lines. As the name suggests, it is primarily a tailor's method and is most suitable on heavy materials, but it has a very general use among dressmakers for all types of material.

Cut off, or snip and fold back, the turning allowance on the pattern, so that the markings can be done exactly on the pattern line. It is best to do this while the pattern is being prepared preparatory to placing on the material.

Use a double length of tacking cotton and a fine darning needle—No. 8 or 9. Have the work flat on the table with the pattern side uppermost.

If liked, pattern lines can be marked through the perforation marks instead of folding back the turning allowance. (Diagram 12 (i)).

Make even stitches about 1 cm in length through double material on pattern lines, but leave loops about 2 cm long after each stitch instead of pulling the cotton right through. When beginning, do not make a back stitch or a knot, but leave a good 2 cm of thread. Finish off in a similar way.

After all the pattern lines and other markings have been thread marked, remove the paper pattern and pull the layers of material apart until the cotton is taut between them.

Cut the strands of cotton in the centre. This leaves tufts of thread on the inside and tacking stitches on the outside. The stitch can be worked on some machines.

Other pattern markings to be transferred to material

Before removing a pattern from the material there are certain pattern markings which must be transferred, whether the pattern lines have been marked or not. Either of the two methods given for transferring pattern lines may be used for the other pattern markings.

NOTCHES
These should have been cut outwards in the turning (see Diagram 11). If they have not, mark the notch with a tack at right angles to the pattern. Diagram 12 (i).

PERFORATION MARKS
Those which mark pleats, tucks, darts, pockets and fastenings are specially important. They can be marked with tailors' tacks in the following way:

Make a small running stitch in double material through a perforation, leaving an end of thread. Take a backstitch over this stitch, leaving a loop.

Cut the end of thread or pass the thread over the paper to the next perforation, where the running and backstitch are repeated. Diagram 12 (i).

CENTRAL LINE OF BACK AND FRONT BODICE AND SKIRT
Tack along the fold, picking up a few threads in single material. Pass over about 2 cm, so that a clear line of tacking will mark these important lines. These, also called tracing tacks, are the last to be removed, as they are needed for reference, until it is finished.

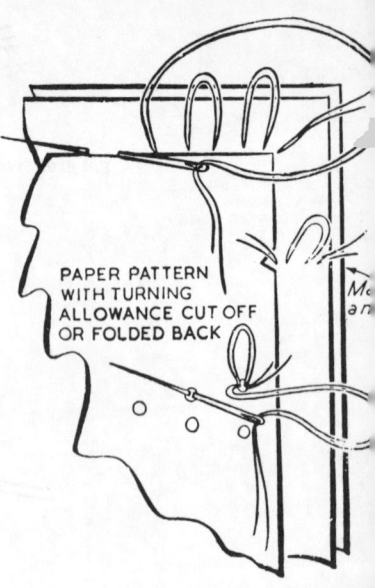

12 (i). To work tailors' tacks along pattern line or through perforation marks

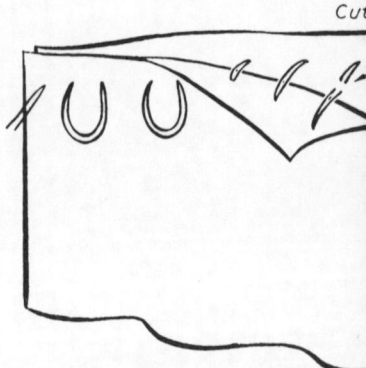

12 (ii). Cutting the strands after pulling the layers of material apart

MARKING PATTERN LINES AND TACKING UP 49

Tacking a garment together

When pattern markings have been transferred, the paper pattern can be removed from each piece as the worker is ready to assemble the sections. It is best to fix the pieces together on a large table, and it is important to pin the pieces together before they are tacked. (TACKING STITCHES, p. 145).

Take each section or unit of the garment and do all the fixing possible on it before joining it to another piece. This will involve tacking in darts, tucks, pleats; putting in gathering threads; working openings, etc. Machining and pressing can be done at this stage unless a fitting is to be given.

There are two methods of assembling the units—the ROUND or the FLAT method.

Order of tacking up the units

THE ROUND METHOD
1. Tack together each main part of a garment:
e.g. bodice—fix yokes, shoulder and side seams,
      sleeve—underarm seam, cuff edge,
      skirt—side seams, hem.
2. Fix the main parts together, the smaller parts to the larger:
e.g. collar to bodice,
      sleeves to bodice,
      bodice to skirt. Diagram 13.

This method is suitable for any style, but particularly those with a waist seam.

THE FLAT METHOD
1. Join shoulder seams so that the work is flat to do the neck line.
2. Complete the neck edge.
3. Set in the sleeves or complete armhole edges.
4. Join the side seams.
5. Finish edges of sleeves and skirt hem.

This method is particularly suitable for garments made in one piece from shoulder to hem. Diagram 14 (i), (ii).

After fitting (see p. 250), the main parts of the garment must be separated to enable seams and other processes to be made and pressed properly.

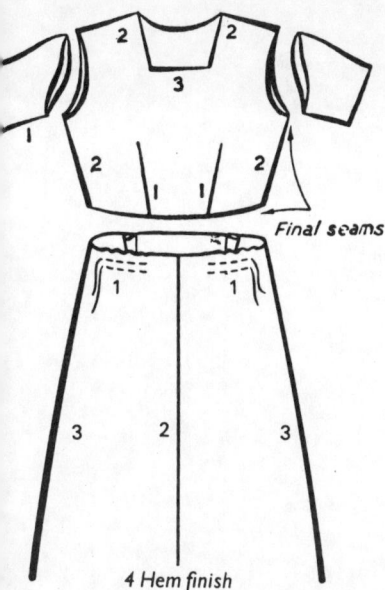

Round method. Numbers show order of work

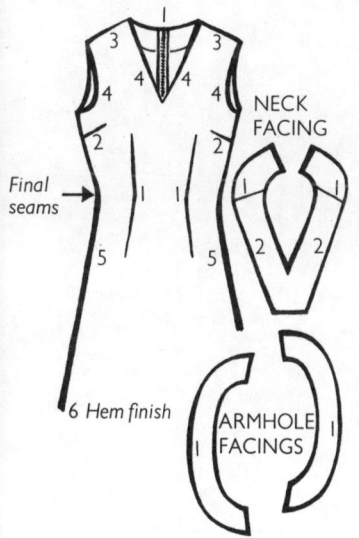

(i). Flat method of work

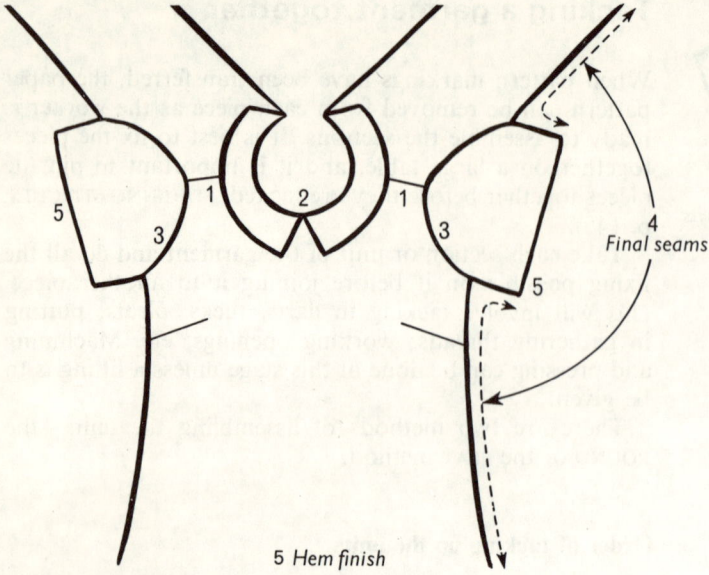

14 (ii). Order of tacking up a garment by the Flat Method. Numbers show the sequence of work

Construction of trousers, shorts, pyjamas and pants

The unit method is used on each section as for other clothing. The order of tacking up and making varies according to the type of garment and style. The general order is:

1. MAKE THE SEAMS. Three methods illustrated on p. 223:
(A) Make the crotch seams separately, then the inside leg and lastly the side seam. Use this method when there is a centre front or back opening and for underwear.
(B) Make inside leg seams, then the crotch seam in one stitching from C.B. to C.F.
(C) Make each leg separately, inside and outside seams, and lastly the crotch seams from C.B. to C.F.

Methods A and B are convenient for putting in side openings, make it easier to keep the crotch seam a good shape and reinforce it, and are the most popular ways of making trousers.

2. MAKE OPENINGS AND POCKETS IN SEAMS.

3. FINISH THE WAIST EDGE.

4. FINISH THE LEG EDGES.

6 Sewing machines

One of the most exciting purchases for a girl to make is a sewing machine—often the purchase of a lifetime. Much thought and discussion must go into choosing the right machine and it is well worthwhile spending as much as can be afforded. With care it will give years of service. One needs to compare similar types of machine made by various manufacturers and note their servicing arrangements. Demonstrations are available in showrooms and, sometimes, it can be arranged to try out a machine at home. Choice depends on price range and the amount and type of use the machine is to have. Weight may be a consideration. A girl living away from home may need a light weight model. One can buy *flat bed* (see front endpaper, which also shows main parts) or *free arm* models Diagram 15 (i), which simplify stitching circular pieces of work e.g. cuff edges. Straight stitch machines have been superseded by swing needle types. However, many people will still be using or buying second-hand straight stitch machines, so they will be in use for some years. Once bought, the machine must be used correctly, kept clean and oiled and be stored in a dry place away from intense heat such as radiators.

Swing needle machines

There are two main classes of machines from which to choose, Automatic and Zigzag. Automatic machines may be fully automatic with a wide range of functional and decorative stitches which, with buttonholes, are worked automatically once controls are set. Other machines are only partly or semi-automatic. For example a machine may work a few embroidery stitches automatically but need alteration to a dial or lever several times during making a buttonhole. Models by different manufacturers vary in what they offer. All do straight stitching.

Zigzag machines (Diagram on front endpaper)
The cheapest swing needle machine is a zigzag model, which meets most sewing requirements of a housewife. It

FOUNDATION METHODS

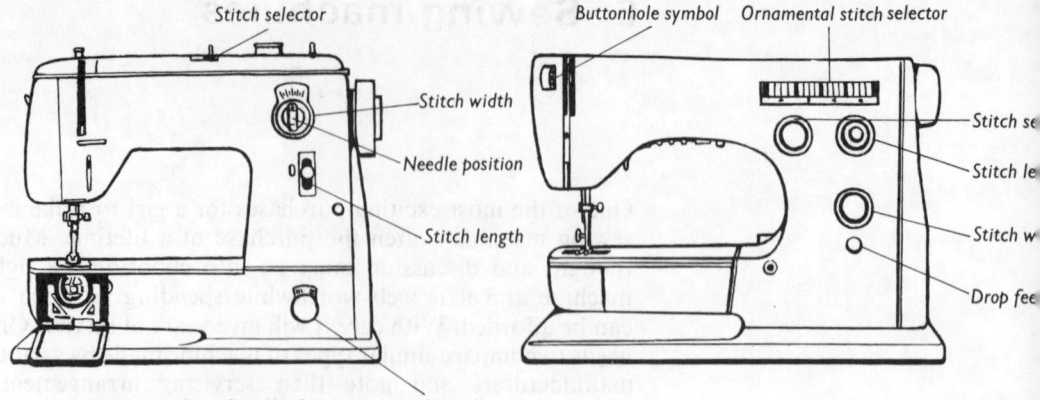

15 (i). Diagram to show controls for swing needle stitching, ornamental stitching and buttonholing

Left. A semi automatic free arm machine which does straight, zigzag and a few ornamental stit Buttonholes made with manual control

Right. A fully automatic free arm machine which, in addition, does ornamental stitches and button automatically after the controls are set

does straight stitching and a zigzag stitch capable of many uses — neatening seams, buttonholes with manual control, satin stitch, some embroidery stitches and mending. The needle swings from side to side to make the zigzag stitch, the shape of which is controlled by length and width setting.

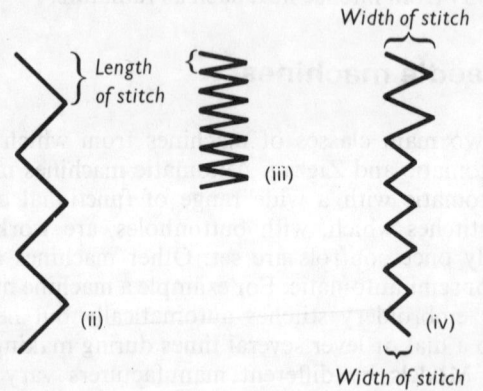

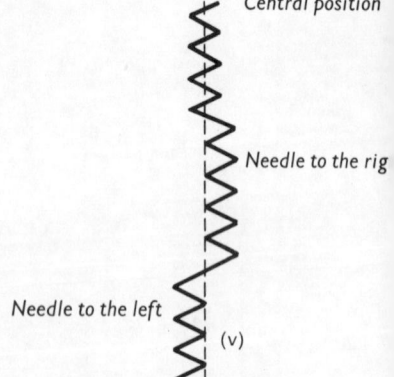

LONG STITCH
When the stitch is set at a long length it gives an *open zigzag* which is used for neatening edges and for ornamentation. Diagram 15 (ii).

15 (ii). Long zigzag stitch
15 (iii). Short zigzag stitch
15 (iv). Various widths of zigzag sti
15 (v). Three positions for the need

SHORT STITCH
When the stitch is set at a short length it gives a *satin stitch*, used for making buttonholes, appliqué work and holding lace and decorative hems and facings in place. Diagram 15 (iii).

A limited number of other stitches can be produced on some machines of this type.

Automatic machines Diagram 15 (i)
Fully automatic models are the most expensive domestic machines. In addition to the work of zigzag types, they do many practical stitches, i.e. tailors' tacks, 3-step zigzag, blindstitch, elastic blindstitch, stretch stitches, overlock stitch (makes seam and neatens in one operation), decorative stitches and buttonholes. These are worked by setting the controls and, for stitches, simply guiding the work.

Although there are a great number of different types of these machines on sale they all have certain characteristics and once one type is understood, one can quickly become accustomed to different models.

All zigzag and automatic machines have certain basic controls, generally knobs or levers, as follows:

STITCH SELECTOR which enables the stitch to be set at zigzag or other decorative stitch. Sometimes cams are inserted.

STITCH WIDTH REGULATOR, numbered to show the possible widths at which the stitches can be made. The needle must always be raised to its highest point *out of the fabric* when this control is altered, otherwise the needle may bend or break. The width of the stitch is known as the bight. Diagram 15 (iv).

STITCH LENGTH REGULATOR, the same gadget as for altering the stitch length for straight stitching. The length affects the closeness of the stitch. Diagrams 15 (ii), (iii).

CONTROL TO ALTER NEEDLE POSITION to left or right of its central position. This is used primarily for buttonholes but also for varying the line of decorative borders. Diagram 15 (v).

To set a machine up for use

1. Wind the bobbin
Loosen the stop motion screw so that the needle does not move while the bobbin is being wound. To do this, steady

the balance wheel with the left hand and turn the stop motion screw towards the worker. Use the same thickness of thread on the bobbin as it is intended to use in the needle. Follow instructions in the booklet concerning the machine, for winding and inserting the bobbin.

2. Set the needle
First see that the needle is the correct size for the type of fabric. For information on sizes to use see p. 29. Notice that the needles for some makes of machines have a groove running down one side and that near the top they are flat on one side. Make certain from the instructions in which direction to face the flat side. Loosen the screw which holds the needle bar and push the needle well up before tightening the screw. Then lower the needle slowly to see that it enters the centre of the hole in the throat plate.

3. Thread the needle
Thread used in the machine should be suited both to the type of work and the thickness of the needle. For information on kinds of thread to use see p. 29. Use the same thickness in needle and bobbin. Follow instructions for threading the needle for the particular make of machine.

4. Test the stitch
Try out the stitch on a double piece of material. Notice the tension and size of stitch.

THE TENSION
In order to judge and alter the tension, it is necessary to understand how the stitch is formed. The stitch is made by the interlocking of the thread which comes from the needle and the thread which comes from the bobbin. This looping should be embedded in the fabric so that the stitch appears the same on both sides of the work. Diagram 16 (i). The tension is the pull on these two threads which can be felt by lowering the presser foot and pulling each thread in turn. When the tension or pull is unequal the interlocking takes place on the surface, either on the top or underside, and the stitches appear to have tiny loops between them. These stitches are not strong and are easily pulled out.

When loops appear on the top surface it shows that the pull from the needle is too strong, drawing up the under cotton. Therefore the top tension is too tight. Diagram 16 (ii).

SEWING MACHINES 55

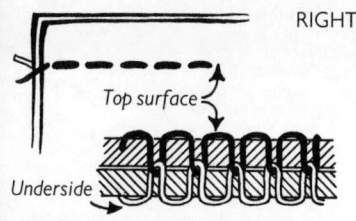

6 (i). Correct tension as stitch should look on both sides

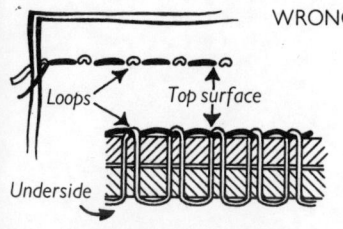

6 (ii). Top tension too tight

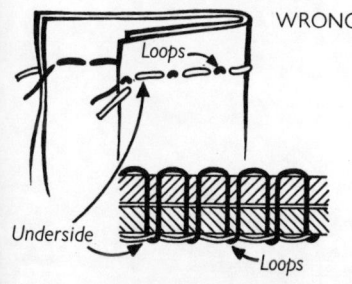

6 (iii). Top tension too loose

Diagrams show machine stitching and how threads loop in the fabric

When loops appear on the underside it shows that the pull from the needle is not strong enough, because the under cotton is drawing the needle cotton down. In this case the top tension is too loose. Diagram 16 (iii).

To alter the top tension tighten or slacken the tension screw which clamps the discs together through which the thread passes. Occasionally it will be found that adjustments to the top tension do not give the desired result. This shows that it is the pull on the under cotton which is too strong or too weak and the under tension has to be altered.

To alter the under tension, tighten or slacken a small screw in the bobbin case which controls the pull of the thread from the case. The instruction booklet will show which is the tension screw.

A further test which is useful in deciding which tension is needing adjustment is to lower the foot of the machine and pull in turn the thread from just above the needle and the thread from the bobbin. If either thread is very tight or slack, it is an indication as to which tension is at fault.

Tensions generally need slackening on synthetic fabrics because the elasticity of synthetic sewing threads tends to draw up the fabric with a tightened result. Loosening the tensions will prevent sewing threads being stretched and keep the stitching flat and unpuckered.

Other adjustments for fabrics made from man-made fibres see pp. 31, 200.

SIZE OF THE STITCH
Alter the size by turning a screw or raising and lowering a lever at the right-hand end of the machine. A diagram in the instruction booklet will show the position and state in which direction to make the adjustment to increase or decrease the size of the stitch. The size chosen depends on the weight and type of fabric. A small stitch looks well on fine materials, such as lawn, but a larger one looks better on woollens and is safer on certain fabrics, which tend to split at the seams if a very fine stitch is used. See p. 31 and Chapter 8.

Directions for working the machine

1. Have the machine in a good light and at such an angle that no shadow is thrown across the work. Sit at a com-

fortable height and square to the machine. Lean forward and rest the arms just below the elbows on the machine table.
2. Always keep feet off the foot control while threading up or making adjustments to electric machines.
3. Place the work in the machine so that the bulk of the material is at the left-hand side where there is room for it.
4. Push both threads towards the back of the foot; lower the needle into the position required; lower the presser foot and begin to machine.
5. Use the sides of the presser foot as a guide to machine straight and watch the foot, not the needle.
6. To turn a corner, stop at the corner with the needle down in the work; raise the foot, pivot the work round, lower the foot and continue machining.
7. To remove work from the machine, raise the presser foot; draw thread from the machine by pulling just above the needle so that it does not bend or break; draw the work out towards the back and cut through the two threads (the needle threads and the bobbin thread) leaving about 12 cm of thread on each side.
8. To end off machining, pull the under thread to bring the top thread through to the wrong side, then tie the ends securely or thread them on to a needle and sew into the back of the stitching. It is not necessary to end off the stitching when the machining finishes at a raw edge. The ends are cut level with the edge.

How to use swing needle machines

1. Always see that the machine is producing a good straight stitch before switching to swing needle work.
2. Obtain a good satin stitch before selecting the embroidery stitch required because many are based on satin stitching.
3. Use fine machine thread for buttonholes and embroidery stitches. This thread is sold specially for the purpose.
4. Experiment with stitch length and width in order to produce a stitch best suited to the fabric and thread. Some slight adjustment of the tension may be needed.
5. Be sure to have the needle at its highest point when making adjustments to the controls especially when altering the stitch width and the needle position.
6. Study the machine handbook carefully and use the

correct foot and plate on the machine for the work being done.
7. Clean and oil frequently because these machines cause fluff to accumulate more quickly than the straight stitching types. Self-lubricating makes never require oiling.

How to machine straight*

Learn to machine straight by practising on paper without thread in the needle or the bobbin. Use lined paper first and practise keeping the sides of a *straight stitch presser foot* level with the lines. Watch the foot, not the needle. Keep the inner side of the small toe of the machine foot level with a line first; then the inner side of the large toe; then the outer sides of both. When machining material any one of these sides can be used as a guide for keeping level, or an even distance from folds and edges. Diagrams 17 (i) (ii). Many machines have lines marked on the throat plate. Edges or folds kept level with these lines ensure straight stitching. See inside front cover. Some machines have a magnetic device to aid in straight stitching.

Now try to machine exactly on the lines, keeping the sides of the foot an even distance from the line. Continue practising without thread, this time doing parallel lines on plain paper. Draw curves, and machine on the lines. When confidence and control of the machine have been gained, thread up the machine and try stitching on material. Skill in machining straight comes with use, so practise as much as possible. Once learnt, it is an art which is never forgotten.

When the machine gives trouble check the following

1. Make quite sure the threading is correct both in the needle and the bobbin. The slightest mistake will upset the stitch.
2. See that the threads in both needle and bobbin are the same thickness.
3. Note that the size of the needle and thread are right for the material.

---

* An alternative method of practice is suggested in *Introduction to Needlework*, p. 3, "Use the machine to scribble".

FOUNDATION METHODS

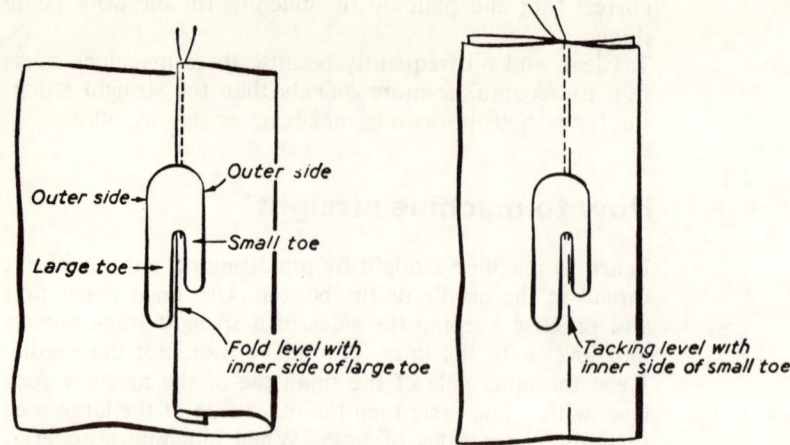

17 (i). How to use the inner sides of a straight stitch presser foot as a guide

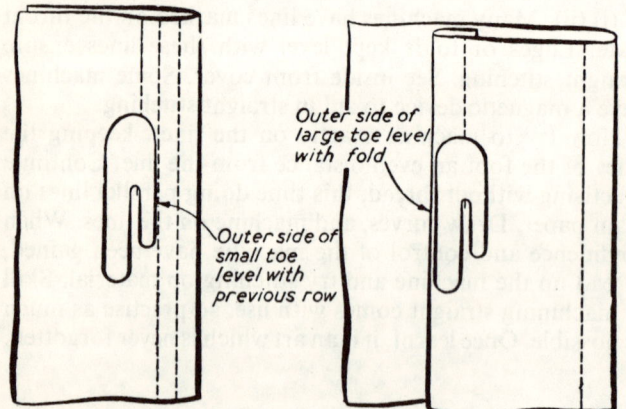

17 (ii). How to use the outer sides of a straight stitch presser foot as a guide

4. See if a new needle is required. Blunt or bent needles cause slipped stitches, when the stitches do not always lock properly and several run together making an occasional long stitch. Also a blunt needle does not pierce the material easily and often strains the threads of the material as it stitches.
5. Make sure that the needle is set correctly. The flat side must face the correct way according to the type of machine, and be well pushed up in the socket.
6. Be certain that the machine is clean and is oiled regularly unless it is self-lubricating.

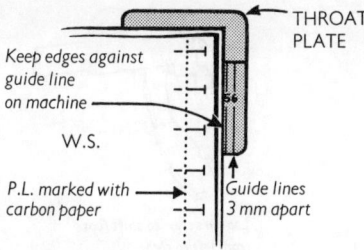

17 (iii). Pins in position for machining a seam without preliminary tacking

Preparation for machining over pins

Sometimes machining can be done without preliminary tacking, for straightforward jobs. Put pins in on the pattern lines and pick up very little fabric so that the points are only just over the P.L.s with heads towards turnings. Use a hinged foot on the machine and machine across the pins holding the work firmly. Use guide lines on the machine only if the turnings are even and the P.L.s are not marked.

To clean and oil the machine

Cleaning
Remove the feed plate and free the feed and bobbin holder of dust and lint. A feather or paint brush is useful for cleaning intricate parts. Lift the machine head and wipe the mechanism beneath in old models. Follow instructions given with new types.

Oiling
Use a reliable machine oil and lubricate the under mechanism first. Place a drop of oil at all those places where one part of the machinery moves against another. A slight turn of the balance wheel will make these apparent.

Replace the head of the machine in position and insert a drop of oil into the small holes in the arm of the machine. Note that the holes in the table part of the machine are intended for screws for machine attachments, not for oiling purposes. Sometimes oiling points are marked.

Place a piece of material under the machine foot and work the machine without thread, to work in the oil. Leave some material under the foot when the machine is not in use to collect any oil which may drain down the needle bar.

Take care not to over oil the machine, but never allow parts of the machinery to become dry.

Machine attachments and accessories

All types of machines have attachments for special work and once good machine control has been gained, any of them can be used successfully. The following are some of the most popular:

The piping or zipper foot
Constructed so that it can be placed on either side of the needle making it possible to stitch very close to a piping cord or near to the teeth of a zip fastener. Diagram 18. Remove the standard foot and put it in a safe place. Attach zipper foot and lower the needle slowly to see it does not scrape the foot. Remember to replace the standard foot afterwards. A special foot is used for invisiible zips, e.g. Alcozip.

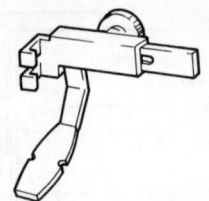

Loosen screw to shift foot from left to right

18 (i). Zipper foot

The hemmer foot
Used to make very narrow hems on fine materials, e.g. on edges of frills.

The gathering foot
Gathers fabric and holds the gathering rigidly in position. Some experimental work must be done first to make sure that the amount of gathering will be correct when it is stitched. This is a particularly useful attachment for gathering slippery materials such as nylon because it holds the gathers in place for setting in.

Left and right hand grooves fit over teeth of zip.

18 (ii). Grooved foot for invisible zips

The ruffler
This looks a complicated attachment but is really very simple to use and saves much time when long lengths of material are to be softly pleated. The depth of the pleats can be adjusted from about 3 mm to 1 cm and can be spaced very close together or spaced out. After screwing on the gadget the cut edge of the fabric is threaded through according to instructions and as the machine works the pleats are pushed into place by a blade and sewn in place. To get the right amount of fullness try out on spare pieces first. The ruffler can also be regulated for gathering.

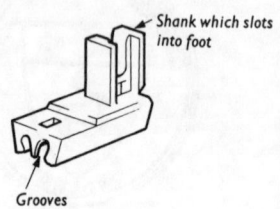

Foot with detachable shank to fit different types of machines

18 (iii). Foot with detachable shank

The quilter
A foot to which a bar is attached, designed to hold layers of fabric together and to be a guide for working even rows of machining. This attachment cannot be used successfully unless the fabric to be quilted has been properly tacked to the wadding and backing material. The quilter is screwed on to the machine with the bar to either right or left of the needle.

The binder
With this, edges are bound with binding with one row of machining which holds all layers in place. After the binder

has been screwed on the needle should be carefully lowered to see that it is in the centre of the needle hole.

Darning attachments
Modern sewing machines require a small adjustment to lower the feed and then after the foot is removed or replaced the machine is ready for darning. (Method of work, p. 293.) Older machines require special plates to cover the feed and needle springs on the needle bar. Once the feed is no longer in action the machine is fed by the operator who guides and controls the work held tautly in an embroidery frame. This is called 'free machining', see p. 293, and is used for modern embroidery as well as darning.

Stitch ripper (See endpaper)
This is mainly for cutting buttonholes after they are made. The point is pierced into the middle of the buttonhole on the W.S. until the cutting edge is against the cloth, and gently pushed towards each end. Control is needed to prevent cutting too far. A pin put in at the end of the buttonhole will act as a buffer. Care is needed to use the tool safely for unpicking faulty machining.

Teflon coated presser foot
Designed to assist the even feed of fabrics with slippery or shiny surfaces, i.e. tricots; for stretch fabrics and for those which resist movement under the foot, i.e. foambacks. Variations of this foot are sold, e.g. one has a ridged surface on the underside which makes it good for stitching pile fabrics such as velvet. It also keeps designs such as plaids in place, because the top surface does not get pushed along during machining.

Roller presser foot
This also helps the feed of fabrics, especially for P.V.C., leather and suede. With any of these special feet, pressure may need adjustment.

Ball point needles
These prevent seam pucker on fine and stretch fabrics. The ball tip tends to part threads without piercing them and so damaging the structure of the fabric. This is particularly important with knit fabrics. Ball points do not blunt as quickly on synthetics as regular ones. Sewing needles with ball points are also available.

7 Arrangement of fullness

One of the first things to be done in making up a garment is to arrange the fullness.

Ways of arranging fullness

Darts
Darts are used at the waist, bust and shoulders of clothing, the points of the darts tapering towards the wider parts of the figure. A well-stitched dart has the point tapering gradually right off to nothing, so that the surface of the material is quite smooth at the end of the dart. As a rule, darts are made on to the wrong side of the work and are pressed to make them as inconspicuous as possible. A dart is made by folding material and stitching a certain distance away from the fold, tapering the stitching in a straight line to end on the fold.

To make a dart. Diagrams 19, 20, 21 (i) (ii)
1. Fold the material so that the right sides face and the pattern lines of the dart are together.
2. Pin and tack the dart on the pattern lines.
3. Stitch from the broad end towards the point bringing the stitching right off the fold. Sew off or knot the ends of thread.
4. Press the dart to one side of the stitching, or if the material is too thick to lie really flat, cut along the fold to within 2 cm of the point and open the turnings.

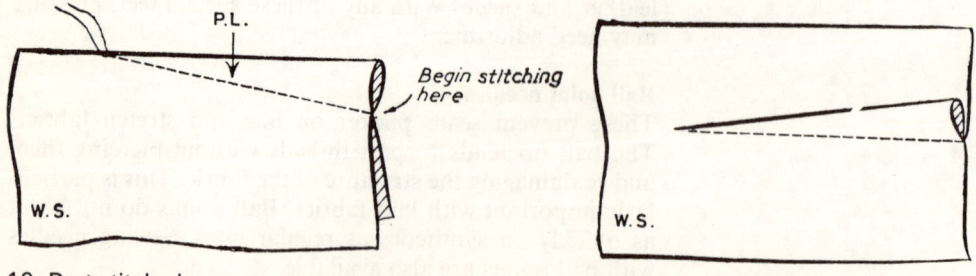

19. Dart stitched

20. Dart pressed to one side

ARRANGEMENT OF FULLNESS 63

Instructions for pressing darts are given in Chapter 13.

DARTS POINTED AT BOTH ENDS

These are made similarly, but a beginner may find it easier to begin stitching darts in the centre of the broad part and stitch towards the points both ways. With practice, the stitching can be started at one point. The dart will have to be snipped in places to allow it to be pressed flat on to the garment.

Tucks

These may serve several purposes:

1. They may provide extra width, e.g. tucks at the shoulders of a bodice give extra width over the bust.
2. They may reduce fullness, e.g. tucks at the waist of a blouse.
3. They may serve as a style feature exclusively, e.g. tucks which are taken throughout the length or breadth of a dress bodice.
4. They may be planned to allow for growth, e.g. on children's clothing.

A tuck is formed by folding material and stitching an even distance from the fold. The fold, except in pin tucks, is pressed to lie flat to the side of the stitching. Tucks are made on fine material and mostly on the right side of material. The depth of a tuck may be very narrow, e.g. a bare 2 mm which are pin tucks or several centimetres wide. Both hand and machine stitching are used to make tucks.

TO MAKE TUCKS. Diagram 22

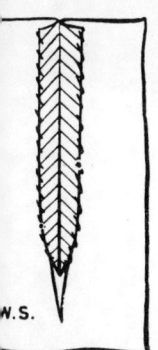

1 (i). Dart cut down, pressed open and neatened

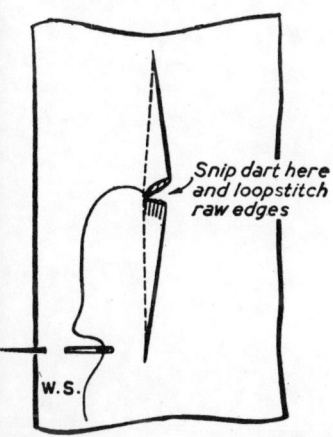

1 (ii). Treatment of a dart pointed at both ends

STEP 1
Tuck pinned in position

STEP 2
Tuck fixed with running stitch and pressed to one side

22. Tucks worked by hand

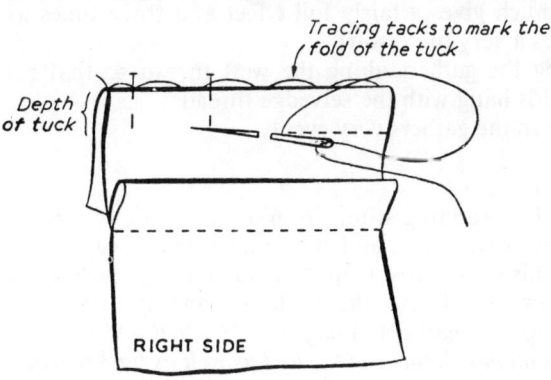

By hand. Fold the material with the wrong side facing and exactly on the line marking the fold of the tuck and pin in position.

Make small running stitches to fix the tuck, stitching an even distance from the fold according to the depth of tuck desired, e.g. 6 mm from the fold for a 6 mm tuck. Work the stitches with the side uppermost which will show when the tucks are pressed, because the stitches are likely to be more even. Use a measuring card as a guide to help in keeping straight. It is a matter of preference if tucks are tacked before stitching, but complete one tuck before fixing the next. The work curls and becomes difficult to handle if all the tucks are fixed before stitching them. Take care not to stretch bias tucks (RUNNING STITCH, p. 145).

When all the tucks are stitched, press them in position.

By machine. Pin and tack each tuck before machining it and complete one tuck before beginning the next one. The machine tucking attachment can be used if liked especially on cotton and linen materials on which the crease made by a tuck marker will show up well. An edge-stitching attachment is very useful for stitching tucks evenly.

Gathers

Of all the ways of dealing with fullness, gathering is probably the most commonly used. The effectiveness of the method depends on:
1. choosing fine or soft materials to gather, e.g. cottons, silks, rayons, fine woollens;
2. having the right quantity of material to gather up, e.g. too much might be bulky even if the material is fine, too little would not be effective. Approximately half as much again as the finished gathered section gives slight fullness; twice as much gives a fairly full effect and three times as much gives a very full result;
3. working the gathers along the weft thread so that resulting folds hang with the selvedge threads;
4. setting in the gathers very evenly.

TO WORK GATHERS
By hand. Use running stitch (p. 63) and work two rows, one on the pattern line and the other 6 mm away in the turning. This second row helps to control the gathers when setting them in. Leave the cottons hanging ready for drawing up the gathers. Diagram 23. *N.B. Make very strong beginnings. Knots can be used as well as backstitches.*

ARRANGEMENT OF FULLNESS 65

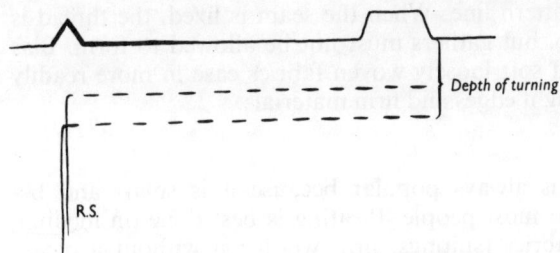

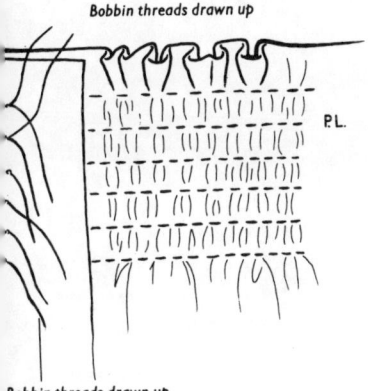

Gathers prepared for setting into band, yoke or seam

Bobbin threads drawn up

Bobbin threads drawn up

Shirring by machine

When a long piece of gathering is to be done, divide the work into sections to avoid using a very long thread, e.g. work a long frill in four sections, a skirt in two or four sections. Threads are ended off after gathers are drawn up and fixed in place. Diagram 31 (v).

By machine. Lengthen the stitch on the machine to the maximum.

Work two rows of machining on the right side of the material. one on the pattern line and one 6 mm away in the turning.

When ready to pull up the gathers, pull up the under cotton on the wrong side of the work.

A machine attachment for gathering, gathers up the material as the machining proceeds and holds it in position firmly gathered.

Shirring is the term given to a number of rows of gathering used to form a block of decoration, e.g. below a yoke or on sleeves.

Work by hand or machine as given above but work a number of rows below the pattern line to give the depth of shirring required. Diagram 24.

Draw up gathers evenly and tie the threads together in pairs with bows. It is best to end off the threads securely *after the gathers are set in* in case the fullness needs to be released or drawn up more tightly.

Easing

Easing means to arrange a slight amount of fullness so that no gather or pleat shows where the fullness is set in, e.g. at the head of a plain sleeve. Expert workers are able to arrange the fullness while fixing the seam by holding the work well rounded over the hand with the full side on top. The threads of the material can then be 'pushed' together as opposed to stretching them. The best way for the learner to ease in the fullness is to put in a running thread on the pattern line. When the seam is fixed, the thread is pulled up, but gathers must not be allowed to form. Bias edges and soft loosely woven fabrics ease in more readily than straight edges and firm materials.

Pleats

Pleating is always popular because it is smart and becoming to most people. Pleating is best done on medium weight fabrics (suitings, firm woollens) without a crease resistant finish. Too many pleats in washable fabric give trouble in laundering. Permanent pleating is only done commercially.

Pleats are used principally on tailored skirts, dress skirts and shorts, giving ample fullness in wear. They are also used on bodices of dresses and blouses where they do not provide extra fullness, but make an attractive style feature, e.g. centre back pleat on a blouse. In both cases the fit of the garment must be easy apart from the width in the pleats, otherwise the pleats will gape open, thus spoiling the set.

A pleat is formed of three layers of material; a fold of material is creased and laid flat on the garment, basted down and pressed. A pleat is held in position by the band or seam into which the pleats are fixed and after the basting is taken out, it swings from the seam. Often the fold of a pleat is stitched part way down its length to help keep it in position, but this is not essential.

KINDS OF PLEATS

According to the direction in which the folds of the pleats are fixed, different kinds of pleats are made. Diagram 25.

Knife pleats have the folds facing in one direction and can be made in groups if liked. The width of the pleat may be very narrow. e.g. 6 mm or up to 5 cm to 8 cm wide.

Box pleats are formed by facing the folds of two knife pleats away from each other in pairs. The folds of the pleats should meet on the wrong side.

Inverted pleats are made by facing the folds of two knife pleats towards each other to meet on the right side.

Other types of pleating are best done commercially by machine, such as:

Accordion pleating which consists of very fine pleats with the folds outstanding.

ARRANGEMENT OF FULLNESS

Sun ray pleating where the folds are outstanding but taper off to nothing at one end. Pleats may be narrow or fairly wide, e.g. 3 cm at the broad end.

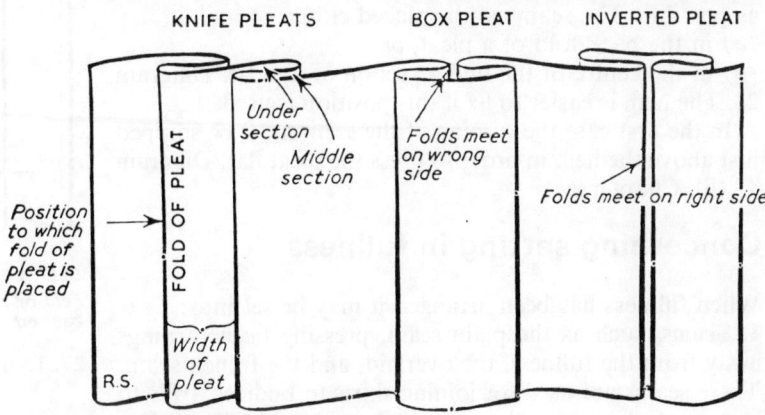

25. To show the construction of pleats

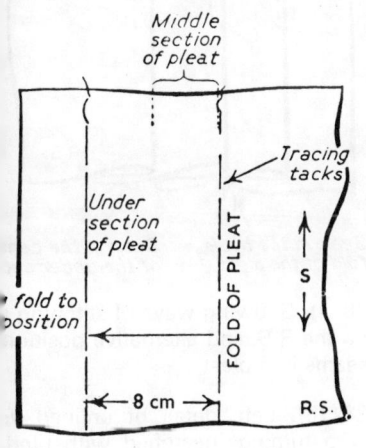

The position of one 4 cm knife marked with tacking

TO MARK THE POSITION OF PLEATS

Two lines should mark the position of each pleat; one to mark the fold of the pleat on the right side and the second to mark where the fold is to be placed on the right side. These two lines must be quite straight. Pleats hang better and keep their creases longer if they are made with the straight selvedge thread along the folds, but this will depend on the position of the pleats, the cut of the pattern and current fashion. Diagram 26.

TO MAKE PLEATS Diagram 27

1. Working from the right side, fold the material on the fold line and pin and tack the fold independently.
2. Place the fold against the next line marked on the right side and pin it down flat. While pinning, watch the weft grain at both ends to make sure that the threads are kept level in all the layers of material. Baste through the centre of the pleat.
3. Press the pleats thoroughly (Chapter 13).
4. If desired, stitch down the fold of a pleat on the right side along a part of its length. This can be done close to the fold or an even distance, e.g. 6 mm or 1 cm away from the fold. Diagram 28 shows three ways in which the stitching may terminate.

SEAMS WHICH FALL IN PLEATS

Whenever possible, complete the seams which fall in the pleats and fix and press the hem before pleating.

Seams should be so placed that they are as inconspicuous as possible. The seam can be placed either:

(a) in the back fold of a pleat, *or*

(b) in the centre of the under section of a pleat. Diagram 28. The hem is easier to fix if this position is used.

In the first case the turning of the seam must be snipped just above the hem in order to press the pleat flat. Diagram 42 (ii), Chapter 9.

Concerning setting in fullness

When fullness has been arranged it may be set into:

1. Seams, such as the plain seam, pressing both turnings away from the fullness, the overlaid, and the french seam. These seams are used for joining skirts to bodices, frills to hem and armhole edges, and sleeves to bodices. For method see Chapter 8.

2. Yokes on bodices of adults' and children's dresses, blouses and jackets and at the waist of skirts and shorts. Yokes, if unlined, may be fixed with plain or overlaid seams. The turnings are either overcast together or the turning on the yoke is folded over to bind the raw edges. Diagram 28 (ii). Lined yokes have the lining attached with the yoke in one step. See p. 231.

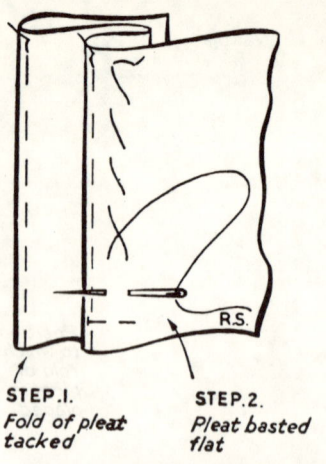

STEP.1.
Fold of pleat tacked

STEP.2.
Pleat basted flat

27. To fix pleats showing the two s

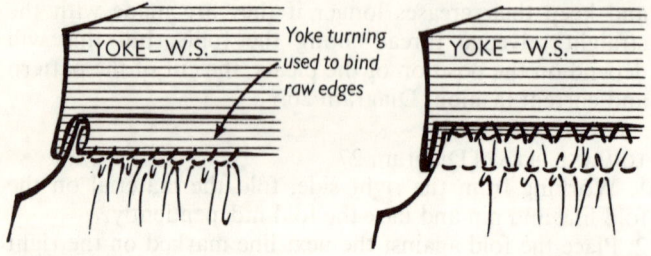

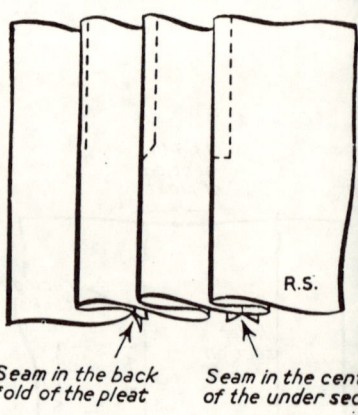

Seam in the back fold of the pleat

Seam in the cen of the under sec

28 (i). Showing ways of stitching on the R.S. and alternative position seams in a pleat

28 (ii). Left, detail of unlined y with turnings neatened with bind or zigzag machining

3. Bands which fasten, e.g. close fitting cuffs on full sleeves, waist bands of skirts and aprons, or closed circular bands as on loose cuffs. Chapters 14 and 16.

4. Binds and facings, e.g. necks of blouses and dresses. Chapter 9.

5. Elasticized edges. The use of elastic (or drawstrings) is a simple way of controlling fullness. Hems or casings can be made at waist, neck, sleeve and leg edges through which elastic is threaded. See p. 190. Also, elastic can be stitched directly on to an edge e.g. on pants, waist slips, skirts. See p. 303.

8 Seams

The line or shape of clothing depends very largely on the way the sections are joined together, that is, seamed. Clothes which fit closely, such as brassières, tightly fitting dresses and jackets, have more seams than loosely fitting clothes. This is necessary because so much curving and shaping is required to make the clothing fit the figure.

Seams can be made so that they are practically invisible, or they can be made to emphasize shape. Certain factors must be considered before the kind of seam is chosen.

When choosing seams consider:

1. THE KIND OF CLOTHING
Some clothes require to be more strongly made than others, e.g. overalls and school blouses are expected to stand harder wear than delicate lingerie and pretty dresses. Therefore very strong seams are needed for clothing which must stand up to hard wear and constant laundering. It should be noted, too, that certain seams are less trouble to iron than others.

2. THE KIND OF MATERIAL
Because materials vary considerably in weight and thickness, seams which are perfectly flat and neat in thin materials may be clumsy in thick ones, e.g. french seams are a good choice on a rayon blouse, but would be unsatisfactory used on a tweed skirt. Some materials fray badly as soon as they are cut; therefore a seam must be wide enough when finished to allow these edges to be adequately protected. The width must be considered in this way also when slippage is likely to occur, so that the seam may stand strain without pulling away. Information on seams to use, see pp. 31, 200.

Whatever seams are chosen they must be:
1. well stitched and pressed, so that the shape and appearance are good;
2. strong, in relation to the type of clothing and the material;
3. flat and neat on both right and wrong side.

As far as possible the same kind and width of seam should be used for the main seams, but this will depend largely on the style chosen.

In order that directions given for seams may be clearly understood, the following is an explanation of the terms used in connection with seams:

The seam allowance or turning is the amount of material allowed outside the pattern line to make a seam. Diagram 29 (i). This may be as little as 0.5 cm or as much as 3 cm to 4 cm. The whole of the turning allowance is not necessarily used for making a seam, as extra is often given to allow for letting out when fitting.

The seam width is the final width of a seam when it has been made, and will vary according to the type of material from 3 mm to 2.5 cm. Diagram 30 (i).

When french and double-stitched seams are being made, this seam width is often alluded to as the 'fell'.

Commonly used seams, their features and directions for making

The open or plain seam. Diagram 29 (iii)
This is a flat seam showing no stitching on the right side, and is consequently used for joins which are meant to show as little as possible, e.g. joins in binding, underarm, shoulder and sleeve seams on clothing of all kinds, made in both thin and thick materials. The turnings may be pressed open or both pressed to one side, according to where the seam is used. Diagram 30 (ii). The seam is not a quick one to launder as the turnings may have to be

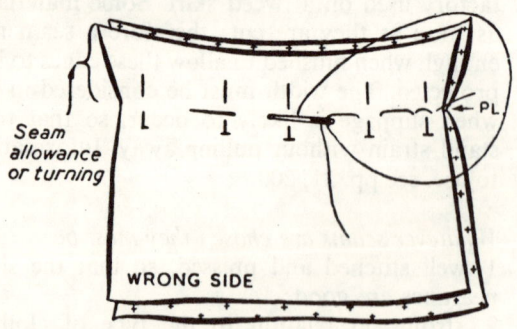

29 (i). To fix an open seam and to show how to work even tacking

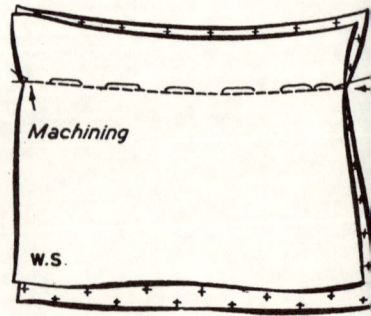

29 (ii). An open seam tacked and stitched

(iii). Open seam pressed and the nings snipped

Straight cuts into the turning on curved edges

Seam width

W.S.

opened with the toe of the iron to press it flat. Therefore it is not a good choice for the main seams of articles which are frequently laundered. The seam width (after neatening) is usually 1 to 2 cm wide.

DIRECTIONS FOR MAKING OPEN SEAMS

1. *Preparation*
If the P.L.s are not marked, trim the seam allowance evenly, so that the line is good, i.e. perfectly straight if it is intended to be straight, a smooth curve if a curved edge.

2. *Fixing*
Place the edges to be seamed with the right sides facing and pin with the edges level. If pattern lines have been previously marked with thread, keep these lines exactly on top of each other. Tack at the depth of the seam allowance and remove the pins.

3. *Stitching*
Machine on the tacking thread. If a seam is to be made by hand, use running stitch with a back stitch at regular intervals, working as close to the tacking as possible. Remove the tackings. Diagrams 29 (i) (ii).

4. *Neatening and pressing*
(i) If the edges are not exposed to wear, e.g. seams in a

facing or a band, there is no need to neaten them in any way. Complete them as follows:
(a) Trim the turning evenly 3 mm to 6 mm in depth.
(b) Press the turnings open with the toe of the iron or press them both to one side.
(c) Snip curves sufficiently to make the seam lie flat. Diagram 29 (iii).
(ii) If the edges are exposed to wear, one of the following methods may be chosen to neaten them:

Pinking, a method suitable for non-fraying materials, is best used on clothing which is not intended to be laundered, e.g. dresses, skirts and trousers made in flannel.
(a) Mark the final width of the seam with chalk.
(b) Cut off the surplus material using pinking shears.
(c) Press the seam.
(d) Snip curves with pinking shears. Diagram 30 (i).

Overcasting, by hand or machine, a popular way of neaten-

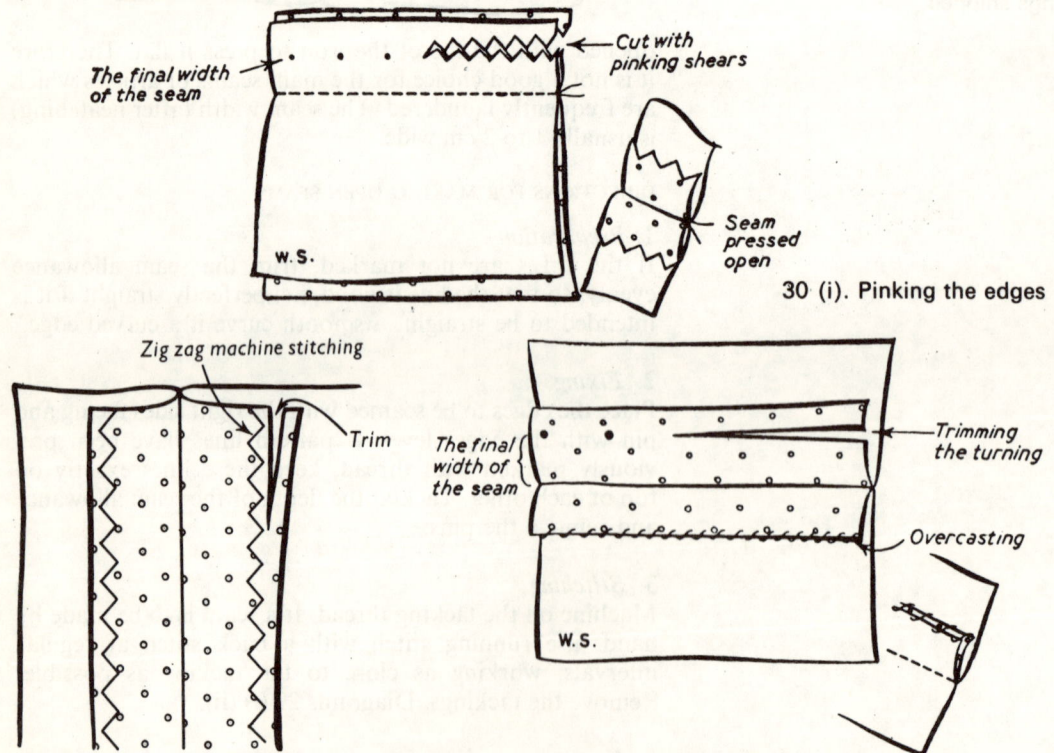

30 (i). Pinking the edges

30 (ii). Overcasting the edges singly or together by machine or by hand

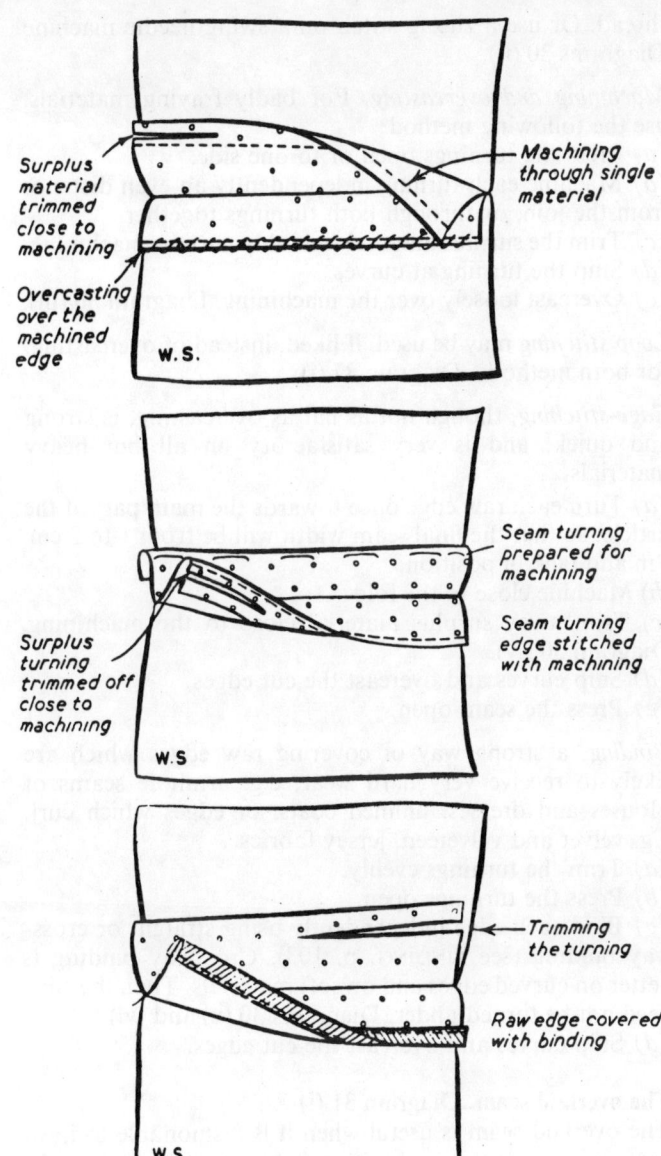

Edges machined and overcast

Edge-stitched turnings

Straight binding

ing the edges of any type of material, giving a very flat and neat finish.

(a) Trim turnings to the width required.
(b) Press the seam and snip the curves.
(c) Overcast each edge loosely by hand using matching

thread. Or use a zigzag stitch on a swing needle machine. Diagrams 30 (ii).

Machining and overcasting. For badly fraying materials, use the following method:
(a) Press the turnings open or to one side.
(b) Machine each turning independently an even distance from the join, or through both turnings together.
(c) Trim the surplus material right down to the machining.
(d) Snip the turning at curves.
(e) Overcast loosely over the machining. Diagram 30 (iii).

Loop stitching may be used, if liked, instead of overcasting, for both methods. Diagram 87 (i).

Edge-stitching, though not as flat as overcasting, is strong and quick, and is very satisfactory on all but heavy materials.
(a) Turn each raw edge once towards the main part of the article, so that the final seam width will be from 1 to 2 cm. Pin and tack in position.
(b) Machine close to the fold.
(c) Trim away surplus material close to the machining. Diagram 30 (iv).
(d) Snip curves and overcast the cut edges.
(e) Press the seam open.

Binding, a strong way of covering raw edges which are likely to receive very hard wear, e.g. armhole seams of blouses and dresses, unlined coats, or edges which curl, e.g. velvet and velveteen, jersey fabrics.
(a) Trim the turnings evenly.
(b) Press the turnings open.
(c) Bind each edge independently using straight or crossway binding (see BINDING, p. 103). Crossway binding is better on curved edges and on soft materials. Then the edge need not be turned under. Diagrams 30 (v) and (vi).
(d) Snip curves and overcast the cut edges.

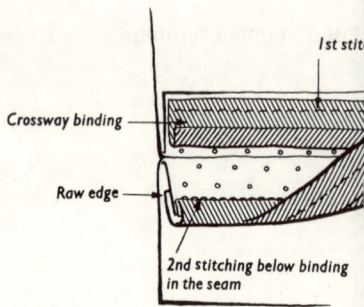

30 (vi). Crossway binding

The overlaid seam. Diagram 31 (i)
The overlaid seam is useful when it is fashionable to have some seams emphasized with stitching on the right side. The seam is strong because it is stitched through three thicknesses of material, is flat for laundering and is quick to make. Fixing panels in bodices and skirts, setting on yokes and bands, are but a few examples of when an overlaid seam can be used, in both under and outer, children's and adults' clothing.

SEAMS

DIRECTIONS FOR MAKING OVERLAID SEAMS

1. *Preparation*

This seam is easier to handle if pattern lines are thread-marked. If this is omitted, see that the turning allowance is even.

Decide which section is to be uppermost, i.e. overlaid on to the under section when the seam is made. The position of the seam will influence this, e.g. skirt panels are fixed with the centre panel overlaid on to the side ones. When one of the sections to be joined has fullness, the plain section is overlaid on to the full part. Diagram 31 (i).

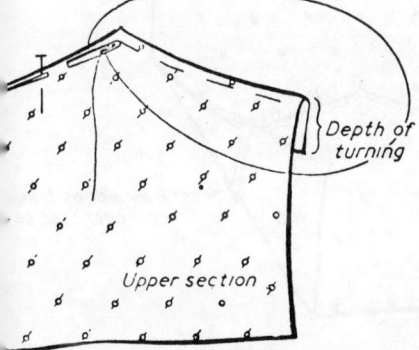

Overlaid seams. How to distinguish the upper and under sections of a seam

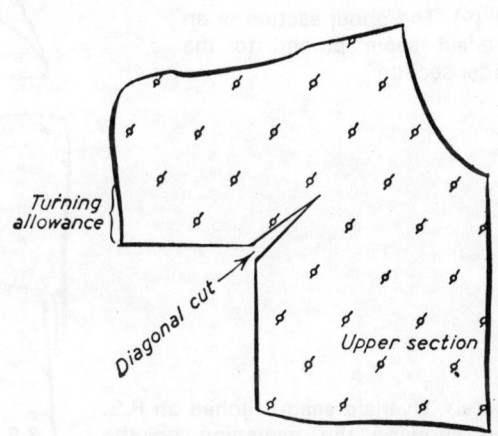

31 (iv). The turning snipped at an inner corner

To prepare the upper section of an overlaid seam

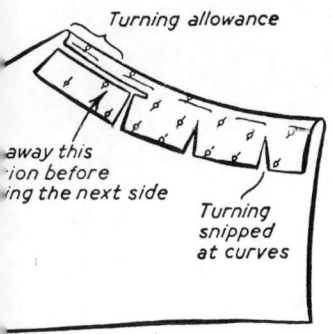

The surplus material cut away at an outer corner

FOUNDATION METHODS

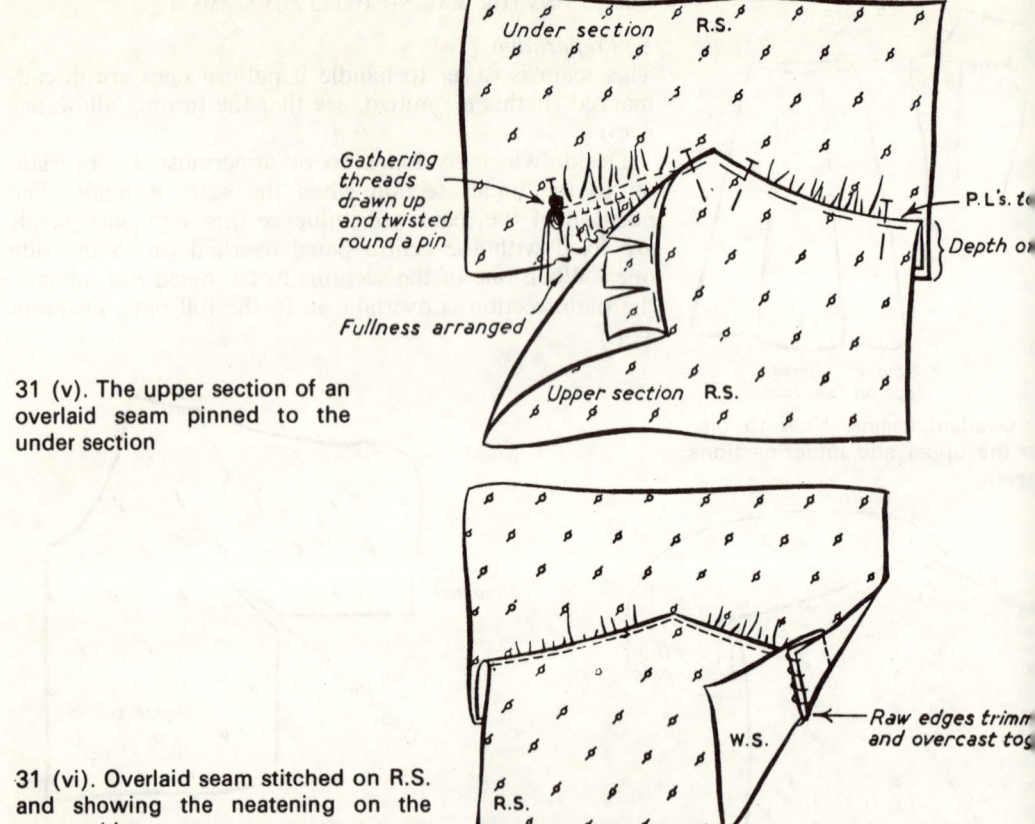

31 (v). The upper section of an overlaid seam pinned to the under section

31 (vi). Overlaid seam stitched on R.S. and showing the neatening on the wrong side

2. *Fixing*
(a) Fold the turning allowance of the upper section on to the wrong side. Pin and tack in position, snipping the turning allowance on curved edges. Have the right side of the material uppermost in the hand while preparing this section. Press the turning on the wrong side. Diagram 31 (ii).

Fix angles neatly in the following way:
(i) Outer corners. Pin and tack one side before fixing the second side.

Cut away surplus material near the corner before turning the second side. Diagram 31 (iii).
(ii) Inner corners. Pin the turning allowance in position, but when the angle is reached, cut diagonally through the turning allowance up to the pattern line. Diagram 31 (iv).

Continue fixing the turning in position, and tack rather closely near the corner.

The corner can be strengthened first in one of two ways. Either stay-stitch (i.e. machine on single fabric) on the P.L. round the corner or face the corner, see p. 184.

(b) Arrange any fullness, if it is provided, in the under section, and press pleats, tucks or darts.

(c) Place wrong side of the upper section on to the right side of the under, with the fold of the upper exactly on the pattern line of the under section.

Pin in position, working from the right side. Pull up gathering threads (if any) and arrange evenly.

Tack closely still working from the right side. Diagram 31 (v).

3. *Stitching*
Machine close to the fold on the right side, or at an even distance from it, e.g. 3 or 6 mm. Diagram 31 (vi).

4. *Neatening and pressing*
Methods used for neatening the overlaid seam may be any of those described for the open seam, except edge-stitching, with the following differences:

(*a*) The seam width is rarely less than 6 mm or more than 2 cm.

(*b*) Both turnings are neatened together, thus speeding up the finishing of the seam. Take special care that the neatening stitch is made loosely, as the set of the seam will be spoilt if the turnings are tightened. Diagram 31 (vi).

The method described for badly fraying materials on p. 74 can be used.

The french seam. Diagram 32.
This is a neat seam about equal in strength to an open seam and is used for similar purposes. It has two advantages over an open seam, in that it is quicker to make and easier to launder, because both raw edges are enclosed in a fell, which is pressed to one side of the seam. The french seam is not as flat as most other seams mentioned in this chapter, so that it cannot be used successfully on any but fine or medium weight fabrics. Because it is quickly made, easily ironed and suitable for thin materials, it is ideal for use on underclothes (with the exception of close fitting clothing worn next to the skin, where the fell might cause discomfort), washing dresses, blouses and overalls.

78 FOUNDATION METHODS

32 (i). A french seam tacked, st[itched] and the turning partly trimmed

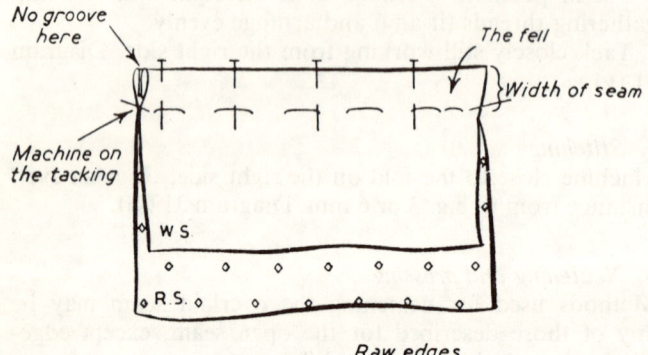

32 (ii). A french seam fixed for the final stitching

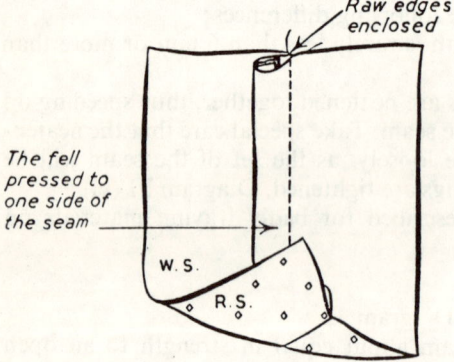

32 (iii). A french seam with t[he] stitching in place and the fell pre[ssed to] one side

DIRECTIONS FOR MAKING FRENCH SEAMS

1. *Preparation*

Decide how wide the fell is to be when finished. On strong fabrics such as cambric, linen and silk, 3 mm is a suitable width, but on materials which are likely to fray quickly or on which slippage is likely to occur, such as viscose and nylon, 5 to 6 mm is safer.

Trim the turning allowances down to twice the width the fell will be when finished, unless pattern lines have been threadmarked, e.g. 1.2 cm turning allowance for a 6 mm fell.

2. *Fixing*
Pin the pieces together with the wrong sides of the material facing and the edges even or P.L.s together. Tack on the pattern line. Try on garment for fitting at this stage.

3. *Stitching a seam the first time*
Stitch outside the pattern line in the seam allowance, making the distance between the tacking and machining equal to the width the fell is to be when finished, e.g. stitch 6 mm away from the tacking if the fell is to be 6 mm when finished. If the seam is to be done by hand, use running stitch combined with back stitch.

4. *Trimming the turnings*
Remove tackings and trim down the turnings to slightly less than the finished fell, e.g. for a 6 mm fell, trim the turnings to a bare 3 mm, so that the raw edges will not show when the seam is completed. Diagram 32 (i).

Snip the turnings on all curved edges.

5. *Finishing and second stitching*
Turn the seam so that the right sides of the material face each other.

Push the seam up with the thumb and forefinger of both hands so that there is no groove along the top, and pin it in position.

Tack the width of the fell from the top, e.g. 6 mm, so that the raw edges are enclosed in the fell. Diagram 32 (ii).

Stitch close to the tacking. This final stitching should fall exactly on the pattern line if the turning allowance has been accurately calculated and the seam well made. Diagram 32 (iii).

Press the seam with the fell to one side, towards the back of the garment.

Double stitched seams. Diagram 33.
These are the strongest seams because the strain in wear is taken by two sets of stitching. Further, they are very flat seams and are the easiest seams of all to launder. They can be used on all but heavy fabrics, and are excellent for clothing which is given hard wear and frequent washing, e.g., on shirts, jeans, underwear and nightwear where flatness is an additional advantage, and on overalls. Other names for these seams are flat felled, machined fell, machined flat seam. Seams can be made on the wrong or right side of the fabric. It is easier to make them on to the

W.S. where only one row of stitching shows on the R.S. (Diagram 33 (iii)), but the effect is not as smart as when the seam is made on to the right side and two rows of stitching show. Diagram 33 (iv).

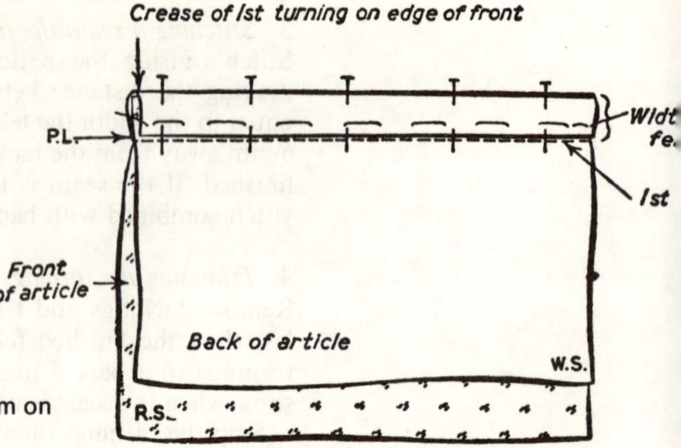

33 (i). To fix a double stitched seam on to the W.S. of the material

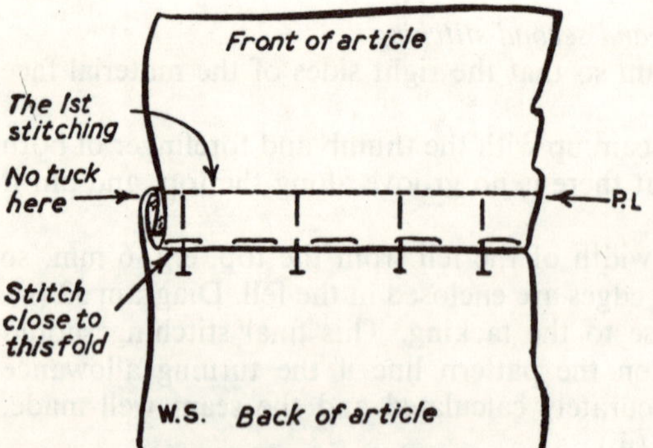

33 (ii). A double stitched seam tacked ready for the final machining

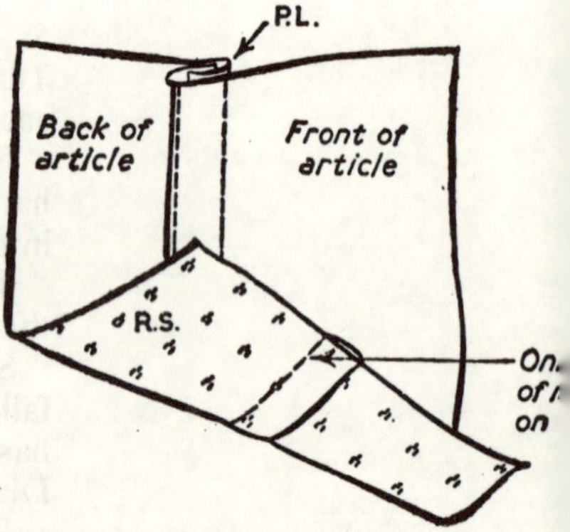

33 (iii). A double stitched seam made on to the W.S. of the material

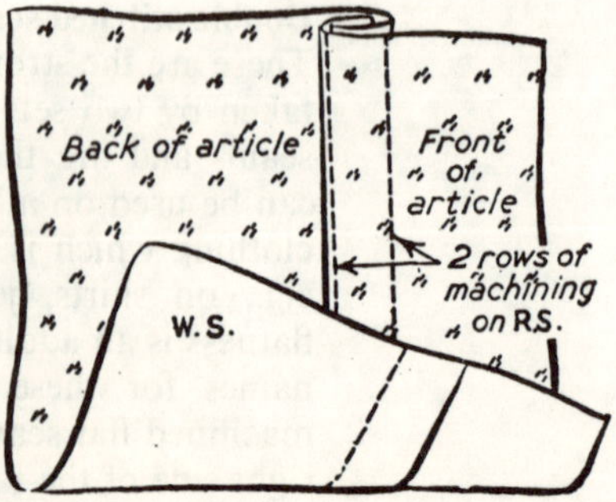

33 (iv). A double stitched seam made on to the right side of the material

A. DIRECTIONS FOR MAKING A DOUBLE STITCHED SEAM ON TO THE WRONG SIDE OF THE MATERIAL*

1. *Preparation*
The average width of the fell of this seam is 6 mm, but it can be made narrower on very thin material, e.g. 3 mm on a baby's cotton pants. The fell is always stitched flat on to the back part of a garment. The diagrams show that the front edge of the garment will require a larger seam allowance than the back, therefore twice the width of the fell is allowed on the front edge, and exactly the width of the fell on the back edge; e.g. for a 6 mm fell, allow 1.2 cm on the front and 6 mm on the back. This distinction need not be taken into account on loosely fitting articles such as overalls when twice the width of the fell can be allowed on both edges.

Trim the seam allowances on both edges to the required depth.

The success of this seam depends particularly upon accurately cut turnings.

2. *Fixing*
Fold the turning on the front edge over to the right side of the material, making the width of the turning equal to the width of the fell. Crease the turning in position.

Place the back edge under this turning with the edge level with the crease and the right sides of the material facing.

Pin and tack through the three thicknesses of material, just above the raw edge. Diagram 33 (i).

3. *Stitching*
Machine just below the raw edge through two thicknesses of material. Diagram 33 (i).

4. *Finishing and stitching the seam flat*
Open out the seam and pin and tack the fell flat on to the back of the article, so that the raw edge is hidden. Pull the pieces well apart so that there is no tuck on the underside. Diagram 33 (ii).

Machine close to the fold; take out the tacks and press the seam. Diagram 33 (iii).†

---

* An alternative method of handling this type of seam where the pattern pattern lines are fixed together before trimming the turnings, is given given in *Introduction to Needlework*, p. 118.

† A quick method to simulate this seam is given in *Introduction to Needlework*, p. 119, Imitation machined fell.

B. DIRECTIONS FOR MAKING A DOUBLE STITCHED SEAM ON TO THE RIGHT SIDE OF THE MATERIAL

The method of making the seam is similar to the method given for seam A except for the following differences in the *fixing*:

1. Fold the turning allowance on the front edge over to the *wrong* side of the material.

2. Place the wrong sides of the pieces of material facing one another when pinning them together, because the fell is to be made on to the right side of the work.

Piped seams Diagram 34.

Piping is an effective way of outlining and strengthening seams and edges—see p. 108, and is also a very hard wearing method. Piping consists of a narrow outstanding fold of material which is inserted into seams at yokes, waists, at neck, collar, armhole, sleeve, cuff and hem edges and on bags, cushions and covers. Piping may be either *flat* or *corded* when a cord is enclosed in the fold of material. The choice depends on whether the piping is to be used on clothing or household articles, whether the material is thick or light weight and whether it will need to be washed frequently.

Flat piping. The usual width is 3 mm, and it can be stitched in without any adjustment to the machine. It is preferable to use flat piping on washable articles and it needs very accurate work if it is to look professional.

Corded piping is easier to do than flat piping but is more difficult to wash. Cord for piping must be bought. It is made in various yarns—cotton—nylon—rayon and in many thicknesses, as fine as twine or as thick as rope. There is a choice of black or white. A special cording or zipper foot must be used on the machine in order to stitch close to the cord unless it is stitched strongly by hand. Cotton cord should be shrunk by washing in hot water.

Fabrics for either kind of piping *must be cut on the true cross*, but they can be contrasting in colour or texture to the main part.

A good result should have an even amount of piping showing, should lie smoothly along the seam without the main part being drawn up or stretched and joins should be as inconspicuous as possible.

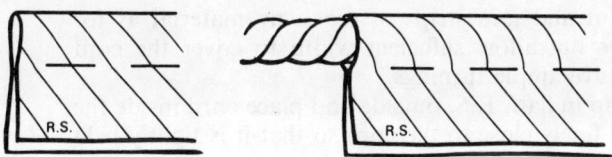

34 (i). Crossway strips prepared for FLAT and CORDED piping

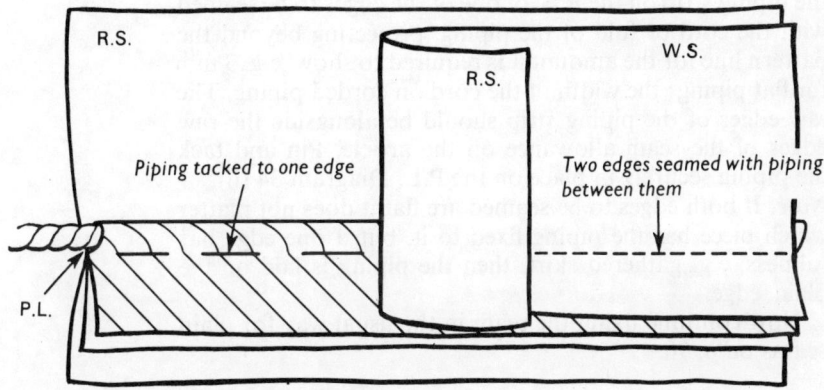

34 (ii). Piped seam prepared and stitched

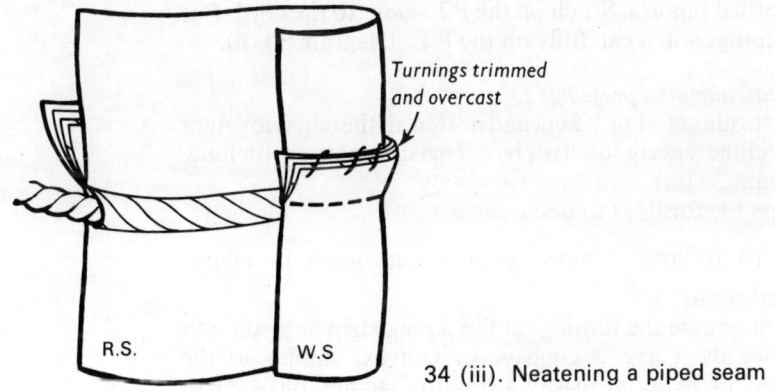

34 (iii). Neatening a piped seam

DIRECTIONS FOR MAKING PIPED SEAMS

1. *Preparation of the piping.* Diagram 34 (i)

Flat. Cut strips of material on the true cross not less than 2.5 cm wide and join them to make sufficient length.

Fold the strip in half with the R.S. outside, pin, tack and press.

Corded. Cut and join strips of crossway material as for flat pipings but allow sufficient width to cover the cord and still leave ample turnings.

Fold strip in half, R.S. outside and place cord inside the fold. Tack finely close to the cord so that it is tightly held inside the strip.

2. *Fixing flat or corded piping into a plain seam*

See that the edges to be seamed are clearly marked. Place the piping strip on the R.S. of one of the edges to be seamed with the cord or fold of the piping, projecting beyond the pattern line for the amount it is required to show, e.g. 3 mm for flat piping; the width of the cord on corded piping. The raw edges of the piping strip should be alongside the raw edges of the seam allowance on the article. Pin and tack the piping securely in place on the P.L. Diagram 34 (ii).

Note. If both edges to be seamed are flat it does not matter which piece has the piping fixed to it, but if one edge has fullness, e.g. gathered skirt, then the piping is laid on the plain edge.

Now continue fixing the seam in the usual way for plain seams on p. 70.

3. *Stitching*

Use a zipper foot on the machine or back-stitch closely for corded pipings. Stitch on the P.L. *close* to the cord. For flat pipings stitch carefully on the P.L. Diagram 34 (ii).

4. *Neatening and pressing*

Trim turnings to 1 or 1.5 cm and neaten all the edges together by machine (zigzag stitch) or by overcasting or loopstitching. Diagram 34 (iii).

Press the turnings to one side.

HOW TO HANDLE CURVES, ANGLES AND JOINS IN PIPING

Curved seams

Stretch or ease the turning on the piping strip according to whether the curve is concave or convex, similar to the method of fixing crossway strips for facings on a curve p. 103. Keep the piping itself flat on the P.L.

Angles

Follow the line of the angle with the piping as closely as possible and ease the piping for about 2 cm each side of the corner. Allow the turning allowance to form a tapered pleat on an outer corner, and snip the turning at an inner corner. Diagram 34 (iv).

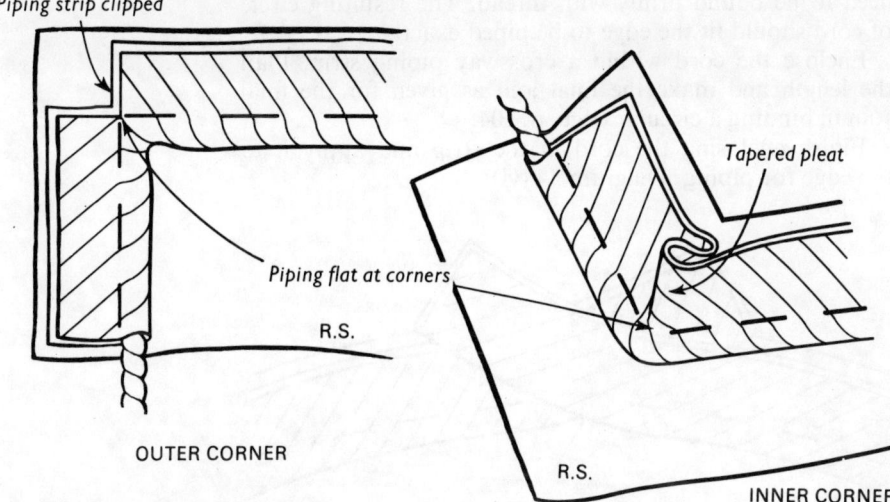

34 (iv). Piping tacked in place at corners

Joins
There are two ways to join piping on a circular edge, e.g. necklines without openings, armholes, cushions. A quick method only suitable for flat and very fine corded pipings and a longer, but invisible method suitable for corded pipings.

Quick method. Make the join in an inconspicuous place. Allow the piping strips to cross each other and slant towards the edge of the seam allowance. Tack right across the piping through all thicknesses but keeping the amount projecting even. Diagram 34 (v).

Invisible join method. This requires accurate measurement and gives a far better appearance than the previous method.

Decide the *exact* length of cord required for the seam and cut the cord this length plus 5 cm for making a spliced join.

Splice the cord and join it by untwisting 5 cm of cord at each end, cutting away half the thickness (one strand from one end of three-ply cord and two strands from the other) and twisting the ends together again. The join will need to be bound firmly with thread. The resulting circle of cord should fit the edge to be piped exactly.

Enclose the cord within a crossway piping strip. Plan the length and make the final join as given for the final join in binding a circular edge, p. 104.

Finish enclosing the cord in the strip and apply it to the edge for piping. Diagram 34 (vi).

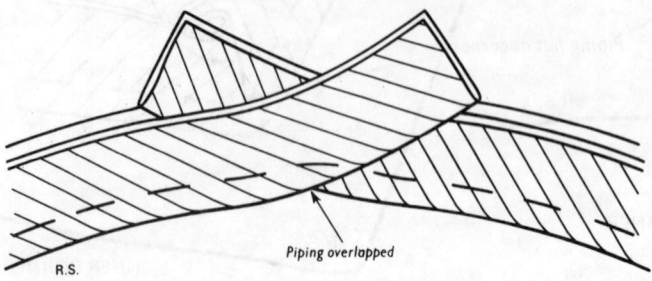

34 (v). Quick method of making a circular join

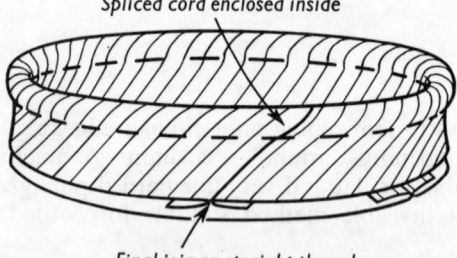

34 (vi). Invisible join. Circular piping ready for placing on article

General points concerning seams

HANDLING
1. Spread the work out and fix the seams flat on the table.
2. When joining a full (i.e. gathered, eased) edge to a plain one, have the full edge uppermost throughout the construction of a seam, so that the fullness can be controlled. An exception to this is when an overlaid seam is being made.
3. When one bias edge is to be seamed to a straight edge, there is danger of the material dropping on the bias side

after the seam is made. To avoid this, fix the seam with the bias edge on top and stretch it slightly when fixing. Smoothing the material down with the hand while pinning will probably cause sufficient stretching.

4. When two bias edges are to be seamed, the stitching is apt to prevent the seam dropping with the threads of the material on each side. This causes the seam to poke out and up at the hem edge, an effect often seen on inexpensive ready-made clothing, e.g. on side seams of flared skirts. Prevent this by slightly stretching the seam while it is being stitched, that is, pulling the work a little as it goes under the machine.

DIRECTION OF FIXING

When several seams are made, fix each one in the same direction, e.g. the seams of a skirt should all be pinned, tacked and stitched from the waist towards the hem.

ORDER OF FIXING AND STITCHING

1. Keep all seams at the same stage of work as far as practical, e.g. pin and tack a number of seams, then stitch them all, and finally do all the neatening. This method will give a more accurate result and is quicker.

2. Complete and press the seams in one section before joining to another section, e.g. finish seams in a bodice and skirt before making the waist seam; finish the centre front and back seams of trousers before making the leg seams.

SEAM JUNCTIONS

1. When seams cross or meet, take particular care when pinning the final seam that the joins are opposite, e.g. when making the waist seam, see that the underarm seams of the bodice and skirt are opposite; pin these together before fixing the rest of the seam.

2. Take care that seam fells and turnings are not caught in tightly to another seam, so spoiling the set on the right side, e.g. the shoulder seam is liable to be drawn in too tightly to the neck finish and the armhole seam, unless care is taken to keep it quite flat on the shoulder.

3. Trim down or cut away turnings at seam junctions whenever possible to avoid bulkiness. Turnings on thick fabrics can be graded (sometimes called layered). See page 211.

9 The finish of edges

When the choice of the best or most effective way of neatening edges of articles and garments has to be made, the worker will be influenced both by the kind of material being used and the particular edge to be neatened. Of the wide selection of finishes from which to choose, some are more suited to thin than thick materials and some are plainer, daintier, stronger or smarter than others. The edges on garments to be treated are—edges of neck lines, armholes, sleeves at wrist or elbow, waist of skirts, aprons, pants, hem edges on all types of articles and garments. The method selected must in each case be strong enough to withstand the kind of wear it will receive. Obviously some edges will require a much more hardwearing finish than others. Most of the methods given here can be used in such a way that they are plain and comparatively inconspicuous or so that they provide a decorative or smart finish.

Hems

A hem is made by folding material twice on to one side of the work, making the first turn a narrow one. The hem is generally turned on to the wrong side of the work, and is held in position with suitable stitches. A smart appearance depends on a good line at the outer fold, an even depth of hem, a flat set and good stitching. The depth of a hem when finished can be narrow, e.g. 3 mm, or wide, e.g. 10 cm.

For all hems prepare the work as follows
1. To calculate the width of material required to make a hem allow the depth of the finished hem plus a turning allowance. The turning allowance varies between 3 mm and 1 cm according to the weight of the material and the final depth of hem; e.g. to make a 3 cm hem on a gingham apron allow 3 cm plus 6 mm, i.e. 3.6 cm; to make a 6 cm hem on a jersey dress allow 6 cm plus 1 cm, i.e. 7 cm.
2. The edge to be turned should be either quite straight or a

smooth curve. When the edge is on the straight thread it is a good plan to pull a thread along the edge and trim down to it, to make quite certain it is true.

Narrow hems

To make narrow hems, i.e. between 3 mm and 2.5 cm wide, used on both straight and curved edges:

1. Fold and crease a narrow turning on to the wrong side of the work along the whole length of the edge, holding the wrong side of the material towards the worker.

The following is a special way to hold the work so that it is easy to keep the turning even and avoid stretching bias edges:

With the thumb of the left hand below the edge, bring the turning over with the first finger. Then hold the crease firmly between the thumb and finger.

Transfer the material to the right hand and as the left hand continues turning and creasing, pleat up the crease two or three times in the right hand. Diagram 35 (i).

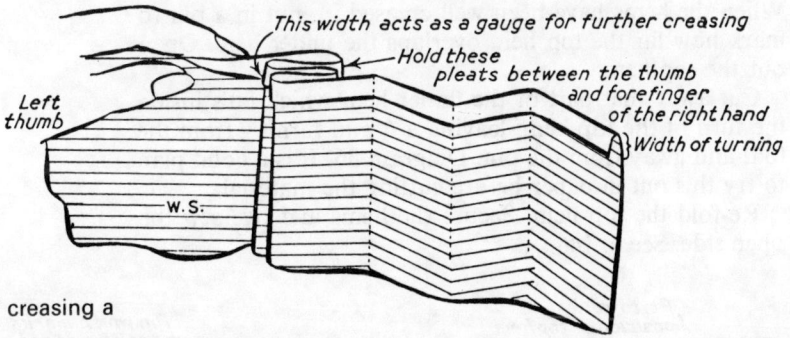

35 (i). The method of creasing a turning on an edge

By this method the turning, having once been measured, acts as a gauge for measuring throughout the creasing. When the material will not crease, pinning and tacking or pressing must be used instead.

2. Fold and crease the material over a second time on to the wrong side of the work, making this second turn the final depth of the hem. Hold and crease the work in the same way as before.

3. Pin this fold in position and tack it down to the garment. Diagram 35 (ii).

4. Secure the fold with hemming stitches, slip hemming, machining or an embroidery stitch according to where the hem is used; e.g. machine the hem on a curtain; use plain hemming on a baby's nightdress; slip hemming on a skirt;

embroidery or decorative machine stitch on a tray cloth.

When several sides of an article are to be finished with a hem, turn the selvedge hems first, then the weft hems, so that the corners will overlap symmetrically.

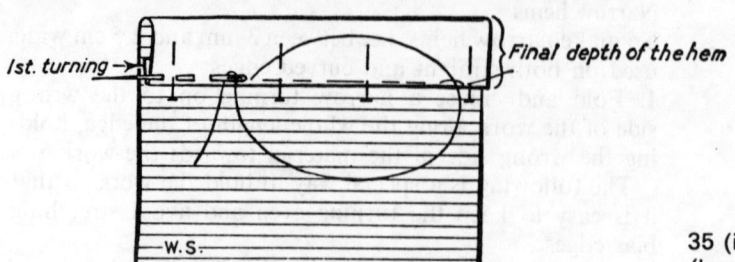

35 (ii). A hem pinned and tacked (long and short tacking)

TREATMENT OF CORNERS

There are two ways of fixing corners:

Method 1. A tailored corner where the underlying material is cut away to thin it down

When the hems have been well creased in, put in a pin to mark how far the top hem overlaps the under hem. Open out the top hem.

Cut away that part of the under hem which falls inside the turn of the top hem, leaving a 6 mm turning from the fold and away from the pin. Diagram 36. It is a good plan to try this out in paper before cutting the material.

Re-fold the top hem. Secure the hems and oversew the open side. See p. 146.

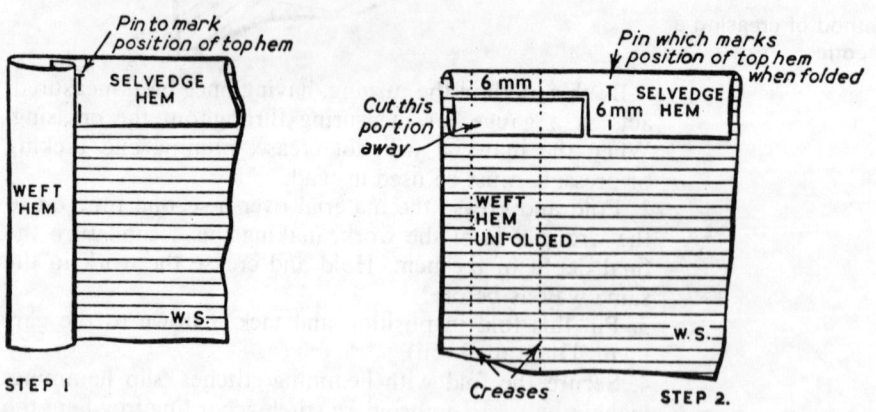

36. A tailored corner showing where cut away the surplus material

Method 2. A mitred corner where a seam is made diagonally from the corner

This is a more difficult corner to handle than the previous one. It is used chiefly on household articles, such as table cloths and curtains.

Crease in the hems on both edges.

Fold the corner to make a diagonal crease from the outer corner of the hem to the inner corner.

Cut off the turnings of the top hem 6 mm away from the crease.

Open out the under hem and cut off the turnings 6 mm away from the crease.

Now, with both hems opened out, press in the 6 mm turning allowance on to the wrong side across the corner.

Re-fold the hems in position and oversew or slip-stitch the diagonal folds together. Diagrams 37 (i) (ii) (iii) (iv).

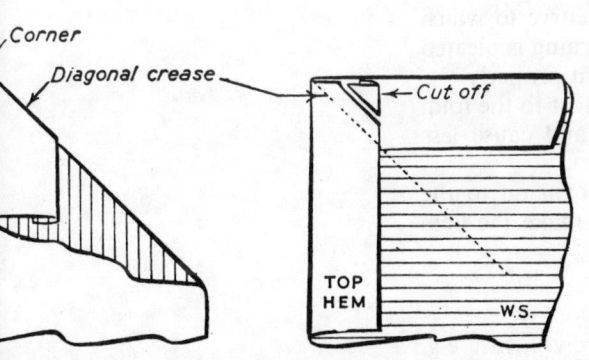

37. A mitred corner

37 (i). Corner creased diagonally

37 (ii). The surplus material cut away from the top hem

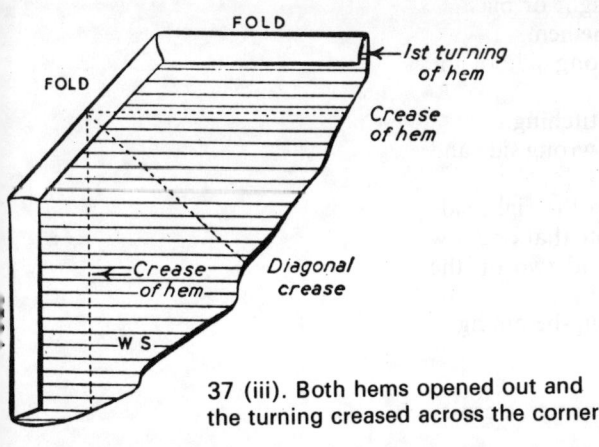

37 (iii). Both hems opened out and the turning creased across the corner

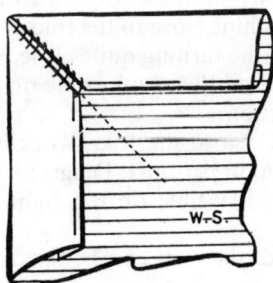

37 (iv). Hems re-folded and the folds oversewn together

CURVED EDGES

Only very narrow hems can be used on deeply curved edges, such as the neck and armholes of children's petticoats and pinafores and the legs of panties, because the fold of the first turning has to be stretched to enable it to lie flat on the garment. Diagram 38 shows that on *concave curved edges* the length of the first turn is shorter than the curve to which it is to be fixed on the garment.

1. Crease in the first turning and snip it at frequent intervals almost to the fold. This will let the turning spread out.
2. Stretch the first fold between the thumb and forefingers, particularly on the bias and crossway parts.
3. Crease in the second turning in the usual way.

Convex curves which are made the other way, such as those on the outside of round collars, flaps of bags, skirts of dresses, bring the opposite difficulty. The length of the fold of the second turn is longer than the curve to which it has to be fixed. In this case the second turning is pleated with small wedge-shaped pleats to make it fit properly.

1. Crease in the first turning and snip it almost to the fold. This will allow the cut edges to overlap and cause less bulk.
2. Crease the second turning and pin it down on to the garment. Form small pleats at the fold to make the hem lie flat.

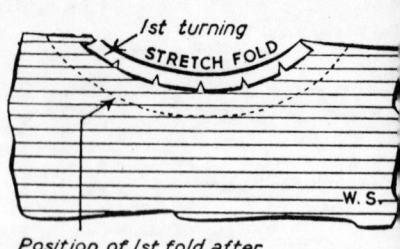

38. Treatment of the first turning of a hem on a concave curved edge

EDGE-STITCHED HEMS

Edge-stitched hems are popular for narrow hems, e.g. hem edges of frills, and flared skirts. It is a neat finish; it is quick to make and simplifies the handling of cross-cut edges, though it is useful on any edge, straight or bias.

1. Allow 1 cm turning allowance to make the hem.
2. Fold over a 6 mm turning on to the wrong side of the work and machine close to the fold.
3. Trim away the turning quite close to the stitching.
4. Make a second turn 3 mm wide on to the wrong side and tack it in postion.
5. Machine close to the fold, working with the right side of the material uppermost. Diagram 39. Note that one row of machining is visible on the right side and two on the wrong.

If preferred, the hem can be fixed with slip-hemming.

Wide hems

Wide hems are chiefly concerned with skirt hems. A cross-

THE FINISH OF EDGES 93

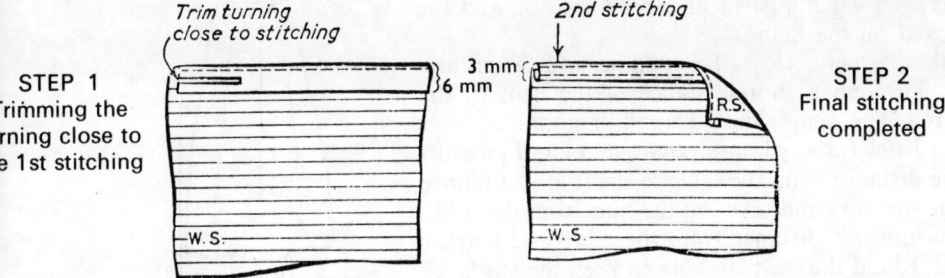

An edge-stitched hem

cut skirt should be allowed to hang for several days before adjusting the length, to allow the threads to drop to their fullest extent. If during the making up a skirt is kept hanging when not being worked upon, it should be ready when the time comes for fixing the hem.

TO ADJUST A HEM LEVEL

Method 1 is used when it is not possible to try a garment on to check the length.

Fold the skirt in half with a fold along the centre back and centre front. Pin the seams together in a few places. Place the garment flat on the table and smooth the material from the waist down towards the hem.

Measure the length of skirt required from the waist line and put in a line of pins to mark the hem level. Take the measurement at right angles from the waist and when there is no waist seam measure from the waist level, which should be thread marked. Diagram 40 (i).

Mark the hem level with tailors' tacks. Measure off the hem allowance and cut off the surplus turning.
turning.

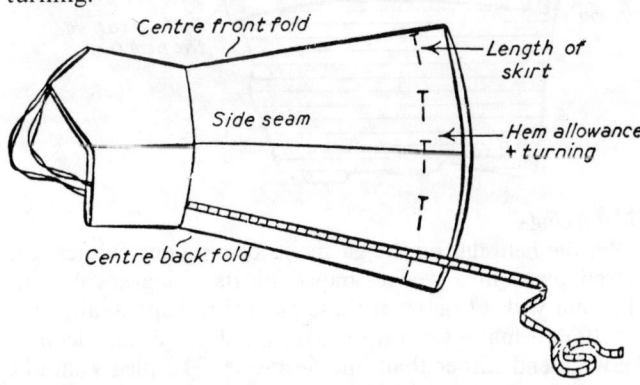

(i). A method of adjusting a hem level on a garment

Method 2 is used when a garment can be tried on and the length checked on the figure.

Put on the garment, close the opening and fasten any belt or tie. Turn up a short distance of the hem to the length desired. The wearer should stand on a table.

Use a yardstick (or any long straight stick) and measure or mark the distance from the table to the fold just pinned up; note the measure and take out the pins from the fold.

Now measure this distance from the table and mark it with pins all round the skirt. Be sure to keep the yardstick upright. A skirt marker which puffs powdered chalk on to the fabric can be used instead. Remove the garment from the figure and substitute a line of tacking for the pins, making the line a good one. Diagram 40 (ii).

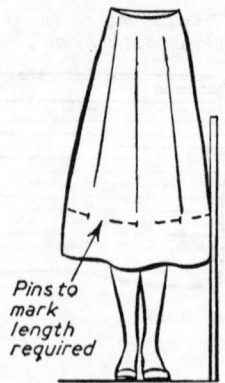

40 (ii). Method of marking the hem level with a yardstick

TO FIX WIDE HEMS

Preliminary fixing. Diagrams 41 (i) and (ii).
1. Fold the whole of the hem allowance over to the wrong side exactly on the line marking the hem level, and pin and tack the fold in place.
2. Tack the turning flat on the garment through the centre of the hem. Try on the garment again to make sure the skirt hangs evenly at the hem.
3. Measure the width of the hem plus turning allowance from the fold, and trim off the surplus material.
4. Fold over and crease or tack the narrow turning allowance on to the wrong side.

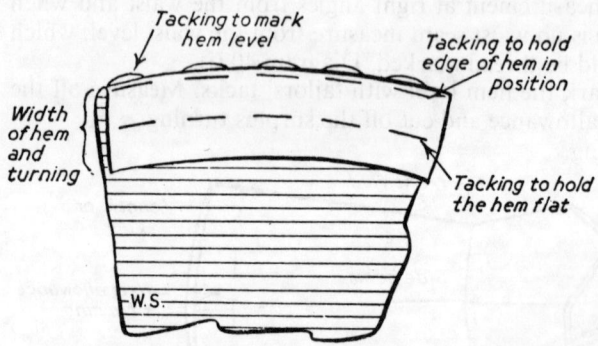

41 (i). Preliminary fixing of a wide hem

Final fixing—
5. Pin the hem flat on the garment forming any fullness on curved parts into wedge-shaped pleats. Diagram 41 (ii). The hem will set better if these pleats are kept small, so it is better to make several, measuring about 6 mm deep at the wide end rather than one deep one. The pleats should

THE FINISH OF EDGES

fold away from the centre front and back.

6. Fix the hem with slip hemming. Hem along the fold of each pleat. Or use machine blindstitch. Diagrams 41 (iii), (iv), 85. Press the hem and remove all tackings.

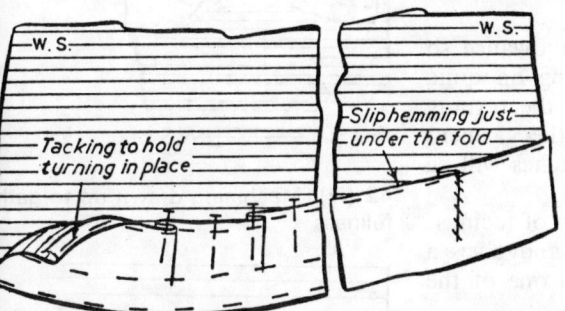

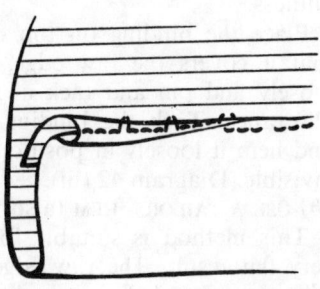

(ii). Hem pinned flat with llness formed into pleats

41 (iii). Hem finally stitched and pleats hemmed flat

41 (iv). Machine blindstitch

ALTERNATIVE WAYS OF TREATING SKIRT HEMS

1. *On springy materials* which do not remain well pressed for long, e.g. some rayons and woollen mixtures, machine stitch the fold of the narrow turning before tacking it down flat. Diagram 42 (i).

2. *When using material which curls at cut edges,* such as velvet, cut off the narrow turning allowance and bind the edge with straight or crossway binding before tacking it down flat. Method B, p. 107. Diagrams 30 (vi), 42 (ii).

3. *On thick materials*, e.g. tweeds, heavy woollens, turn the hem once only and either cover the raw edge with a flat binding or catch stitch or herringbone it in position. Either a straight or crossway binding can be used.

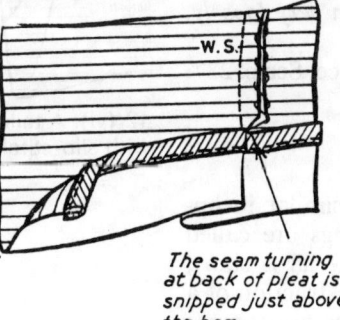

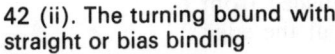

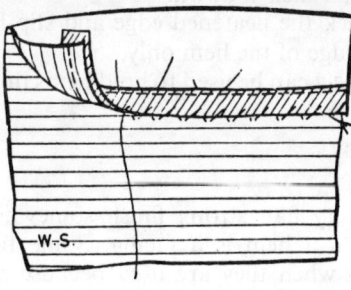

2 (i). The turning dge-stitched

42 (ii). The turning bound with straight or bias binding

The seam turning at back of pleat is snipped just above the hem

42 (iii). The edge covered with flat binding

Hemming stitches made very loosely

(a) USE A FLAT BINDING:

Arrange fullness in the hem before applying the binding. Either form the small pleats and press and hem them in position or gather the fullness by machine, draw up the bobbin thread until the hem sets flat, and shrink away the fullness.

Place the binding on top of the turning allowance so that it covers the raw edge. Ease the binding on quite loosely and pin and tack and machine it to the turning allowance. Tack the binding down flat on the garment and hem it loosely in position so that the stitches will be invisible. Diagram 42 (iii).

(b) USE A TAILORS' HEM (also for use on edges of facings).

This method is suitable for any material and gives a very flat result. The raw edge is neatened in one of the following ways before it is slip-hemmed in place:

Overcasting by hand, suitable for firm materials. The stitches can be drawn up to gather in fullness on curves. Fraying materials can be machined first before overcasting.

Overcasting by machine, suitable for any material. A zig-zag stitch is used on the machine and a gathering thread put in by hand or machine to draw up the fullness.

Pinking, or machining and pinking, for fabrics which do not fray.

Method

Mark hem depth and cut evenly. Diagram 41 (i). Neaten the cut edge independently in one of the ways described above. Draw up fullness on curves. Diagram 42 (iv).

Drop the hem down and press the neatened edge. Shrink away fullness on woollens, p. 161. Replace the hem in position and tack it down.

Fold back the neatened edge and slip hem *very loosely*. Press the edge of the hem only.

BONDING WEB can be used to hold hems in place. See p. 237.

Facings

Another very flat, strong finish somewhat similar in appearance to a hem is a facing. Some facings are called false hems when they are used because material is short, instead of hems. In spite of this fact, the construction of a facing is very different from a hem and it has many more uses and possibilities. A facing can be distinguished from a hem by the fact that there is always a seam at the edge

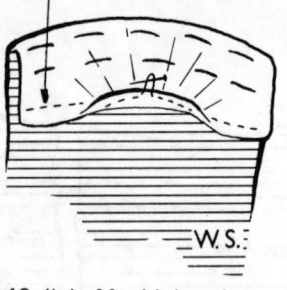

42 (iv). Machining drawn up to gather fullness

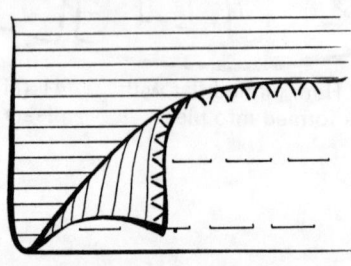

42 (v). Tailor's hem with turning zigzagged

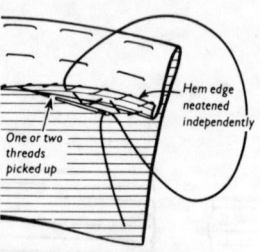

42 (vi). A tailors' hem held in place with slip-stitching

THE FINISH OF EDGES

in place of a fold because an extra or 'false piece' of material is sewn on to make the facing. It is called a facing because the false piece 'faces' one side of the article and is not visible from the other side.

Uses of facings

Facings can be made on to the right or wrong side of an article using the same material or a material of contrasting colour or texture. Therefore a plain or decorative effect can be produced both by the material used to make a facing and the kind of stitch used to hold it down. Any of the stitches used to fix hems can be used to fix facings. The depth of a facing is not generally less than 1 cm. Facings can be used on almost any edge of a garment, both under and outer wear, as well as on household linen and articles of all kinds.

Kinds of facings and how to cut them

STRAIGHT FACINGS

Straight facings have the facing cut on the straight of the material and the edge to be faced is quite straight, though not necessarily to a thread, e.g. a facing at the top of a pocket, at a square neck, at the hem edge of a straight cut skirt. Diagram 112 (i).

To cut a facing:

Cut a straight strip of material along the selvedge threads:
   Length—the length of the edge to be faced plus two turnings.
   Width—the final depth of the facing plus two turnings.

Ribbon, tape or braid can be used instead of material, and is applied without turnings being made.

SHAPED FACINGS

These are cut the same shape as the edge to be faced and on the same grain, so that close examination will show that the threads of the facing are exactly in line with those of the article. These facings are often quite wide, e.g. the facing on the front of a blouse. Diagram 99 (ii).

A paper pattern is required for the facing, which is obtained from the pattern of the article. Diagrams 145 (ii), 146. Commercial patterns will include the facing pieces.

Turnings must be allowed when cutting out unless they are already allowed on the pattern. There are occasions when the facing is cut on a different grain from the article, in order to get some special effect, as in the use of striped material.

CROSSWAY FACINGS

These have the facing cut on the true cross. These can be recognised by looking at the facing carefully, when it will be seen that the straight threads slant across the facings. This type of facing is not as a rule made wider than 3 cm because it becomes more difficult to keep flat. Crossway facings can be used on any edge, straight or curved, but are particularly suitable for curved edges because the facing, being on the cross, can be stretched and eased to fit the edge. Diagram 111.

Cut strips of material on the true cross to make the facing (Diagram 10) or use commercial bias binding. The width of the strip must be the final depth of facing plus two turnings, plus 0.5 cm to spare, to allow for the narrowing of the strip when it has to be stretched, e.g. 3.5 cm strip is needed to make a 2 cm facing. Join up the strips to make it fully the required length plus turnings.

To prepare the edge of an article to be faced
Trim an even turning on the edge, making it the same depth as the turning allowed on the facing. Alternatively, mark the pattern line. See that the line is a good one before attaching the facing.

General directions which apply to fixing all types of facing
(Study these directions first and then the section which applies to the particular kind of facing being made.)
1. Place the right side of the facing on the opposite side of the material to which it will be finally fixed, e.g. place the right side of the facing on the right side of the garment if the facing is to be made finally on the wrong side.

Keep the edges of facing and garment level, and pin and tack them together. Machine at the depth of the turning or on the pattern line if it has been marked. Diagram 43 (i).
2. Trim a 6 mm turning, snip all curved edges and right into the corner of angles. Diagrams 44 (ii) and 47.
3. Turn the facing over to the opposite side of the work. Hold the work just below the seam between the thumb and first finger of both hands and roll the seam up to the top and slightly over to the wrong side of the work. Pin this seam to hold it at the edge and tack it there. Diagram 43 (ii).
4. Tack through the centre of the facing if it is wider than 2 cm.

THE FINISH OF EDGES 99

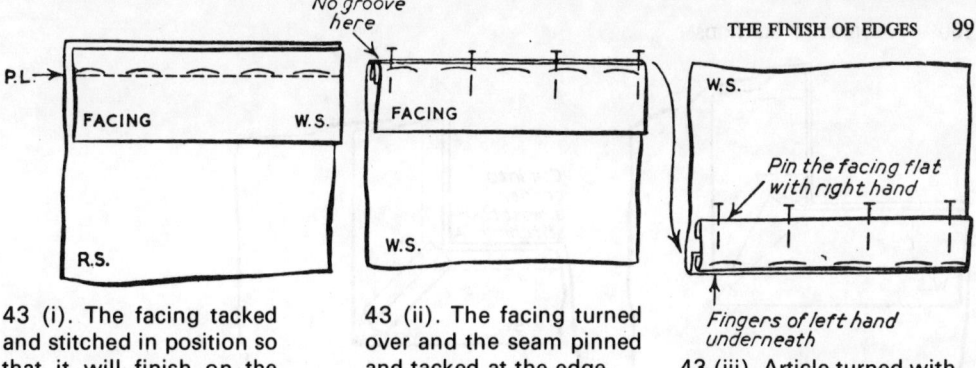

43 (i). The facing tacked and stitched in position so that it will finish on the wrong side of the work

43 (ii). The facing turned over and the seam pinned and tacked at the edge

Fingers of left hand underneath

43 (iii). Article turned with edge towards worker, to pin facing flat, ready to be tacked in place

5. Crease and turn under the free edge of the facing, making certain that the final depth of the facing is accurate. Pin the facing flat on to the article. To do this successfully, the seamed edge should be held towards the worker with the facing uppermost in the hand. Smooth the article with the fingers of the left hand and flatten and pin the facing with the right. Diagram 43 (iii). Tack down the facing on to the article and fix it with a suitable stitch, e.g. slip hem the facing at the neck of a woollen dress; machine the front facing on an overall; use an embroidery stitch on edges of a table mat.

DIRECTIONS FOR STRAIGHT FACINGS

1. *Crease the turnings* on both edges of the facing before applying the facing to the article. This simplifies the process for a beginner, if cotton or linen material is being used.

2. *When a corner is to be faced, seam the strip across the corner as follows:*

(a) Inner corners, e.g. corner of a square neck.

Pin the strip along one side as far as the corner. Keeping the strip quite flat on the article, bring it round the corner, forming a fold diagonally across the corner, with the wide end at the inner corner. Pin across the strip below the fold to make an open seam close to the article.

Tack and machine the seam; trim the turnings to leave 6 mm and press the seam open. Diagram 44 (i) and (ii).

(b) Outer corners, e.g. corner of a table cloth.

Pin the strip along one side as far as the corner.

Fix the strip round the corner keeping the edges of the article and facing exactly level, and allow a fold to form from the corner.

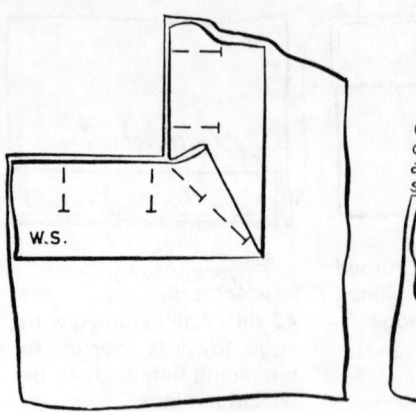

44 (i). An inner corner with a facing pinned in place

44 (ii). Facing seamed across the corner and turnings trimmed and pressed open

Pin below the fold and make a seam as for the inner corner. Diagram 45 (i) and (ii).

3. *To apply ribbon, braid or tape as a facing:*
(i) Fold the turning allowance on the article over to the side of the material on which the facing is to be finally fixed. Crease or tack it in place and press.
(ii) Place the wrong side of the facing strip over the turning, pinning and tacking the folded edge of the garment level with the edge of the facing, i.e. ribbon, braid or tape.
Now tack the free edge of the facing flat on the article.
(iii) Secure the facing by machining both edges, or if the facing is on the wrong side and is to be stitched by hand, oversew the outer edge and hem the lower. The hand method is often used on baby clothing. Diagram 46 (i), (ii) and (iii).

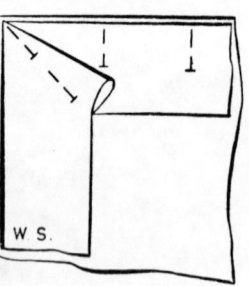

45 (i). An outer corner with the facing pinned in position

DIRECTIONS FOR SHAPED FACINGS
1. *Make the seams which occur in shaped facings,* e.g. shoulder seams on a neck facing, before the facing is attached to the garment. Plain seams should be used, and the turnings trimmed to 6 mm and pressed open.
2. *Fold the turning allowance of the lower edge of the facing* (the last to be fixed flat on the garment) on to the wrong side before applying the facing. Diagram 47. When this edge is to be left free inside the garment, the fold is machined independently and the turning trimmed to 3 mm. Alternatively, finish with zigzag stitching, diagram 137, machining and overcasting or pinking.

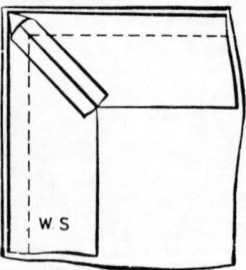

45 (ii). Facing seamed across the corner

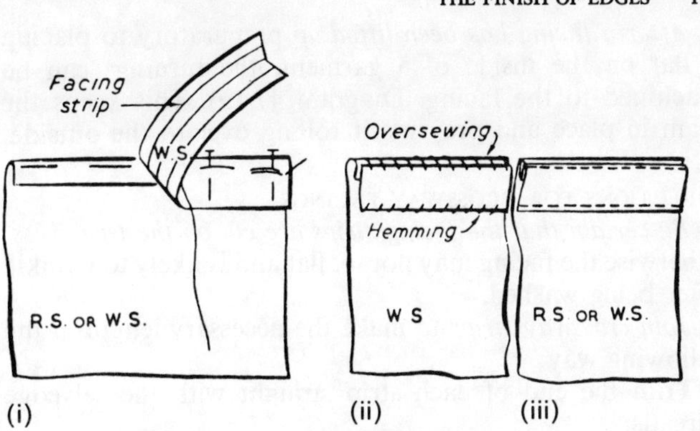

THE FINISH OF EDGES 101

(i). Edge prepared and straight braid or ribbon facing being applied

(ii). Facing fixed by hand

(iii). Facing fixed by machine

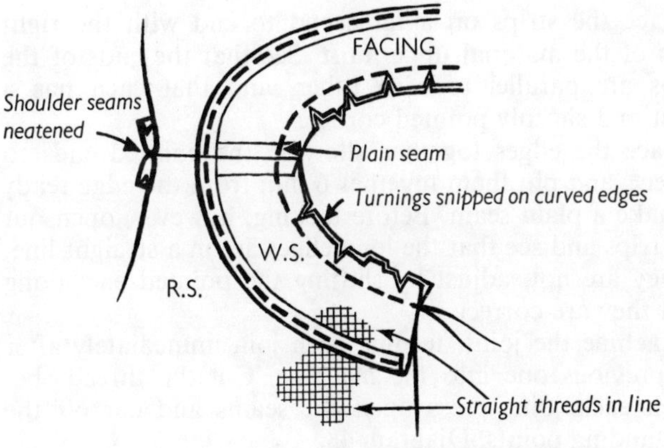

(i). A shaped facing machined in place, showing treatment of turnings ready for hemming

(ii). Understitching (optional) — turnings machined to facing

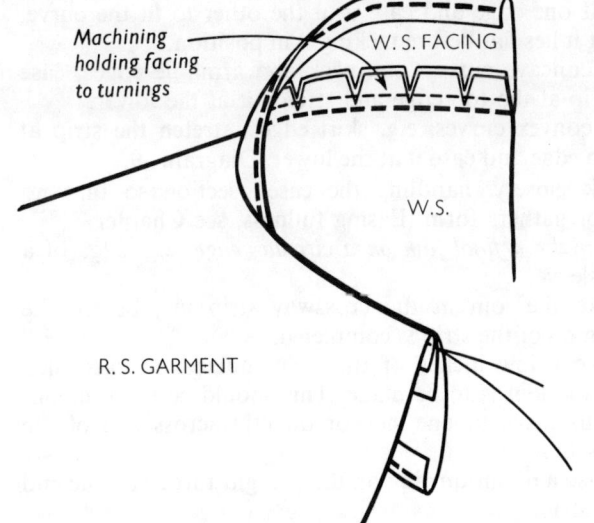

3. *After a facing has been lifted up* preparatory to placing it flat on the inside of a garment, the turnings can be machined to the facing. Diagram 47 (ii). This keeps the seam in place and prevents it rolling over to the outside.

DIRECTIONS FOR CROSSWAY FACINGS

1. *Be certain that the facing strips are cut on the true cross,* otherwise the facing may not set flat and is likely to wrinkle after being washed.

2. *Join crossway strips* to make the necessary length in the following way:

Trim the end of each strip straight with the selvedge threads.

Place the strips on a table end to end with the right sides of the material uppermost. See that the ends of the strips are parallel to each other, and that each has a blunt and sharply pointed corner.

Place the edges together allowing the pointed ends to project, and pin them together 6 mm from the edge ready to make a plain seam. Before tacking, however, open out the strips and see that the long edges are in a straight line. If they are not, adjust by shifting the pointed end along until they are correct.

Machine the joins, feeding each join immediately after the previous one into the machine. Cut the threads between each join; press open the seams and cut off the outstanding points. Diagram 48.

3. *To fix crossway facings to curved edges,* stretch the strip at one edge and ease it at the other to fit the curve, so that it lies flat before tacking it in position.

On concave curves, e.g. neck and armhole edges, ease the strip at the top edge and stretch it at the lower.

On convex curves, e.g. skirt edges, stretch the strip at the top edge and ease it at the lower. Diagram 49.

Tack closely, handling the eased section so that no pleat or gathers form. Easing fullness, see Chapter 7.

4. *To make a final join on a circular edge,* e.g. edge of a short sleeve.

Make the join in the crossway strip just before the tacking on of the strip is completed.

Leave a few inches of the strip unfixed on each side where the join is to be made. This should be in an inconspicuous place to one side or directly across one of the main seams.

Crease a 6 mm turning on the straight thread at one end of the strip.

THE FINISH OF EDGES

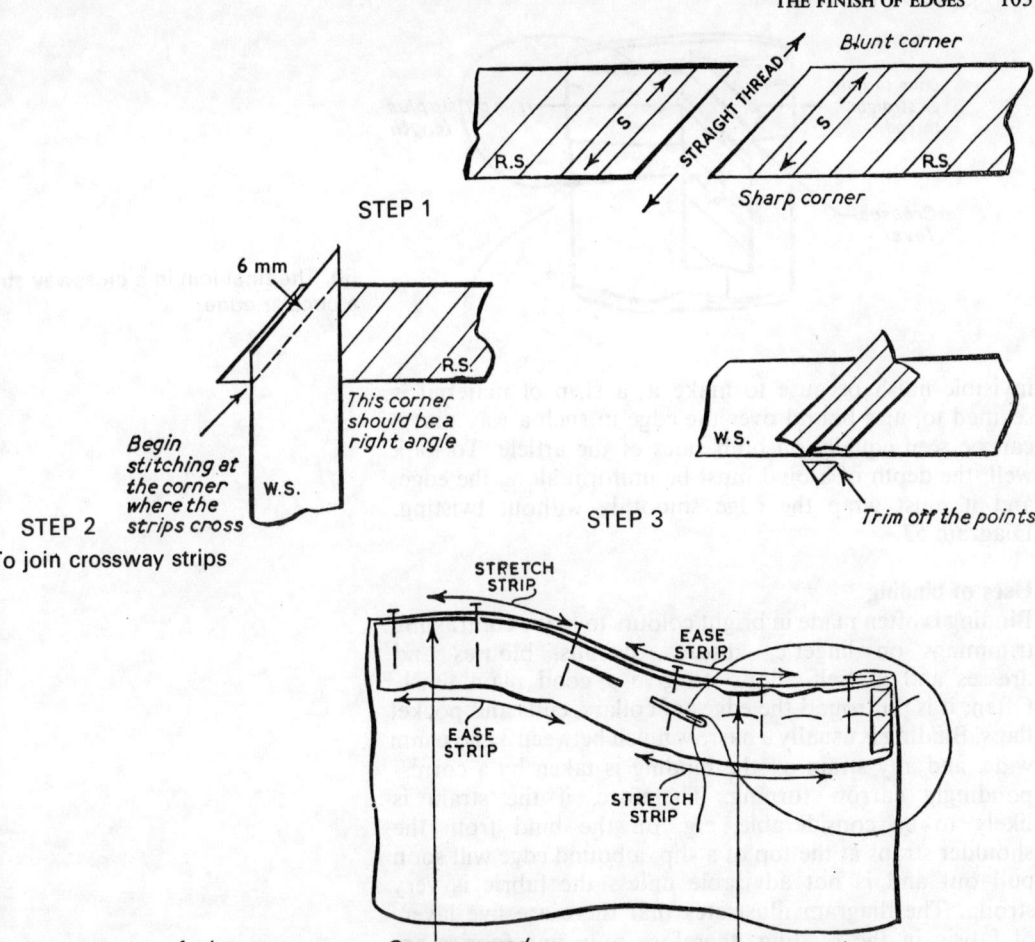

Crease back the other end of the strip so that the creases of both ends are level. Join these two folds with an open seam or oversew them together. Trim off the surplus turning and press the seam.

Complete tacking the strip in position across the join. Diagram 50.

N.B. Fix corners as given on p. 100.

Binding

Binding an edge, though not as strong a finish as a hem or facing, can be decorative. It can never be used as an

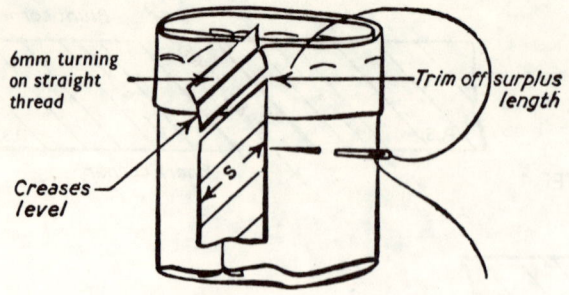

50. The final join in a crossway strip a circular edge

invisible finish because to make it, a strip of material is seamed to, and bound over the edge in such a way that it can be seen equally on both sides of the article. To look well, the depth of a bind must be uniform along the edge, and it must wrap the edge smoothly without twisting. Diagram 52.

Uses of binding

Binding is often made in bright colours to make contrasting trimmings on lingerie, aprons, overalls, blouses and dresses and in 'self-colour' to give a good plain finish. Often, it is put round the edges of collars, cuffs and pocket flaps. Binding is usually a narrow finish between 3 and 6 mm wide, and any strain on the binding is taken by a correspondingly narrow turning. Therefore, if the strain is likely to be considerable, e.g. on the bind from the shoulder straps at the top of a slip, a bound edge will soon pull out and is not advisable unless the fabric is very strong. The diagram illustrates that there are five layers of fabric in the binding, therefore only fine fabrics are suitable for binding. There are two types of binding, CROSSWAY, where the binding strip is cut on the true cross, and STRAIGHT when ribbon, braid or seam binding is used, but crossway has a more general use.

CROSSWAY BINDING: METHOD A

Method A is suitable for binding of not less than 0.5 cm in depth when finished. No stitching shows on the right side.
1. *To prepare the binding strip*
Cut strips of material on the true cross (Chapter 4) making them four times the width the binding will be when finished.
   Join the strips to obtain the required length plus turnings.
   Fold and crease the strip in half with the wrong side of the material inside. Open the strip out and turn in the raw

THE FINISH OF EDGES

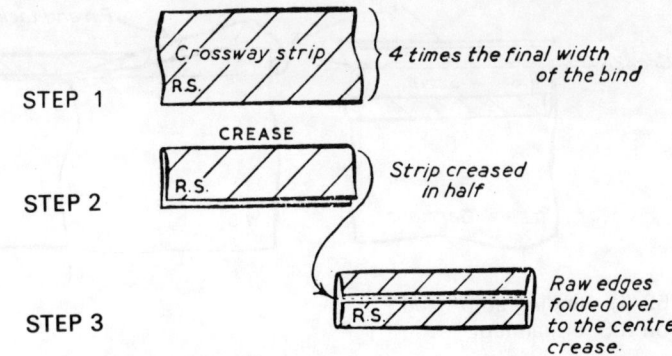

prepare a crossway strip for an edge

STEP 1

STEP 2

STEP 3

edge on to the wrong side as far as the centre crease. Crease the folds and press in with an iron.

Iron the strip to stretch it slightly. Diagram 51.

2. *To prepare an edge for binding*

Trim off the turning allowance making the line a good one. Diagram 52 shows that the position of the pattern line when the bind is finished is on the top. This explains why no turning is needed on the edge to be bound.

3. *To fix the binding strip to an edge*

Open out the binding and pin the strip on to the right side of the article with the edge of the binding level with the edge of the article (or with the pattern line if it has been marked).

Tack just above the crease in the binding.

Machine exactly in the crease. Take out the tacking threads.

Trim off any frayed edges level with the edge of the binding.

Fold the binding over to the wrong side of the work and pin and tack the second fold in the binding just above the first line of stitching.

Hem the binding in position, taking care that the stitches do not show through on the right side. The hemming stitches can be taken into the machine stitches. Diagrams 52 (i) and (ii).

Additional directions for:
(a) Fixing binding to curved edges

When the binding is first pinned to the edge, whether concave or convex, keep the crease nearest the edge quite flat on the article without any fullness forming at the crease. Be prepared for the binding either to curl up or to flute from the article on one side of the crease according

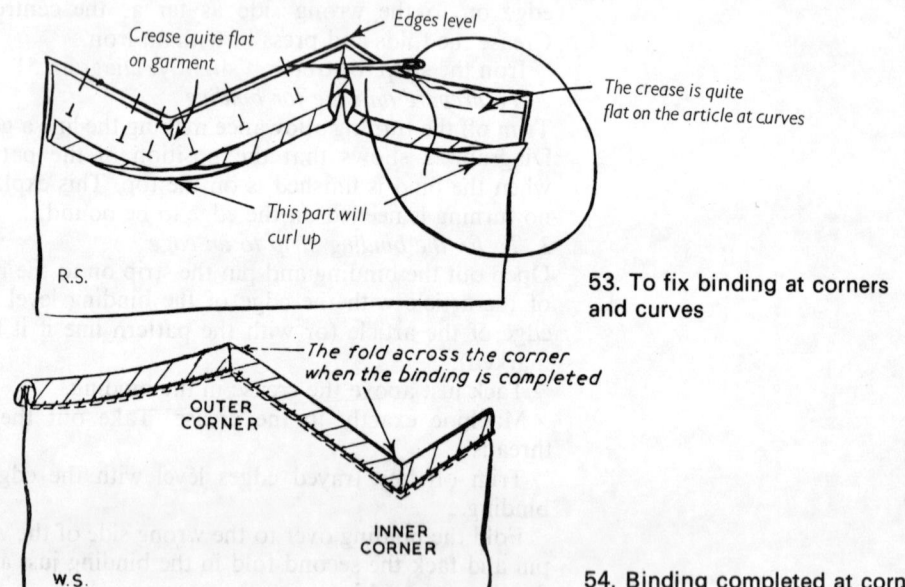

52 (i). Binding strip fixed on R.S. of garment

52 (ii). Binding partly fixed down on W.S. with hemming

53. To fix binding at corners and curves

54. Binding completed at corner and curves

to the kind of curve. When the strip has been bound over the edge it will be found to set perfectly well. Diagrams 53 and 54.

(b) Turning corners with the binding. Diagrams 53 and 54 *Outer corners.* Keep the binding strip level with the edge of the article on both sides of the corner and allow a fold to form from the corner. Do not make a seam in the binding strip across the corner.

Keep the fold upright while the binding is being tacked and machined to the edge. The diagram shows how the needle should be slipped through the fold. To machine the corner, leave the needle down in the work at the corner; lift the machine foot; turn the work and lift the diagonal fold and lay it under the foot towards the back. Lower the foot and continue machining.

It will be found that the fold spreads open when the binding is turned to the wrong side, so that the binding is quite flat where it is hemmed to the stitching.

Inner corners. Fix the binding round the corner so that the crease in the binding nearest the edge is kept quite flat on the article. This will cause the rest of the binding strip to curl up sharply from the garment, but the binding will set well when it is fixed on the wrong side.

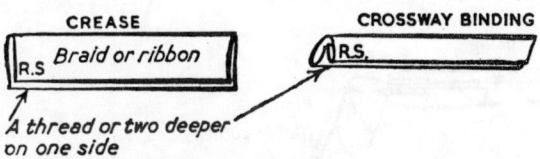

Straight or crossway binding ready for binding an edge

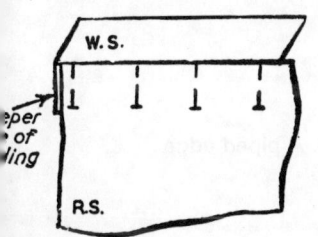

Binding pinned of article

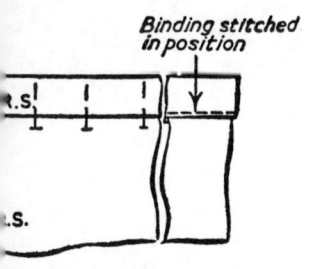

Binding folded over and pinned or tacking and stitching

CROSSWAY BINDING METHOD B

Method B (Diagrams 55 (i), (ii) and (iii) is a quick way of attaching binding, and is useful for treating seam turnings and edges on quickly made clothing and articles. It is the method to use also for straight bindings such as tape, ribbon, braid and prussian binding. The binding is fixed with one row of machining which shows on both sides of the work.

1. *To prepare the binding strip*

Fold the binding strip almost in half, making it a thread or two deeper on one side, with the right side outside. Press the crease in well.

2. *To prepare the edge of an article* proceed as given for Method A.

3. *To fix the binding.*

Place the edge of the article inside the binding level with the crease, and with the deeper side of the binding on the wrong side of the article.

Pin the under side of the binding to the article, working with the right side of the article towards the worker.

Fold the binding strip on to the right side of the article and transfer the pins to hold both edges of the binding to the article.

Tack and machine close to the edge of the binding on the right side.

Piping

For general information on piping see PIPED SEAMS. p. 82.

Piping at edges of necks, sleeves, belts and hem edges is often fashionable for trimming as well as strengthening. A fine corded piping is popular on toddlers' clothing. The piping is generally inserted into the seam formed by joining on a facing—straight, shaped or crossway. Therefore once the method of constructing a facing is known it is a simple matter to insert a piping into the join. Diagram 56. The method can be followed for piped seams on p. 82. *Note.* Attach the piping to the main part of the garment and place the facing on top.

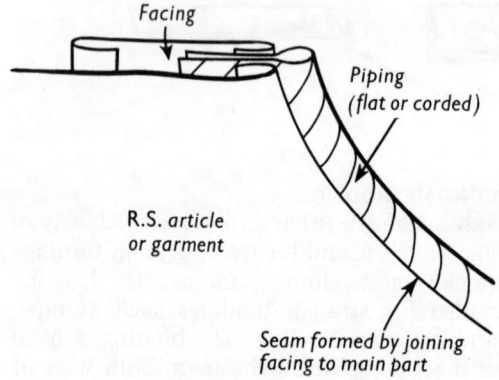

56. A piped edge

Edges finished with lace

Lace is made of many yarns, but mostly cotton, linen and synthetics. It can be bought as an edging in a narrow or wide width, or as 'piece lace' for appliqué and insertions. Piece lace is sometimes used to make the whole garment, because it is sold as wide as single width material. Real lace, that is, hand-made lace, still made in many countries, notably France, Belgium, Spain, Italy, England and Ireland, is very expensive. However, excellent machine-made copies of, for example, Valenciennes and embroidered net laces can be bought cheaply. To judge if a lace edging will be satisfactory in wear, the shaped edge should be examined. This should be firm and well finished. A poor quality will soon pull away from the net and become ragged. The

THE FINISH OF EDGES 109

straight edge of the lace which is attached to the garment generally has a fine thread worked into it, which can be pulled up in order to ease and gather the lace when required. It will be noticed that on the right side of the lace, the design is raised.

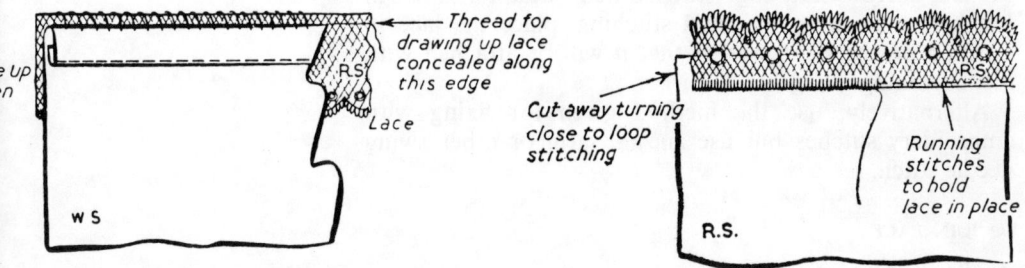

Lace fixed with oversewing   57 (ii). Lace fixed with an embroidery stitch

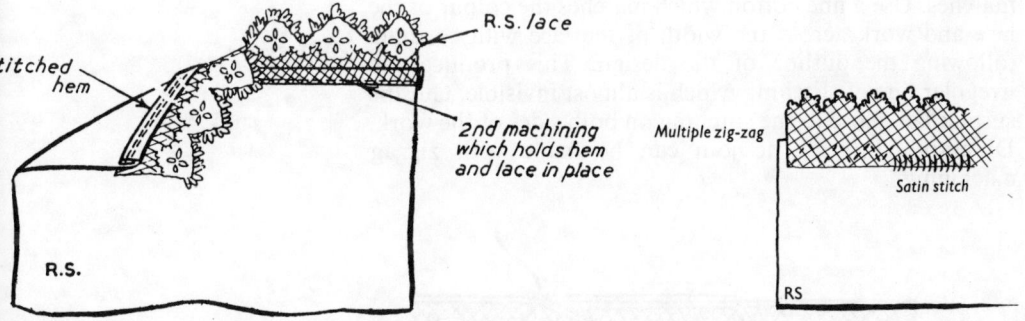

Lace fixed by machine

1. Methods of attaching lace to edges

(a) BY HAND

Oversew the lace to the edge after it has been previously neatened with a hem or facing. Draw up the gathering thread in the lace if it is to be frilled on, but avoid making it very full. Place the right side of the lace against the right side of the edge and pin it in position. Oversew the lace to the garment very closely. Flatten the join and press well. Diagram 57 (i). *Or*

Use an embroidery stitch to fix lace. Place the lace on the right side of the garment over the raw edge, with the right side of the lace uppermost. Fix lace first with running stitches and then with strong embroidery stitches worked closely together over the edge, e.g. fine loop stitching, or pin stitch. Cut the fabric close to the lace on the wrong side on fine strong materials which will not pull away from the stitching in wear, otherwise leave a narrow turning and overcast the edge. Diagram 57 (ii).

(*b*) BY MACHINE
Fix lace with the machining which holds a hem in position. Make a narrow, flat, edge-stitched hem (Chapter 9, p. 92) but before working the final stitching, place the lace in position on the right side so that it will be attached with the machining. Diagram 57 (iii).

Alternatively, use the method given for fixing with embroidery stitches but use zigzag, satin or other swing needle stitch.

TO JOIN LACE

Appliqué join
Lay one end of the lace over the other so that the design matches. Use a fine cotton which matches the colour of the lace and work across the width of the lace with cording, following the outline of the design. This produces an irregular line of stitching which is almost invisible. Cut the surplus lace close to the stitching on both sides of the work. Diagram 57 (iv). The join can be made with zigzag machining.

57 (iv). Appliqué join in lace

Embroidered edges
These are decorative edges which are made with embroidery stitches forming the edge, e.g. loop stitching closely worked to give scalloped edges, corded edges, etc.

10 Openings

Openings are likely to wear out before any other part of a garment or article because they are handled so frequently and are subjected to much strain. Therefore, openings must be made as strong as possible.

THE STRENGTH OF AN OPENING DEPENDS ON:
1. *The length.* Too short an opening causes wrenching and strain in use which will soon tear the base.
2. *The kind of opening* which is chosen. Some openings are much stronger than others and it is important to choose one which is strong enough for the article. The information given on each kind of opening in this chapter will show whether it is one which will stand hard wear, or whether it is more suitable for lighter wear.
3. *The stitching,* especially at the base of the opening.
Sometimes openings are intended to show as little as possible and sometimes they are part of the design of a garment and they should be smartly conspicuous. Therefore openings must always set well.

THE SET AND APPEARANCE OF AN OPENING DEPEND ON:
1. *Flatness*
(a) Both sides of an opening must be the same length so that the opening will lie flat when fastened.
(b) The wrap of an opening must be wide enough to prevent gaping and to take the fastenings easily.
(c) A thinner material can be used to neaten an opening on woollen materials (if it can be done without showing on the right side), thus avoiding unnecessary thickness.

2. *Neat stitching and well-placed fastenings*
An opening must be made carefully and stitched and fastened accurately.

GENERAL POINTS ON MAKING OPENINGS
1. When an opening is put into a slit cut in a garment, the opening should be worked before the seams are made; e.g. the wrist opening in the back of a sleeve should be made before fixing the underarm seam.

FOUNDATION METHODS

2. When an opening is put into a seam, the seam should be made before the opening, leaving that part of the seam unstitched which is to have the opening inserted.
3. The opening must be made long enough to allow the garment to be put on and taken off easily. (For lengths of openings, see Charts, pp. 162–164.)
4. The position of an opening should be such that it can be fastened conveniently. Front openings should lap right over left for women and left over right for men.
5. The opening should be planned so that fastenings can be sewn on double material.

Openings designed with a wrap

The majority of openings used in needlework are made so that the two edges of the opening overlap. The upper part is termed the overlap, the under part the underlap, and the double part where the two overlay is called the wrap. Diagram 58. Useful openings which have a wrap are the hem openings, the continuous wrap, a side opening for a dress and the skirt placket.

Hem openings: overlapping hems or false hems

These very simply made and strong openings are used widely on all types of clothing and on household articles, e.g. they can be seen on the fronts and shoulders of blouses, dresses, pyjama coats; in sleeves, on cushions, loose covers and pillow cases, to mention only a few instances. The fastenings may be buttons and buttonholes or loops, press studs or Velcro.

OUTLINE OF CONSTRUCTION
The hem opening is made in a seam or through the entire length of a garment, e.g. the front edge of a bodice from throat to waist, and is formed by making a hem on both edges and overlapping the two hems. Sometimes the top hem is turned on to the right side of the material. Diagram 58. When there is not enough material to make a hem, a false hem is seamed on one or both edges. (FALSE HEMS, see p. 97.)

DIRECTIONS FOR MAKING HEM OPENINGS
1. Plan the hems to be wide enough to take the fastenings, e.g. consider the size of a buttonhole that will have to be made in the hem, if buttons are to be used for fastening.

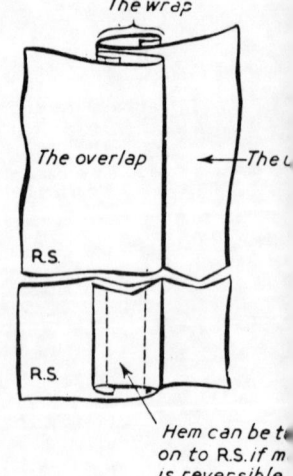

58. To show the construction of opening formed with overlapping hems

2. Fix the hems in position (Chapter 9) and secure with machining or with hemming if the garment is hand-made. On outer garments such as blouses, the first turn is frequently machine stitched independently and left free. The fastening holds the hem in place. For further information see Chapter 15.

Continuous wrap opening
Though not as strong as the hem openings the continuous wrap is a hard-wearing opening when properly made. It has many uses for:
(a) Side openings of shorts and skirts made of thin material, slips and dresses.
(b) Sleeve openings on school and shirt blouses.
(c) Neck openings for girls' blouses and dresses.

OUTLINE OF CONSTRUCTION
The opening can be made in a seam or in a slit cut in the garment. The cut edges are neatened with a continuous band which is folded back on the overlap and remains projecting on the underlap. In some cases part of the band is cut away underneath the overlap and it is fastened down on to the garment to form a facing. The final width of the wrap is between 1 and 2 cm wide. Diagrams 59 (vi) and 60 (ii). The opening is fastened with buttons and buttonholes, press studs, hooks and bars or Velcro.

DIRECTIONS FOR MAKING

1. *Prepare the garment*
To put the opening into a seam, complete the seam as far as where the base of the opening is planned. Cut across the seam turnings at this point and loop stitch the raw edges of the seam. Diagrams 59 (i) and (ii) show exactly where to make the cut on different types of seams and hold good for other kinds of openings. Trim the turning allowance on the opening down to 6 mm.

To put the opening into a slit, make a straight cut in the garment, exactly the length of the opening required.

2. *Prepare a strip for the continuous band*
Cut a strip of material for the band, making it twice the length of the opening plus two turnings, by twice the finished depth of the band plus two turnings. Diagram 59 (iii). Turnings of 6 mm are satsfactory, but rather less gives a better result in the set of the opening. The selvedge threads should run the length of the strip. Crease and press

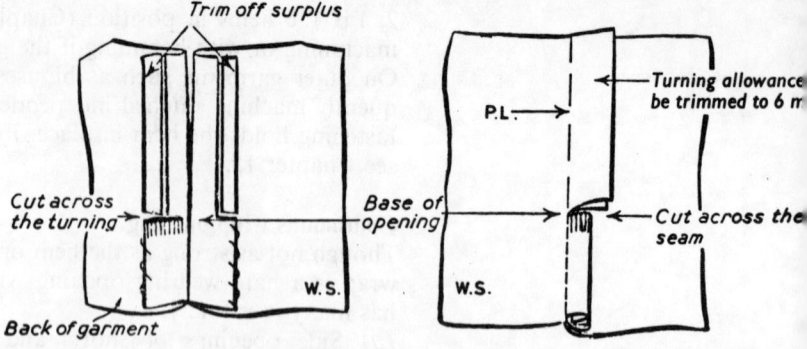

59 (i). Section of an open seam into which the continuous wrap opening is to be inserted

59 (ii). Section of a french seam prepared for inserting the opening

the turnings on the long edges, on to the wrong side of the strip.

3. *Fix the strip to the garment*
Method of fixing the strip in a slit. Place the right side of the strip on to the right side of the garment with the raw edges together, and begin pinning them together from the top of the opening. Keep the edges level until 1.5 cm away from the base of the slit. Now let the turning on the garment taper off to nothing at the base, but keep an even turning on the strip. Pin and tack in the crease of the strip as far as the base. Diagram 59 (iii).

Open the edges of the opening so that they are horizontal and pin and tack the strip along the second side, shaping the turning on the garment to correspond with the first side. Diagram 59 (iv).

Machine in the crease of the strip and take out the tacks.

Method of fixing the strip into a seam is the same as for the slit except in the following respect—the turning will not have to be tapered on the garment at the base of the

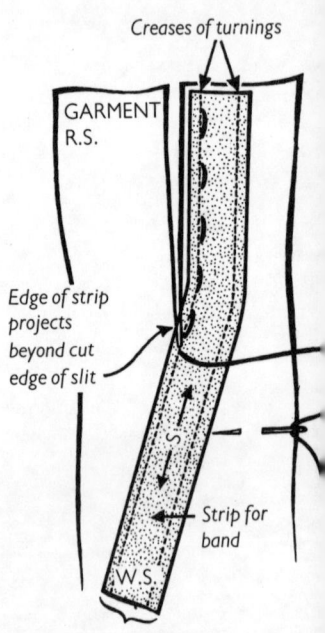

59 (iii). The strip fixed to one side of slit for a continuous wrap

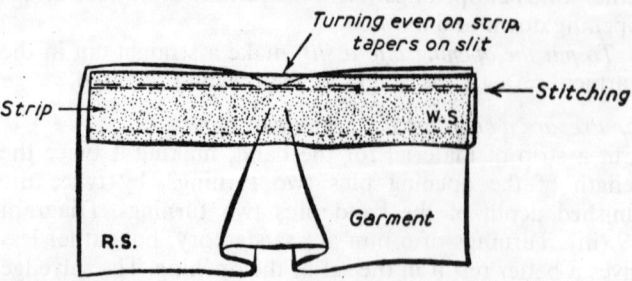

59 (iv). The strip fixed to the second side of the slit

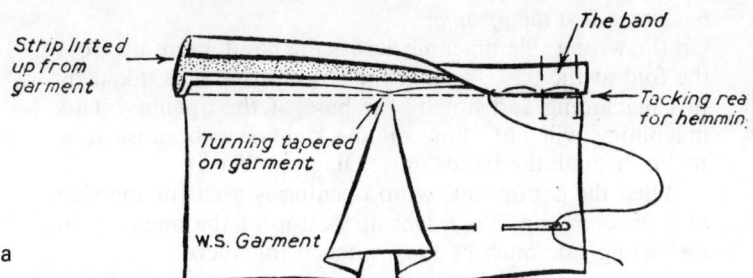

v). The strip folded over to form a

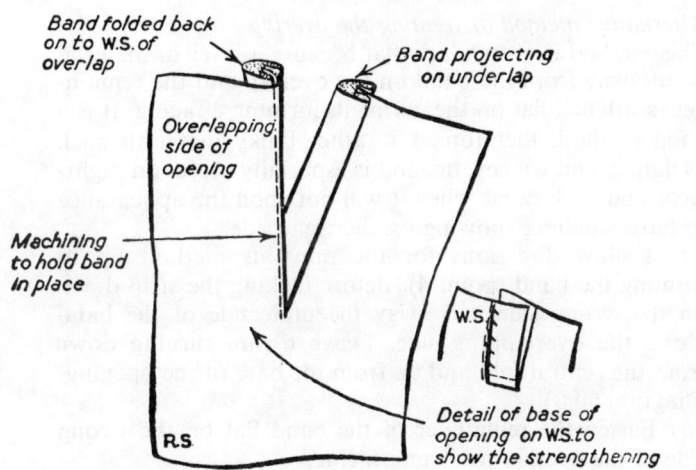

vi). The band folded to form the
inuous wrap opening

opening, because an even turning allowance has been left along the whole length of both sides.

4. *Form the band*
Lift the strip up from the garment, fold it over to the wrong side and place the crease of the turning allowance level with the machining, so that the raw edges are all enclosed in the band. Pin, tack and hem the band along both sides of the opening. Do not allow the hemming stitches to show through to the opposite side. Diagram 59 (v). Press the band.

5. *Form the opening*
Fold and tack the band back on to the wrong side of the garment on the overlap and leave it projecting from the garment on the underlap.

Machine close to the edge of the overlap from the top to the base to hold the band in position. (This stitching may be omitted where buttonholes are to be worked through all thicknesses of the overlap.)

6. *Strengthen the opening*

On the wrong side machine across the band 3 mm up from the fold at the base, so that the strain in wear is taken by this machining and not by the base of the opening. This machining will not show on the right side because it is taken through the bands only. Diagram 59 (vi).

When the continuous wrap opening is used for the side of a dress or slip, raw edges at the top of the opening on the wrong side must be loop stitched together.

Alternative method of treating the overlap

This method is particularly flat because a layer of material is cut away from the band on the overlap and the remainder is stitched flat on the garment, forming a facing. It is a good method, therefore, for rather bulky materials such as flannel and winceyette, and is especially useful on nightwear and underwear when it will not spoil the appearance to have stitching showing on the right side.

(a) Follow directions for the previous method up to forming the band (point 4). Before tacking the strip down on the wrong side, cut away the underside of the band along the overlapping side. Leave 6 mm turning down from the central fold and up from the base of the opening. Diagram 60 (i).

(b) Fasten the remainder of the band flat on the wrong side of the overlap to form a facing.

(c) Machine the facing in position and continue machining across it at the base of the opening. Diagram 60 (ii).

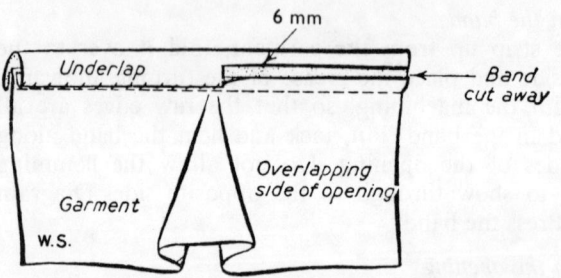

60 (i). Part of the band cut away on a continuous wrap opening (alternative method)

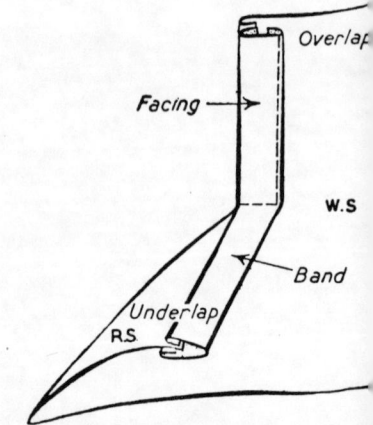

60 (ii). The facing machined flat on continuous wrap opening

Skirt placket

This is good for skirts and trousers of thick and medium

weight fabrics to give a flat opening, and it saves the cost of a zip* Diagram 61 (iv).

OUTLINE OF CONSTRUCTION

The opening is put into a seam and the seam turnings are used to make the opening. These should be wide enough to make a hem on the overlap and allow a wrap on the underlap. The wrap should not be less than 2 cm when finished, so that there is no danger of the opening gaping over the hip when the garment is close fitting. When material is short a facing can be used instead of a hem. Because the line of the opening is a shaped one and consequently on the bias, part of the opening is 'stayed' to prevent stretching. The opening is generally fastened with press studs, but sometimes buttons and buttonholes are used.

DIRECTIONS FOR MAKING

1. *Prepare the garment*

Work and neaten the seam up to the bottom of the opening; snip across and neaten the back turning. Diagram 61 (i).

See that pattern lines are clearly marked on both sides of the opening and that there is sufficient turning allowance to make the wrap and neaten the opening. Reference to diagram 61 (iii) will show that the width of the wrap plus a turning allowance is required on both edges.

2. *Stay the opening*

Cut two lengths of straight binding such as prussian or cotton seam binding, making them exactly the length of the opening.

On the overlap, baste one stay on to the garment on the wrong side with the edge level with the pattern line. Hem the stay along the pattern line on the overlap. Diagram 61 (i).

On the underlap, baste the second stay on to the wrong side of the wrap with the edge to the pattern line. Fastenings will eventually be sewn through this stay, so that there is no need to hem it in place. Diagram 61 (ii).

3. *Neaten the edges of the opening*

Overlap. Fold and tack the turning allowance on to the wrong side to make a hem. Cover the raw edge with a flat binding and slip-hem it to the garment. Diagram 61 (iii) (Chapter 9, p. 95). If there is insufficient turning to

---

* Another opening which saves buying a zip is the Pocket opening described in *Introduction to Needlework*, p. 120.

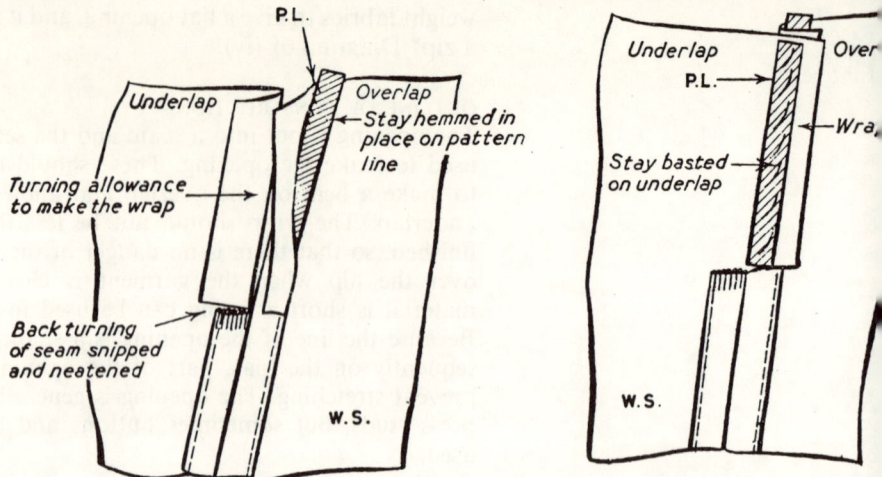

61 (i). The seam prepared and the stay fixed in place on the overlap of a skirt placket

61 (ii). The stay fixed on the W.S. of the underlap skirt placket

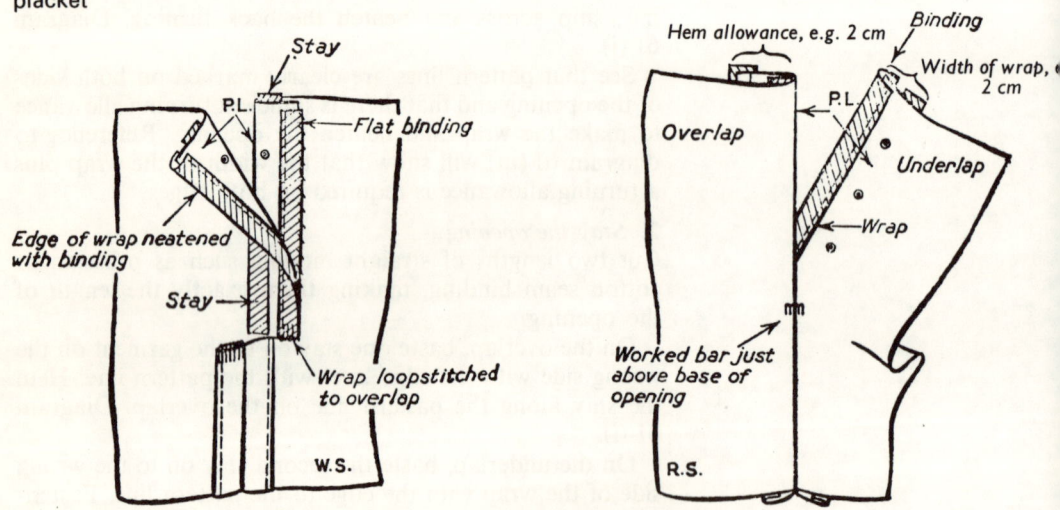

61 (iii). To neaten the skirt placket on the W.S.

61 (iv). To strengthen the skirt placket on the R.S.

make a hem, the edge should be neatened with a shaped facing (p. 97).
Underlap. Bind the edge of the wrap with straight or crossway binding, using Method B, p. 107. Diagram 61 (iii). This way of treating the wrap produces an extremely flat opening, but is not suitable for loosely woven woollens.

It is better when using these to neaten the wrap with a shaped facing and to bind or machine stitch the free edge. There is no need to hem it down on to the garment because the fastenings will hold it in place.

4. *Press and strengthen the opening*
Press the overlap and the underlap thoroughly and close the opening with pins, with the edge of the overlap to the pattern line of the underlap.

Work a small bar across the opening on the right side just above the base of the opening. Diagrams 61 (iv) and 77 (ii).

On the wrong side, stitch the end of the wrap to the overlap.

Sew on the fastenings.

Openings designed without a wrap

These openings have the two edges just meeting without any lap and may be termed slit openings. Often they are fastened at the top only, and are on the whole more suitable for adults' than for children's clothing. Slit openings are: the faced, the bound, and the zipped opening. With the exception of the zipped opening, they are less strong than openings which have a wrap.

The faced slit opening

This is a very popular opening at the front or back of the neck on blouses and dresses, whether they are collarless or with a collar. Diagram 146. A further use is for a wrist opening on full gathered sleeves. The opening can be worked successfully in any weight of dress material, but is not suitable on transparent fabric, because the facing shows through.

OUTLINE OF CONSTRUCTION
The opening is formed by a slit in the garment which is neatened with a shaped facing. The neck facing is frequently cut in one with the facing for the opening. The facing is usually made on to the wrong side of the garment, but can be finished on the right if it is designed as part of the style of a garment. The facing should extend at least 2 to 5 cm below the base and side of the opening. The opening is fastened with a button and loop at the top or all the way down the slit, or with a hook and eye at the top only.

DIRECTIONS FOR MAKING

1. *Prepare the garment*

Mark the line of the opening with tacking on the right side of the garment.

2. *Prepare the facing*

(Usually a pattern piece is provided for the facing.)

Cut a strip of material with selvedge threads along the length:

    Length of strip = the length from the neck or shoulder to the base of the opening plus at least 4 cm

    Width of strip = at least 8 cm

(Further directions on cutting shaped facings which are to include the neck facings will be found in Chapter 21.)

Fold the turning allowance along one short and two long sides, on to the wrong side of the facing, and tack and press in place. If the edge is to be left loose inside the garment when the opening is finished, machine stitch close to the fold. Alternative treatment of edge, see p. 175.

3. *Fix the facing to the garment*

Lay the right side of the facing on the right side of the garment, with the centre of the facing in line with the tacking which marks the position of the opening. Pin the facing flat, watching that the threads are in line with the threads of the garment and keep it in place with several rows of basting. Diagram 62 (i).

Turn the work to the wrong side where the tacking line which marks the opening should be visible. Machine 3 mm away from this tacking along both sides, tapering to a

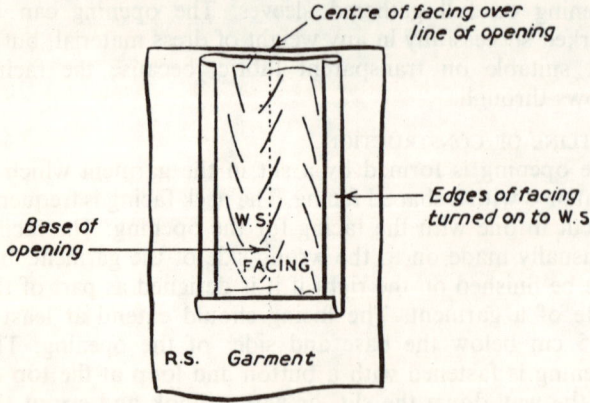

62 (i). Facing basted in position for a faced slit opening

OPENINGS 121

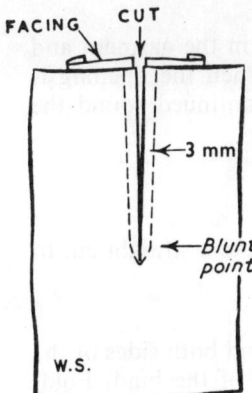

(i). The stitching completed the opening cut ready to the facing through to the site side

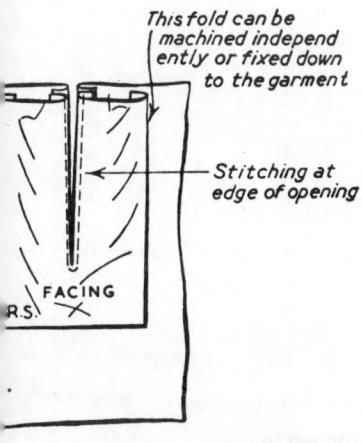

(ii). The faced slit opening d flat and the edge of the ing machined

blunt point at the base. Do not begin to taper until about 1 cm away from the base or the point will be too sharp. Diagram 62 (ii).

4. *Cut the opening*
Take out the bastings and cut down the opening on the central tacking between the machining. Be sure to cut right down to the bottom of the opening to within a thread of the machining. Unless this is done it is impossible to make the opening set well.

5. *Finish the facing*
Turn the facing through to the opposite side of the garment and tack the seam at the edge (Chapter 9, p. 99).

Baste the facing flat on to the garment, watching the direction of the grain in both, to keep the threads in line.

Fix the free edge of the facing on to the garment with slip hemming, machining or an embroidery stitch. If the edge is stitched independently and left loose, stitch all round the edge of the opening to keep the facing in place. In any case, this stitching can be done if liked to strengthen the opening. Diagram 62 (iii).*

The bound opening
This is used as an alternative to the faced slit but is suitable only for thin materials. It would be a good choice for transparent materials. The method of fastening is the same as on a faced slit opening.

---

* An adaptation of this opening to make a wrapped opening is given in *Introduction to Needlework*, p. 123. Faced wrap opening.

OUTLINE OF CONSTRUCTION

The opening is made by cutting a slit in the garment and neatening it with a crossway bind. When the opening is used at the neck, the bind is often continued round the neck edge.

DIRECTIONS FOR MAKING

1. *Prepare the garment*

Mark the depth of the opening and make a straight cut to this point.

2. *Prepare the binding strip*

Cut a crossway strip long enough to bind both sides of the cut and four times the finished depth of the bind. Fold, crease and iron the binding. Chapter 9, pp. 104, 105.

3. *Fix the binding strip to the cut edges*

Place the right side of the binding to the right side of the garment with the edges level, and begin to pin from the top of the cut towards the base.

When about 1 cm from the base, begin to taper off the turning on the garment to a few threads at the base. Tack the binding as far as this point, keeping the tacking stitches in the crease of the binding all the way along. The

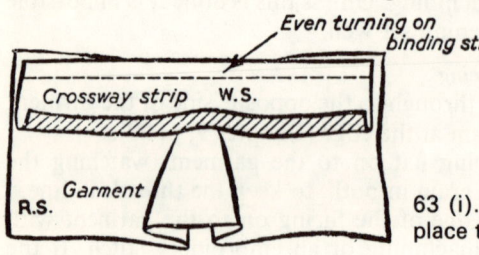

63 (i). A crossway strip stitched in place to make a bound opening

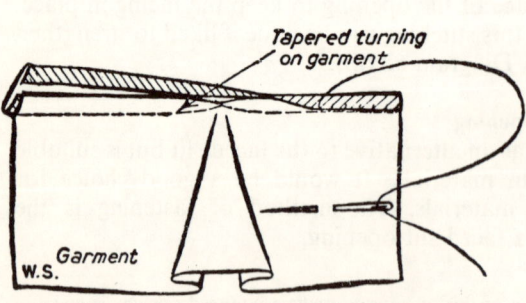

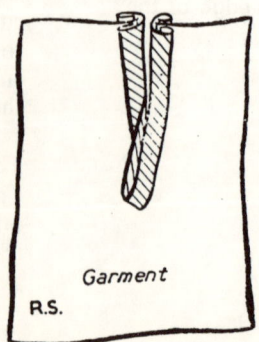

63 (ii). Binding the slit for a bound opening

63 (iii). A bound opening

handling is the same as for fixing the strip in the continuous wrap opening. Diagrams 59 (iii) and (iv).

Open the slit out so that the two edges are in a horizontal line and pin and tack the binding along the second side, shaping the turning on the garment to match the first side. Note that the turning on the crossway strip is kept an even depth all the way along both sides.

Machine close to the tacking. Diagram 63 (i).

4. *Form the bind*
Fold the crossway strip over to the wrong side so that it binds the edge, and hem it in position, level with the machining (Chapter 9, p. 106). It is usual to leave the bind to project at the base of the opening as it is quite narrow and not unsightly. Diagrams 63 (ii) and (iii).

The zipped opening
This method of combining opening and fastening is used widely on children's and adults' outer clothing, on adults' underclothing, on all kinds of cases and bags and on loose covers. The popularity of zips is due to the fact that they are quick and easy to insert and that they wear well. On clothing they are used chiefly at the neck, sleeves, side and back openings of dresses, skirts, shorts and trousers.

CHOICE OF ZIPS
Zips are made of both metal and nylon and can be bought in a number of lengths, colours and weights for various purposes.

Lengths are measured from the top of the slider to the bottom of the teeth and it is essential that the correct length is bought. Too short a zip causes strain on it every time the clothing is put on and taken off.

Colour. It is preferable to match the colour to the garment as nearly as possible but if the zip is inserted well the colour of the tape will for most methods not be visible, so that a near match or neutral shade will usually be satisfactory.

Weight. It is most important to buy the correct weight for the purpose. Too light a weight on a heavy tweed will not wear well—too heavy a one on a thin, light woollen will sag. Zips are manufactured for special purposes—correct weights and types for skirts, dresses, cushions, bags; open ended ones for jackets; curved ones for trousers; feather weights for use on very light weight fabrics.

124 FOUNDATION METHODS

OUTLINE OF CONSTRUCTION

Zips may be inserted in the following ways:

1. *Into a slit cut in the material.* The zip and the tape show, therefore it is a method used principally for bags and cases (METHOD A).

2. *Into a seam* so that the zip is either:

SEMI-CONCEALED (METHOD B), where the zip lies just under two meeting folds of material and a row of stitching shows all round on the R.S. The tape cannot be seen but the zip itself may show slightly. With this method the zip can be stitched in with an ordinary machine foot. Or,

CONCEALED (METHOD C), where the zip cannot be seen at all but one row of stitching shows down one side and across the bottom. A zipper foot is needed for stitching in the zip if this method is used.

INVISIBLE METHOD. No stitching shows at all with this method and the zip is invisible when closed. A special type of zip is used, e.g. Alcozip, which has the teeth set at an angle into the tape instead of flat. This type of zip can be set in by hand, otherwise a specially grooved zipper foot is needed. Direction for setting in see p. 224.

The semi-concealed, concealed and invisible methods are suitable to use in any position on clothing. Methods A, B and C follow.

SPECIAL NOTES

1. A fly-flap can be attached to the turnings on the inside after the zip has been inserted or attached to the tape of the zip before it is inserted. This prevents underclothes catching into the zip.
2. In all methods the material of the garment must be eased slightly on to the zip in order that it will set properly. The top of the zip is best placed below the pattern line at waist or neck, e.g. 6 mm to 1 cm. Therefore the zip should be 1 cm shorter than the length of the opening.
3. All pressing must be done *before* the zip is tacked in as it will be impossible to press heavily *over* the zip once it is inserted.
4. There should always be a strong fastening above the top of the zip so that there is no strain on the slider.

DIRECTIONS FOR INSERTING ZIPS

METHOD A—*To insert a zip into a slit. Zip and stitching are*

OPENINGS 125

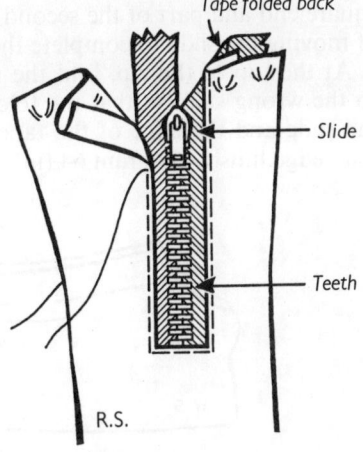

). Opening marked tacking and cut

64 (ii). Opening tacked ready for inserting a zip

64 (iii). To show a zip fixed to a slit in the garment. Method A

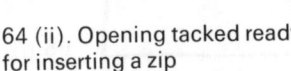
visible on R.S.

1. *Prepare the garment or article.*

Mark the depth of the opening with tacking, making it 3 mm longer than the zip—more. if top is to be below P.L.

Measure across the widest part of the slide on the zip, and put two rows of tacking this distance apart, so that the line marking the opening will be exactly between them.

Cut along this central line to within 6 mm of the bottom of the opening, and from this point cut in a diagonal direction to the bottom of the outer tackings. Diagram 64 (i).

Fold the turning on both sides and on the bottom of the opening over to the wrong side, and tack and press it in position. Diagram 64 (ii).

2. *Fix in the zip*

Place the zip underneath the opening with the top of the slide level with or 6 mm below the pattern line which marks the top edge. Work with the right side of the article uppermost and pin the article to the tape of the zip. Ease in the slight extra length on the garment. Notice how the distance between the teeth of the zip and the material of the garment leaves room for the slide to move freely up and down.

Machine the garment to the zip close to the fold. To begin the stitching, move the slide part way down the zip and machine down to this point. Leave the needle down in the work, raise the machine foot, move the slide back to the top, and continue machining along one side, the square end and part of the second side. Repeat the process of moving the slide to complete the stitching.

At the top of the zip, fold the tape back diagonally on to the wrong side, so that the fold is level with the top of the slide and the edge of the tape can be caught into the final edge finish. Diagram 64 (iii).

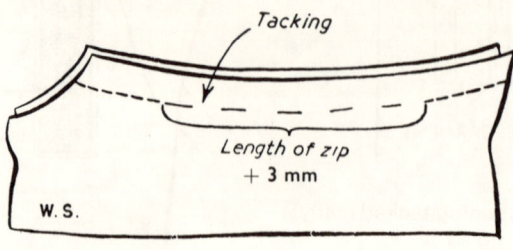

65 (i). Seam prepared for inserting

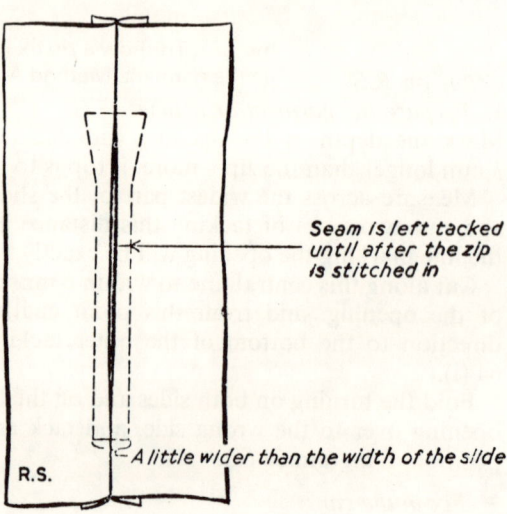

65 (ii). A zip stitched into a seam (semi-concealed). Method B

METHOD B—*To insert a zip into a seam so that it is semi-concealed. Stitching shows all round the zip on the R.S.*

1. *Prepare the garment*

Mark the length of the opening making it 3 mm longer than the zip. Work the seam and neaten it as far as the opening. Leave at least 1 cm turnings on the edges of the opening.

Tack the pattern lines of the opening together along the length of the opening, as though preparing an open seam. Press this tacked seam open. Diagram 65 (i).

2. *Fix in the zip*

Although it is better to have the tape of the zip matching

the colour of the material, it is not essential for this method.

Place the right side of the zip against the wrong side of the tacked seam, with the centre of the zip in line with the join. Pin from the garment side, easing in the extra length. The seam can be pulled apart sufficiently to see that the zip is kept in the right position.

Tack the garment to the tape along both sides and across the bottom.

The machining will have to be far enough from the metal of the zip to allow the slide to move freely.

Decide this measurement and machine an even distance from the tacked seam and across the bottom of the zip. Widen the stitching at the top of the zip to make room for the slide, shaping it as shown in diagram 65 (ii).*

Trim down the turnings of the garment on the wrong side so that they are covered and protected by the tape of the zip. Remove all tacking threads.

METHOD C—*To insert a zip into a seam so that it is concealed and only one line of stitching shows*

1. Prepare the garment

Make the seam to the bottom of the opening and press it open.

Fold the front edge of the opening to the W.S. on the P.L., tack and press it.

Fold and tack the back edge of the opening 3 mm *outside* the P.L. in the turning allowance. This will give a 3 mm lap when the zip is fixed in. Press the fold.

2. Fix in the zip

Place the zip behind the back edge of the opening with the fold almost up to the teeth and the top 6 mm below the P.L. Tack and machine it in place using a zipper foot. Diagrams 18, 65 (iii).

Now lay the front edge flat over the zip with the fold level with the P.L. on the back of the garment. Pin and tack this fold firmly in place. Note that the stitching is now concealed. Diagram 65 (iv).

Next, tack through the front of the opening to the zip tape about 1 cm away from the fold. The stitches should just clear the teeth of the zip. Diagram 65 (v). Machine on the tacking and straight across the base. It will be seen that a small pleat has been formed on the W.S. at the

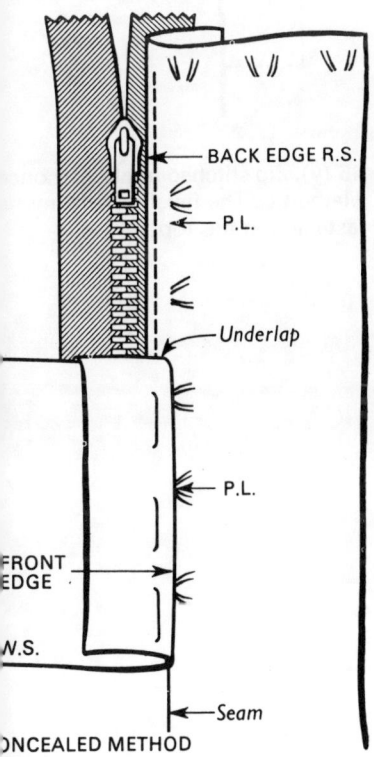

ii). Zip machined to back edge of ing. Front edge prepared

ONCEALED METHOD

* A method of fixing zips by hand is given in *Introduction to Needlework*, p. 124.

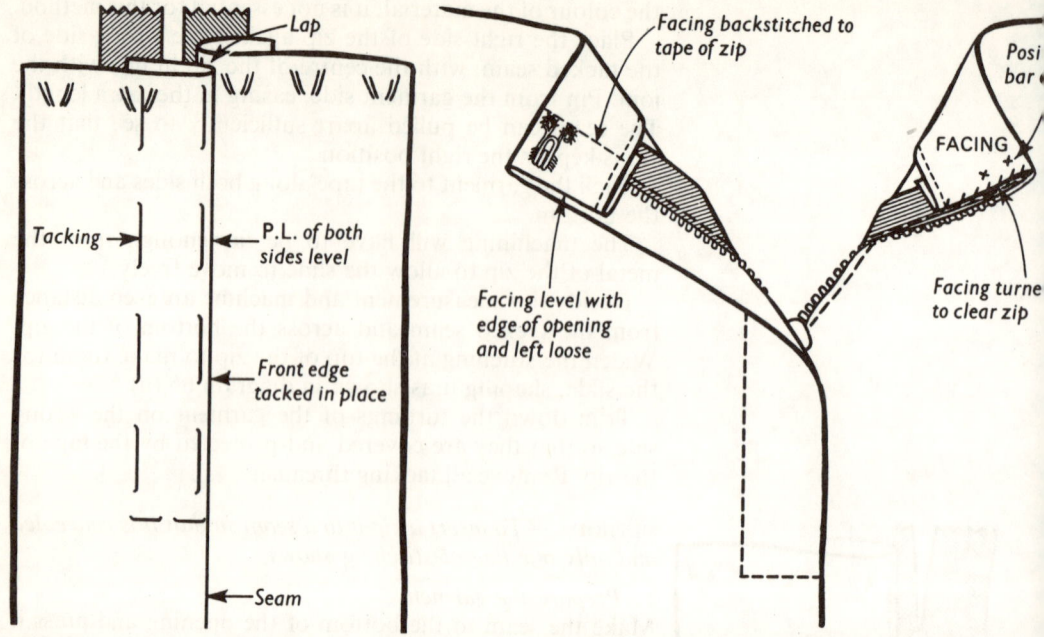

65 (iv). Front edge of opening tacked in place ready for machining

65 (v). Zip stitched in place (conce Method C. The finish of a facing a fastening at the top*

base of the opening which is held flat with the machining.
Complete as given for Method B.
If the zip is to be stitched by hand, use the hand-picking stitch, see p. 155.

A FLY-FLAP. (Optional, see p. 124)
1. *Make the flap* the length of the zip and 4 to 5 cm wide. On thick fabrics make it in single material and neaten the cut edges with zigzag machining or overcasting. With thinner fabrics cut the strip wide enough to fold in half lengthwise. Neaten the cut edges together.†
2. *Attach the flap* with one long edge to the tape of the zip on the back of the opening. See that the width of the flap lies across the zip teeth. Machine or hem the flap to the tape and stitch it in place at both ends to keep it flat during wear.

---

* Two other methods of finishing the top are shown in *Introduction to Needlework*, p. 125.

† A method of making a fly-flap in thin fabric is given in Introduction to Needlework, pp. 74, 75.

11 Fastenings

When an opening has been completed and pressed, it is ready to have the fastenings attached. The kind of fastenings to be used will have already been decided while planning the opening. Fastenings can be put on so that they show, or they may be concealed between the over and underlap of the opening. Buttons and loops or buttonholes, eyelets and strings, tie strings, zip fasteners, can be put on in either way. Others are always concealed, such as press studs, hooks and eyes, or bars, and Velcro.

CHOOSE FASTENINGS SO THAT:
1. They are suitable in size. Openings with narrow wraps require smaller fastenings than those with wide wraps or made in heavier materials.
2. They are suitable to the type of garment or article, e.g. non-metal fastenings are preferable on undergarments and children's clothing, plain buttons look better on patterned materials than decorative ones.

FIX FASTENINGS SO THAT
1. They are sewn on double material.
2. They are sufficient in number to keep the opening closed. (Close-fitting clothes, therefore, will require more fastenings than loose ones.)
3. They are sewn exactly opposite one another in order that the opening will be flat when fastened.

Buttons and buttonholes

Buttonholes are needed on all types of articles and clothing, and should be made before sewing on the buttons which fit into them. There are bound and worked buttonholes, but the worked are the stronger and more useful kind. Contrary to the general rule, the bound variety are made before the opening is worked, early in the construction of the garment. Worked buttonholes, on the other hand, are made after the opening is finished and often when the article is otherwise completed. Worked buttonholes can be made quickly and effectively on a swing needle machine or with a special attachment on a straight stitch machine. Instructions are supplied with the machines.

DIRECTION OF BUTTONHOLES
Buttonholes are made in a horizontal or vertical position according to the amount and direction of the strain they will undergo in wear.

Horizontal
Buttonholes are made in a horizontal direction when there is strain in that direction, such as on closely fitting bands, cuffs, yokes and dress bodices. Diagram 66 (i).

Vertical
Buttonholes are made in a vertical direction:
(a) when there is strain or pull in a vertical direction, such as at the waist of a skirt or toddlers' trousers, which button on to the blouse,
(b) when the garment is loosely fitting and there is little or no strain in either direction,
(c) when the hem or facing on the opening is made on to the right side of the garment, e.g. at the front of a shirt blouse, so that the buttonholes can be placed centrally. Diagram 66 (ii).

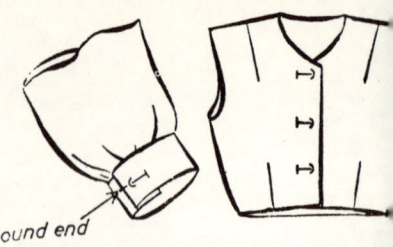

66 (i). Buttonholes in horizontal positions

POSITION AND SIZE OF BUTTONHOLES
The length of a buttonhole should equal the width of the button plus 3 mm to allow the buttonhole to slip easily over the button.

The space between the edge of an opening and the buttonhole should be at least half the width of the button, so that the button does not project beyond the edge when fastened.

The position of the buttonholes should be marked with a crease, pins or tacking and they should be evenly spaced. When a number of buttonholes are to be made horizontally, e.g. on the front opening of a blouse, two lines of tacking to mark the length of the buttonholes will ensure that they are exactly in line. Diagram 67.

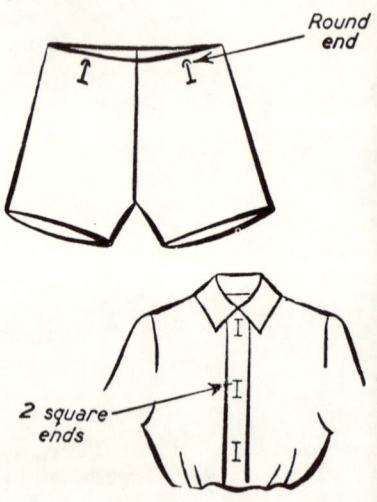

66 (ii). Buttonholes in vertical position

Worked buttonholes
Worked buttonholes are made by cutting a slit in double material and working buttonhole stitch—a strong knotted stitch—to cover the raw edges. Accurate work, care and a little practice will soon give the skill required to make

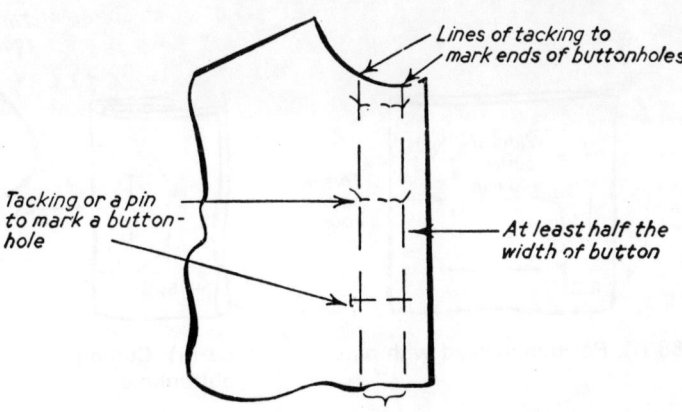

. How to plan and mark the position buttonholes

buttonholes with confidence.* It is essential for a needlewoman to be able to make them easily because they are so widely used and are excellent on children's clothing, underclothing and household articles. Worked buttonholes may be made in three different ways:

(a) Buttonholes with one round and one square end
These are used whenever there is sufficient strain to pull the button to one end of the buttonhole. A buttonhole should be planned with the round end nearest the edge of the opening, so that it will take the shank of the button when fastened. Diagram 68 (viii).

(b) Buttonholes with two square ends, which are used when there is no strain on the buttonhole in any direction and the button will remain in the centre of the buttonhole when fastened. Diagram 69.

(c) Buttonholes with two round ends
These are rarely used to fasten buttons unless there is liable to be strain at both ends of the buttonhole. They are used chiefly for working slots for ribbon, braid and elastic. Diagram 111.

INSTRUCTIONS FOR WORKING

A. BUTTONHOLES WITH ONE ROUND AND ONE SQUARE END
Mark the position of the buttonholes. If only one buttonhole is to be made, e.g. on a cuff, mark the length with pins; crease the material between them on the straight

* Button-through styles can be made with a fly-flap on which buttonholes are worked by hand or machine *(Introduction to Needlework,* pp. 74, 75). Then the buttonholes, if not very good, will not show.

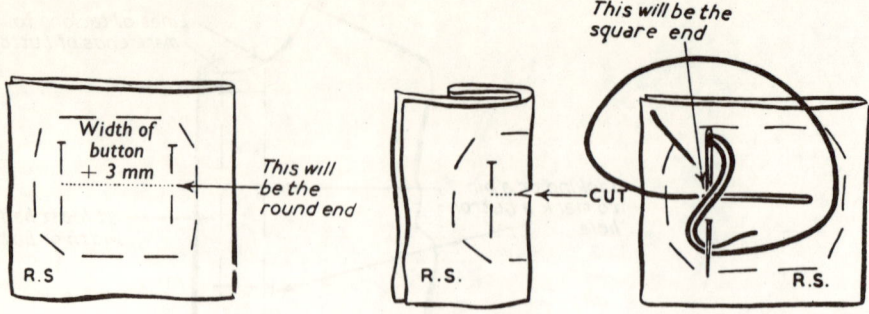

68 (i). Position marked with pins

68 (ii). Cutting a buttonhole

68 (iii). To begin working the first side

thread to mark the position for the cut, and baste round this position to hold the layers of material together while working. Diagram 68 (i).

Make a clean straight cut along the crease, using small, sharp, well-pointed scissors. Pierce the material with the point of the blade at what will be the round end of the buttonhole and cut towards the square end; or, fold the material across the crease and snip a small cut in the centre of the crease at the fold, open the material flat again and cut from the snip to each end. Diagram 68 (ii). Work the buttonhole immediately after it is cut and before cutting the next one.

Use a thread for working which is a little heavier than the threads of the material, e.g. Drima on viscose, heavy duty or button thread on thick woollens. Have the thread long enough to complete the buttonhole.*

1. *The first side*
Begin working at the end of the cut which will be the square end of the buttonhole. Slip the needle between the two layers of material and bring it out level with the cut and a thread to the left of the end, on the right side of the work. Work buttonhole stitch closely along the cut from left to right, making the last stitch at the end of the cut. Diagram 68 (iii), (iv). (Buttonhole stitch, see p. 147.) Take care that the stitches are not too deep, but that they are deep enough to secure both raw edges properly.

2. *The round end*
Put the needle behind the cut as though to make a buttonhole stitch, but bring it through to the right side without

---

* A graded method of learning buttonhole stitch is given in *Introduction to Needlework*, p. 113.

FASTENINGS 133

68 (iv). The first overcasting stitch at the round end

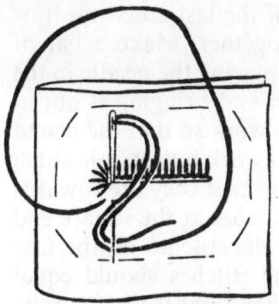

68 (v). The last overcasting stitch and the first buttonhole stitch on the second side

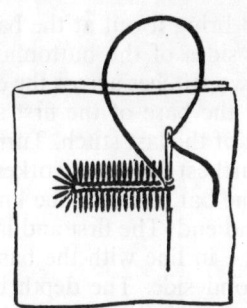

68 (vi). Drawing the edges together at the square end

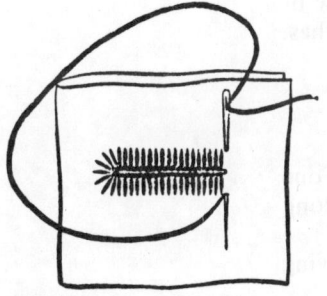

68 (vii). Stitches across the square end

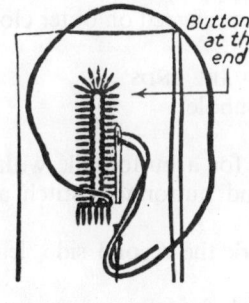

68 (viii). Working the square end

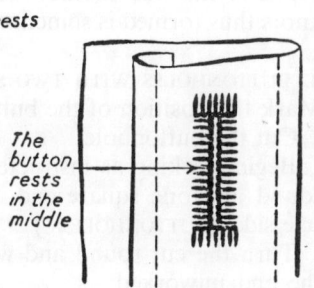

69. Buttonhole with two square ends

twisting the thread round the needle, thus making an overcasting stitch. Continue working overcasting stitches round the end, spacing them evenly and making them form a good round shape. There should be an odd number of stitches, so that one stitch can be made directly in line with the cut. When the needle is in position for the last overcasting stitch, twist the cotton round the needle so that the first buttonhole stitch on the second side is formed at the same time. Diagrams 68 (iv), (v).

3. *The second side*
The first buttonhole stitch just described should be exactly opposite the last one on the first side. Work buttonhole stitch along the second side to the end of the cut.

4. *The square end*
Put the needle into the knot of the first stitch on the first

side and bring it out at the base of the last stitch to draw the two sides of the buttonhole together. Make a bar of one or two stitches across the end, placing the needle in the work at the base of the first stitch and bringing it out at the base of the last stitch. Turn the work so that the round end is furthest from the worker and work buttonhole stitch across the bar, forming the knots so that they are towards the round end. The first and last stitches at the square end should be in line with the base of the stitches on the first and second side. The depth of the stitches should equal those at the sides and should be taken right through to the back of the work. Diagrams 68 (vi), (vii), (viii).

N.B. In dressmaking, the stitches along the square end are made very small, instead of making them equal to the depth of the side stitches. The appearance of the row of knots thus formed is sometimes preferred on outer clothes.

B. BUTTONHOLES WITH TWO SQUARE ENDS

Mark the position of the buttonhole.

Cut the buttonhole.

Begin working as instructed for a buttonhole with one round and one square end, and buttonhole stitch along one side. (BUTTONHOLE A.)

Turn the cut round and work the second side, leaving the end unworked.

Work the end as instructed for the square end in BUTTONHOLE A.

Take the thread through to the back of the work and slip the needle under the stitches to the opposite end.

Bring the needle out in the knot of the last stitch and work a square end. Diagram 69.

C. BUTTONHOLES WITH TWO ROUND ENDS

Work exactly as instructed for BUTTONHOLE A, but finish with a second round end in place of the square end.

Suggestions for working buttonholes on material which frays readily

1. Machine or backstitch round the crease which marks the position for a buttonhole, leaving 3 mm between the stitching. Diagram 70, *or*

2. cut the buttonhole and overcast the cut edges before working buttonhole stitch. Both these methods are suitable for beginners to use on any material, *or*

3. cut a thread of the material in the centre of the crease marking the buttonhole, and draw it out to each end of

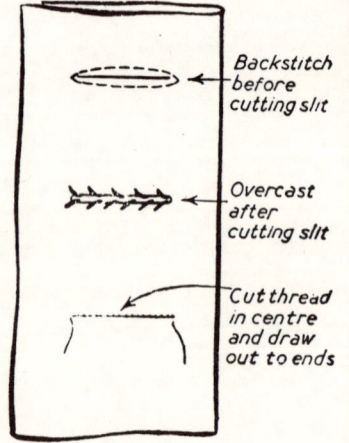

70. Three ways of minimizing fraying

the crease. Diagram 65.

Do not cut the buttonhole, but instead, work buttonhole stitches into the space left by the drawn thread. Complete the working. Turn the buttonhole to the wrong side and cut the material through the centre of the buttonhole between the stitches. Use a stitch ripper, see p. 61.

BUTTONHOLES BY MACHINE, see p. 235, p. 236.

Bound buttonholes

Bound buttonholes are not as strong as worked buttonholes and are not very satisfactory on garments which are constantly washed. They are used chiefly on adults' clothing, particularly outer clothes. Buttonholes can be bound with self or contrasting material, either in colour or texture, and are often designed to be a style feature. The bind is approximately 3 mm in depth when finished, but can be made wider if liked. The buttonhole is worked on single material preferably backed with interfacing and is neatened on the wrong side by a facing or hem.

INSTRUCTIONS FOR WORKING

1. *Mark the position of the buttonholes* with tacking on the right side of the material. Make a back stitch at the beginning and end of this tacking which marks the length of the buttonhole, so that the length will be visible on the wrong side as well. Diagram 67.

2. *Cut strips for the binding* 5 cm wide and at least 2 cm longer than the buttonhole. The strips should have the selvedge threads along the length or they should be cut on the true cross.

3. *Baste the strip to the right side of the garment* so that the centre of the strip is directly over the tacking which marks the length of the buttonhole. The right side of the strip should be against the garment. Baste over the whole of the strip. Fix all the strips in position. Diagram 71 (i).

4. *Machine all the strips in position.* Turn the work to the wrong side and machine round the tacking which marks the length of the buttonhole. Keep the stitching 3 mm away from the tacking but do not stitch beyond each end of the tacking. The ends should have square corners so that when finished a neat rectangle of stitching is seen on both sides of the work. It is best to begin stitching in the middle of one side so that the ending off does not occur at a corner. Diagram 71 (ii). When a wider bind is required the stitching must be done a corresponding distance from the tacking, e.g. 6 mm away from the tacking to give a 6 mm bind.

5. *Cut and bind each buttonhole.* Cut through the strip and garment from the centre of the tacking to within 3 mm of each end.

From this point cut diagonally right into the corners up to the stitching. Diagram 71 (ii).

Turn the strip through to the wrong side, wrapping the strip closely over the raw edges and lay the strip flat on the wrong side. Pull the ends well over to the wrong side and form a small inverted pleat at each end. Pin in position, and tack all round the buttonhole. Diagram 71 (iii).

Secure the strip in place either:

(a) with small running stitches taken through the strip and the turnings inside the bind, taking care that the stitches do not show on the right side. (Make one or two firm stitches across the pleats to hold them together.) Diagram 71 (iv). *or*

(b) with machining round the buttonhole on the right side, working the stitches in the seam, or on the edge of the seam. (See A BOUND POCKET, p. 193).

Draw the edges of the buttonhole together with fishbone tacking. Diagram 71 (v).

Press all the buttonholes and trim down the strip to extend about 1 cm beyond the slit. (FISHBONE TACKING p. 296.)

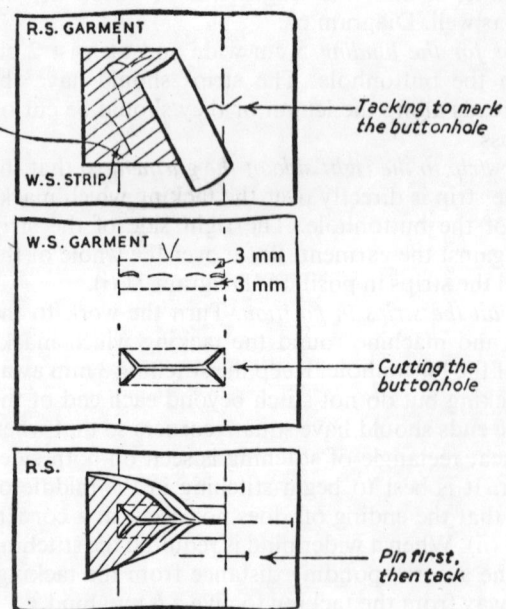

71 (i). Strip basted in position for bound buttonhole

71 (ii). Stitching the buttonhole from the W.S. of garment

71 (iii). Pushing the strip through to the W.S. to fix the binds

(iv). Fixing the binds on the W.S.

(v). Pins to mark the position for the cut in the facing

(vi). To neaten the back of the buttonhole with the facing

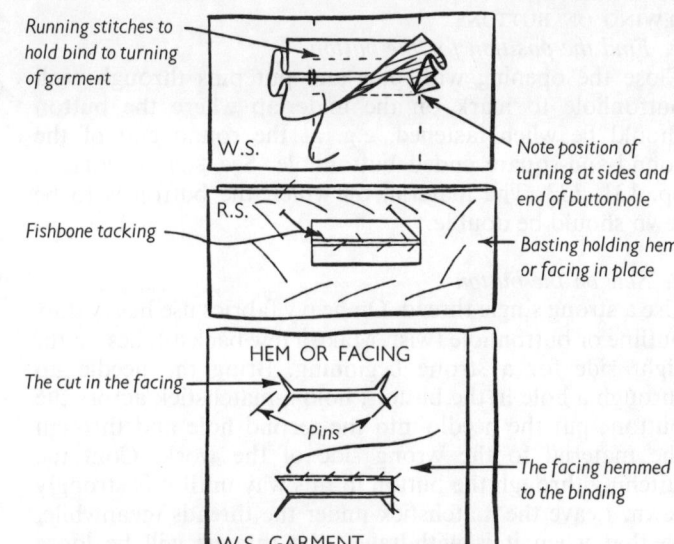

6. *Fix the facing in position at the back of the buttonholes.* Fix the facing to the garment and baste it flat over the buttonholes.

Put a pin in each end of the buttonhole to show its length in the facing. Cut through the facing only, between the pins to within an 3 mm of them. From this point cut diagonally to the depth of the bind at the corners of the buttonholes. Note that the cut is the same shape and size as the one made when the buttonholes were cut. Diagram 71 (v), (vi).

Turn under the cut edges and hem the facing closely to the binding. Take special care that the facing is not drawn down tightly because this would spoil the set of the buttonholes on the right side.

Buttons

Buttons are made in a wide variety of materials, including metal, bone, wood, rubber, plastics, leather, linen. Some are flat buttons pierced with two or four holes, and others have a shank underneath through which stitches are taken to sew on the button. The purpose of the shank is to make a space between the material and the button to allow for the thickness of the overlap when the button is fastened. Flat buttons are always sewn on so that a shank is formed with thread.

SEWING ON BUTTONS

1. *Find the position for the button*
Close the opening with pins and put pins through each buttonhole to mark on the underlap where the button should be when fastened, e.g. at the round end of the round-and-square ended buttonhole. See BUTTONHOLE A, pp. 131, 133. The material on which the button is to be sewn should be double.

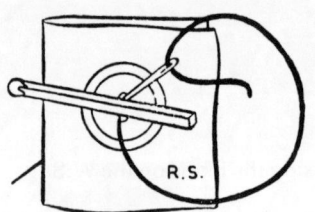

72 (i). Sewing on a button over a matchstick

2. *Sew on the button*
Use a strong single thread. On heavy fabrics use heavy duty outline or buttonhole twist. Make a few backstitches on the right side for a strong beginning. Bring the needle up through a hole in the button; hold a matchstick across the button; put the needle into the second hole and through the material to the wrong side of the work. Continue stitching through the button in this way until it is strongly sewn. Leave the matchstick under the threads meanwhile, so that when it is withdrawn, the threads will be loose enough to make a shank. Diagram 72 (i).

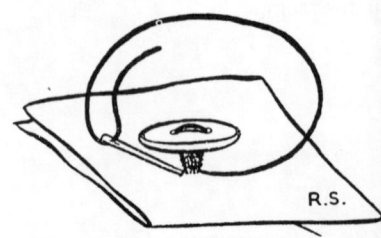

72 (ii). The shank made and the needle taken through to W.S. to finish off

3. *Make the shank*
After making the final stitch in sewing on the button, bring the needle out between the button and the material and remove the matchstick.

Wind the cotton tightly round the threads beneath the button until it forms a firm shank. Take the cotton through to the wrong side and fasten off securely. Diagram 72 (ii).

Buttons and loops

The loop to fasten a button is generally made on the edge of an article or garment, but occasionally it is concealed by working it on the wrong side of the overlap a short way in from the edge. Diagram 73 (i).

Worked loops
Worked loops are made when the opening is completed and after the buttons have been sewn on.

1. *Mark the position for the loops*
Pin the opening together and put pins in the edge opposite the centre of each button. These mark the centre of each loop.

The space across the loop should equal the width of the

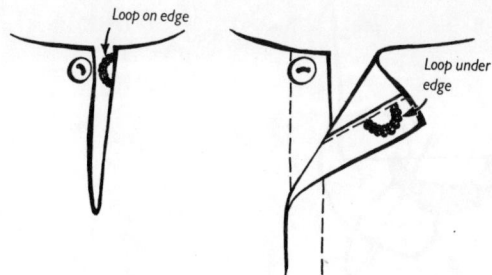

(i). Positions of loops on openings

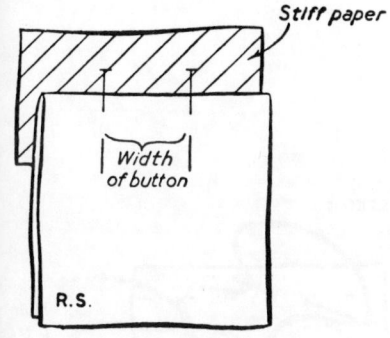

(ii). Edge of opening pinned to paper ready for working a loop

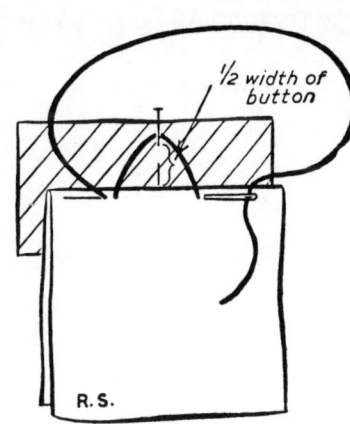

73 (iii). Stranding the loop

button. Mark each end with pins and take out the central pin. Diagram 73 (ii).

Pin or tack the edge of the article (wrong side down) to stiff paper for support while working the loop. Put a pin in the paper half the width of the button away from the edge of the article and between the pins which mark the width of the loop. Diagram 73 (ii), (iii).

2. *Work the loops*

Slip the needle through the double material and bring it out at one pin. Return the needle to the material at the second pin, leaving a loop which should pass under the head of the pin on the paper. Diagram 73 (iii).

Pass the needle along the fold and bring it out at the first pin. Continue making loops in this way until enough strands have been formed to give the required thickness. The pin in the paper is a guide to make all the strands the same size.

Loop stitch the strands together closely, working from left to right with the right side of the work uppermost. Take the first and last stitches into the material. The rest of the stitches are made more easily if the needle is reversed and the eye put first into the loop to make the stitches. The loop should be very firm when finished. Diagram 73 (iv).

Eyelet holes, strings and ribbons

Eyelet holes

One of the simplest methods of fastening is by making eyelet holes in the fabric and threading ribbon, cord or tape through them to tie. This form of fastening is popular on babies' and children's clothing, especially at neck openings because the size is then easily adjusted. It is, of

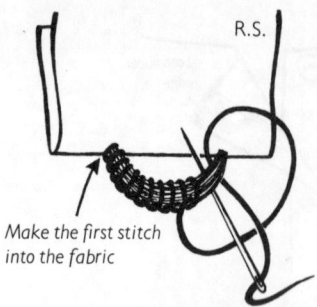

Make the first stitch into the fabric

R.S.

73 (iv). Working the loop with loop stitches

course, stronger to work the eyelets on double material, but this is not always possible.

TO WORK EYELET HOLES

Mark the position for the eyelet with a pencil dot.

Make a ring of small running stitches surrounding the pencil dot. The top of a pencil pressed down on the material will give an imprint of a circle for a guide.

Pierce through the centre of the circle with a stiletto and oversew tightly and closely over the running stitches on the right side. Use sewing thread. Diagram 74.

N.B. A slot for ribbon or elastic can be worked in a similar way, over the edges of a slit cut in the material.

Tie strings

These are a practical fastening on children's clothing and articles of household use, such as pillow slips, mattress covers, cutlery cases. When a very strong fastening is needed, tape is the best to use for the ties. Ribbon, braid, webbing and seam bindings can be used as strings for other purposes. When the edges of an opening meet, as in a faced slit opening, both tie strings are fixed on the edge of the opening. When there is a wrap on the opening, the tie string on the overlap is fixed on the edge and the tie on the underlap placed in from the edge. Diagram 75 (ii).

TO ATTACH TIE STRINGS

Cut one end of the tape straight and fold over 3 mm. Place in position so that a square of tape is concealed under the opening, as shown on the overlapping side in diagram 75 (i).

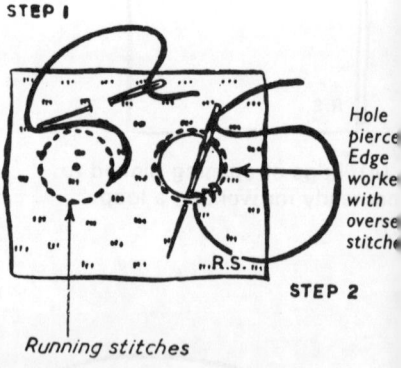

STEP 1

Hole pierced Edge worked with oversew stitche

Running stitches

STEP 2

74. How to work eyelet holes

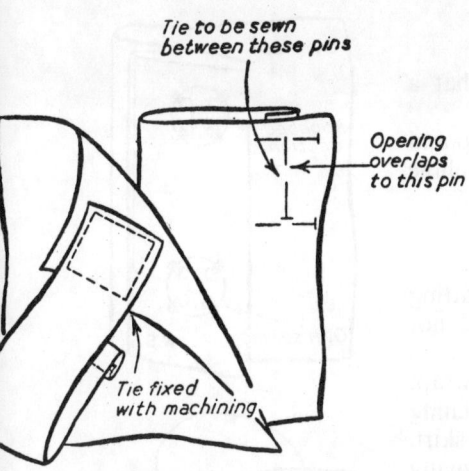 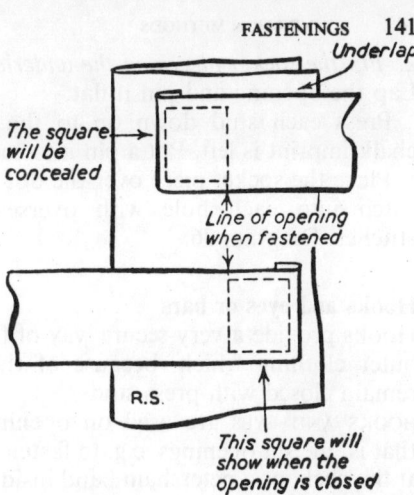

(i). A tie string fixed by machine and position marked the opposite tie string on the underlap

75 (ii). Ways of fixing tie strings on the underlap

Machine neatly in place.

The opposite tape is placed either under the edge or for openings with a wrap, as shown in diagram 75 (ii).

If a machine is not available, oversew the tape to the edge of the opening and hem the remaining three sides of the tape flat to the article. Alternatively use back-stitching.

Press studs, hooks and eyes or bars

Press studs

These provide a convenient and quick method of fastening. They are used on all types of clothing but need careful handling during laundering to prevent them becoming bent and broken. Of the two parts of a press stud, one has a knob on a flat base, which should be sewn to the overlap and the other has a socket, and is sewn on the underlap.

1. *Fix the studs on the overlap*

Put in pins to mark the position for the studs on the wrong side of the overlap, spacing them evenly.

Hold the knobbed half in place 3 mm from the edge of the overlap or in the centre of the hem or facing. Sew on with oversewing or buttonhole stitch into each hole. Fix all the studs on the overlap and rub chalk on to each knob preparatory to finding the positions for the other halves of the press studs.

2. *Fix the socket pieces on the underlap*
Lap the opening and pin it flat.

Press each stud down on to the underlap so that a chalk imprint is left. Put a pin into each dot.

Place the socket piece over the dot on the underlap and stitch into each hole with oversewing or buttonhole stitches. Diagram 76.

Hooks and eyes or bars

Hooks provide a very secure way of fastening close-fitting outer clothing which, because of the strain, would not remain closed with press studs.

HOOKS AND EYES are used on openings without a wrap, that is, the slit openings, e.g. to fasten a bound slit opening at the neck, or a petersham band inside the waist of a skirt.
1. Fix the hook behind one side of the opening—usually the right-hand side, with the bend of the hook a bare 3 mm from the edge.

Bring the needle up through one of the holes in the hook and work round this hole and the next with oversewing or buttonhole stitch.

Pass the needle through the material up to the bend of the hook, and secure it with several straight stitches passing across the hook just below the bend. Diagram 77 (i). In most cases none of the stitches must be taken through to the right side.

2. Fix the eye underneath the opposite edge of the opening so that the eye just projects beyond it, thus allowing room for the hook to fasten into the bend.

Oversew or buttonhole stitch all round both holes.

Bring the needle through the material near the edge and stitch across each side of the eye, just below the edge, to hold the eye in place. All the stitches can be taken through double material. Diagram 77 (i).

HOOKS AND BARS are used on openings which have a wrap. Either metal or worked bars may be used, but worked bars are a little flatter and are especially suitable for delicate fabrics.
1. Sew the hook on to the overlap as described for hooks and eyes.
Lap the opening and pin it closed. Put a pin in the underlap just level with the bend of the hook. This gives the position for the centre of the bar.
3. Fix the bars.

Metal bars. Fix so that the bend in the bar is towards the

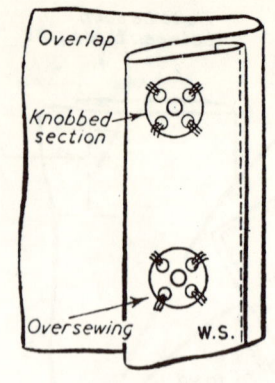

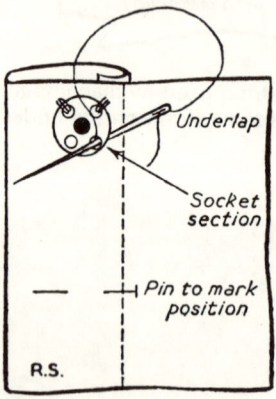

76. To sew on press studs

FASTENINGS

edge of the opening. Oversew or buttonhole stitch round each hole. Diagram 77 (ii).

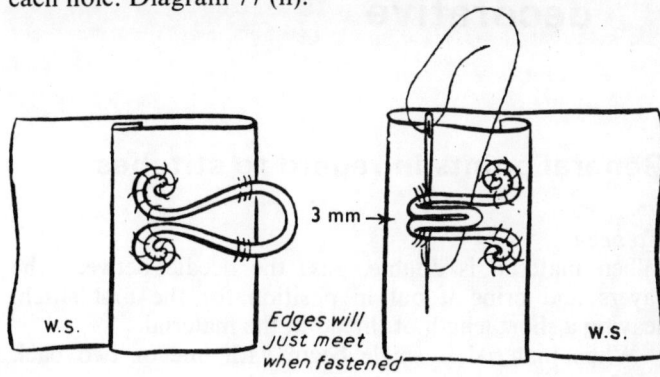

77 (i). To sew on hooks and eyes

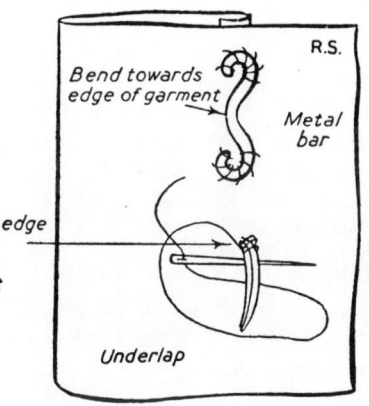

(ii). To sew on bars and make a worked bar

Worked bars. Make strands with thread across the pin, making the strands the length of a metal bar and working a sufficient number to give a bar which will be proportionate in thickness to the hook. The usual number is 4 to 6 strands.

Loop stitch the strands together so that the stitches are close and the looped edge is towards the edge of the opening. Diagram 77 (ii). It is easier with needle reversed.

Velcro

Velcro is a nylon 'touch and close' fastening composed of two strips which cling together because the surface of one is covered with minute nylon hooks and the other with correspondingly small loops. The strips can be bought in a variety of colours and can be used in long lengths, e.g. to close covers and cushions, or in short lengths in place of buttons and buttonholes or other fastenings, e.g. to close skirt bands, blouse and dress fronts or bags and cases. Two widths are available, 2.5 cm and 1.5 cm.

1. Complete the opening and plan the position of the strips so that they will not show when the opening is closed and so that the opening will lie flat.

Fix the softer side underneath the overlapping side of the opening.

2. Machine round each piece or hem strongly. Diagram 78.

A new Velcro which can be ironed on is now available and is washable.

During laundering, the fastening should be kept closed to prevent surfaces from collecting fluff.

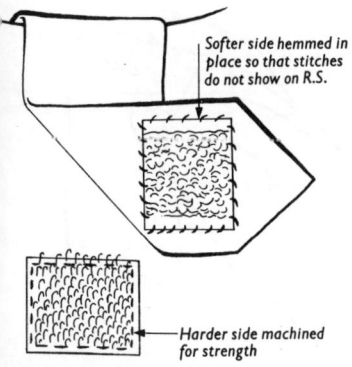

Velcro used on a tab

12 Stitches, plain and decorative

General points in regard to stitches

To begin
When material is double, pass the needle between the layers and bring it out in position for the first stitch, leaving a short length of thread in the material.
When material is single begin with one or two back stitches.

To join on a new thread
Bring in the new thread in such a way that the regularity of the stitches is not interrupted. Often a few double stitches are made for strength by working over the old ones with the new thread.

To end off
Make one or two stitches over the final stitch, pass the needle between the layers of fabric and cut it close, or weave the needle through the stitches on the wrong side for a short distance, before cutting the thread close.

Position in which to hold the work
Unless otherwise stated the work is held in the following way—Take the edge to be sewn between the thumb and first finger of the left hand and a little further along between the second and third fingers. A flat taut surface is spread between. The bulk of the work should be below the hand. The stitching is done over the first finger. Diagram 79.
For certain stitches, the work is held level with the forefinger as shown in Diagram 82.

Stitches for preliminary fixing

Tacking stitches
Use tacking cotton which is cheap, and being unglazed, is soft and therefore easy to remove.

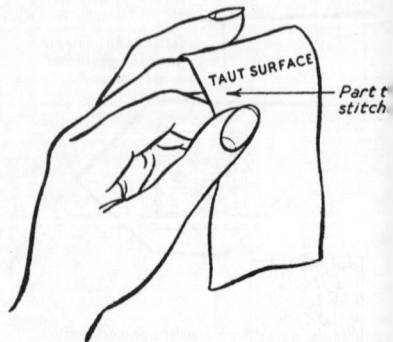

79. How to hold the work

Use a fine darning needle, e.g. No. 8 or 9.

1. EVEN TACKING. Diagram 29 (i)
The stitches, approximately 1 cm long, are the same size on both sides of the work.

2. LONG AND SHORT TACKING. Diagram 35 (ii)
Two short stitches, approximately 6 mm long, are taken on the needle together followed by one long stitch.

3. BASTING. Diagram 27
Used for fixing layers of material together because the stitch can be worked over the surface in any direction without moving, and thus disturbing, the work. Basting is done with the work flat on the table. The amount picked up on the needle is approximately 1 cm.

4. FISHBONE TACKING. Diagram 171
Used for drawing edges together temporarily.

5. SLIP TACKING. Diagram 123
Used to tack seams from R.S. to match designs.

Stitches for joining

Use sewing thread of a suitable thickness and the finest needle which can be threaded without difficulty, e.g. a No. 8 or 9 needle with a No. 40 or 50 Sylko.

Backstitch. Diagram 80
This is a strong stitch used in place of machining. It has a similar appearance to the machine stitch on the right side, but on the wrong side it resembles stem stitch. Backstitch is also used to make strong beginnings and endings for other sewing stitches.

Notice that the space over which the needle is taken back equals the space it is brought forward.

Always put the needle into the work exactly at the end of the last stitch made.

Running stitch. Diagram 22
This is used for joining seams by hand and for working tucks.
Work small even stitches. The size should be the same on both sides of the work. A better result will be obtained if one stitch is worked at a time. To take several stitches

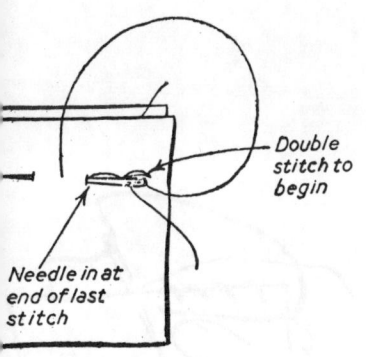

To work backstitch

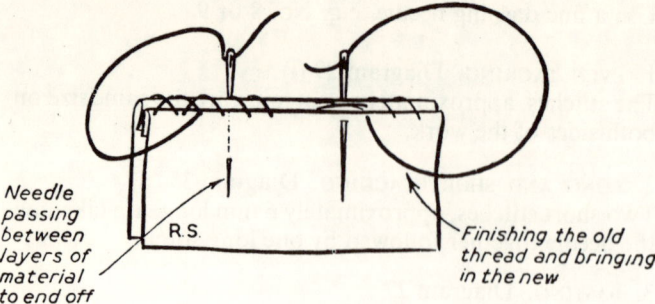

Needle passing between layers of material to end off

R.S.

Finishing the old thread and bringing in the new

81. Oversewing. To join on a new thread and to end off

on the needle together causes uneven and weak stitches.

Oversewing. Diagram 81.
A strong, tight stitch used to join finished edges together; e.g. the open sides of a hem at the corner of an apron.

Hold the work with the forefinger behind the edges to be joined and level with them. The stitch is worked on the right side of the work. Diagram 82 shows how to hold the work although it illustrates another stitch.

Work from right to left and put the needle in quite straight from back to front, making small shallow stitches across the two edges. Work the stitches closely and tightly.

To join on a new thread unpick half a stitch and tuck the short end of cotton down between the two edges.

Bring in the new thread at the front edge and tuck the short end down between the edges.

To end off, work in the reverse direction over two or three stitches forming cross stitches.

Stitches to neaten raw edges

Use sewing thread for these stitches.

Overcasting. Diagram 82
Worked over single edges or to neaten several edges together.

Hold the work with the raw edge level with the forefinger.

Work from left to right and put the needle in from back to front, a few threads down from the edge, so that a slanting stitch is made over the edge. Slant the needle slightly towards the left and keep the stitches loose.

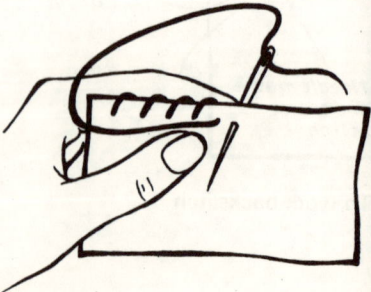

82. Overcasting, showing how to hold the work

Loop stitch
Sometimes used in place of overcasting for neatening, but it is also used for making bars for hooks and as a decorative stitch. It is worked with sewing thread except when it is used as an embroidery stitch. Directions for working are included with embroidery stitches.

Buttonhole stitch. Diagram 83
This stitch gives a firm knotted edge and is used principally for worked buttonholes. Use sewing thread or buttonhole twist.

Hold the work with the edge upright between the thumb and first finger and work the stitch from left to right on the right side of the material.

Put the needle in from back to front a few threads from the edge. Pass the double end of cotton, which comes from the eye of the needle, under the point of the needle from left to right. Pull the needle through and draw the thread upwards, so that the knot which has been formed lies on the raw edge.

Work the stitches closely, but because knots take up more room than stitches space them sufficiently to avoid overcrowding.

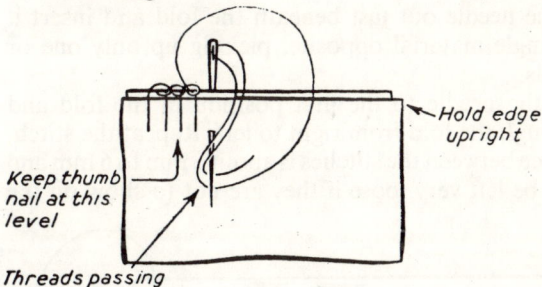

Buttonhole stitch

Stitches to hold edge finishes in place

Hemming. Diagram 84 (i)
Used on household linens and children's clothing to hold folded edges in position. The stitch shows equally on both sides of the work.

Put the needle into single material below the fold and bring it out a few threads above the fold a little to the left. The slant of the stitches should be similar to the sides of a 'V' and should appear the same on both sides of the work.

To end off, work in a reverse direction for two or three

84 (i). Hemming

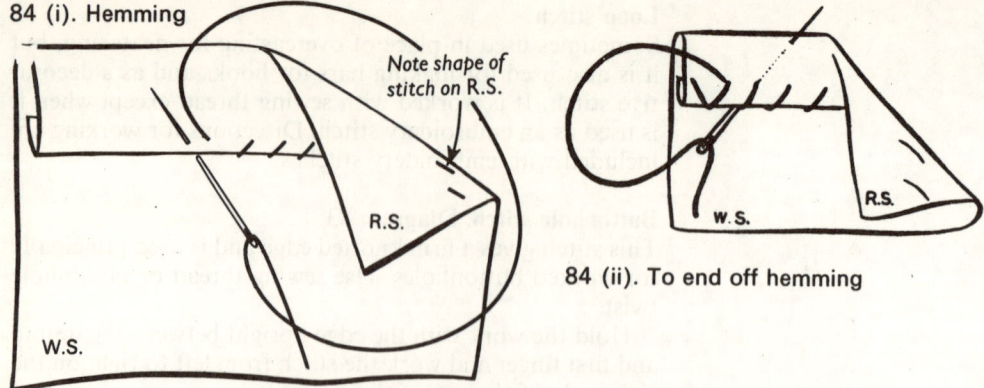

84 (ii). To end off hemming

stitches forming V's on both sides of the work, and bring the needle out in the hem. Diagram 84 (ii).

Slip-hemming. Diagram 85
Not as strong as hemming, but on the right side it shows very little, and on thick materials is invisible.

Turn the bulk of the material down from the hem so that the fold to be stitched projects 3 mm. Hold the fold level with the first finger.

Bring the needle out just beneath the fold and insert it into the single material opposite, picking up only one or two threads.

Return the needle to the first position in the fold and slip it through the fold from right to left. Repeat the stitch. The distance between the stitches is about 3 mm to 6 mm and they must be left very loose if they are not to show on the right side.

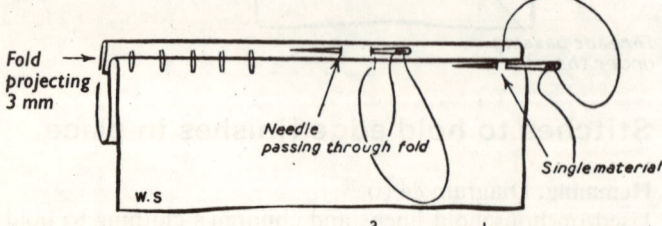

85. Slip-hemming

Another way of slip-hemming is used when the hem turning is single—see p. 96. This is called *slip-stitching* when used for other purposes, e.g. slipstitching a facing in place on the right side, when it is pulled close.

Herringbone stitch. Diagram 86
Worked over a raw edge on materials which do not fray

much, e.g. flannel. The stitch is strong and shows on both sides of the work. It is used chiefly to hold facings in place under linings and for embroidery.

Begin with a backstitch in double fabric. Make a running stitch in single material just below the raw edge and a little way to the right.

Take the next running stitch in double material, a little to the right, so that the needle is brought out above the end of the first running stitch. Continue working running stitches in this way, making stitches alternately in double and single material. On the right side, two rows of running stitches will be seen with stitches immediately above or below the spaces.

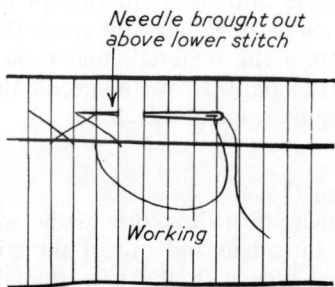

Herringbone stitch

Stitches for decorative purposes and embroidery

The following form the foundation of more elaborate stitches. Most of the stitches in the previous categories can also be used for decoration. Begin embroidery stitches

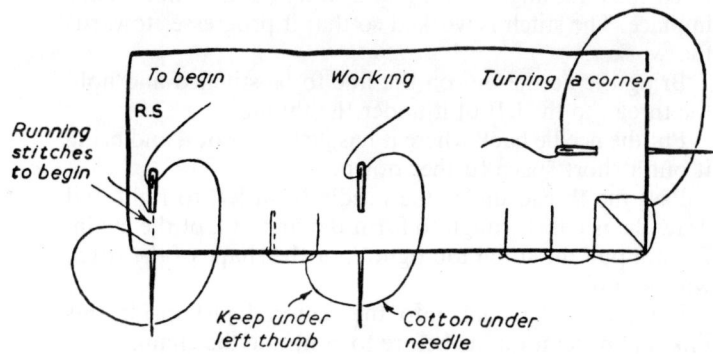

i). Loop stitch (To work)

by making a few running stitches along the line to be stitched, so that they will be covered with the embroidery. Ending-off is done by weaving the ends of thread through the stitches on the wrong side of the work. All joins and endings must be strong but not apparent from the right side.

Loop stitch. Diagram 87 (i), (ii)
Used in varying sizes and shapes to form effective borders; spaced evenly to decorate edges or worked closely for scalloping, eyelets and cut-work. The stitch is generally made over a raw edge. This edge is held towards the worker and the stitch is worked from left to right.

Place the needle into the right side of the material at the depth of stitch required. Pass the single thread of cotton which comes from the material, under the point of the needle from left to right. Draw the needle through so that a loop lies along the edge of the cloth.

To join on a new thread
Complete a stitch; turn the work to the wrong side and weave the old thread in and out of the stitches just beneath the edge. Weave in the new thread towards the last stitch and bring it out on the right side just inside the last loop.

To turn a corner
Make a stitch three times into the same spot, one diagonally to the corner.

Chain stitch. Diagram 88
Used for outlining or filling in a design and to hold hems in place. The stitch is worked so that it progresses towards the worker.

Bring the needle out on the line to be stitched and hold the thread to the left of it under the thumb.

Put the needle back where it has just come out, and bring it out a short space further down.

Pass the thread under the needle from left to right and draw the needle through to form the first link of the chain. Do not pull the stitch too tightly, or the shape of the stitch will be spoilt.

Put the needle back into the material just inside this link and bring it out as before to continue the chain.

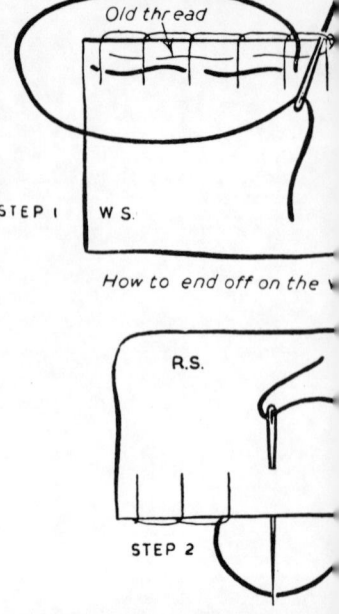

How to end off on the w

The first stitch with the new thread
87 (ii). Joining on a new thread

STITCHES, PLAIN AND DECORATIVE 151

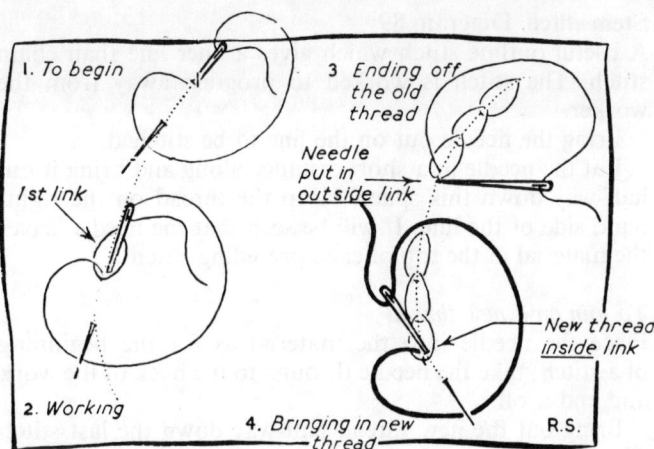

Chain stitch

To join on a new thread
Complete a stitch. Put the needle back into the work just outside the link to hold it down when the thread is pulled through to the wrong side.

Bring out the new thread inside the last link and continue working.

Chain stitches may be worked singly for petals and leaves of flowers or as part of a border.

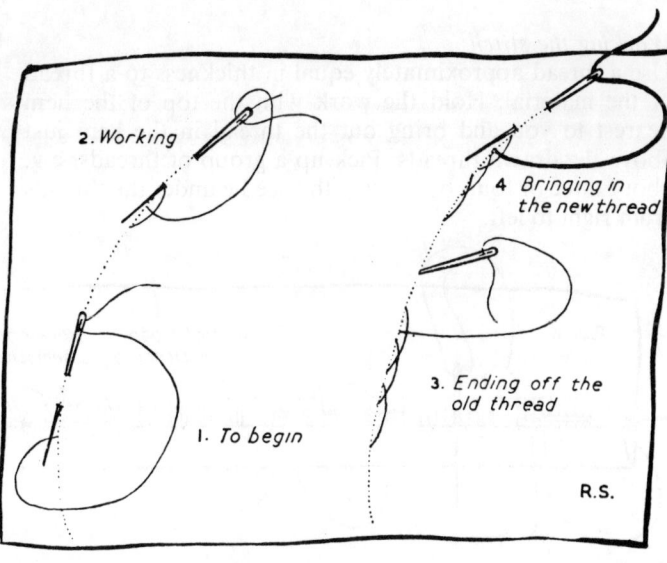

Stem stitch

Stem stitch. Diagram 89

A useful outline stitch which gives a finer line than chain stitch. The stitch is worked to progress away from the worker.

Bring the needle out on the line to be stitched.

Put the needle in a short distance along and bring it out half-way down this space. Keep the thread on the right-hand side of the line. It will be seen that the needle leaves the material at the top of each preceding stitch.

To join on a new thread

Place the needle into the material as for the beginning of a stitch; take the needle through to the back of the work and end it off.

Bring out the new thread half-way down the last stitch where the old one would normally be brought out, and continue working.

Hemstitching. Diagram 90 (i), (ii)
A decorative way of holding hems in position.

To prepare the material

Draw threads from the material according to the depth of hemstitching required, e.g. sufficient to give a 2 to 3 mm space of drawn threads.

Fold the hem on to the wrong side of the work so that the fold is just above the drawn threads. Tack in place.

Working the stitch

Use a thread approximately equal in thickness to a thread of the material. Hold the work with the top of the hem nearest to you and bring out the thread in the hem just above the drawn threads. Pick up a group of threads, e.g. about three or four, by passing the needle under the threads from right to left.

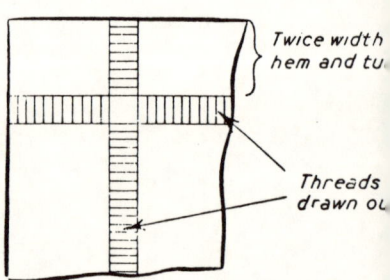

90 (i). To prepare material for hemstitching

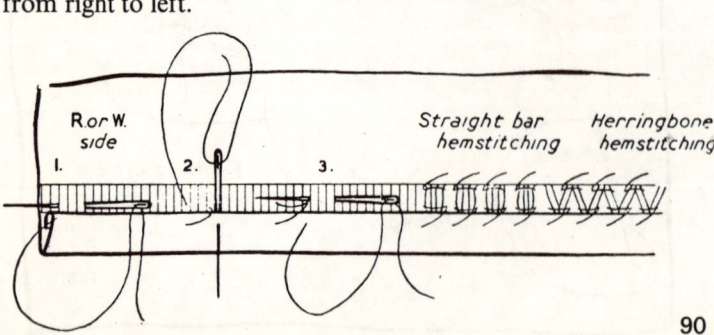

90 (ii). Hemstitching

Hold the thread taut under the left thumb and make a small vertical stitch, putting the needle in the space to the right of the group of threads, and bringing it out in the hem, so that it passes through the three thicknesses of material.

When hemstitching has been worked along one side, work the opposite side in a similar way. The diagram shows how a herringbone effect is achieved by picking up half of two bundles of threads when working the second side.

Pin stitch or mock hemstitching. Diagram 91

Used to hold down hems and facings, to attach lace to an edge and to fix decorative seams on handwork. The stitch (unlike hand hemstitching, which can only be worked on the straight threads) can be worked in any direction with, or across, the grain of the material.

Use a sewing thread or fine embroidery cotton with a coarse needle, so that an open-work effect is obtained as the stitch is made. Experiment with different thicknesses of needles to obtain the best result. A No. 4 needle may be suitable; even a needle as thick as a carpet needle is sometimes used.

Bring the needle out in single material below the hem.

1. Make a backstitch in the single material.

2. Place the needle in the material again as though to make another backstitch over the previous one, but bring the needle out above the fold of the hem over the first position of the thread.

3. Return the needle to the hole in the single material below, and make a running stitch.

Repeat from (1) and take care that the needle enters the

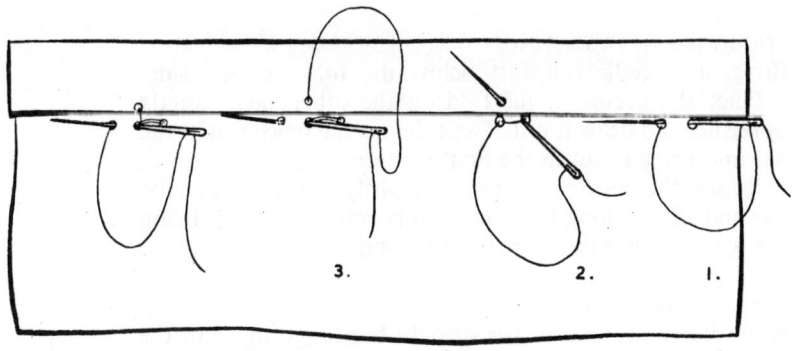

Pin stitch or mock hemstitching

same hole in each case, so that a punched effect is obtained. Draw the thread tightly after each stitch.

Faggoting stitch. Diagram 92 (i), (ii)
Used to join seams or to fix a band, strap, or rouleau to an edge. Tack the edges to be joined on to stiff paper with a space between them, e.g. 3 to 6 mm.

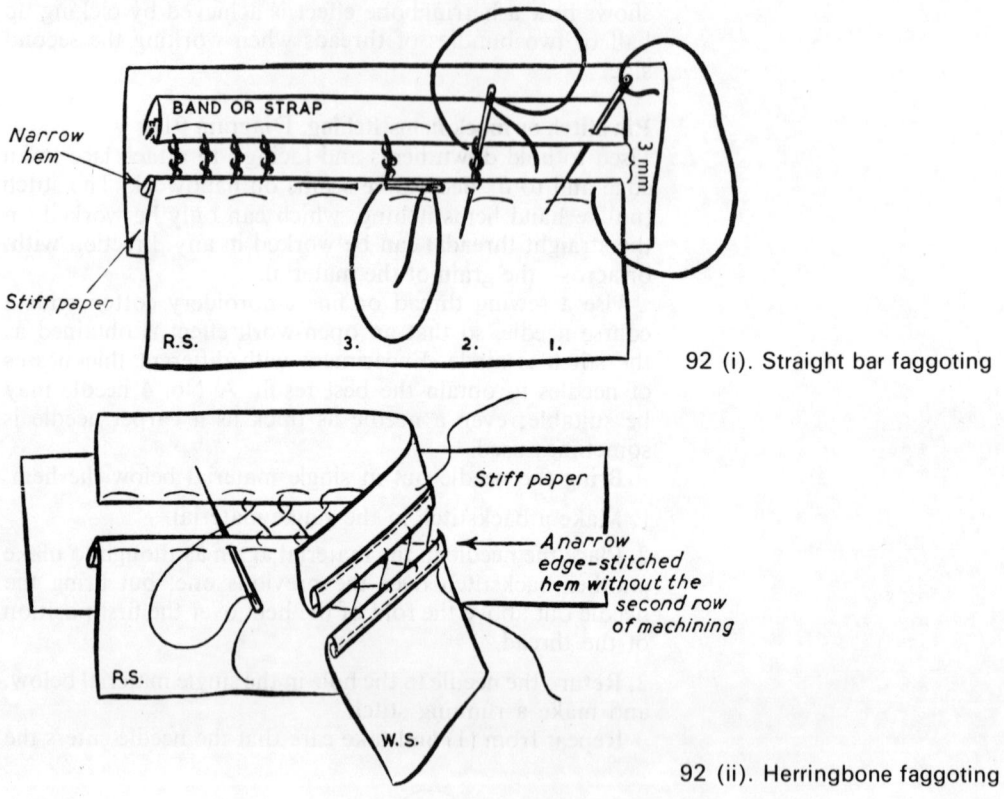

92 (i). Straight bar faggoting

92 (ii). Herringbone faggoting

STRAIGHT BAR FAGGOTING
Bring the needle out just below the fold on one side.
 Place the needle in the fold on the other side, exactly opposite, and draw it out. Twist the needle twice round the bar and bring it out in the first position.
 Return the needle to the work slightly to the right of the bar and slip it along the fold a short way to the left. Bring the needle out ready to work a second bar.

HERRINGBONE FAGGOTING
Bring the needle out as for straight bar faggoting. Put the

needle in the upper fold as before, but slightly to the left.

Without twisting the needle over the thread, make a stitch in the lower fold, again slightly to the left, so that a slanting stitch is formed each time. Keep the thread on the left-hand side and keep it under the needle for each stitch.

Cording
A stitch used for outlining designs in fine embroidery and for attaching lace to edges.
1. Pad the line to be corded by making small running stitches with a soft embroidery thread.
2. Use embroidery thread (single strands are best) and work small straight stitches closely across the line of padding. Work from left to right or right to left and keep the stitches very regular. Keep the tension of the stitch even, so that the roll is smooth. Diagram 57 (iv).

Saddle stitching
This is a running stitch worked with embroidery thread an even distance in from an edge or seam to give a decorative trimming, e.g. round collars, cuffs, pocket flaps.
1. Experiment with different thicknesses of embroidery thread. Use a contrasting or toning colour, e.g. white on navy, brown on fawn. Tack a guide line an even distance from the edge or seam to be trimmed. Work on the R.S.
2. Take even running stitches about 3 to 5 mm long, picking up slightly more on the needle than is passed over. It is not necessary to take the stitches right through unless the fabric is a light weight one. Keep a loose tension and practise until the result is an even, decorative trimming. Diagram 93.

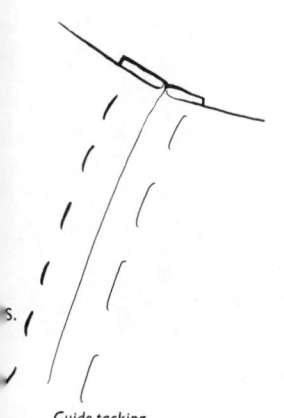

Guide tacking

Saddle stitching on a seam

Hand-picking
This is a spaced backstitch used for outlining edges such as collars revers to give a tailored, hand-stitched finish. It is also used for stitching in zips by hand. Work on the R.S.
1. Use matching, or slightly darker, sewing thread.
2. Make a small backstitch over two or three threads and bring the needle forward about 6 mm. Take the stitch through all thicknesses—if necessary stab the needle through. Repeat, keeping the stitches an even distance from the edge. In some soft fabrics, the stitches will be almost invisible, but slight hollows will show the even path of the thread. Diagram 94.

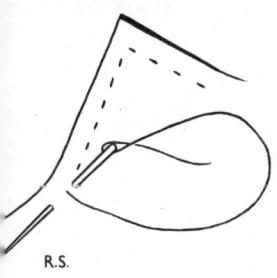

Hand-picking on a collar

13 Pressing

One of the secrets of a professional finish in needlework and dressmaking is to learn the art of pressing, and to press each piece of the work as it proceeds, before it is joined to another section. Equipment needed for pressing (Chapter 2, p. 3) should be collected at the same time as the workbox, and the worker should be prepared to use it constantly.

General points with regard to pressing

1. Remove tacking threads before pressing whenever possible. When this is unavoidable, it may be necessary to remove the imprint of tackings on the surface afterwards by steaming, p. 161.

2. Test the heat of the iron on a scrap of the same material, not only to avoid scorching but also because some man-made materials melt, shrivel or harden under excessive heat. As a general guide, use a fairly hot iron for linens, cottons and for pressing over a damp cloth; a medium hot iron for viscose fabrics; a warm iron for Terylene, nylon, acetates and woollens (unless damp pressed) and a cool iron for silks and acrylics.

3. Press work on the wrong side, so that the surface on the right side is not spoilt by iron marks.

4. To press correctly, hold the iron down on the work for a short while; lift it up and press it down a little further along. Note that the iron is not pushed along as in ironing. Vary the pressure on the iron according to the weight and thickness of the material. Thick woollens need longer and greater pressure than cottons. Too much pressure on viscose and synthetic and woollen mixtures causes shiny marks which are difficult to remove. Experience will teach how to adjust the heat of the iron and the amount of pressure for the material.

How to damp press

METHOD A
Dip a damping muslin in water and wring it out tightly. Place the muslin over the work on the wrong side and give a preliminary pressing. Remove the damp muslin and complete the pressing over a dry muslin. Be certain that the fabric is quite dry as well as properly pressed.

METHOD B
Dip the tips of the fingers into water and pass them along the part to be pressed on the wrong side. Press immediately and lightly without a muslin. Cover with a dry muslin and complete the pressing. This is a particularly good method for pressing seams.

To press woollens, worsteds and wool mixtures

1. Press on the wrong side using a cloth between the fabric and the iron, because prolonged pressure of even a moderately hot iron is likely to scorch wool.

2. Use water for pressing, but test the effect on a scrap of material first, to see whether it causes shrinkage or water-marking.

3. Use heavy irons for thick fabrics. 2 to 2.5 kg is a medium weight.

To press fabrics made from man-made fibres

It is particularly important with these fabrics to experiment with the heat of the iron on spare material before pressing the work. The fabric may be a mixture or a blend or it may have a finish which will make some difference in the heat and pressure required. Some of these fabrics are springy and resist pressing. A safe method of work is the following:

1. Test a spare piece of fabric with a cool, dry iron on the wrong side.

2. Increase the temperature gradually to find the most effective heat, but remember—when the iron becomes too

hot viscose fabrics scorch, acetates melt and shrivel and synthetics glaze on the surface and the iron sticks.
3. Use a well wrung out damp cloth on synthetics (Method A) because they do not shrink or water mark and note the result. Courtelle, however, should not be pressed with a damp cloth. It will stretch out of shape if handled while steam is in the fabric.
4. After deciding the temperature of the iron, amount of pressure needed and if a damp cloth is to be used, press the work. Take particular care not to make incorrect or unnecessary creases with the iron, because a higher temperature will be needed to remove them, with the result that it may become impossible to smooth the fabric without causing damage.

To press pile, napped and brushed fabrics

Pile fabrics
Aim to flatten pile as little as possible. Use thick Turkish towelling on the ironing board or a spare strip of velveteen, pile side up. Place work to be pressed with pile side face downwards.

Velveteen, corduroy, needlecord
Press on wrong side using as little pressure and moisture as possible.

Velvet
Velvet (whether of silk or synthetic fibre) requires special treatment. Press with pile side down on a needle board—steel needles angled on a flexible base, allowing the pile to fall between the needles. Press with a cool dry iron. There are other methods of pressing velvet without a velvet board but they are difficult methods for inexperienced workers. See p. 289.

Napped and brushed fabrics
Place nap or brushed side down on a piece of flannel or light coloured woollen cloth on the ironing board. Press lightly using a damp cloth if fabric is suitable. While the fabric is still steaming brush lightly on the right side. Napped fabrics should be brushed with the nap.

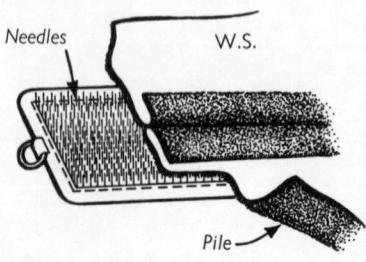

95 (i). Needle board used for pressing velvet

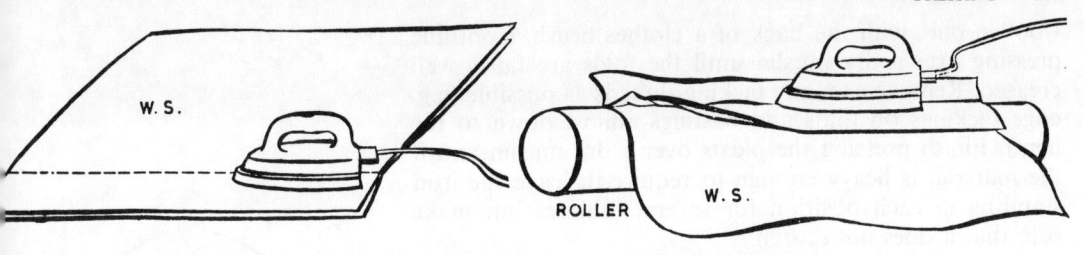

(ii). Pressing to flatten the stitching and turning

96 (i). To press a seam open

Directions for pressing

Seams
Press the turnings or fell first, including the stitching. Diagram 95 (ii). Next place the seam right side down on a covered roller, and press the join, pulling the two sides well apart with the fingers of the free hand. Diagram 96 (i). Look from time to time to see that the seam is being opened properly and pressed quite flat. An advantage of using a roller is that the material on each side of the seam does not become marked by the iron or the turnings, because the iron is only in contact with the actual join. A sleeve or skirt board can be used instead, however, or an ironing table. In such cases, pass the iron along the material underneath the turnings when the pressing is finished, and press lightly to remove any imprint of the turnings.

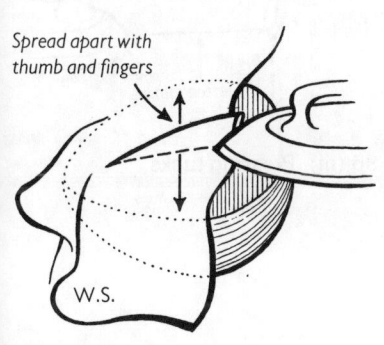

(ii). Pressing a dart on a tailor's ham pressing cushion

Darts
First press the fold of the dart and then press it to one side, treating it like a seam, and using a covered roller or a pressing cushion or pad. Press the fold upwards towards the armhole for underarm bust darts; towards the neck for shoulder darts; towards the centre front or centre back for darts at the waist of bodices, pants and skirts, and towards the armholes for elbow darts in sleeves.

If the material is too thick to give a flat result by pressing the fold to one side, cut along the fold until width from fold to stitching is 6 mm, open the turnings flat and press the dart like an open seam.

Pleats
Place the pleated section, right side down and quite straight, on a skirt board or table. Cover it with a damp muslin, unless water is injurious to the fabric. Press lightly; remove the muslin and beat the steam back into the fabric, if it is a

woollen one, with the back of a clothes brush. Continue pressing over a dry muslin until the folds are fairly well creased. Remove as many tacking threads as possible (e.g. edge tackings on folds and bastings almost down to the hem). Finish pressing the pleats over a dry muslin and if the material is heavy enough to require it, leave the iron standing in each position for several minutes but make sure that it does not scorch.

Tucks

Press in the fold of each tuck. This must be done on the right side, but take care that the iron only comes in contact with that part of the tuck which will eventually lie against the garment.

Stand the iron up on end or ask someone to hold it with the ironing surface facing upwards. Draw the wrong side of the tucked section over the iron, pulling it from side to side across the tucks. This flattens out the section and is sufficient pressing for pin tucks which are too narrow to press to one side. Place wider tucks right side down on the ironing table and finish by pressing each tuck flat, with the fold placed to one side of the stitching.

Sleeves

The seam used for setting a sleeve into the armhole is pressed in the same way as other seams, except that it cannot be done over a roller because it is a deep curve. Instead, after preliminary pressing of the turnings and stitching, place the bodice with the top of the sleeve over the wide end of a sleeve board and press a short section of the seam at a time. Diagram 97. Press the turnings or fell towards the sleeve and move the sleeve round as each part of the seam is pressed.

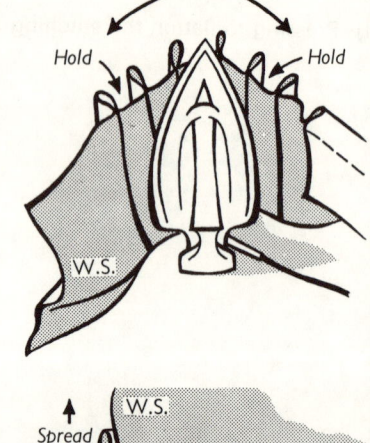

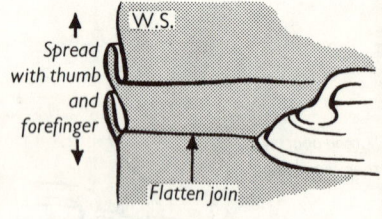

96 (iii). Pressing tucks

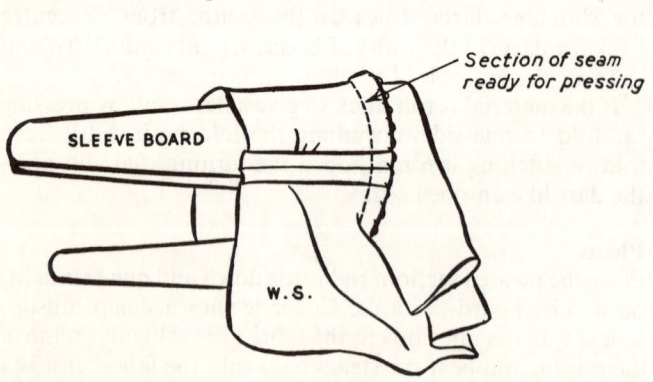

97. To press an armhole seam

To remove shine caused by pressing

Shiny marks caused through pressing are sometimes unavoidable. When they occur on woollen material they can be removed, when the pressing is finished by steaming, in the following way:

1. Place a damp muslin over the marks on the *right* side of the work, having the muslin wetter than when it is wrung out for ordinary pressing.
2. Hold a very hot iron *close to* the wet muslin until steam rises. Note that the iron does not actually touch the muslin.
3. Remove the muslin and brush the surface of the material lightly. Marks caused by the imprint of tacking threads and turnings can also be removed in this way.

To shrink fullness

Sometimes it is necessary to shrink away fullness in order to flatten work, e.g. on a curved skirt hem. This can only be done, of course, on material which will not spoil if water is used for pressing.

1. Place a fairly damp muslin over the full part on the wrong side of the work.
2. Press with a hot iron, at first lightly, until the material begins to shrink, then more firmly.
3. Continue pressing until the muslin and the fabric are both quite dry.

The final press

If each piece of work is carefully pressed as the sewing progresses, it will be found that the final press takes very little time. Each seam should be flat and edges crisp, so that it only remains to iron over the whole garment on the wrong side. At this stage *ironing,* i.e. pushing the iron backwards and forwards, is necessary to remove creases and freshen the material. Attend to the smaller sections of the garment first, such as the collar, cuffs and sleeves, so that the main parts will not become crushed through handling. Allow the garment to hang for a few hours before it is stored away.

OUTLINES FOR MAKING STANDARD CLOTHES

Garments	Quantity of single width material	Main seams	Openings	Fastenings
Nightdress and all-in-one suits *For children*	Allow twice the length from nape of neck plus 20 cm for short sleeves or 50 cm for long sleeves. Allow 20 cm extra for turnings	Double stitched seams made on to the wrong side of the garment or french seams	A hem or a continuous wrap opening at the centre back. The length of the opening 20 to 25 cm	Flat buttons and button-holes. A drawstring at the neck for babies. Zips or studs down front hems and under legs for all-in-one suits
Nightdress *For adults*	Twice the length from nape of neck plus 30 cm for short sleeves or 70 cm for long sleeves. Allow 20 cm extra for turnings	French seams	An opening is not usually required. For a style with a high neck, use a hem, faced or bound openings.	Buttons and buttonholes. Buttons and loops. Drawstring
Pyjamas Track Suits	*For the trousers*, allow twice the length of the leg measured from the waist to the ankle. For 'shorties', measure to the length required. *For the jacket*, allow twice the length of the jacket plus an allowance for sleeves as given for a nightdress. Allow 20 cm extra for the turnings on the two garments	Double stitched seams made on to the right or wrong side of the garment, for both the trousers and the jacket. French seams may be used for women's pyjamas if the material is thin. The same type of seam used for the trousers	*Trousers.* A hem opening at the front of boys' pyjamas. Styles for girls are made without an opening. *Jacket.* A hem or faced opening at the centre front. On blouse tops, use a faced, bound or a continuous wrap opening	A braid or cord threaded through a casing. Elastic threaded through a casing. Buttons and buttonholes. Button and loop or ribbon ties on slit openings
Housecoats Dressing gowns *For children and adults*	As for nightdresses	Open or plain seams, french seams or imitation machined fell	Faced fronts, overlapping hems or zips	Buttons and buttonholes. Zips. Cord round waist

OUTLINES FOR MAKING STANDARD CLOTHES — continued

Garments	Quantity of single width material	Main seams	Openings	Fastenings
Slips *For children*	Twice the length, measured from the nape of the neck to the hem plus 10 cm for turnings	Double stitched seams made on to the right or wrong side of the garment, or french seams	As given for children's nightdresses	As given for children's nightdresses
For adults	Twice the length measured from the nape of the neck or the underarm, or the waist, according to style. Allow 20 cm extra for turnings	French seams	For fitted styles a continuous wrap opening or a zip fastener at the left-hand side, 20 cm to 32 cm long or at centre back 50 cm–60 cm	Press studs. Zips
Blouses **Shirts** **Tops** **Jackets** **Anoraks** **Waistcoats** **Jerkins** **Cardigans**	Twice the length from the nape of the neck plus an allowance for sleeves, as given for a nightdress. 20 cm extra for turnings	French seams. Doublestitched seams made on to the right side for shirt and tailored styles Imitation machined fell seams (see p. 81) Plain and open seams	Hem or faced openings through the length of the centre back or centre front; or bound, or faced slit at the neck 10 cm to 20 cm long. Sleeve openings 10 cm to 14 cm long. Hem opening in the seams or bound, faced, or continuous wrap in the back of the sleeve. Zips	Zips Buttons and buttonholes. Buttons and loops. Hook and eye Buttons and buttonholes or press studs
Skirts **Shorts** **Trousers** **Dungarees**	Twice the length from the waist to hem or ankle plus 20 cm for turnings Allow extra for depth of bib Plus 10 cm for turnings	Open or french seams according to the fabric Double stitched on R.S. or W.S.	Zip fastener at centre front, centre back or left hand side. Length of opening 18 cm to 23 cm	Hooks and eyes at the waist. Press studs below or buttons and buttonholes Zips Velcro

OUTLINES FOR MAKING STANDARD CLOTHES – continued

Garments	Quantity of single width material	Main seams	Openings	Fastenings
Dresses **Pinafore dresses** **Coats** **Overalls**	Twice the length of the bodice from the nape of the neck to the waist, plus twice the length of the skirt. Allow twice the length for garments without a waist seam. Allowance for sleeves as given for a nightdress. 20 cm extra for turnings	French seams on washable dresses, otherwise open seams. Double stitched seams on to the right or wrong side on overalls	For children, at the centre back, as given for slips, and zips. For adults. The openings given for blouses. For a side opening, use the continuous wrap opening or a zip fastener, 20 to 32 cm long Back or front zips, 50 to 60 cm	Buttons and buttonholes As given for blouses A hook and bar at the waist and press studs above and below

N.B.

1. Allow an extra 20 to 50 cm if the material has an 'up and down' or a large pattern.
2. The allowances for turnings include seam and hem allowances.
3. Less material is required when double width material is used, sometimes half as much. This depends on the style and how much of the garment can be cut from the width. Two-thirds to three-quarters of the length of single width material required gives a rough estimate for double width material. (Single width 70 to 90 cm; double width 115 to 140 cm and over.)

FIGURE TYPES APPROVED FOR PATTERNS BY THE MEASUREMENT STANDARD COMMITTEE OF THE PATTERN FASHION INDUSTRY

Type	Height (m)		Size symbols
Misses'	1.65–1.68	Average, well proportioned and developed	Sizes 6–20
Miss Petite	1.57–1.63	For the shorter MISS figure	Sizes 6mp–16mp
Women's	1.65–1.68	Larger, more fully mature	Sizes 38–50
Half Size	1.57–1.60	Fully developed with short nape to waist	Sizes $10\frac{1}{2}$–$24\frac{1}{2}$
Junior Petite	1.52–1.55	Well proportioned small figure	Sizes 3jp–13jp
Young Junior Teen	1.55–1.60	Teen and pre-teen developing figure with high bust line	Sizes 5/6–15/16
Girls'	1.27–1.55	Young, immature with no defined bust line	Sizes 7–14
Chubbie	1.32–1.55	For growing girl who is over average weight for age and height	Sizes $8\frac{1}{2}$c–$14\frac{1}{2}$c
Children's	0.79–1.17	Sizes refer to age 1–6 years	Sizes 1–6
Toddlers	0.71–1.02	For figures between a baby and a child. Sizes $\frac{1}{2}$–4 refer to age	Sizes $\frac{1}{2}$–4
Babies	0.43–0.61	For babies 1–3 months weighing 3–6 kg	1–3 months
	0.31–0.87	6 months weighing 6–8 kg	6 months
Boys and	1.22–1.73	Youths no longer classed as children – comparable to GIRLS' sizes	Sizes 7–12
Teen Boys			Sizes 7–14–20
Men	1.78	Average mature adult 0.87 to 1.22 m chest	Sizes 34–48

The measures of these patterns are listed in pattern catalogues. Compare measurements taken from the figure with the lists and decide which figure type to choose, by considering the height, nape to waist measure and general contour of the figure.

Patterns for dresses, suits and coats are selected by the bust measure. Skirts, trousers and shorts are chosen by the waist measure unless the hips are much larger in proportion. In this case it may be better to buy the right hip size and alter the waist size.

Shirts for men and boys are selected by neck measurement. Jackets and coats by chest measurement.

Fibre content labelling of textile products

No doubt you have noticed that all clothes now have attached to them information giving the fibre content of the yarns used in manufacture. If only one kind of fibre has been used, just the name may be given, e.g. wool, possibly preceded by 100 per cent, 'all' or 'pure'. When more than one kind of fibre has been used, each is named with the percentage content, e.g. 7 per cent camelhair, 93 per cent wool; 85 per cent viscose, 15 per cent nylon. Sometimes this information is on sewn in or adhesive labels, sometimes a swing label or on wrappings. In fact in the U.K. not only clothing but practically all textile goods must by law [Textile Products (indications of fibre content) Regulations 1973] be labelled with the fibre content. It applies to rolls of fabric, clothing, yarns, bedding, curtains, upholstery and other household goods.

This type of labelling has been done for a number of years in some European countries and it is to conform with EEC regulations that the law has come into force in the U.K. Furthermore, with international consultation there has been agreement on names of fibres so that they are standard in member countries.

It is not only very interesting but extremely helpful to know what you are buying. With basic knowledge of the qualities of textile fibres and the fabrics made from them, you are able to make the right choice for the purpose in mind. You will know, too, the best way to care for the fabrics and how to clean them. Years ago, one could tell the fibre content by the appearance and feel of a fabric. This is no longer possible so the enforcement of the 1973 law has many advantages to the consumer if not to the manufacturer.

Fibre content labelling is often accompanied on clothing by size details and perhaps fabric care. See the International Textile Care Labelling Code p. 274. Though not required by law yet, it is being very widely used in the U.K. and conforms to the International Care Labelling Code for Textiles.

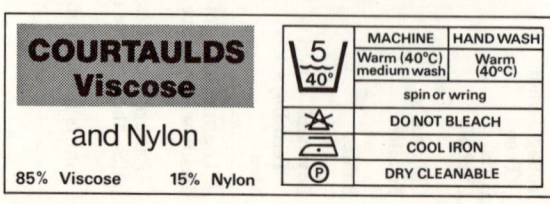

Part II
Constructing clothes

14 Collars and cuffs

Collars are a style feature which is always popular. They may be fixed permanently to the bodice or they can be detachable and can be made of double or single material.

Collar styles can be divided mainly into two classes:
1. *Flat collars* of the Peter Pan type which lie quite flat on the shoulder. These collars are circular in shape, the neckline being the same shape as the neckline of the bodice. The width may be quite narrow or it may extend to the width of the shoulder and the shapes are varied. Diagram 147.
2. *Turnover collars* which stand up in the neck at the back and roll over to the shoulder. These collars fit the neck snugly and are cut with the neck edge quite straight or slightly curved. They may be worn fastened high at the throat or opened and laid back on the shoulders in front to form the collar for a rever front. Diagram 148.

Directions for making and fixing collars to neck edges

Make the collar. Diagrams 98 (i), (ii)
For flat or turnover types.
   Place the two collar pieces together with the right sides of the material facing, and pin them (quite flat), on the pattern line at the outer edge. Leave the neck edge open. Tack and machine the outer edges on the pattern line.

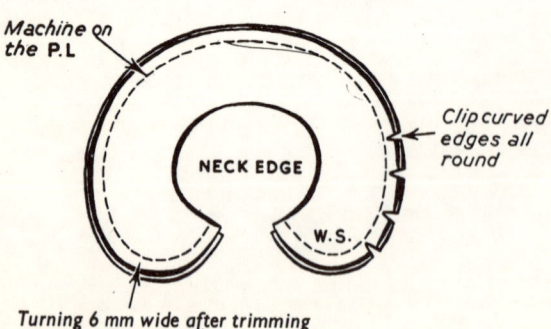
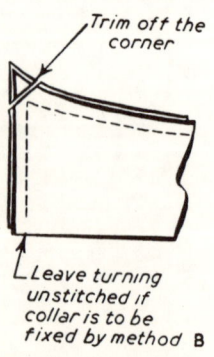

98 (i). To make a collar

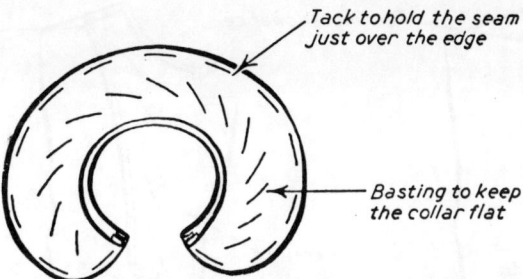

(i). Collar prepared for fixing
  bodice

Trim the turnings to about 6 mm and snip curved edges.

Turn the collar through to the right side, and pin and tack the seam so that it is slightly over the edge to what will be the underside of the collar.

Baste the collar through the centre to keep it flat while fixing it to the bodice.

Trim with machining, if desired, at this stage, if Method A for applying the collar is to be used. Press the collar.

II. Prepare the bodice ready for attaching the collar

1. Make the opening; if there is a wrap which extends beyond the centre front or centre back, neaten the neck edge of the wrap in the following way. Diagram 99 (i):

(a) Fold back the hem on to the outside of the garment so that the right side is against the right side of the bodice.

(b) Machine along the neckline as far as the point to which the collar is to be attached (marked on the pattern with a notch or perforation). This point is usually the centre back or front. If the opening is made with a facing, this stitching will be done when the facing is attached to the garment.

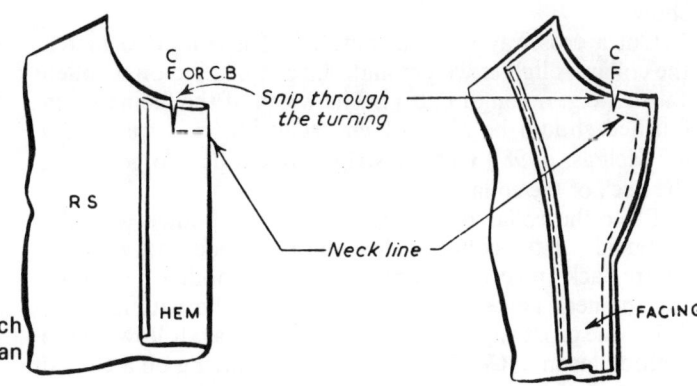

(i). To neaten the wrap which projects beyond the C.F. or C.B. of an opening

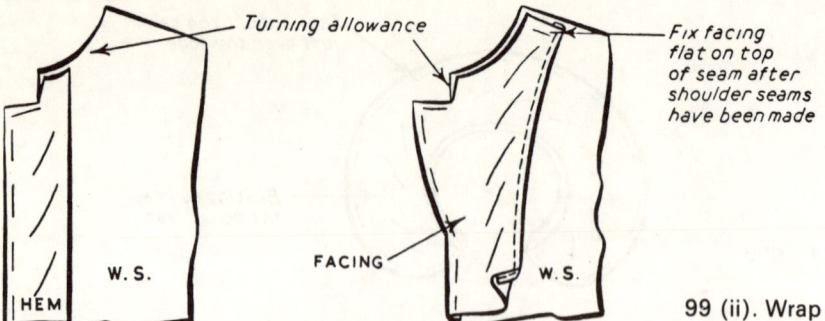

99 (ii). Wrap and opening neaten

(c) Snip through the turning of the neckline down to where the stitching finishes. Trim and snip the rest of the turning outside the stitching.

(d) Turn the hem or facing on to the wrong side of the work and tack the seam at the edge (see FACINGS, p. 99). Baste the hem or facing flat on to the bodice. Diagram 99 (ii).

2. Complete and press the shoulder and underarm seams of the bodice.

III. Fix the collar to the bodice

The collar should be attached to the bodice before the sleeves are set in, because the garment is more convenient to handle at this stage. There are two standard ways of attaching a collar:

METHOD A. Diagrams 100 (i), (ii), (iii)

The collar is fixed with a crossway strip which forms a facing on the inside of the neck. This method can be used to attach any type of collar but is not suitable for a turnover collar which is worn open, because the facing would show.

1. Cut a crossway strip in material of a colour to match the collar. A lighter weight material can be used on woollen fabrics, e.g. rayon or cotton. The width of the facing when finished should be about 1 cm. (Cutting crossway strips for facings, p. 98.) Cut the strip long enough to go round the neck of the collar.

2. Place the collar on to the neck of the bodice with the underside of the collar against the right side and with the centre back and centre front of collar and bodice matching. Pin the neck edges together. Tack along the pattern line.

3. Pin the crossway strip on top of the collar, following the method given in Chapter 9 for making a facing on a curved

COLLARS AND CUFFS 171

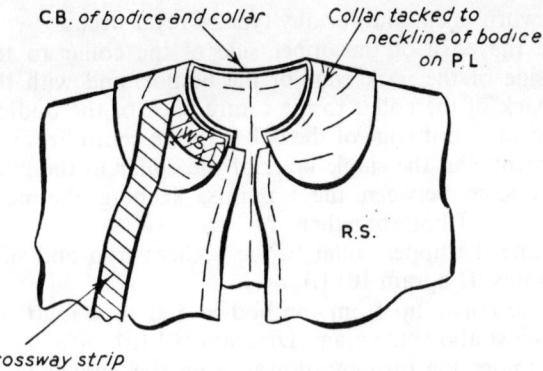

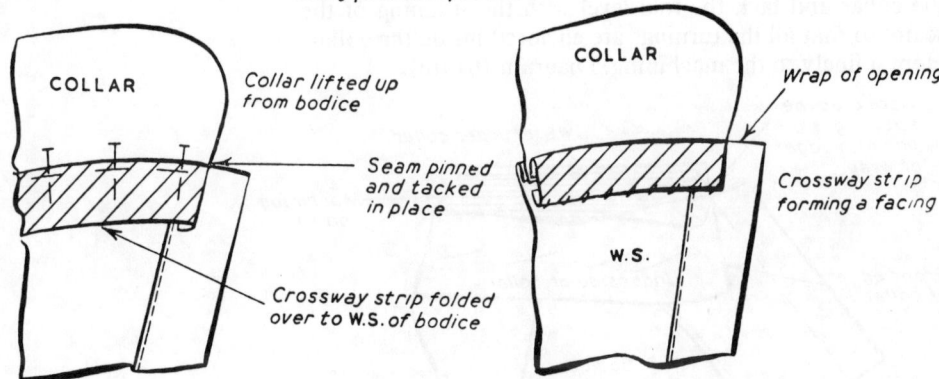

(i). Preparation for stitching the collar and crossway strip to the bodice Method A)

(ii). The collar stitched and the crossway strip laid flat on the inside of bodice

100 (iii). The collar neatened at the neck with a crossway facing

edge, making sure that by easing and stretching, the strip lies quite flat. Tack it in position.
4. Machine the collar and crossway strip to the bodice on the pattern line, working with the bodice side uppermost.
5. Trim the turning to 6 mm and snip the curved parts.
6. Lift the collar up from the bodice and fold the facing over to the wrong side of the work, pulling the bodice and facing down from the seam. Pin and tack this seam in place. Diagram 100 (ii).
7. Turn under the free edge of the crossway strip and pin and tack it flat on to the bodice. Hem or machine it down. Diagram 100 (iii).

METHOD B. Diagrams 101 (i), (ii), (iii)
The collar is attached like a band, the neck edge of the bodice being inserted between the two collar pieces. This method is particularly suitable for a turnover collar which

is to be worn open, and for any type of rever neck.

1. Place the edge of the upper side of the collar to the wrong side of the neck edge of the bodice, and with the centre back of the collar to the centre back of the bodice. Next pin the front edge of the collar to the centre front of the garment. Pin the single layer of the collar to the neck of the bodice between these points, keeping the neck pattern lines of both together.
2. Machine the upper collar to the bodice; trim and snip the turnings. Diagram 101 (i).
3. Lift the collar up from the bodice and tack it to the turnings just above the seam. Diagram 101 (ii).
4. Fold under the turning allowance on the underside of the collar and tack the fold level with the stitching of the seam, so that all the turnings are enclosed inside the collar. Hem it finely to the machining. Diagram 101 (iii).

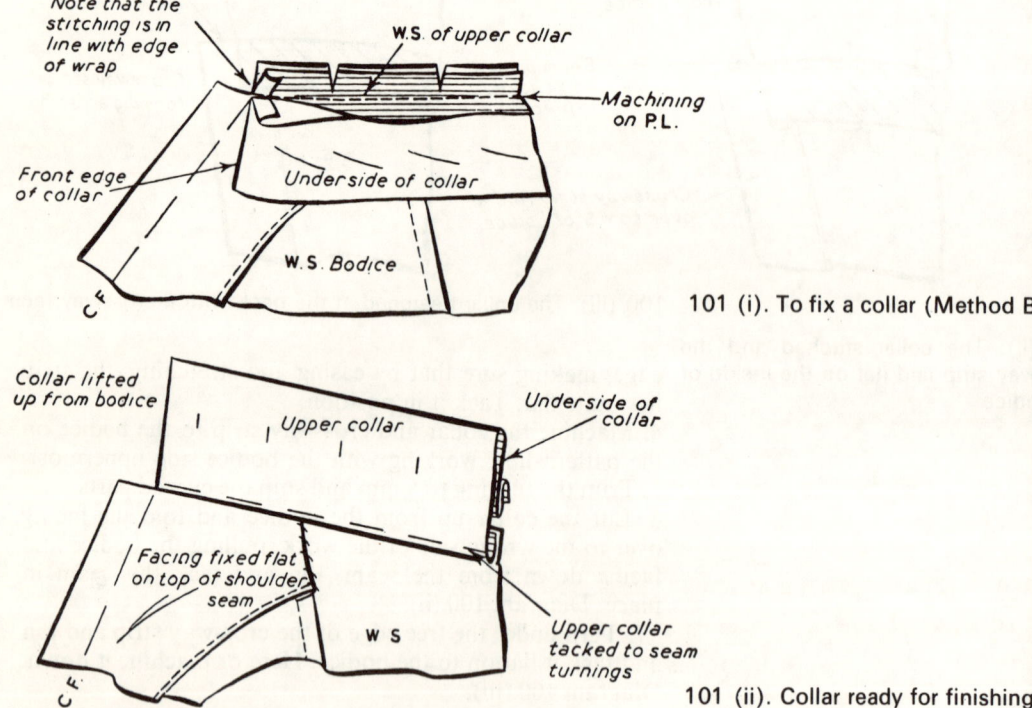

101 (i). To fix a collar (Method B)

101 (ii). Collar ready for finishing

ALTERNATIVE METHODS OF ATTACHING COLLARS
Diagrams 102 (i)–(iv)
These methods are to some extent a combination of the standard methods A and B. In both Methods *(a)* and *(b)*

COLLARS AND CUFFS 173

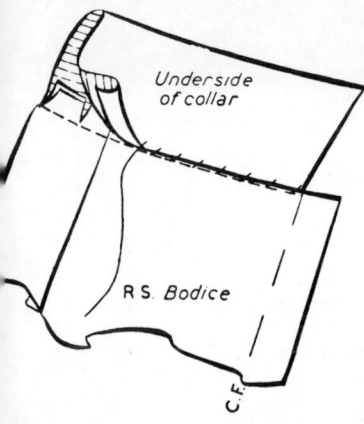

iii). Finishing the collar (Method B)

below it will be seen that the collar is attached to the front neck up to the shoulder seam between the garment and the front neck facings. The back of the neck is neatened with either a crossway facing or a shaped facing or as a band. Diagrams 102 (ii), (iv).

One advantage of these methods is that the process of neatening the front edge and extension first (p. 170) is bypassed since this part is done as the collar is stitched on.

A disadvantage is that unless work is done accurately the facing may not set flat when the process is finished.

To be certain that the facing will set properly check that the pattern lines at the neckline of garment and facing are exactly the same. Place one on top of the other, to do this, before starting to attach the collar. (It is best to have pattern lines marked for these methods.)

METHOD (*a*). Diagrams 102 (i), (ii). The collar is fixed with a shaped facing.

1. Place collar on to the outside of the bodice with the underside of collar against the R.S. of the garment and with C.B. and C.F. of both' matching. Pin and tack the collar securely to the garment on the pattern lines.
2. Join the back neck facing to the front facings at the shoulder seams and neaten the outer edge — see p. 100.
3. Place the facing on the R.S. of the bodice on top of the collar with R.S. down and C.F. and C.B. matching these points on the bodice. See that the facing is quite flat and tack through all thicknesses exactly on the pattern line of the garment.
4. Machine facing to garment in the usual way, trim turnings to 6 mm and clip. Turn facing over to W.S. lift collar up and tack through all thicknesses just below the seam.
5. Smooth and pin facing flat on to garment. Baste in place and hem it loosely to the turnings of the shoulder seam. Fastenings will hold the facing in place along the front edges.

METHOD (*b*). Diagrams 102 (iii), (iv). The collar is attached with a facing at the front up to the shoulder seam and is fixed like a band across the back.

1. Place collar on bodice as for Method *(a)* but *tack through both* thicknesses of collar and the garment from the front edge to the shoulder seam and through the *under layer only* across the back of the neck. Machine this one layer of collar to the garment across the back of the neck only.
2. Exactly at the shoulder seam clip through the turning

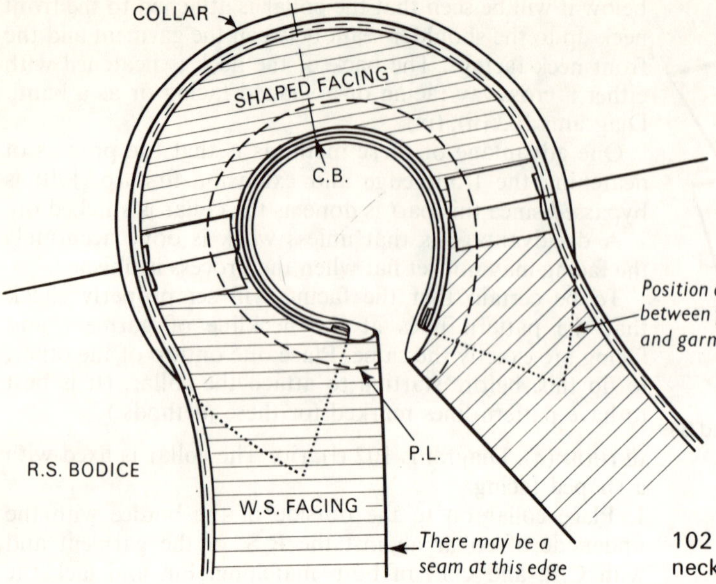

174 CONSTRUCTING CLOTHES

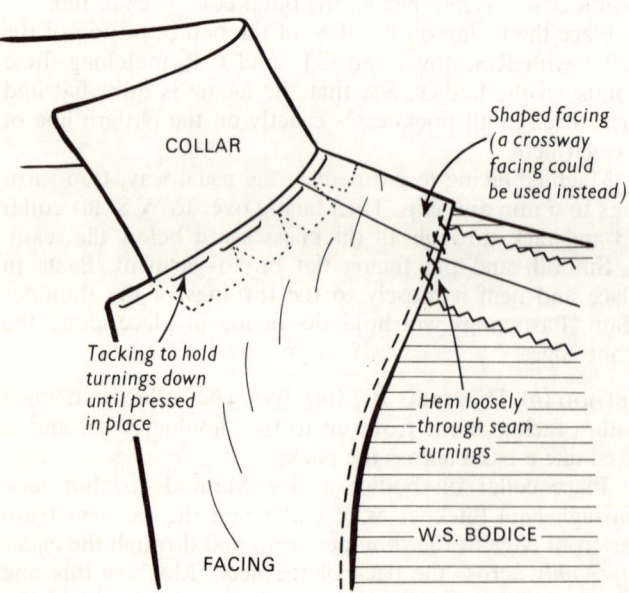

102 (i). Collar and facing maching neckline

102 (ii). Facing basted flat and attached to shoulder seam. ALTERNATE METHOD (a)

COLLARS AND CUFFS 175

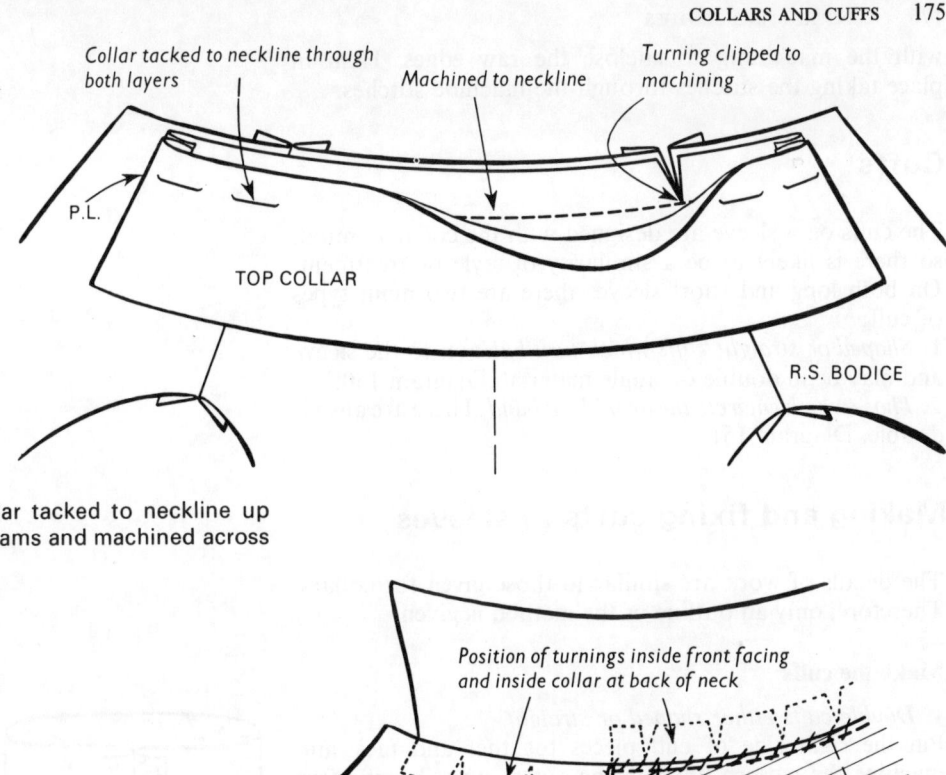

(iii). Collar tacked to neckline up shoulder seams and machined across neck

(iv). The finish on the inside. Collar is a band across the back neck. ALTERNATIVE METHOD (b)

allowance of garment and under layer of collar leaving the top unclipped. Diagram 102 (iii) shows how this clip has released the turnings so that they may stand up inside the collar across the back of the neck.
3. Place the front facing in position as for Method (*a*) and machine up to the shoulder seam through all thicknesses.
4. Trim and clip turnings in usual way and turn and place the front facings flat on to the W.S. of the garment.
5. Now turn in the free edge of the collar and bring it level

with the machining to enclose the raw edges. Hem in place taking the stitches through the machine stitches.

Cuffs

The cuffs on a sleeve are designed with the collar in mind, so there is likely to be a similarity of style or treatment. On both long and short sleeves there are two main types of cuff:
1. *Shaped or straight cuffs which turn back* on to the sleeve and may be in double or single material. Diagram 150.
2. *Those which encircle the arm like a band*. These are always double. Diagram 151.

Making and fixing cuffs to sleeves

The details of work are similar to those given for collars. Therefore, only an outline of the method is given.

Make the cuffs

1. *Double cuffs either shaped or straight*
Pin the right side of cuff pieces together and tack and machine the pattern lines on the outer edges, leaving free edges which are to be joined to the sleeve.
   Trim and snip the turnings and turn the cuff through to the right side. Tack the seam at the edge and baste through the centre as shown on a collar. Diagram 98 (ii).

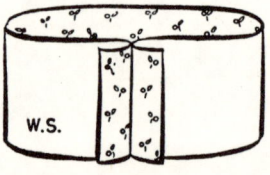

STEP 1

2. *Circular cuffs with no opening*

Join the two short sides of the cuff to form a circle, and press open the seam.
   Fold and tack the cuff in half with the right side outside. Diagram 103.

Prepare the sleeves for attaching the cuffs
Make and press the underarm seam and opening (if any) and arrange the fullness at the cuff edge in both sleeves, Chapter 15, p. 180.

Fix the cuffs to the sleeves
The cuffs are tacked to the sleeves before fixing the sleeves into the bodice, but they need not be machined until after the sleeves are set in and fitted, in case an adjustment in

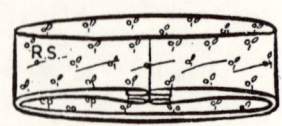

STEP 2

103. To make a circular cuff

length is needed. Methods for fixing cuffs are comparable to the same method given for collars.

METHOD A

The cuffs are attached with a crossway strip. This method is used for turn back cuffs. Instead of a crossway strip, a straight or shaped facing can be used.

1. Tack the cuff to the sleeve with the underside of the cuff on the right side of the sleeve and the raw edges together.
2. Cut a crossway strip long enough to make a facing along the edge and to measure about 1 cm wide when finished. Tack the strip on top of the cuff with the edge level with the edge of the sleeve, and machine through the strip, cuff and sleeve on the pattern line. Diagram 104.
3. Pull the cuff down from the sleeve and turn the strip on to the inside of the sleeve. Tack through the strip and sleeve just below the seams as shown on a collar. Diagram 100 (i), (ii).
4. Turn under the free edge of the facing strip and fix it flat on to the sleeve, so that the turnings are covered. Hem or machine it in position. Diagram 100 (iii).
5. After a final pressing, turn the cuff back on to the right side, letting the roll of the cuff be 3 mm down from the join of the cuff and sleeves. Press in this fold.

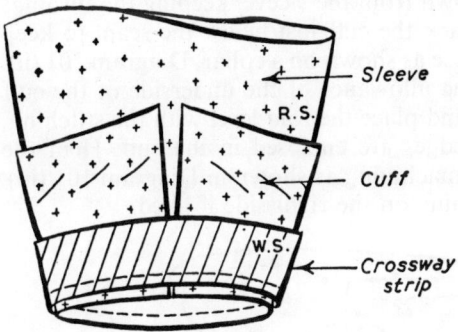

A cuff and crossway strip stitched to the sleeve ready for finishing

METHOD B

The cuff forms a band into which the sleeve is inserted. The cuff can be fixed with a plain seam so that no stitching shows on the right side, or it can be fixed with stitching to show on the right side, e.g. by trimming with machining or by using an overlaid seam.

To fix the cuff with a plain seam. Diagram 105
1. Place the right side of the upper side of the cuff to the

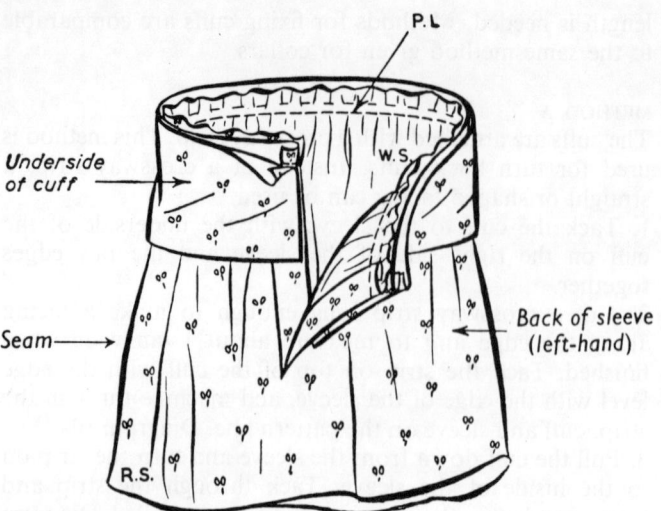

105 (i). A cuff stitched to a sleeve a plain seam

right side of the sleeve with pattern lines level, and the edges of the opening (if any) in line with the ends of the cuff. If there are gathers, regulate them so that the sleeve is a little fuller at the back than at the front. Stitch through the sleeve and the upper side of the cuff exactly on the pattern lines. Diagram 105.

2. Pull the cuff down from the sleeve, keeping the turnings inside the cuff. Tack the cuff just below the seam to keep the turnings in place as shown on a collar. Diagram 101 (ii).

3. Fold the turning allowance of the underside of the cuff on to the inside, and place the fold level with the stitching, so that the raw edges are enclosed in the cuff. Hem the fold finely to the machining as shown in Diagram 101 (iii). Trim with machining on the right side if liked.

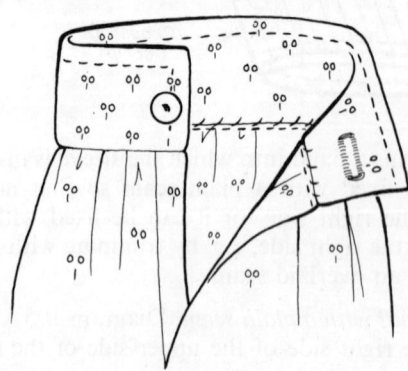

105 (ii). Cuff completed with bu and machine made buttonhole

15 Sleeves

Directions for making sleeves

Make the pair of sleeves, working on them simultaneously, so that they are both kept to the same stage of work.

Preparation
1. Notice the shape of the sleeve opened out flat. The head has a slight, rather shallow curve at the back, a well-rounded crown and a hollowed front. The curve at the cuff edge is longer and deeper at the back than the front. Diagram 165.
2. Mark the right sides of the sleeves with a pin and see that they are a pair. When sleeves (either flat or with the seams fixed) are placed on the table with either both right or wrong sides facing up, the backs or the fronts of the sleeves should face. Diagram 106. The topmost curve is called the crown of the sleeve.

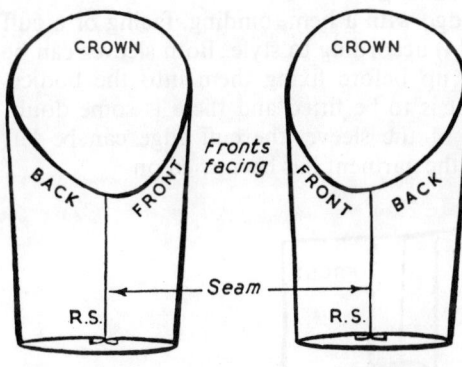

106 A pair of sleeves

The opening
1. Plan the position of the opening which should lap over from the back of the sleeve on to the front. Diagram 107 (ii). An opening can be in one of the following positions:
(a) in the sleeve seam, in which case a portion of the sleeve seam will be left unstitched from the wrist edge, and the turning allowance will be used to make a hem

opening, Diagrams 107 (i), (ii), (iii);
(b) cut in the back of the sleeve, approximately a quarter of the measurement across the sleeve from the seam. The opening will be made more conveniently before the sleeve is seamed up. Diagram 165.

2. Mark the length of the opening, making it long enough for the sleeve to pass easily over the hand. An average length is 9 cm to 12 cm including the depth of the cuff, if any. See Chart, p. 163 for types of openings to use on sleeves, and Chapter 10 for method of making openings.

The sleeve seam
Make the long underarm seam using the type which has been planned for the main seams of the garment.

Fullness in the cuff edge and the head
1. Arrange the fullness at the cuff edge in gathers, pleats, darts or tucks according to style. A short sleeve may be left plain so that it is loose, or made to fit the arm with pleats or tucks or set into a band or cuff.
2. Fix the fullness in the head of the sleeve. If the sleeve head is to be smooth without apparent fullness, put in a running thread along the crown, to facilitate easing.

The finish of the cuff edge
Neaten the cuff edge with a hem, binding, facing or a cuff (Chapters 9 and 14) according to style. Both sleeves can be completely made up before fixing them into the bodice, but if the garment is to be fitted and there is some doubt about the length of the sleeve, the cuff edge can be left tacked until after the garment has been tried on.

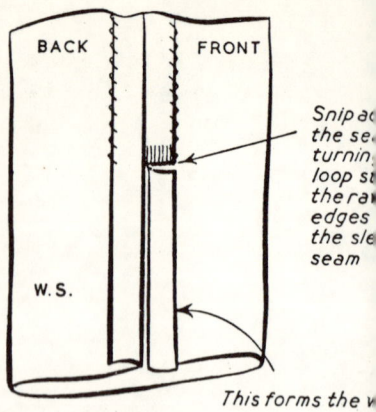

107 (i). A sleeve prepared for a hem opening in the seam

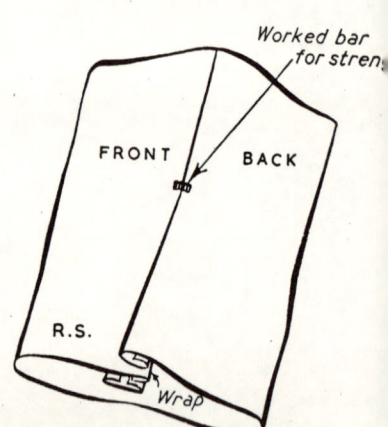

107 (ii). The hem opening complete the R.S. showing how it laps from to front (righthand sleeve)

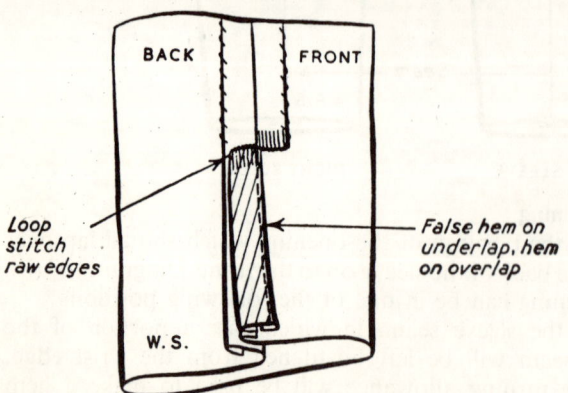

107 (iii). The hem opening on the W showing the wrap finished with a f hem

PREPARATION FOR SETTING IN SLEEVES TO A BODICE
1. Mark the right- and left-hand sleeve. Test by slipping the sleeve on the arm and notice if the deeper curve of the head is at the front of the arm. Diagram 106.
2. Make sure that the lines of the head are good, i.e. a smooth shallow curve at the back and a deep curve at the front.
3. Measure the length of the pattern line of the head of the sleeve and make a note of it, because this measurement will have to be compared with the armhole measurement of the bodice. The most accurate way to measure the curve is to hold the tape measure upright on edge, instead of flat, along the curve, with one edge on the pattern line.

To set sleeves into an armhole

The aim of a dressmaker is to put in sleeves so that they are comfortable to wear, set well on the shoulder and hang well. The round method of setting in sleeves follows:*

Preparation of bodice
1. Complete the side and shoulder seams.
2. Attend to the neck finish. This may be stitched, or only tacked, ready for testing the set of the collar.
3. See that the armhole line is a good one—a smooth flat curve at the back and a deeper one in front—and that it is a comfortable fit.
4. Measure the armhole of the bodice on the pattern line and compare it with the corresponding measurement taken on the sleeve head. *The armhole line of the sleeve must be at least 2.5 cm and not more than 4 cm larger than the armhole line of the bodice.* This is essential to enable the sleeve to be eased in to the bodice over the shoulder, e.g.

Armhole of bodice 43 cm.
Armhole of sleeve 45.5 to 47 cm.

(The only exception to this rule is a gathered sleeve.)
If through alteration in fitting, or inaccurate construction, there is not the correct difference between the two, alter the pattern lines of the sleeve, by raising or lowering the line of the crown or underarm curves, until the right measurement is achieved. If there is still too much discrepancy between the measurements, it may be possible to let out or take in the seam of the sleeve.

---

* The flat method of setting in sleeves is given in *Introduction to Needlework,* pp. 80, 81.

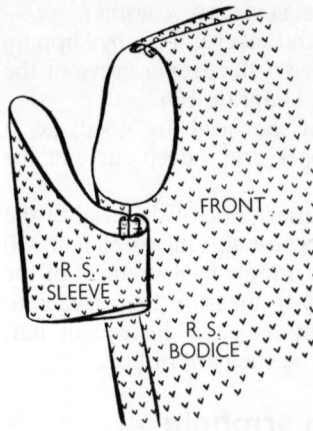
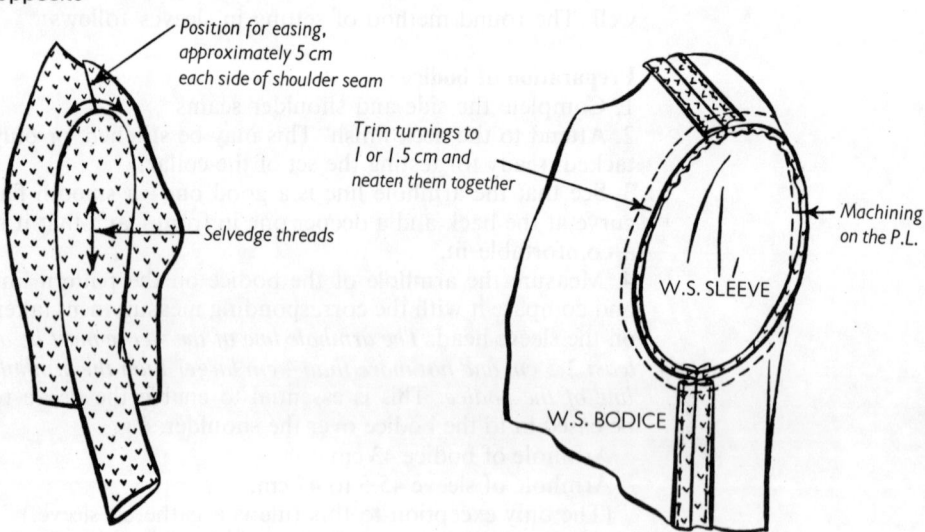

107 (iv). The sleeve fixed in place on the bodice with the seams opposite

107 (v). The sleeve pinned into the armhole of the bodice with the fullness eased across the shoulder

107 (vi). To test the set of a sleeve

107 (vii). The sleeve stitched into the armhole and ready for neatening

Setting in a sleeve with a plain seam

FIXING

1. Place the right-hand sleeve to the right armhole of the bodice, right sides of material facing, and pattern lines together. Pin notches or balance points together or if these are not marked, pin the seams opposite one another. Diagram 107 (iv).

2. Pin the rest of the sleeve to the armhole working from inside the bodice. There is no need to turn the bodice inside out. Pin round the underarm section, keeping the sleeve uppermost in the hand and the two layers of material quite smooth. Put the pins close together, on the pattern line and placed horizontally, in order to judge the set.

3. Next, fix the crown of the sleeve, easing in the fullness across the head (EASING, p. 65 and FULLNESS IN SEAMS, p. 86). Diagram 107 (v).

4. Hold the sleeve with the head over the hand and notice how it hangs. If correctly set, the sleeve should hang with the selvedge threads dropping straight down or very slightly forward, from the shoulder seam. Diagram 107 (vi). If the hang appears to be wrong, move the sleeve round in the armhole, but the seam of the sleeve must not be allowed to fall behind the seam of the bodice, or more than 4 cm in front, because it would not be comfortable to wear.

5. Tack the seam with small stitches and set in the left sleeve up to this point.

STITCHING
Machine the sleeve to the bodice exactly on the pattern line and having the sleeve uppermost in the machine, so that the fullness can be regulated. Diagram 107 (vii).

NEATENING
Trim the turnings to 1 to 1.5 cm and neaten them both together as a plain seam, p. 160. Diagram 97.

FINAL PRESSING. See Chapter 13.

Other ways of putting in a sleeve are with a french seam, or an overlaid seam (the bodice is overlaid on to the sleeve), or with a double stitched seam. Details of making these seams are given in Chapter 8, but the same general procedure is followed for setting in the sleeve as when a plain seam is used.

Raglan sleeves
These have the sleeve set into the bodice from underarm to neck, two seams to each sleeve, as used on many overcoats and raincoats. The sleeves are put in by the Flat method, p. 49. Patterns provide ease in the seams so that the sleeves will set properly over the shoulders. Therefore sleeve edges will be longer than bodice edges and notches

must be matched with fullness eased between them.

Magyar sleeves are described on p. 246.

To strengthen curved underarm seams
Curved seams which are clipped in order that they will be flat can be strengthened against wear, e.g. the curved part of the seam under the arm on magyar shapes.
1. Cut a strip of tape the length of the curved section. Place it over the seam on the W.S. and tack in position.
2. From the R.S. machine 3 mm each side of the seam line. Diagrams 107 (viii).

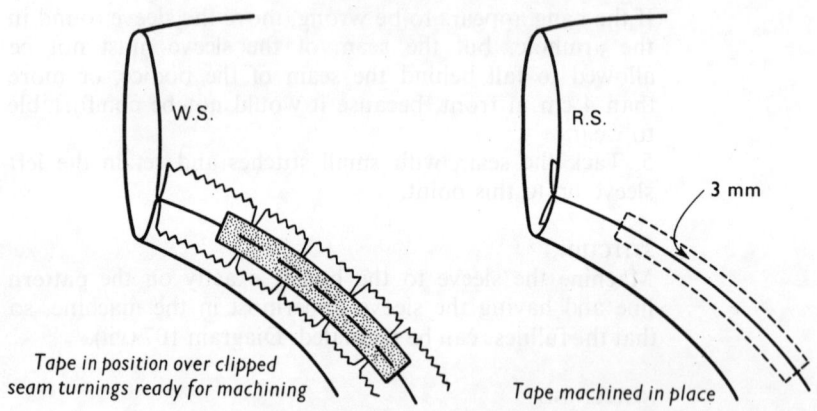

107 (viii). Strengthening curved se

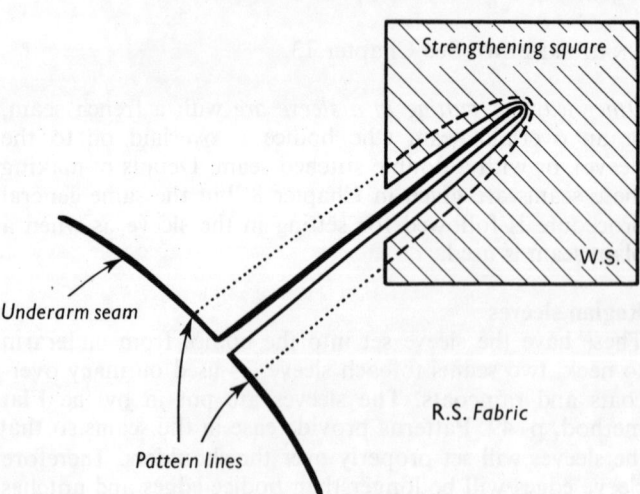

107 (ix). Strengthening a poir corner. Fabric stitched in place clipped up to the point

To set in underarm gussets

Magyar shapes are often made with underarm gussets which may be cut so that strain is taken on the cross of the fabric. They give strength and extra room under the arm. Gussets may be cut in one-piece (diamond shaped) in which case they are put in after the underarm seams are made or two-piece (triangular) when they are inserted before the underarm seams are completed. *Two-piece gussets* are much easier to put in. There will be four gussets to fix, one on the front and one on the back under each arm.

Each gusset is fixed in the following way:

1. Place a straight piece of fabric about 5 cm square on the R.S. of the garment where the point of the gusset is to be inserted. Fabric of thinner texture than the garment can be used but the colour should match or tone. Machine on the P.L. for at least 2 cm each side of the point. Keep the shape of the point a blunt one.
2. Slash through centre of gusset markings and clip up to the stitching.
3. Fold strengthening fabric on to the W.S. and press flat with the seam just under the edge. Fold the remainder of the turning on the garment on to the W.S. and press in place. Trim strengthening fabric to 1 cm.
4. Lay the prepared edge of the garment on to the P.L. of the gusset (as for an overlaid seam) and tack in place. Top stitch close to the edge.
5. Trim turnings to 1 cm and overcast them together.
6. Complete each gusset and then make the underarm seams in the usual way. Diagrams 107 (ix, x, xi, xii, xiii).

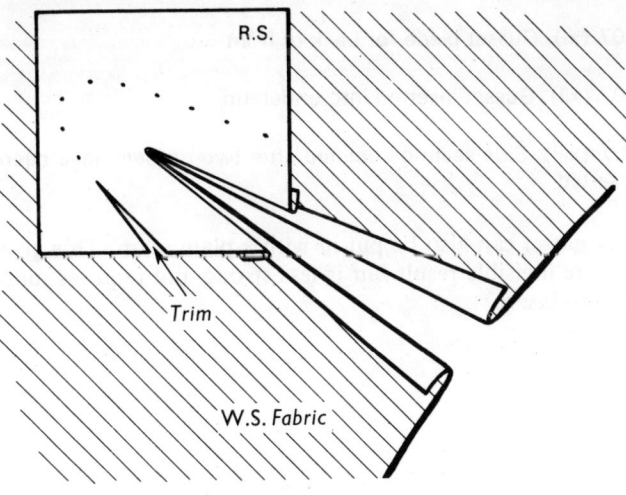

(x). The finish on the wrong side.
le is now strengthened with a
ng

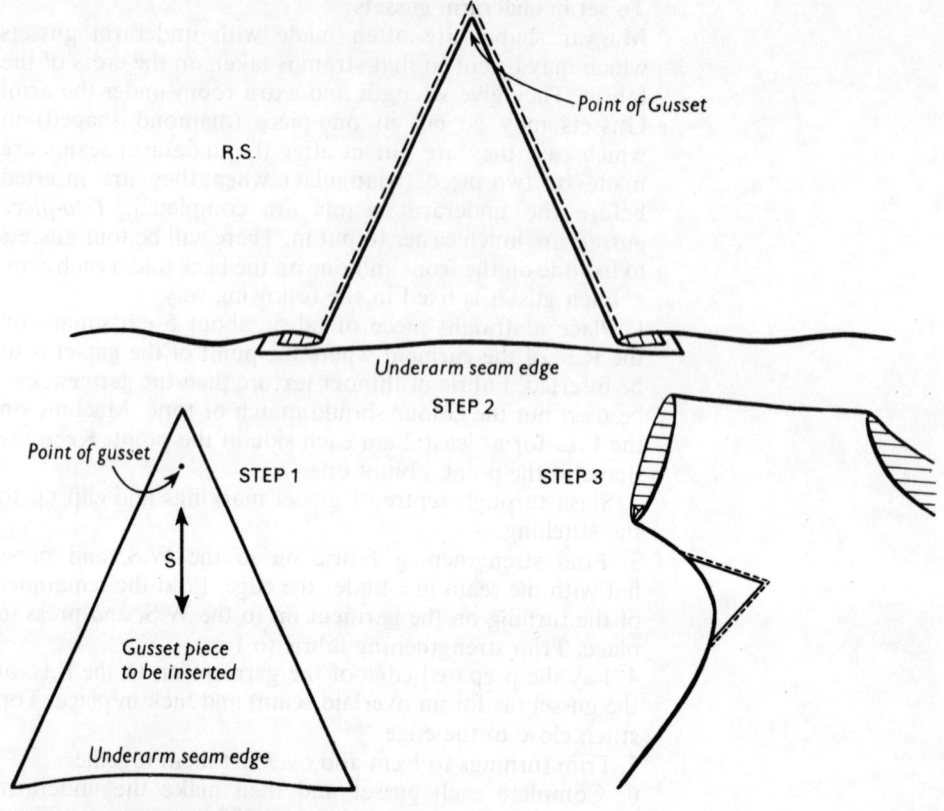

Inserting a two-piece gusset

107 (xi). Gusset piece for back or front

107 (xii). Gusset inserted into underarm

107 (xiii). Side seam completed after two gussets have been inserted

A gusset can also be put in with a plain seam. This gives a more invisible result but is less strong and requires more skill to insert.

16 Waist finishes

The waists of skirts, shorts and slacks must be finished in such a way that they grip the waist comfortably and do not stretch in use. A popular method is to insert the waist into a stiffened band. Another is to make a shaped facing, see p. 227.

To set a waist edge into a stiffened band

The band should be stiffened by interlining with canvas, calico, vilene or belting, so that it will keep flat in wear and is less likely to stretch.

1. Interline the band
1. Cut a strip of interfacing the exact length and width the band is intended to measure when finished, including the width of the wrap on the opening.
2. Pin and baste or iron-on the interfacing strip on to the wrong side of strip for the band, so that one long edge is level with the centre of the band, and there is an even turning at each end. If it is planned to finish the band finally with rows of machining, the interlining strip can be left basted at this stage. If, however, a plain finish is intended, machine the strip to the fabric in zigzag lines to fix it securely and give added stiffness. After this, the stiffened side will be considered as the back of the band. Diagrams 108 (i), (ii).

2. Make the band
Fold the band lengthways with the right side inside and close the two ends with machining. Trim the turnings and turn the work so that the right side of the material is outside. Tack the seams and the fold in position; tack through the centre and press the band. Diagrams 108 (ii), (iii).

3. Fix the band to the waist edge of the garment. Diagrams 109 (i), (ii).
1. The band can be fixed with a plain or an overlaid seam.

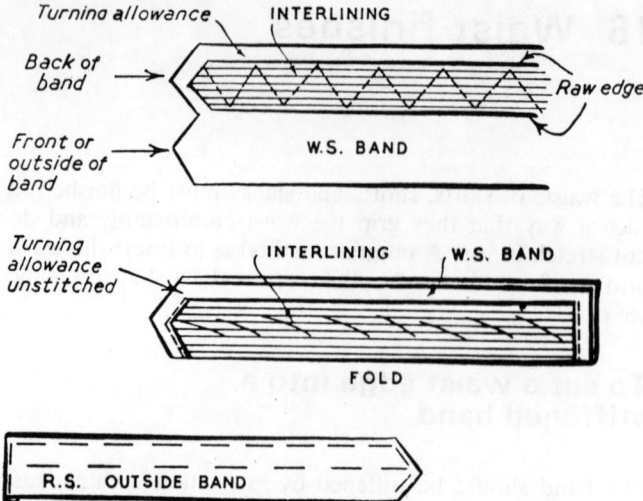

108 (i). The interlining fixed to material for the band (showing interlining machined in place)

108 (ii). The material folded seamed (showing an interlining ba in place)

108 (iii). The band turned inside and prepared for fixing to the waist

The decision will depend on whether it is desired to have machining showing on the outside. If an overlaid seam is to be used, prepare the open edges of the band by tacking and pressing the turnings back on to the wrong side.

2. Place the front or outside of the band to the waist edge of the skirt or pants, fixing the edges together according to the kind of seam being used (Chapter 8). Match the centre back and front of the band and garment, ease in any surplus fullness on the garment and note that the ends of the band are in line with the ends of the opening. Machine the outside of the band to the garment, press the seam and trim the turnings.

3. Fix down the back of the band so that the raw edges are enclosed in the band and hem the fold level with the machining.

4. Trim with machining on the outside, if wished, by machining once all round the band an even distance from the edges. Fasten the end of the band with a button and buttonhole, or hooks and bars.

To fix a skirt to a top

Generally a plain or overlaid seam is used to fix a skirt to a bodice, e.g. a dress or slip. An overlaid seam is often chosen when the bodice is plain and the skirt has gathered fullness or thick pleats. When both bodice and skirt have fullness arranged, a plain seam will be more successful.

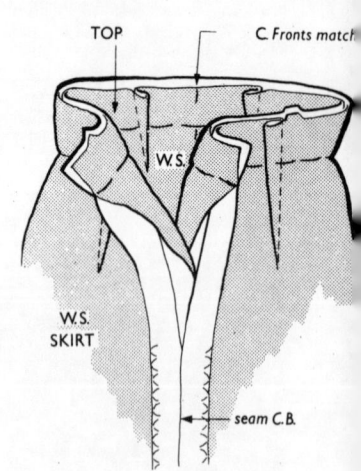

110 (i) Skirt and top tacked together

WAIST FINISHES 189

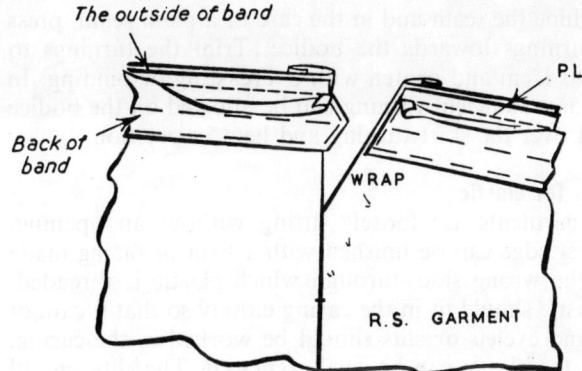

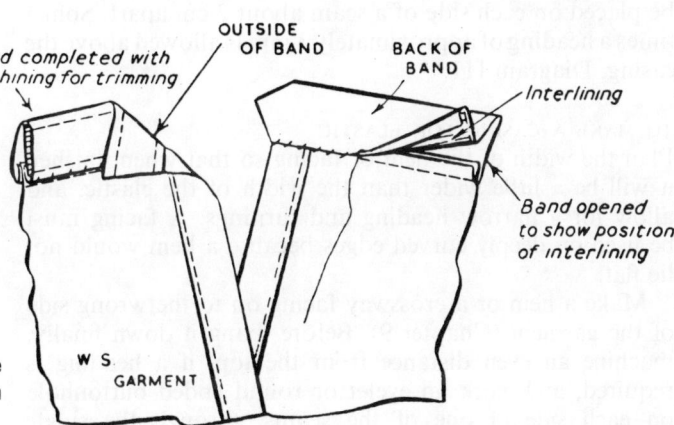

(i). The band fixed to the waist of the garment with a plain seam

(ii). The finish of a band on the Diagram shows a plain and a \[mac\]hined finish

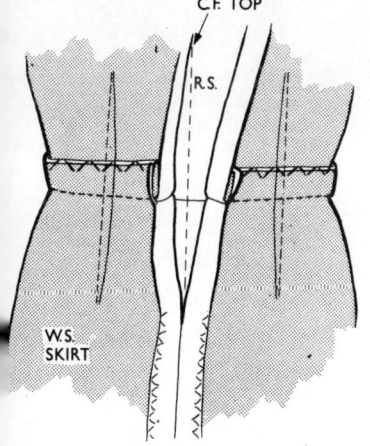

(ii). Skirt and top seamed and \[fast\]ened with a plain seam

When to fix a bodice and skirt together

The bodice should have the neck opening and seams completed and the neck edge and sleeves either finished or fixed temporarily ready for fitting. If there is to be a side opening the seam should be left unstitched on the left side for 10 cm to 12 cm above the waistline.

The skirt should have the seams completed except the section left unstitched for an opening, and the hem tacked up.

Method of attaching a skirt to top

1. Decide the type of seam to be used and place the waist edges of the bodice and skirt together, matching the pattern lines and matching the centre fronts and backs. If there is to be a side opening, see that the seam lines of the opening are opposite. Equalise any fullness and tack the seam preparatory to machining.

2. Machine the seam and in the case of a plain seam, press both turnings towards the bodice. Trim the turnings to 6 mm to 1 cm and neaten with overcasting or binding. In some cases sufficient turning can be allowed on the bodice to bind over the skirt turning and hem in position.

Casings for elastic
When garments are loosely fitting without an opening, the waist edge can be finished with a hem or facing made on to the wrong side, through which elastic is threaded. The elastic should fit in the casing closely so that it cannot twist, and eyelets or slits should be worked in the casing, so that the elastic can be easily renewed. The slits should be placed on each side of a seam about 2 cm apart. Sometimes a heading of approximately 3 mm is allowed above the casing. Diagram 111.

TO MAKE A CASING FOR ELASTIC
Plan the width of the hem or facing so that when finished it will be a little wider than the width of the elastic, and allow for a narrow heading and turnings. A facing must be used on deeply curved edges because a hem would not lie flat.

Make a hem or a crossway facing on to the wrong side of the garment (Chapter 9). Before fixing it down finally, machine an even distance from the top, if a heading is required, and work an eyelet or round ended buttonhole on each side of one of the seams, through the single thickness of the casing. Eyelets are used for narrow elastic.

Complete the hem or facing and thread elastic through the casing, using a bodkin or safety pin. Overlap the ends of the elastic and machine or backstitch them securely.

N.B. The casing for elastic at leg and sleeve edges of garments is made in a similar way.

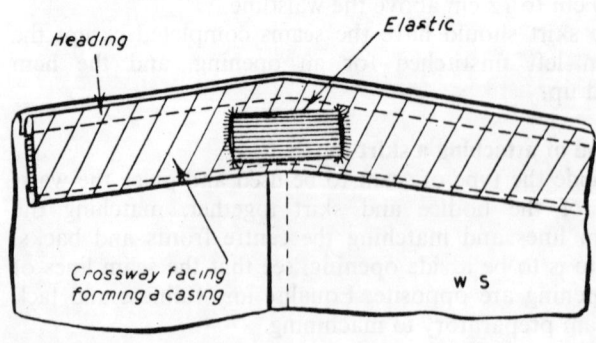

111. Section to show the construction of a casing at the waist

17 Pockets and finishings

Pockets

A patch pocket

This consists of a rectangular piece of material stitched flat on to the outside of a garment leaving one side open. Rounded corners at the bottom of a pocket are more practical than square or pointed, because they are easier to wash. Decorative pockets can be any suitable shape.

DIRECTIONS FOR MAKING. Diagrams 112 (i), (ii), (iii)

1. Cut out the pocket and neaten the top edge. This may have a hem or facing, a bind or some other edge finish which fits in with the style of the rest of the garment.*

Turn in the remaining edges of the pocket on to the wrong side. Tack, press and snip the turnings and trim them to 6 mm in depth. Cut away the thickness at the corners. (See Chapter 9, p. 90.)

2. Pin and tack the pocket in place on the garment, easing it slightly on all sides. If it is placed quite flat it will be too tight when in use and will not set properly.

3. Machine the pocket to the garment. Fix it with one or two rows of machining close to the edge of the pocket. In any case, put double stitching at the corners to make them strong. The diagrams show alternative ways of arranging the stitching.

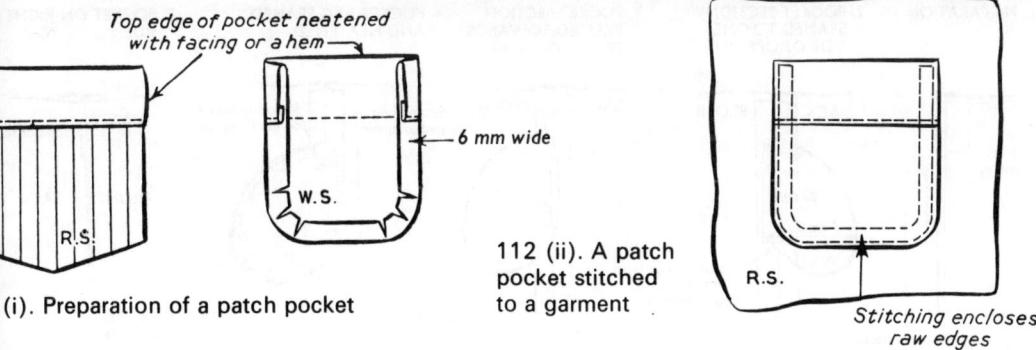

(i). Preparation of a patch pocket

112 (ii). A patch pocket stitched to a garment

Stitching encloses raw edges

* Another method of making a patch pocket is given in *Introduction to Needlework*, p. 143.

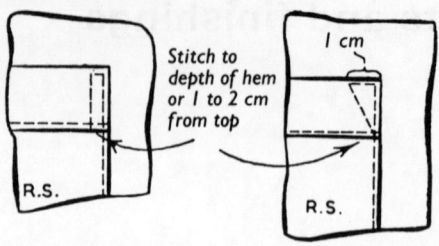

112 (iii). Ways of stitching the corners of a patch p

Pocket in a seam

This pocket can be made on skirts, dresses or trousers. It does not show because it is made in a plain or open seam. Two pocket sections are seamed to the turnings on the inside of the pocket mouth and then stitched together to form a bag which is pressed towards the front of the garment.

DIRECTIONS FOR MAKING. Diagrams 113 (i)–(v)
1. If a pattern is not provided, cut two pocket sections to about the sizes given on the diagram. These include 1 cm turnings.
2. Tack up the entire seam including the pocket mouth. Machine above and below the mouth and press the turnings open.
3. Seam one pocket section to the seam turning of the mouth, a little way from the P.L. This will prevent this seam being noticeable on the R.S. Take the machining a little above and below (about 1.5 cm) the mouth of the pocket. Fold the pocket section away from the mouth and press this plain seam.
4. Seam the second pocket section to the opposite turning

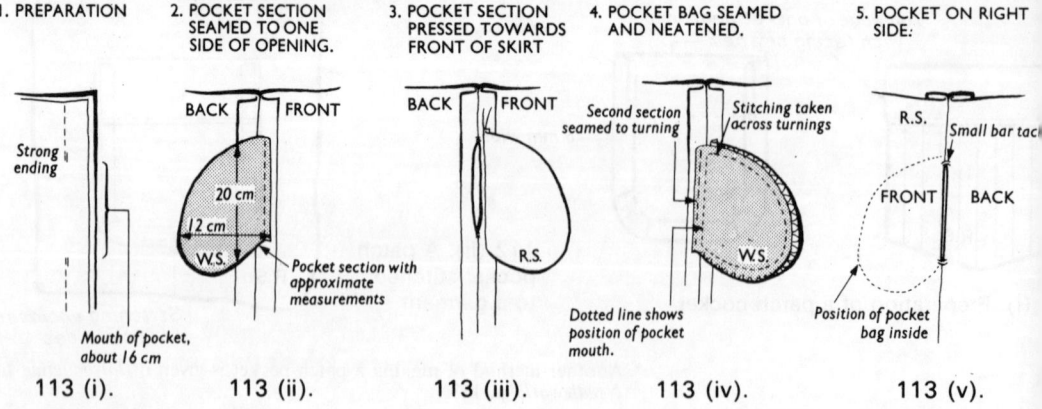

on the opening a little distance from the P.L.

5. Place pocket sections smoothly together. Recut and shape the edges as necessary and stitch all round the pocket bag 1 cm from the edges. Take the machining across the seam turnings.

6. On R.S. work small neat bar tacks at each end of the pocket opening for strength and to keep the pocket bag in place.

A bound pocket

This pocket has the effect from the front of a large bound buttonhole. Two layers of material at the back of the work are stitched together to form the pocket. The method of making the pocket is similar to the method used for making bound buttonholes, which should be clearly understood before attempting the pocket. (See p. 135).

DIRECTIONS FOR MAKING. Diagrams 114 (i), (ii)

1. Mark the position of the pocket with a line of tacking on the garment.

2. Cut a straight strip of material to bind the pocket opening, making it wide enough and long enough to bind the

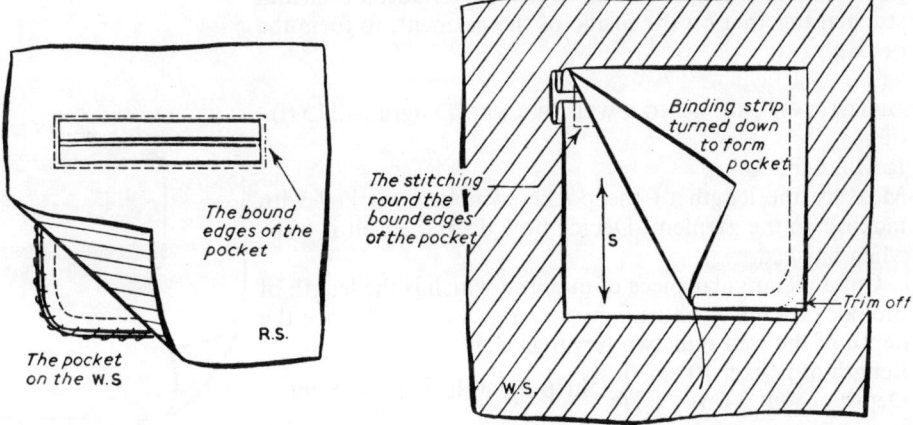

114 (i). A bound pocket on the R.S.

114 (ii). To show the construction of the bound pocket on the W.S.

slit and provide amply for the pocket section back and front; e.g. to make a pocket 10 cm long and 12 cm deep, cut a strip 14 cm by 25 cm.

3. Place the strip right side down on the outside of the garment, to cover the tacking so that more than half its length is above the tacking. Baste the strip in position.

4. Stitch the strip to the garment and cut and bind the slit according to the directions given for bound buttonholes. The bind is usually made a little wider than for buttonholes, e.g. 6 mm wide.

5. Press the bound slit well and draw the edges together with fishbone tacking. The bind can be finished, if liked, with machining on the right side.

This completes the part of the pocket which shows on the outside of the garment.

6. Now make the pocket itself on the wrong side of the garment. Form the pocket by turning the section of the strip above the slit downwards on top of the lower section. Pin the two sections together, trim off any surplus material so that the edges are level. Round off the corners. Machine 6 mm or 1 cm away from the edges and overcast the edges to neaten them.

A welt pocket

A welt pocket is one which has a band or "welt" showing on the right side. The welt, generally at least 1.5 cm deep, is often 2 cm or 2.5 cm; is made separately and is stitched on to the right side of the garment with the pocket sections. The pocket sections are pushed through a cut in the material and stitched together on the inside of the garment, to form the pocket.

DIRECTIONS FOR MAKING A WELT POCKET. Diagrams 115 (i)–(iii)

1. Make the welt.

Measure the length of the pocket which is marked with tacking on the garment. Decide how deep the welt is to be when finished.

Cut a rectangular piece of material which is the length of the pocket plus two turnings (selvedge way) and twice the depth of the welt plus two turnings, e.g.

Length of pocket 10 cm
Depth of welt 2 cm } Strip for welt = 11 × 5 cm

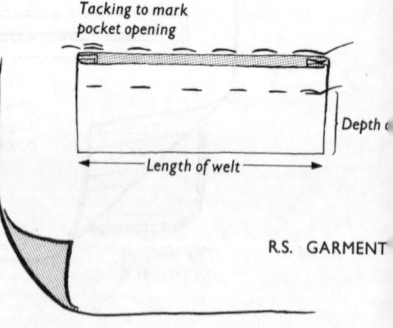

115 (i). Welt prepared and tacked place

Fold the strip in half lengthways with the right side inside and stitch across the two ends.

Trim turnings; turn the welt inside out; tack the seams and fold at the edges and press well. Check accuracy of depth of welt and mark with a chalked line. Tack welt through this line.

2. Tack welt to the outside of the garment below the line of tacking and with the cut edges level with the tacking. Tack

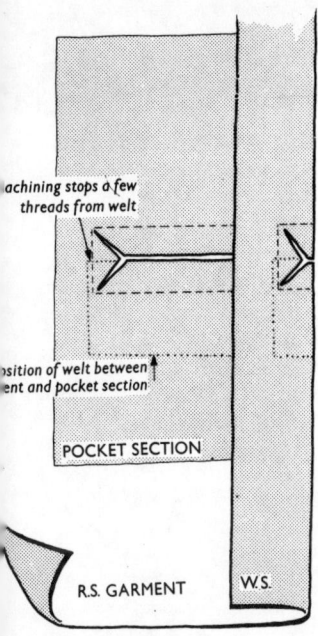

(ii). Pocket section in position, pocket opening machined and cut

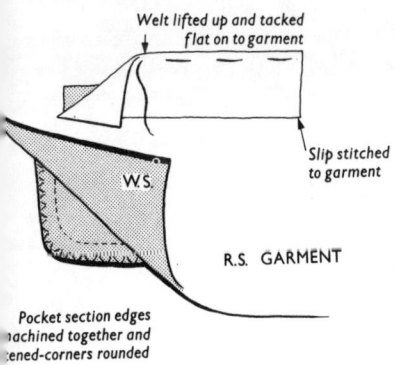

(iii). Completing a welt pocket

firmly in position on the chalked line.
3. Cut the pocket sections and place in position.
Cut one straight strip of material for the two sections of the pocket, i.e. back and front. The width of the strip should equal the length of the welt plus 4 cm for two ample turnings. The length of the strip should be twice the depth of the finished pocket plus two turnings, e.g.

Length of welt 10 cm } Strip for pocket sections
Depth of pocket 12 cm } = 14 cm × 25 cm

Place the right side of the strip on top of the welt so that the centre is directly over the tacking which marks the pocket. Baste the strip in position.
4. Stitch the welt and pocket strip to the garment.
Turn the garment to the wrong side (where the tacking which marks the pocket can be seen) and stitch 0.5 cm away from the tacking exactly as the stitching is made for a bound buttonhole, but do not let it extend as far as the sides of the welt. Turn the corners just a few threads short of the sides. Diagram 115 (ii).
5. Cut the slit for the pocket.
Cut a slit in the garment and pocket strip in the middle of the rectangle of stitching to within 6 mm of each end. Slash into the corners.
 Push the pocket strip through to the wrong side of the garment bringing both ends of the strip down below the cut.
6. Stitch the welt to the garment.
Lift the welt up and place it flat on the garment above the slash, tacking it in position along the top and sides.
 Slip stitch the sides of the welt invisibly and securely to the garment.
7. Make the pocket section.
On the wrong side of the garment pin the two ends of the pocket strip together to form the back and front of the pocket. Trim off the surplus turnings to make the pocket a good shape with rounded corners.
 Machine the two edges together and overcast or zigzag edges to neaten, unless the garment is to be lined.

Finishings

It is surprising how long the finishings take on a garment when it is apparently almost completed. Unless due attention is given to these details, the article will not have a professional appearance. The following include some of the finishings which may be required.

Tie belts

These can be made of double or single material. When single, the edge must be neatened with a hem or bind before the tie is attached to a garment. If a tie is to be cut double, the material is cut in one strip with the selvedge along the length.

TO MAKE A TIE BELT OF DOUBLE FABRIC

Fold the material along the length with the right side inside. Seam the long and one short end, leaving the other short end open. Turn the belt through to the right side, by pushing the closed end through to the open end with the top of a pencil. Tack the seam at the edge, and turn in the raw edges and slip hem them together, unless the tie is to be fixed permanently to the garment by this end. Diagrams 116 (i), (ii), (iii).

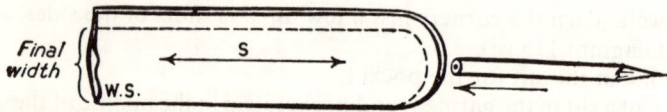

116 (i). Belt or strap stitched ready for turning R.S. out

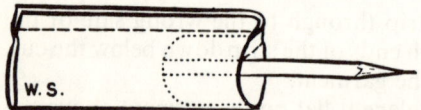

116 (ii). Turning R.S. out by pushing the pencil through to the open end

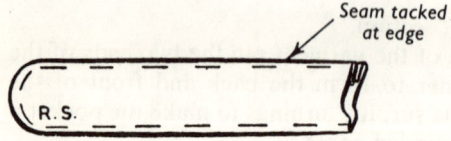

116 (iii). Ready for pressing (and trimming by machining if liked)

Rouleau can be used for ties. See method of making rouleau, p. 212.

Belts

Belts can be made with or without an interlining to stiffen them. If it is to be stiffened, an interlining is attached and stitched in the same way as given for a stiffened band in Chapter 16. The method of making a belt is similar to that

POCKETS AND FINISHINGS

given above for making a double tie belt. Diagrams 116 (i), (ii), (iii).

Attach the buckle to one end. At the other, make eyelets with an eyeletting tool called a spreader.* Encircle the belt with a narrow strap of material (made like a belt carrier) to support the end which passes through the buckle. Diagram 117.

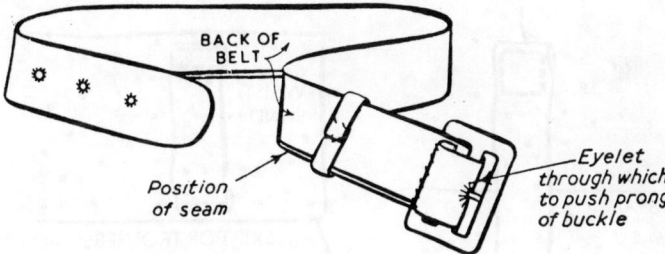

To show the finish of a belt ●ned with a buckle

Belt carriers

Used on skirts, trousers and dresses to keep belts and ties in place at the waist. They must be long enough to allow the belt to pass through easily and should be fixed on each side of the garment over the side seam. Carriers should be placed so that one end is half the width of the belt below the waist level, with the result that the belt is kept in the right position on the waist. When there is an opening in the side seam, the carrier is stitched on the back portion of the garment just by the opening. Carriers can be made of the same material as the garment or they can be worked with thread as a worked bar is made.

TO MAKE FABRIC BELT CARRIERS. Diagrams 118 (i), (ii), (iii). Make a straight strap of the same material as the dress, to

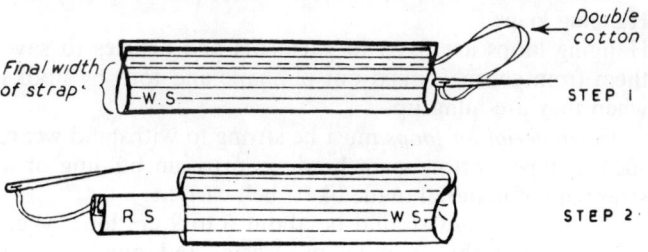

118 (i). To turn a narrow strap inside out

---

* Method of using a spreader is illustrated in *Introduction to Needlework*, p. 57.

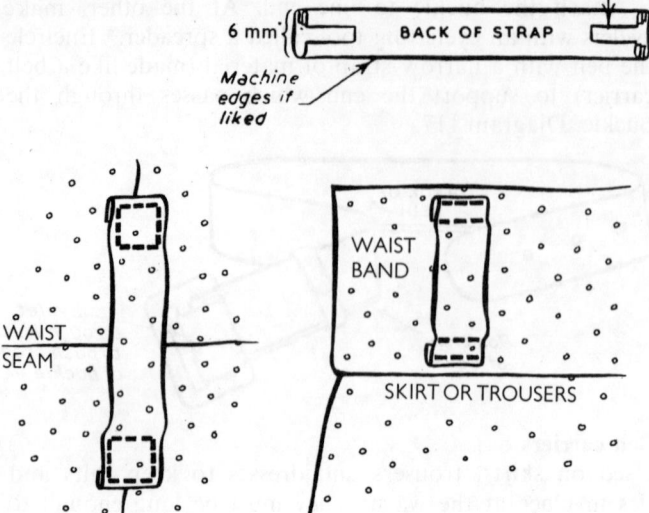

118 (ii). Strap for belt carrier or hang loop prepared for fixing to garment

118 (iii). Belt carriers in position at waist seam and on waist band showing two ways of stitching them

measure 6 mm wide and 2 cm longer than the width of the belt.

Fold back 6 mm at each end of the strap and press well. Cut away some of the material from the back of the strap.

Place the strap in position on the garment so that it is not quite flat, thus allowing for the thickness of the belt when it is slotted through. Fix the strap at each end with a square of machining or two rows 6 mm apart or slip hem it firmly.

Hanging loops
Hanging loops are fixed to garments and articles to save them from getting poked out of shape and torn by hooks when they are hung up.

The material for loops must be strong to withstand wear, such as tape, cotton seam binding, prussian binding or a strapping of material made like a belt carrier.

The size of loops should be about 6 to 9 cm long when fixed, so that they can be put easily and quickly over pegs, and not more than 1 cm wide. A wider loop would crease when in use.

The position of loops should be in a convenient and inconspicuous place on double material if possible. The following are the usual positions:

POCKETS AND FINISHINGS

The centre back of the neck, just above the seam if there is a collar, or just below the neck edge if the bodice is collarless, on coats, blouses, overalls and dress tops.

At the waist of skirts and shorts, one at each side attached to the bottom of the band or petersham.

At opposite corners of towels and tea cloths, or in the middle of both short sides, to distribute wear.

The fixing of loops can be done by hand or machine, but must be very strong, so that a loop will not tear from the garment when it takes the weight.

Loops can be made in two ways, to be flat, or projecting from an edge. Both can be used in most positions, but sometimes the projecting type cannot be chosen because of the possibility of the loop showing on a garment in wear.

TO MAKE FLAT LOOPS. Follow the method given for belt carriers. Diagrams 118 (i), (ii), (iii).

TO MAKE PROJECTING LOOPS. Form loop so that one cut edge is 6 mm above the other. Turn over and press this turning. Place and stitch as given for ties, p. 141.

Outline stitching

A popular way of outlining seams and edges such as collars, cuffs, yokes, pockets, belts. It can be done by hand, using saddle stitching or hand-picking, (p. 155), or by machine, using ordinary sewing thread (pp. 178, 231) or, for a more decorative effect, with heavy duty polyester threads such as Bold Stitch, Outline.

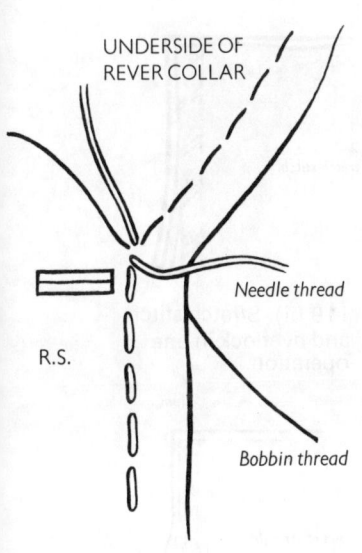

118 (iv) Stitching with outline thread on a rever collar and front edge

TO MACHINE WITH HEAVY 'OUTLINE' THREAD

1. Do the stitching before any edge tacks are removed and after a preliminary pressing. Put in a line of tacking if necessary, to hold the layers of fabric in place.
2. Wind the bobbin with *ordinary sewing thread* matching the colour of outline thread. Thread the needle with outline thread (use a thicker needle than usual). Set to a long stitch and try out on a scrap equal in thickness e.g. two layers of fabric and interlining. Alter the tensions if necessary.
3. *Machine with R.S.* up keeping an even distance from edge or seam. Remember to reverse work when part of the edge turns back as on a rever – see diagram.

If the outline thread is too thick to use in the machine needle, follow the method given for ELASTIC YARN FIXED WITH A STRAIGHT STITCH p. 303, but with the following differences in points 1 and 3.

1. Wind outline thread instead of elastic on the bobbin and wind smoothly by hand without tension.
3. *Machine with W.S. up*. This will give a flat result with a decorative straight machine stitch on the R.S.

18 Special dressmaking techniques

Much good, straightforward work can be done without studying the contents of this chapter, all of which require a little extra trouble, more thought, or greater skill. For example, a dress made in plain fabric is much quicker to cut out than a plaid and it is not essential to interface the neck edge. Ambitious girls will want to go further than the simple work already considered and will be interested in tackling more challenging skills.

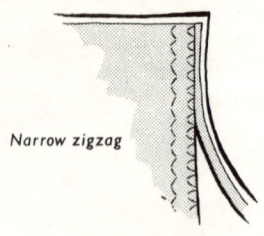

119 (i). Narrow zigzag

Fabrics requiring special treatment

Stretch fabrics
These include suitings, denims, poplins, towelling, knits.

Elasticity is given by use of a proportion of elastomer yarns and/or by the treatment of the yarn itself (p. 9) and by the construction of the fabric (p. 12).

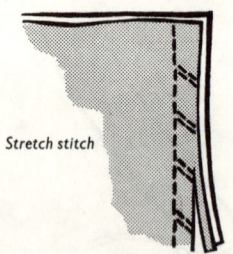

119 (ii). Stretch stitch and overlock in one operation

When buying stretch fabrics check that the stretch is in the correct direction for the clothing being made, e.g. in a horizonatal direction on a skirt (weft stretch fabric); in a vertical direction on pants (warp stretch fabric). Two-way stretch fabrics are used for swim suits. Stretch fabrics should be spread out on a table top for a few hours before placing the pattern to allow the yarns to relax. Care must be taken to avoid stretching the fabric by keeping the weight of it on the table or machine top so that it is not pulled out of shape. In planning the lay of pattern the direction of stretch must be considered so that it is correct in each pattern piece. Check if it has an 'up and down'.

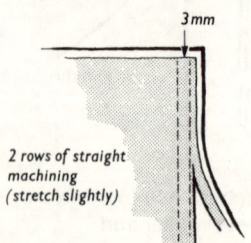

119 (iii). Straight stitch

Stretch fabrics are best stitched with a narrow zigzag stitch which allows seams to stretch with the fabric. Some machines have a stretch stitch setting. When a straight stitch has to be used it is best to loosen the tensions while still maintaining a good strong stitch and to hold the work stretched slightly under the machine foot. Use a fine ball point needle, an average sized stitch and synthetic thread. A Teflon presser foot helps. Fabrics can be pressed with a steam iron if the fabric is one which will not water mark.

P.V.C.

VINYLS (see p. 27) are not easy fabrics to work on because they cannot be pinned, are weakened with too much stitching and can be rather unwieldy to handle. Styles should be carefully planned with a minimum of seaming. Simple lines are the most successful. Pattern lines can be marked with pencil on the wrong side (pattern held in place with weights). The pattern can be marked out and then turned over to mark the second half, e.g. front pattern marked from C.F. and turned over to complete the front. Sections can be held together for fitting or seaming with Sellotape or paper clips. Thread should be chosen to suit the backing fabric and, in order to avoid splitting at the seams, a fine to average needle is necessary with a rather large stitch. Fabric glue can be used to hold hems, facings and seam turnings in place. When machining has to be done on the right side of P.V.C. it will be found easier for the work to pass under the machine foot if the surface is lightly smeared with oil in front of the needle as stitching proceeds. Or, use a roller presser foot. Speed of machining should be kept slow.

Foam backed fabrics

The bulkiness of these fabrics and the rough surface of the foam backing present a number of problems. First, the style must be chosen with care to avoid complicated construction. Simple styles are best and seams should be avoided where possible, e.g. a pattern with a straight seam at centre back can be cut in one piece by omitting the seam; a facing on front edges can sometimes be cut in one with the main front sections. Work is simplified if complete patterns are prepared from the pattern tissues, e.g. two jacket fronts, one in tissue and one cut in paper instead of using one pattern tissue for both fronts. Then patterns can be placed on the fabric side and marked out with tacking because it is not possible to mark easily or stitch on the foam backing. If fabric is folded for cutting, the fabric sides should face. Sections may be pinned and tacked together for fitting in the usual way. Facings, undercollars and buttonhole strips can be cut from ordinary fabric to match the fabric laminated to the foam as closely as possible. Information given on p. 31 for kind of seams for brushed fabrics are applicable to foam backed fabrics.

For machining, a Teflon or roller foot is best. If not available a hinged foot will ride over the thickness of the fabric. Foot pressure may have to be released slightly and thin paper placed under the fabric to prevent the foam backing being in contact with the machine feed, otherwise the foam would catch in the teeth. A strip of tissue paper can be placed on top under the foot if a foam surface is uppermost. Paper is torn away carefully when stitching is completed. A large stitch and fine ball point needle (to avoid too many and large needle punctures) with a loose tension should be tried first when experimenting for a good stitch.

Glass fibre fabrics
Curtains made of these fabrics should not be lined. They are reversible and hang well without a lining. Very sharp scissors are necessary for cutting the fabric and side and bottom hems look better sewn by hand. Fine needles are required and thread made from Terylene or spun nylon should be chosen.

Plaids, checks and stripes
Plaids are chequered or tartan woven designs. They are used on many different kinds of fabrics. Originally plaid was the name of the outer article of Highland costume made of woollen twill and it was patterned according to the clan of the wearer. Copies of these designs and many variations are used in textile designing and cloths woven with these designs need special attention in dressmaking.

A study of plaid designs shows that they fall into one of the following groups:

Even or balanced plaids. Diagram 120 (i)
In these the design is symmetrical in both directions of the fabric. With this type it is possible to fold fabric with warp or weft and match the plaid lines in the two layers of cloth.

Uneven or unbalanced plaids. Diagram 120 (ii).
1. Uneven up and down. Here the design is not symmetrical when folded with the weft.
2. Uneven across. Here the design is not symmetrical when folded with the warp.
3. Uneven both ways. Here the fabric cannot be folded either way to obtain a symmetrical design.

The following points must be considered when using plaids.

STYLING
Choose simple styles with few seams. Note whether plaids are recommended on the pattern envelope.

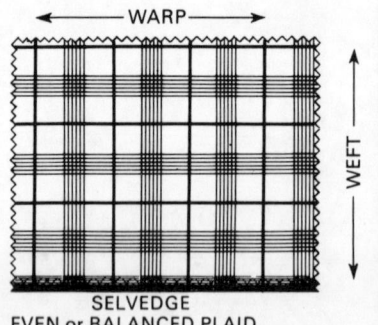

120 (i). Even or balanced plaid. N position of black lines in the design

SPECIAL DRESSMAKING TECHNIQUES 203

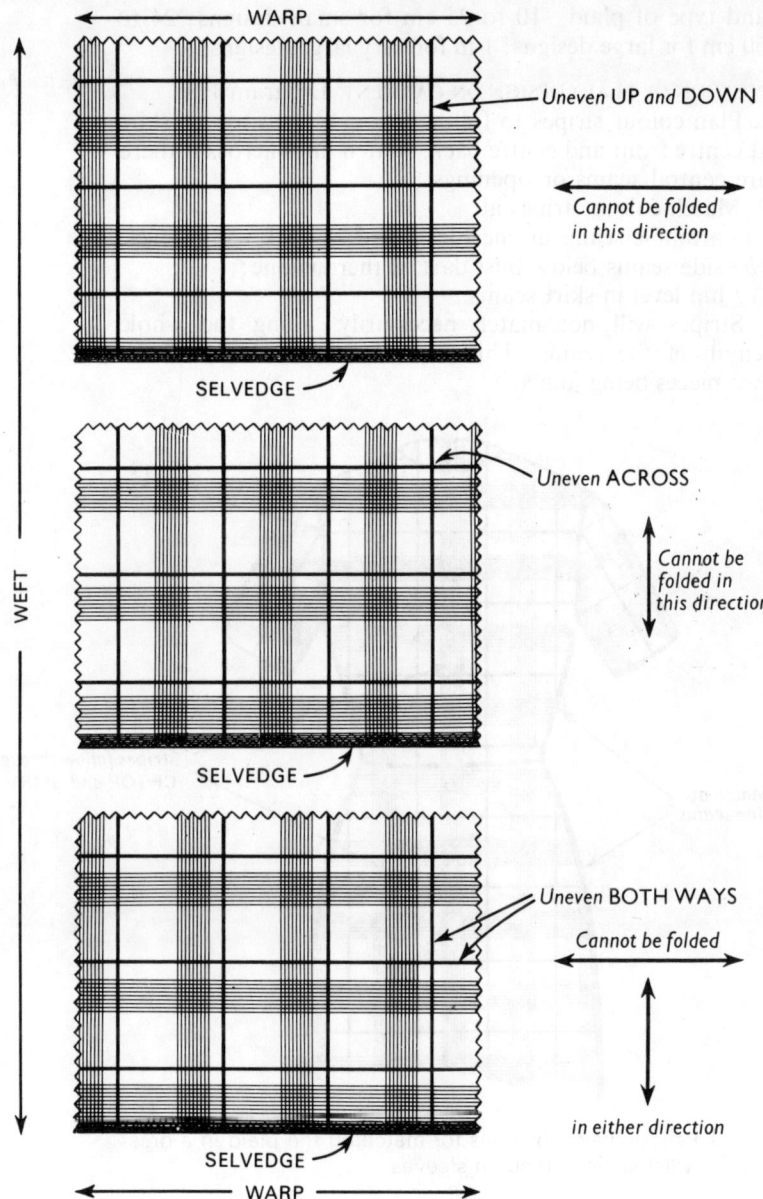

120 (ii). Uneven or unbalanced plaids. Note position of black lines in the design and compare with Diagram 120 (i)

METRAGE

Buy extra fabric to allow for matching according to size

and type of plaid—10 to 25 cm for small designs; 24 to 50 cm for large designs; 1 m for very large designs.

POSITION OF PLAID DESIGN ON GARMENT. Diagram 121.
1. Plan colour stripes to follow through from top to skirt at centre front and centre back. Match lines across if there are central seams or openings.
2. Match colour stripes at
(a) armhole seams at chest level and/or back width level;
(b) side seams below bust dart, if there is one;
(c) hip level in skirt seams.

Stripes will not match necessarily, along the whole length of the seams. This depends on the slant of the two pieces being joined.

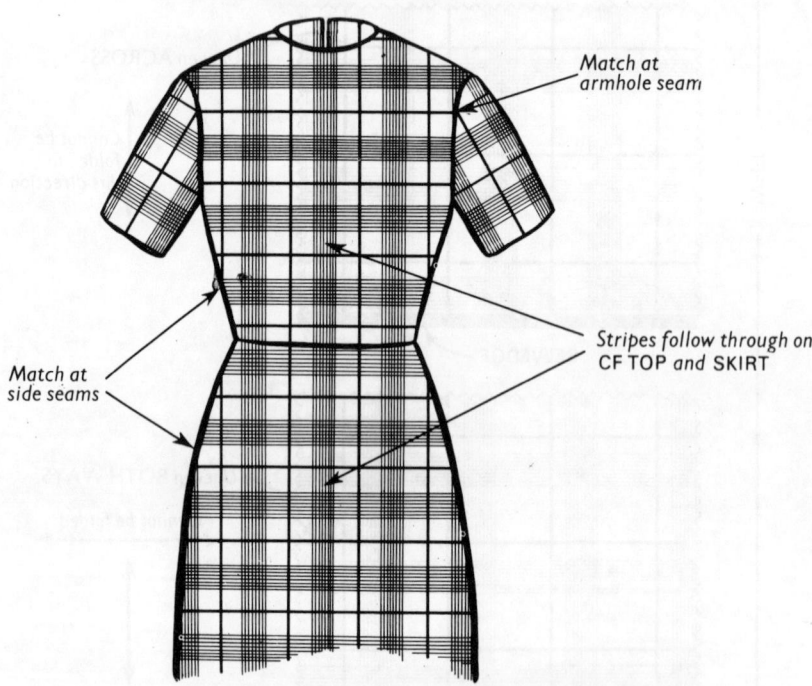

121. To show main positions for matching the plaid in a dress with a waist seam and set in sleeves

3. Plan stripes to follow through in smaller sections such as collars (C.B. to match C.B. of garment) cuffs, pockets, belts, facings. Often, styles are designed with some of these sections cut on the cross for decorative detail.

PLANNING LAY-OF-PATTERN FOR EVEN PLAIDS. Diagram 122. Consider each piece as it is placed to see that colour stripes will match at the required places both through length of garment and across. Use the notches on pattern pieces to match stripes—if notches are in exactly the same position on the plaid in the two pattern pieces, they will match when seamed.

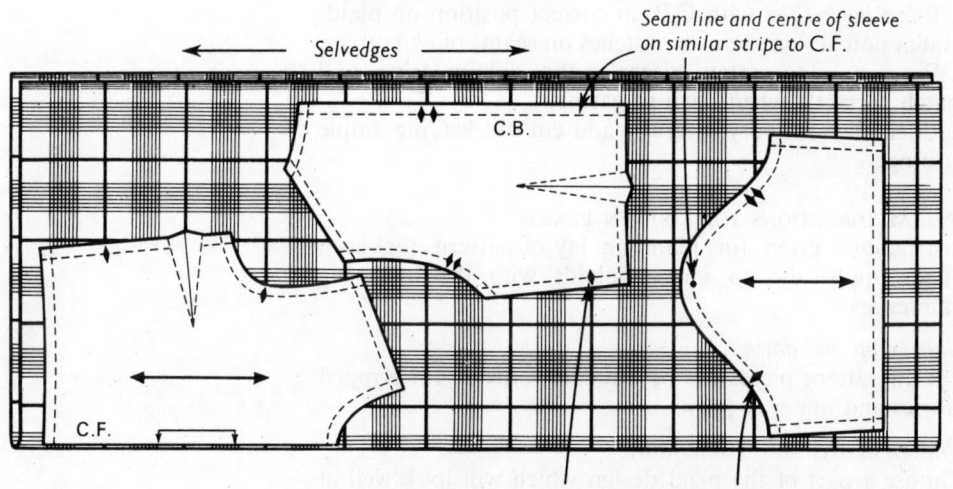

122. To show how to place patterns on an even plaid

Always work in the following order:
1. Decide which part of the plaid is to be at the centre front—usually the centre of one of the conspicuous bars of colour between the bold stripes. Fold fabric through the middle of this bar and pin layers together in places along the plaid lines.
2. Place *front* pattern in position with centre to fold. Consider position of strong coloured stripes going across the body. Usually it is best to site one at chest level.
3. Place *back* pattern to similar fold. If there is a seam or opening at C.B. then place so that seam line is in the middle of the conspicuous bar to make a complete bar when joined.

Shift *back* pattern until notches on side seam match notches on *front* side seam.
4. Place *sleeve* pattern so that plaid design is symmetrical on each side of middle of sleeve.

Move pattern until notches on head of sleeve match notches on *front* armhole (or *back* armhole).

For magyar shapes with shoulder seams, match *back* shoulder hotches to *front*.

5. Lay *front skirt* to similar fold used for *front* pattern with C.F. waist seam at same position on plaid as C.F. waist seam of *front* pattern.

6. Place *back skirt* with C.B. in correct position on plaid. Match notches on seams to notches on seams of *skirt front*.

7. Pin remaining pattern pieces so that colour stripes will match correctly when sewn to garment.

8. Check lay-out very carefully and cut out leaving ample turnings.

SPECIAL DIRECTIONS FOR UNEVEN PLAIDS

Instructions given for planning lay-of-pattern for even plaids apply also to uneven plaids with the following differences:

Uneven up and down
Cut all pattern pieces in one direction only as for napped fabrics and one-way prints.

Uneven across (reversible fabric)
Choose a part of the plaid design which will look well at the centre of the garment and use this for other central positions of the pattern (centres front and back of *front, back* and *skirt*). The plaid design will be different on left and right sides because it is impossible to make the plaid symmetrical unless seams are made at centres front and back.

If there are to be seams at C.F. and C.B. proceed in the following way:

Cut one half *front* in single fabric (leave a seam allowance at C.F.).

Place this section down in another position (reverse side of cloth may be used) so that plaids match. Repeat this method with each pattern section for front and back of garment.

Uneven both ways (reversible fabric)
Follow direction for plaids unbalanced across but, in addition, place all pattern pieces in one direction on the cloth.

Note: Most plaids are reversible, but if the fabric has a definite right and wrong side, e.g. brushed rayon, then problems in matching and cutting are greater. Non-reversible fabrics with uneven plaids are a suitable choice only for workers with considerable knowledge and experience.

Checks and stripes

Designs with checks or stripes over 6 mm in width should be matched at seams and treated as even plaids. If the designs are uneven they fall into the same categories as uneven plaids. Many self-patterned designs woven in fabric, form lines and blocks of design which must be considered for matching when planning pattern-lays. Use slip tacking on seams to match designs and a Teflon foot for machining.

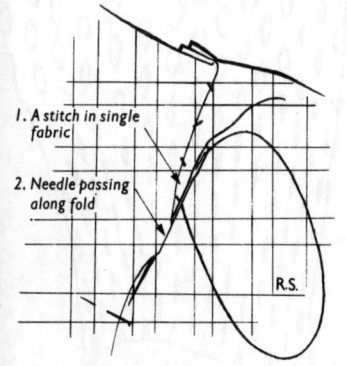

1. A stitch in single fabric
2. Needle passing along fold

(i). Slip tacking helps to keep d in position. Machine from W.S. sual way

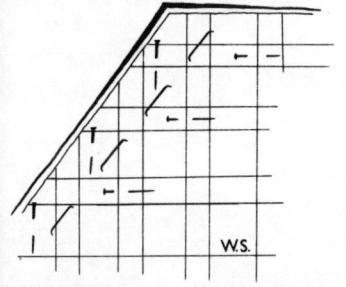

Pin plaid lines together each side of seam

(ii). To prevent fabric shifting e machining

Interfacing

Interfacing or interlining is to put a layer of material between the main part of the garment and the hem or facing.

REASONS FOR INTERFACING ARE:
1. to make edges crisp, as on collars and cuffs;
2. to make edges firm and strong and to prevent stretching, as on front edges of blouses, jackets and belts;
3. to give body to a part of a garment, as on a pocket, a big collar or the fronts of a jacket.

Interfacings, properly fixed, improve the look of a garment and can give a very smart professional appearance. Good results depend much on the correct choice of interlinings for the fabric of the garment.

Materials used for interfacings

Materials must have certain qualities if they are to give flat results. The fabric must be:
1. thin, to avoid bulkiness and firm to hold the shape of the part being interlined;
2. non-fraying, so that it is not difficult to handle;
3. inexpensive, so that it does not add greatly to the cost;
4. washable, on clothing which will need to be washed.

Fabrics which fulfil these requirements are:
Woven cottons and linens, such as organdie, lawn, cambric, holland, canvas, linen.
Bonded fabrics, made mainly from man-made fibres

processed and pressed into thin sheets, such as Vilene. These are sold in a number of thicknesses, mainly in black and white and in various widths, 46 cm, 90 cm. See p. 12.

A soft 'sew-in' Vilene, 'Superdrape', made with stretch quality is useful on knitted fabrics. The Vilene is pierced with small cuts all over the surface in one direction thus allowing it to stretch across the cuts, diagram 124 (i).

Most of these fabrics, both woven and bonded, can be bought with an adhesive backing when they are known as fusible or iron-on interfacings.

Choice of material for interfacing
Selection of the right type and weight of an interlining is very important. The wrong choice can cause bulky, clumsy edges and also make the clothing uncomfortable. Either woven or bonded can be used.

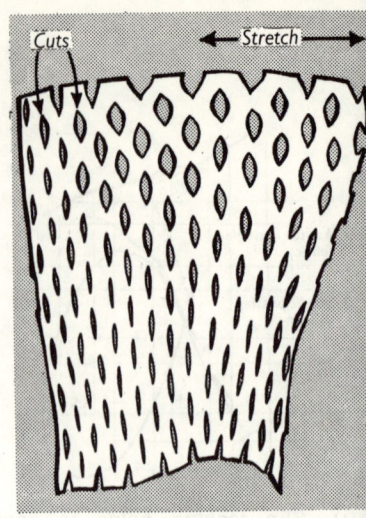

124 (i). Stretch Vilene

CHOOSE THE RIGHT WEIGHT
Generally the heavier the fabric of the garment, the heavier the interlining required to hold it. Therefore, tailors use canvas and heavyweight Vilenes on thick tweeds and worsteds; dressmakers use lightweight interfacings—lawn, organdie, cambric, paper-thin Vilene for rayons, linen, light flannels and suitings. In all cases, though, the fabric of the interfacing must be lighter in weight than the fabric of the garment.

CONSIDER THE EFFECT REQUIRED
The style will influence the choice according to whether a rather firm tailored effect is required or a slight crispness, e.g. a thicker interlining is needed on a belt or stand-up collar than on a soft roll collar, so that thick Vilene might be the choice for a belt; lightweight Vilene or calico for the stand-up collar and lawn for a roll collar.

CONSIDER WHETHER TO USE PLAIN OR IRON-ON INTERFACINGS
It is always a matter of preference which kind is used but iron-on types can only be used in the following circumstances:
1. On fairly small areas, such as collars and cuffs. On larger areas the interfacing may not adhere evenly.
2. On firm materials. If used on soft fabrics such as Tricel jersey, foulards, soft woollens or loosely woven materials the interfacing holds the threads of the fabric too rigidly and will spoil the characteristic appearance and texture of the material.

3. On sections cut on the straight. If used on cross cut sections, e.g. roll collars, the stretching quality of the cross cut will be destroyed and the style spoilt.

Cutting interfacings

1. Interfacings are cut exactly the same shape as the part to be interfaced. Usually a pattern is provided—if not, the pattern of the garment can be used.
2. If a woven interfacing is used it is cut on exactly the same grain as the garment. When bonded types are used the pattern can be placed in any direction to cut economically. Stretch Vilene is placed with cuts lengthwise.
3. Turnings are allowed as when cutting out the garment unless the interfacing is to be placed against a folded edge, as on a cuff. Then no turning is needed.
4. Joins can be made to save material, e.g. a long front opening on a dress can have a join in the interfacing. The join should be made by overlapping the two edges and machining twice through the middle of the overlap making the rows 3 to 6 mm apart. The edges are trimmed close to the machining. Diagram 124 (ii). Darts are made in a similar manner.
5. Pattern lines need not be marked except for darts.

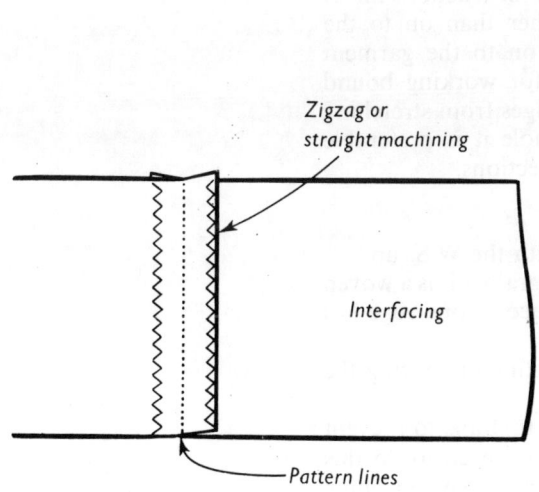

124 (ii). A join in interfacing

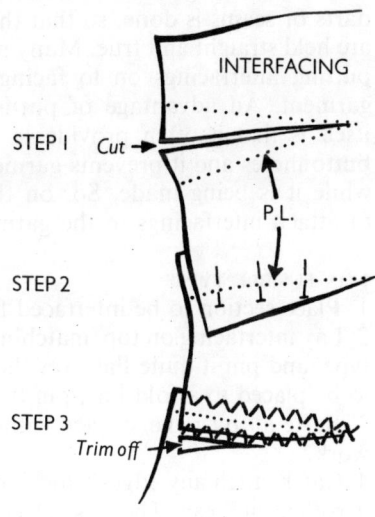

124 (iii). A dart in interfacing made with a flat join

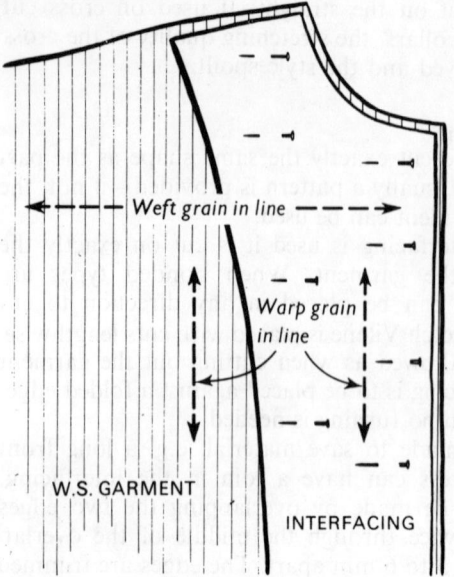

125 (i). Interfacing pinned in place

125 (ii). Interfacing basted in place and one edge being catch stitched in position

To apply interfacings. Diagrams 125 (i), (ii).
It is important to place interfacings in position while sections of the garment are flat *before* any tacking up of darts or seams is done, so that the threads in each section are held straight and true. Many pattern instructions direct putting interfacings on to facings rather than on to the garment. An advantage of putting it on to the garment itself is that it often provides a stay for working bound buttonholes and it prevents garment edges from stretching while it is being made. So, on the whole it is preferable to attach interfacings to the garment sections.

NON-FUSIBLE TYPES
1. Place section to be interfaced flat with the W.S. up.
2. Lay interfacing on top, matching the grain if it is a woven type, and pin it quite flat over the surface. If one edge has to be placed to a fold line, pin this first.
3. Baste all over the surface without lifting or shifting the work.
4. Catch stitch any edges which go to a fold line to prevent it rolling in wear. There is, of course, no need to do this if it will be securely held in place later on with machine trimming or fastenings.

IRON-ON TYPES
1. Test the effect of the interfacing by ironing on a piece to a spare piece of the garment fabric. Use heat suitable to the fabric. If the result is satisfactory handle the work as given for non-fusible interlinings placing the adhesive side down on to the W.S. of the fabric. Pin in place, being very careful that the threads in the garment sections are kept absolutely straight or they will be ironed and set permanently out of the true.
2. Remove a few pins at a time and press the interlining carefully on to the fabric.
   Warning. Do not press interfacing over tacking, e.g. tailors' tackings, because it will be difficult to pull them out.
3. On edges of collars and cuffs the turning allowance on the interlining can be cut off before it is ironed on so that there is less bulk at the edges. On corners the interlining can be cut off just below the point for the same reason. Diagram 125 (iii).

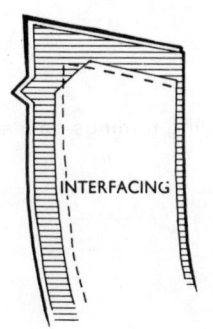

(iii). Interfacing with corner cut and turning trimmed

Stitching interfacing in place
Once interfacings are basted or ironed in place the garment is put together and made up in the usual way, treating the interlined section as though it is one piece of material. When the seams have been made, special treatment in trimming the turnings is necessary to give flat, thin edges, especially on thicker dressmaking fabrics such as woollens and heavy rayons.

Trimming and grading seams. Diagram 126.
1. After machining, press the stitching to flatten it in the usual way.
2. Trim the turnings on the interfacing almost down to the machining.
3. Trim one turning on the garment to 6 mm and the second to 1 cm then clip the curves and corners.

The interfacing is now completed and the making up of the garment is carried out according to instructions. It is as well to leave in the basting which holds the interlinings in place until the garment is ready for its final press so that it cannot shift out of position during the work.

Interfacing should not be confused with *underlining*, where whole sections are lined before the garment is assembled. The purpose of underlining is to give body to a thin, loosely woven or transparent fabric, e.g. lace underlined with taffeta. Pattern pieces are cut out twice, once in

the main fabric and one in the underlining fabric. The pieces are basted together on the central and seam lines; ironed all over the surface on the W.S. and then made up as one fabric.

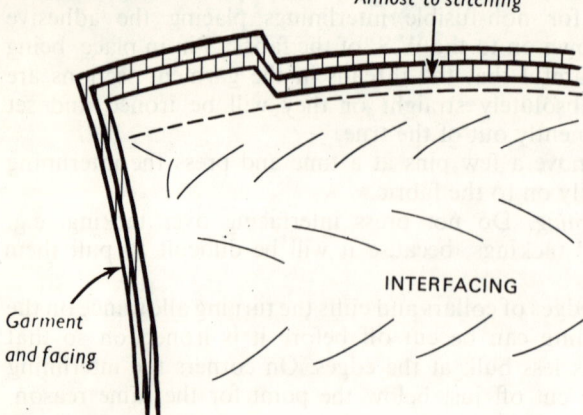

126. Grading turnings on a seam

Rouleau

Rouleau is the name given to narrow tubes of fabric used for trimming edges, for insertions, for ties and for making loops on openings. Fabrics used should be thin and not fray much such as fine dress woollens. Materials with a slippery surface are the easiest to handle, e.g. satin, nylon, tricot and soft taffeta.

Rouleau loops have a very smart appearance and are used mainly on outer clothes. They are made and fixed in the seam in the opening during its construction.

1. MAKE ROULEAU FOR THE LOOPS
Cut crossway strips 2.5 cm wide.
   Fold strip in half lengthwise with R.S. inside. Pin and tack edges together.
   Machine 0.5 cm away from fold using a large stitch and stretching the work through the machine. This allows the rouleau to be pliable and prevents the thread snapping later. If finer rouleau is required, stitch nearer the fold. It helps in turning the rouleau through if the depth of the stitching is widened at one end. Diagram 127.
   Trim turnings to 3 mm and turn rouleau right side out as given for straps, p. 197. It helps to get this process started if the end is trimmed to a point and the easing through is done with a light touch.

SPECIAL DRESSMAKING TECHNIQUES 213

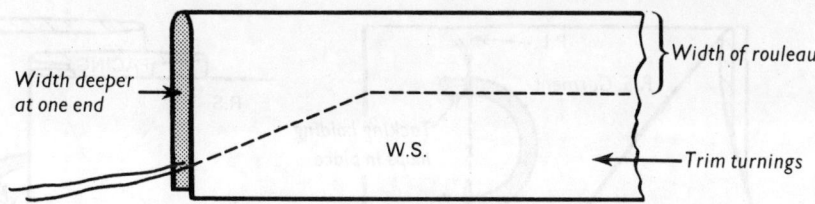

127. Crossway strip folded and stitched for a rouleau

2. FORM LOOPS WITH THE ROULEAU

The loops are fixed to the garment before the facing is attached and project beyond the edge when the opening is completed.

Plan size of loops by testing a length of rouleau pinned on to a piece of material and slipping it over a button. Estimate size as for worked loops but allow extra for domed buttons.

Mark the size of the loops on a piece of squared pattern paper and pin loops in place. Machine through loops and paper (diagram 128 (i)), and tear paper away. The loops are now ready to fix to the opening.

3. FIX LOOPS TO THE GARMENT

Place loops on the R.S. of the main part of the garment with cut edges towards the turning allowance and the line of machining on the P.L. Tack firmly on the P.L. and then complete the opening with a facing in the usual way. Diagrams 128 (ii), (iii).

To trim an edge with rouleau, see p. 154.

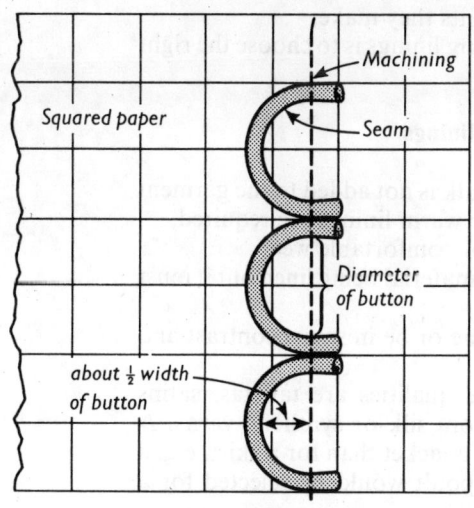

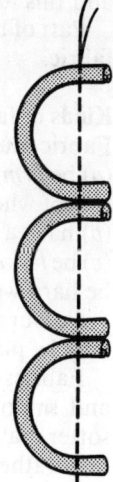

). An easy method of
g the loops accurately

214 CONSTRUCTING CLOTHES

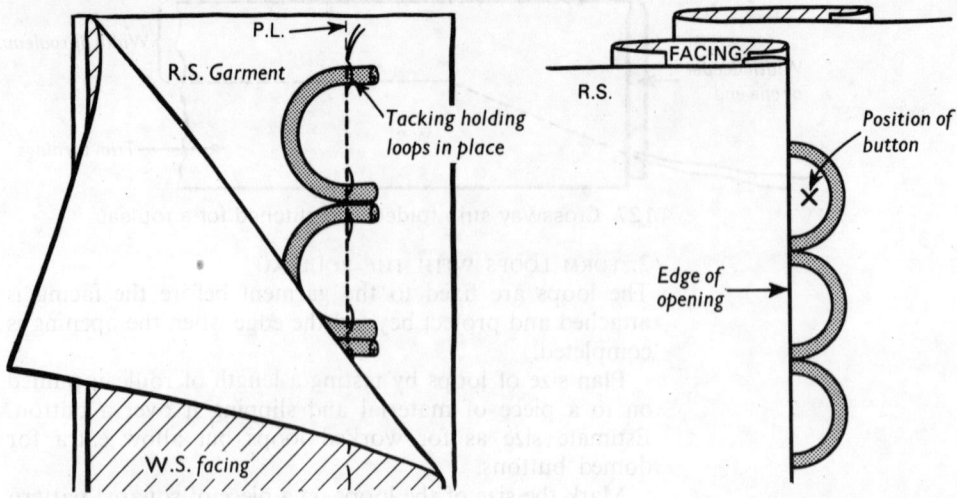

128 (ii). Loops tacked to edge of opening and facing being placed on top

128 (iii). Rouleau loops completed in a fa

Linings

To put a lining in clothing adds *warmth* and *comfort* in wear, improves the *hang*, helps in keeping *shape* and gives *longer life*. Linings also add to the cost but are always well worth while. Because many quite inexpensive dresses, skirts and jackets sold now are lined, many home dressmakers like to add this luxury to the garments they make.

Part of the success of making linings is to choose the right fabric.

Kinds of fabric to choose for linings
Fabric must
(*a*) be *firm* but *thin*, so that bulk is not added to the garment except when quilted or other warm linings are required.
(*b*) have a *slippery* surface for comfortable wear.
(*c*) be *less expensive* than the material being lined but it must be hard wearing.

Colours should match, tone or be in smart contrast and may be plain or printed.

Fabrics which have these qualities are taffetas, satins and smooth crepes made from silk or synthetic yarns. A softer material is needed for a jacket than for a skirt, e.g. a firm rather hard taffeta or poult would be selected for a skirt, while a softer paper taffeta or satin might be chosen for the coat.

A good lining fits smoothly but with slight fullness, not dropping below hem edges (too slack a lining) or drawing the hems upwards (too tight). A dressmaker's method of lining varies according to the style of the garments but details of work are always given in pattern instruction sheets. There are, however, certain things which can be done at each stage of work, whatever the style, to ensure success. These helps to success are given below:

Cutting out and making linings

Linings should always be cut *larger* than the garment because lining materials being firmly woven do not, as a rule, 'give' as much as the fabric of the garment being lined. If a special pattern is provided for the lining this extra size will have been allowed. If not, use the paper pattern of the garment and allow for a 1.5 cm pleat at the centre back of jackets and coats, Diagram 129 (i) and allow an extra 3 mm on the side seams of skirts and tops.

1. Place the C.B. of the pattern 1.5 cm away from the fold.
2. Place and cut out all pattern pieces. Allow plenty of turning allowance, 2 to 3 cm if possible at fronts, neck and hem edges of sleeves and jackets and side seams of skirts.
3. Mark pattern lines—if carbon paper is used be sure to have the markings on the W.S.
4. Tack along the C.B. pleat line and press the pleat to one side. Hold it in place with two short lines of machining or backstitching *across* the pleat, one at yoke and one at waist level. Diagram 129 (ii).
5. Tack, stitch and press darts.
6. Join up the pieces as the pattern instructions direct for the style. There is no need to neaten seam edges except on skirt linings unless the material frays much.

Points on inserting linings

Jackets and coats can be finished and pressed before the lining is put in, but skirts are often lined before the waist finish is applied and dresses before the neck and armhole finishes are made.

1. When pinning in the lining keep the grain of lining and garment level both weft and warp ways.
2. Allow slight ease in both the length and the width as the lining is pinned. Diagram 129 (iv).
3. Where practicable, and if the style is such that it is

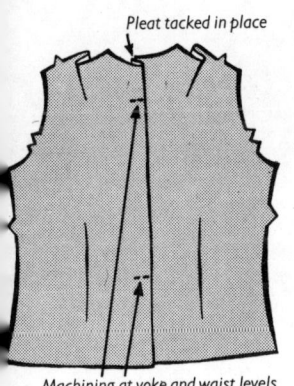

(i). Back pattern placed to allow at centre back

(ii). Back lining prepared for to front units

possible, loosely baste some of the seams of the lining and garment together to hold the lining in place. Diagram 129 (iii).
4. Make sure that linings form a good line down the fronts and round the neck of jackets.
5. When linings hang free at the hem, work a french bar tack to anchor the seam turnings of lining and garment a few inches above the hem. Diagram 130 (iv).
6. Use slip stitching to hold the lining in place with small neat stitches, being careful that they do not come through to the R.S.

To line a jacket or coat

Cut out lining and make the C.B. pleat. Diagrams 129 (i), (ii). Make darts, underarm and shoulder seams. Make up both sleeves. Press lining.

BACK AND FRONTS
1. Place jacket with back flat on table with right side down. Place C.B. pleat of lining on C.B. of jacket and pin down the centre, easing it in the lengthwise direction.
2. Spread lining towards seams and armhole, pinning over the surface and easing it both ways. Match darts and seams in lining and jacket.
3. Fold back fronts and baste side seams, turnings together. Diagram 129 (iii).
4. Arrange front lining sections over the jacket, easing and pinning over the surface. Tack lining to jacket all round about 5 cm from edges. Baste armhole turnings together.
5. Turn in edges of lining along fronts, back of neck (turnings need snipping on curves) and above the hem. Slip stitch in place. Diagram 129 (v).

SLEEVES
6. Select correct sleeve lining and slip it over jacket sleeve with wrong sides facing and darts or shaping placed correctly to match.
7. Tack lining to sleeve 5 cm below armhole and 5 cm above wrist. Remember to ease lining through the length. Diagram 129 (v).
8. Turn under cuff edge of lining about 2 cm to 3 cm from edge and slip stitch in place.
9. Turn in sleeve head round armhole, ease across crown and hem firmly in place.

SPECIAL DRESSMAKING TECHNIQUES 217

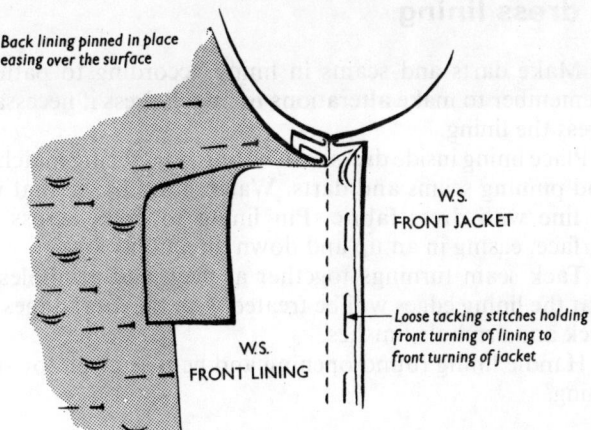

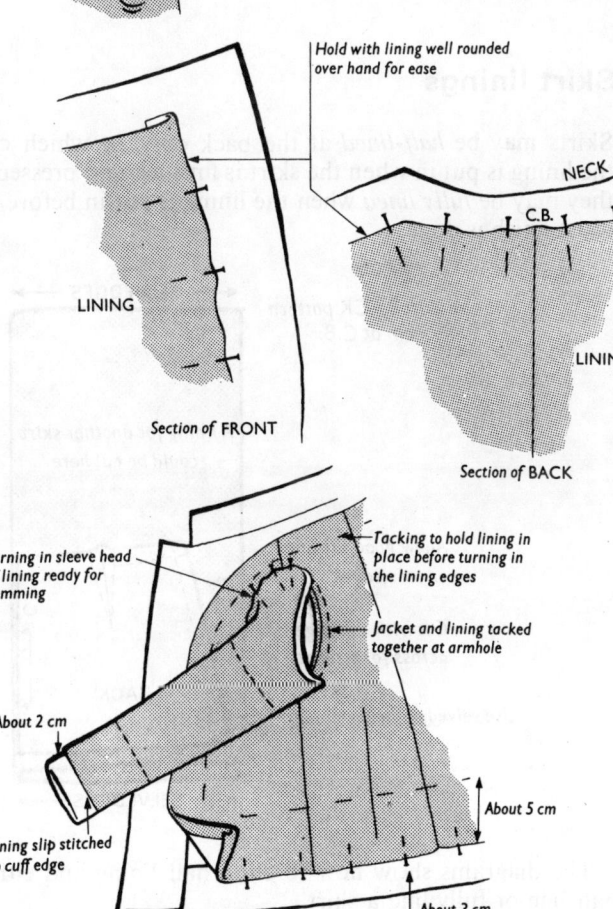

(iii). Method of tacking seam of jacket and lining together

(iv). Examples of ease in length and width

(v). Lining being fixed in place

A dress lining

1. Make darts and seams in lining according to pattern. Remember to make alterations to match dress if necessary. Press the lining.
2. Place lining inside dress with wrong sides facing matching and pinning seams and darts. Watch grain to see that it is in line with dress fabric. Pin lining to dress across the surface, easing in an up and down direction.
3. Tack seam turnings together at neck and armholes so that the lining edges will be treated with the dress edges for neck and armhole finishes.
4. Handle lining round opening and hem as given for skirt linings.

Skirt linings

Skirts may be *half-lined* at the back only, in which case the lining is put in when the skirt is finished and pressed or they may be *fully lined* when the lining is put in before the waist finish is done.

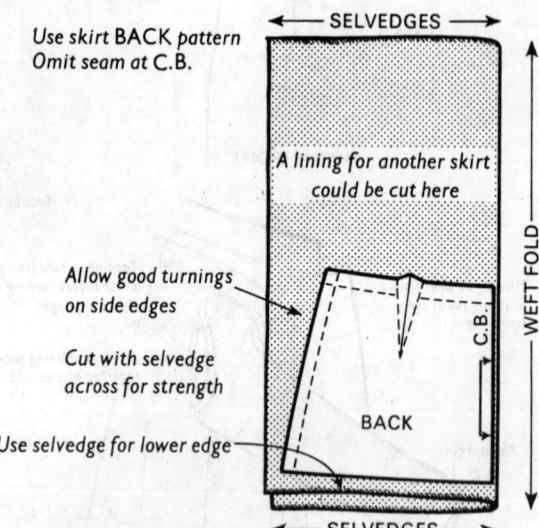

130 (i). Lay of pattern for H LINING the back of a skirt. Lining 2 skirts can be cut from approxim 60 cm.

The diagrams show how to cut a half lining and either half line or fully line a skirt.

SPECIAL DRESSMAKING TECHNIQUES

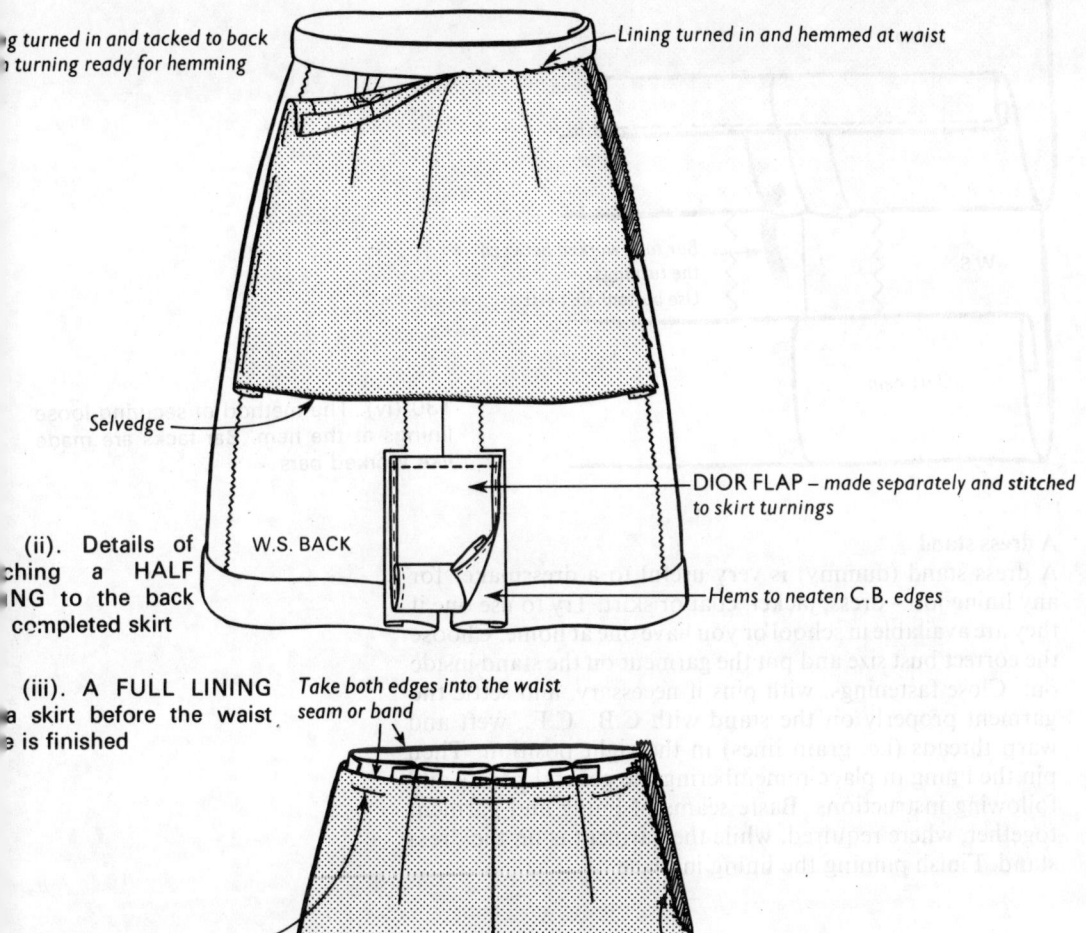

(ii). Details of attaching a HALF LINING to the back of completed skirt

(iii). A FULL LINING in a skirt before the waist line is finished

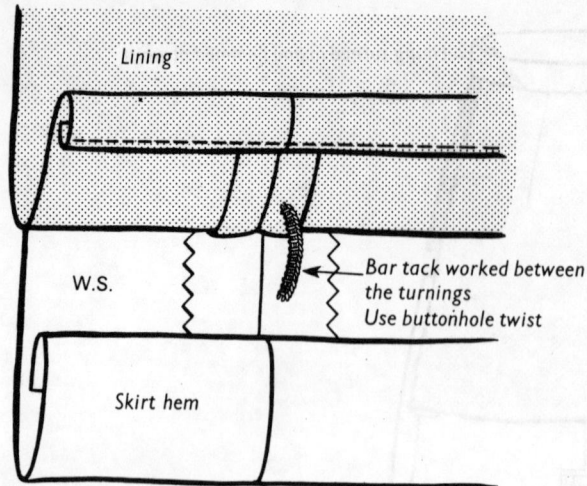

130 (iv). The method of securing loose linings at the hem. Bar tacks are made like worked bars

A dress stand

A dress stand (dummy) is very useful to a dressmaker for any lining job – dress, jacket, coat or skirt. Try to use one if they are available in school or you have one at home. Choose the correct bust size and put the garment on the stand inside out. Close fastenings, with pins if necessary, and settle the garment properly on the stand with C.B., C.F., weft and warp threads (i.e. grain lines) in the right position. Then pin the lining in place remembering the general points and following instructions. Baste seams of lining and garment together, where required, while the garment is on the dress stand. Finish pinning the lining in place.

19 Trousers

Trousers, pants, slacks—whatever the popular name—have taken fashion by storm and are here to stay as a basic item of womens' wardrobes. They have been proved comfortable, practical and warm; can be worn for work and sport as well as for elegant occasions, and can be made in an infinite variety of fabrics from denims to lace. Styles change each season: straight legs, tapered legs, flared legs, wide legs, tubular legs, waist pants, hip huggers, plain styles, styles with decorations of all kinds. Fortunately the basic principles of cut and fit remain for all types and that is the important thing for a home dressmaker to learn about.

Choice of style and fabric

Style
Trousers can be becoming to most figures if carefully chosen and worn with the right tops. Obviously tall slim figures have a great advantage but plump figures can be camouflaged with straight hanging trousers which do not cling to the thighs and by avoiding tight-fitting styles. Tunics and tops which just cover the seat are best for plump figures. Short figures should beware of turn-ups, which shorten the apparent length of leg, and wide legs which widen and shorten the figure. Lengths vary with fashion and purpose—to the instep, just off the ground, above or below the knee or very short.

Fabrics
Trousers are rather more tricky to make than skirts because of the legs and the shaped seams from C.B. to C.F. so choose an easy-to-work fabric, such as jersey in a plain colour or a small all-over design, for a first attempt. Stripes, plaids and checks are more difficult to make up and fit. Generally, fairly substantial fabrics wear and hang well, so the choice for pants is very wide—denims, cords, velveteen, polyester and cotton or wool, woollens, worsteds, Crimplene and many others.

Trousers. Pattern and alteration

Buy patterns by waist measure unless hips are large in proportion, when it is better to go by the hip measure and reduce the pattern at the waist. The following body measures are required to check the pattern.

MEASURES	ADDITION FOR EASE (cm)
Waist } Take as for skirts	2–4
Hips	5
Side length from waist to ankle (or length required)	
Thigh Round widest part of leg. Diagram 131 (i)	6
Crotch depth Take in sitting position from side waist to chair seat. Note length from waist to this level. Diagram 131 (ii).	

Measure the pattern, compare with body measures plus ease and decide alterations to be made.

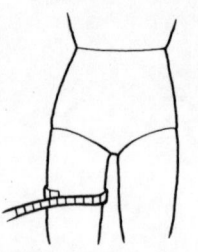

131 (i). Thigh measure

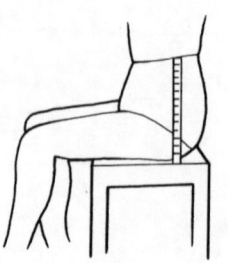

131 (ii). Crotch depth

Alterations to pattern
The general principles of pattern alteration apply: lengthening with insertions, shortening with tucks and adding or reducing by small amounts at seam edges. Also the position of alterations applies, see pp. 38, 39.

WAIST AND HIPS. Alter first at side seam as for skirts and if necessary at C.B. and C.F. seam and in darts. Take in or let out equal amounts on each seam edge.

CROTCH DEPTH
The comfort of trousers depends largely on this measure so check carefully from side waist to fork level. Shorten or lengthen on line indicated on pattern.

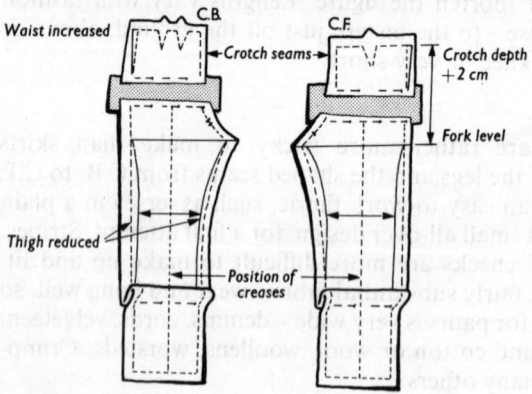

132. Some pattern alterations: crotch depth lengthened, leg shortened, waist increased at side seams, leg reduced at thigh

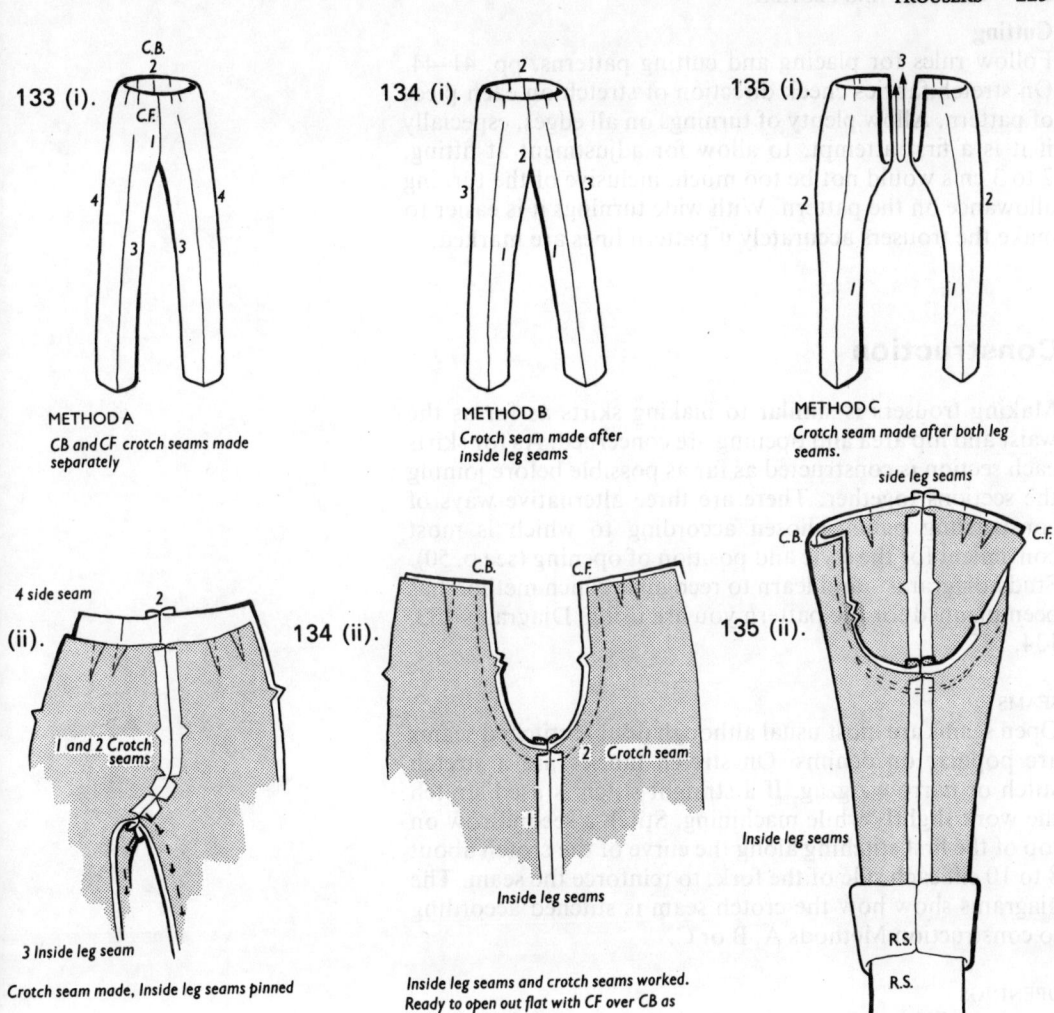

133, 134, 135. Ways of constructing trousers. Details of working crotch seams for alternative methods of construction

THIGH

Measure across the two leg pattern pieces at the distance from waist noted in measurement list. Alter width equally on side and inner leg seams and taper lines towards fork and ankle, e.g. if the thigh width needs to be 2 cm smaller, reduce by 0.5 cm at four seam edges, Diagram 132.

Cutting

Follow rules for placing and cutting patterns, pp. 41–44. On stretch fabrics check direction of stretch on each piece of pattern. Allow plenty of turnings on all edges, especially if it is a first attempt, to allow for adjustment at fitting. 2 to 3 cms would not be too much, inclusive of the turning allowance on the pattern. With wide turnings it is easier to make the trousers accurately if pattern lines are marked.

Construction

Making trousers is similar to making skirts as far as the waist and hip area and opening are concerned. As for skirts each section is constructed as far as possible before joining the sections together. There are three alternative ways of constructing pants, chosen according to which is most convenient for the style and position of opening (see p. 50). Study diagrams—and learn to recognize which method has been planned for the pattern you are using. Diagrams 133, 134, 135.

SEAMS

Open seams are most usual although double stitched seams are popular on denims. On stretch fabrics use a stretch stitch or narrow zigzag. If a straight stitch is used stretch the work slightly while machining. Stitch a second row on top of the first stitching along the curve of the crotch about 8 to 10 cm each side of the fork, to reinforce the seam. The diagrams show how the crotch seam is stitched according to construction Methods A, B or C.

OPENINGS

Position will be at C.F., C.B. or in the left side seam. Length, 18 to 23 cm according to size for waist pants. Hipster styles require a shorter opening. Zips are the usual choice—the semi-concealed method for front and back openings; the concealed method for central and side openings (see pp. 126–127) and the invisible method for side openings. (Diagrams 136 (i)–(v).

INVISIBLE ZIP e.g. Alcozip, Optilon, Lightning.

This type of zip is constructed so that the teeth are upright instead of flat. When properly inserted the zip is not visible on the R.S. and the opening looks like a seam.

TROUSERS 225

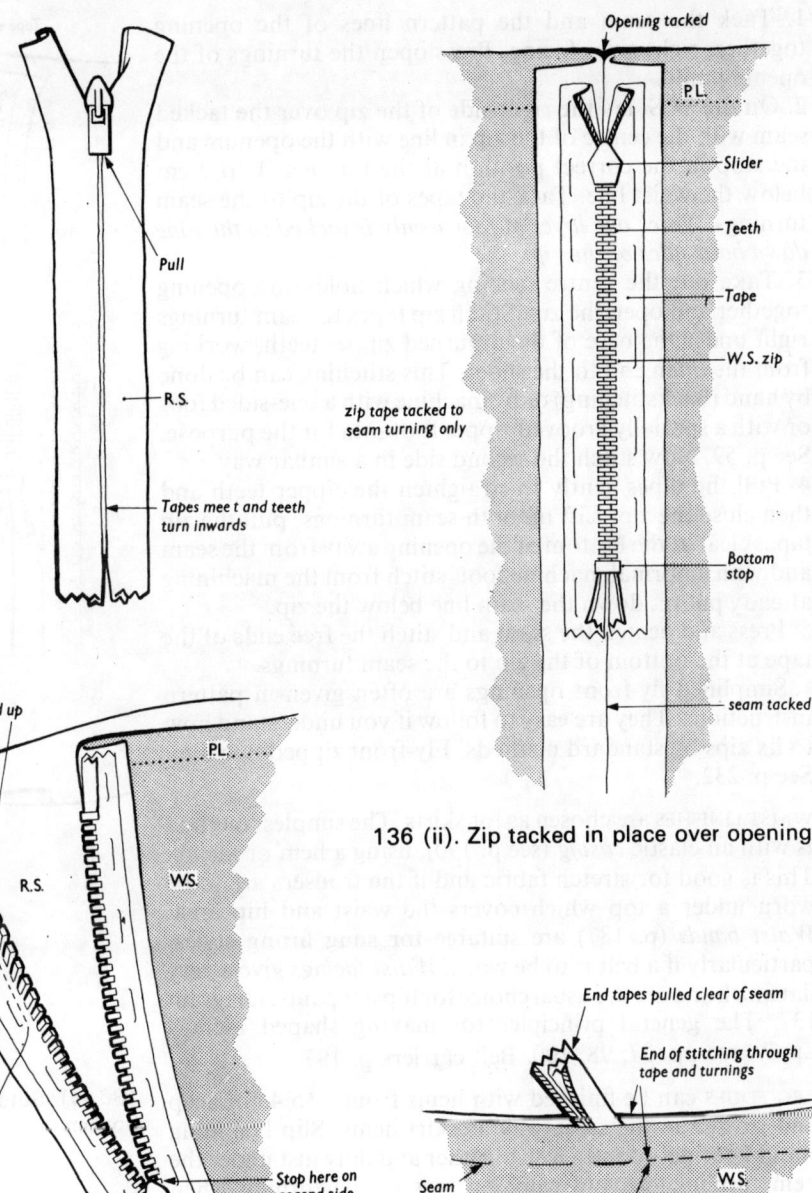

(i). Invisible zipper

136 (ii). Zip tacked in place over opening

(iii). Zip being stitched on first side

136 (iv). Treatment at base of zip

1. Tack the seam and the pattern lines of the opening together, right sides facing. Press open the turnings of the opening only.
2. On the W.S. lay the right side of the zip over the tacked seam with the centre of the zip in line with the opening and the stop in the correct position at the top, e.g. 1 to 2 cm below the waist line. Tack the tapes of the zip to the seam turnings. *Note: one layer of fabric only is tacked to the tape down both sides of the zip.*
3. Take out the centre tacking which holds the opening together and open the zip. Stitch zip tapes to seam turnings right under the base of the upturned zipper teeth, working from the open end to the slider. This stitching can be done by hand (backstitching) or by machine with a one-sided foot or with a specially grooved zipper foot sold for the purpose. See p. 59. Now stitch the second side in a similar way.
4. Pull the tapes gently to straighten the zipper teeth and then close the zip. Lift up both seam turnings, pull the zip tapes clear at the bottom of the opening away from the seam and with a normal machine foot, stitch from the machining already put in, down the seam line below the zip.
5. Press and neaten the seam and stitch the free ends of the tape at the bottom of the zip to the seam turnings.

Simplified fly-front openings are often given in pattern instructions. They are easy to follow if you understand how to fix zips by standard methods. Fly-front zipped opening. See p. 232.

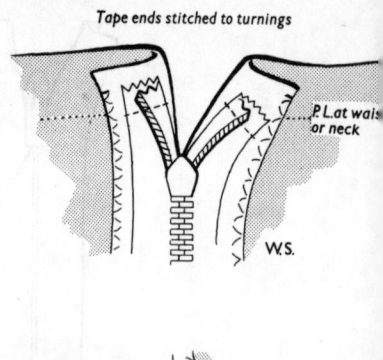
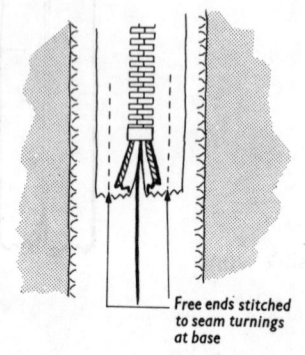
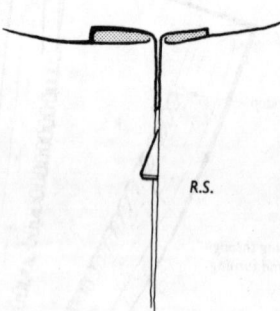

136 (v). Stitching tapes at top and bottom

WAIST FINISHES are chosen as for skirts. The simplest method is with an elastic *casing* (see p. 190), using a hem or facing. This is good for stretch fabric and if the trousers are to be worn under a top which covers the waist and hip area. *Waist bands* (p. 187) are suitable for snug fitting styles, particularly if a belt is to be worn. *Waist facings* give a very flat finish and are the usual choice for hipster pants. Diagram 137. The general principles for making shaped facings apply, see pp. 97, 98, 100. Belt carriers p. 197.

LEG EDGES can be finished with hems from 2 to 4 cm deep and treated in the same way as skirt hems. Slip hemming should be finely done, close together and only just under the hem turning to avoid catching toes in the turning when trousers are put on. Jeans are often made with a narrow hem (about 1.5 cm) and machined in place.

Turn-ups are formed from deep hems and extra length must be allowed to make them. Diagram 138. Bar tacks hold the turn-ups in place on the seams (p. 220).

TROUSERS 227

CREASES. These may be pressed in before making darts or tucks at waist. Fold each leg piece in half with W.S. facing, tack and press in the crease. The front creases are put in almost to the waist line and the back to about fork level. If preferred the creases can be put in when the trousers are finished, in the way mens trousers are pressed. On fabrics which resist pressing the front creases can be edge stitched when the trousers are finished. Fitting trousers see p. 260.

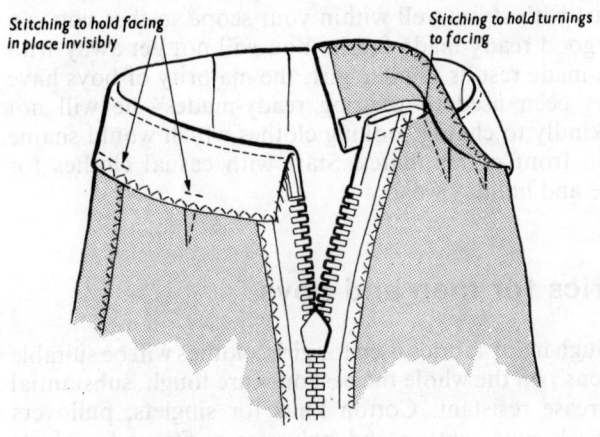

137. Shaped facing on to wrong side at waist

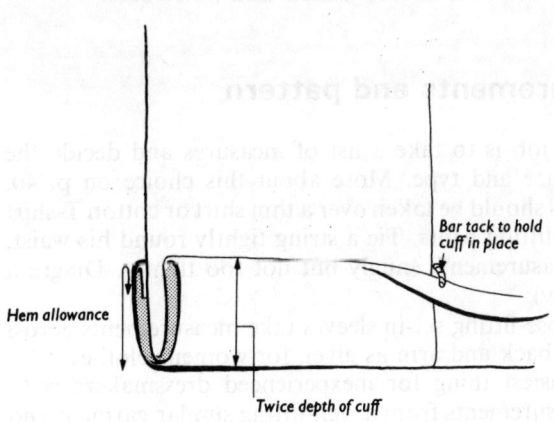

138. Section to show construction of turn-ups

20 Clothes for him

Now that unisex clothes are popular and men's clothing simple in design, girls can make things for boy friends and relatives. It is wise to let the man help choose the fabric and to start with styles well within your scope so that you can get a good ready-made finish. You will not get away with home-made results. Unlike girls the majority of boys have always been used to wearing ready-mades—he will not take kindly to clumsy looking clothes which would shame him in front of his mates. Start with casual clothes for leisure and holiday wear.

Fabrics for men and boys

Although many fabrics used for girls' clothes will be suitable for mens', on the whole the best ones are tough, substantial and crease resistant. Cotton knits for singlets, pullovers and track suits; cotton and polyester mixtures for shirts and shorts; denims and corduroys for trousers; towelling or Viyella for wraps, are all good fabrics to start with. Skilled workers will use more difficult fabrics, e.g. quilted nylon or velvet for leisure jackets and waistcoats.

Measurements and pattern

The first job is to take a list of measures and decide the pattern size and type. More about this choice on p. 40. Measures should be taken over a thin shirt or cotton T-shirt and well-fitting pants. Tie a string tightly round his waist. Take measurements snugly but not too tightly. Diagram 139 (i), (iv).

For close-fitting set-in sleeves take measurements across width of back and arm as given for womens clothes.

The easiest thing for inexperienced dressmakers is to take measurements from a well-fitting similar garment and adjust the pattern to them. Remember that these measures will include ease.

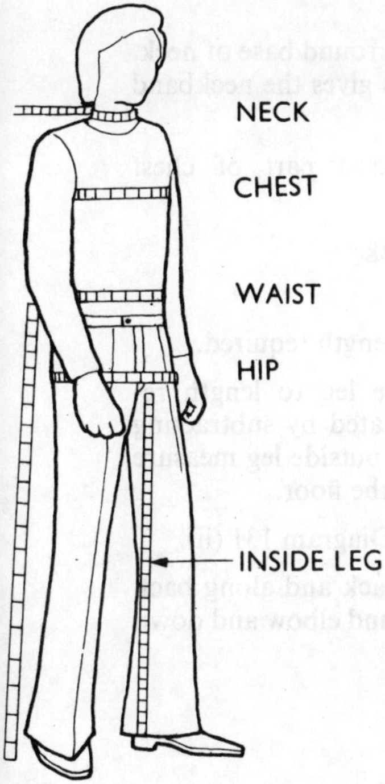

CONSTRUCTING CLOTHES 229

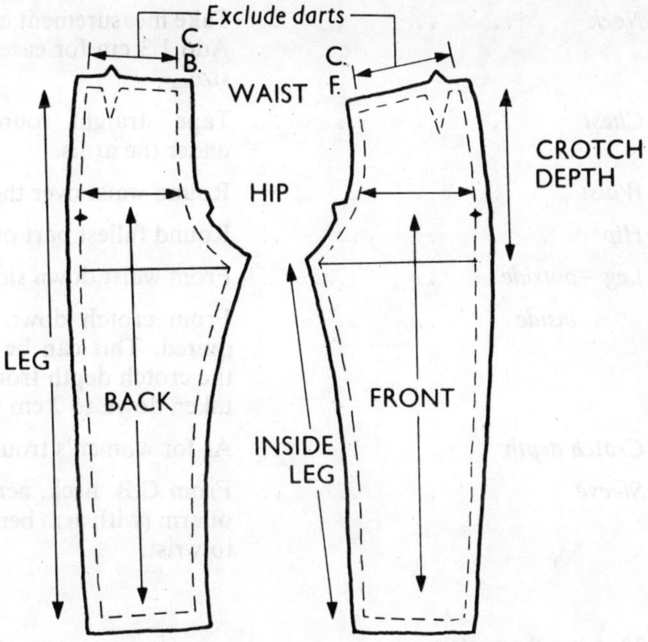

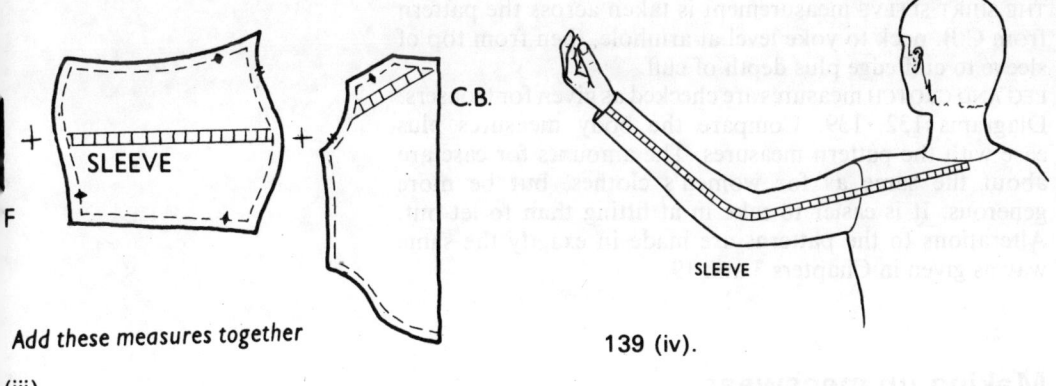

139. Taking body measurements and measuring the pattern

230 CONSTRUCTING CLOTHES

Measures required	How to take them
Neck	Take measurement closely round base of neck. Add 1.3 cm for ease. This gives the neckband size.
Chest	Tape straight round widest part of chest under the arms.
Waist	Round waist over the string.
Hip	Round fullest part of seat.
Leg—outside	From waist down side to length required.
inside	From crotch down inside leg to length required. This can be estimated by subtracting the crotch depth from the outside leg measure taken down to 2 cm from the floor.
Crotch depth	As for women's trousers, Diagram 131 (ii).
Sleeve	From C.B. neck, across back and along back of arm (with arm bent) round elbow and down to wrist.

Measure the pattern

Here again there is little difference about measuring patterns for either sex—the same rules apply as given on p. 36.

NECK, CHEST, WAIST AND HIP are measured across the back and front pattern pieces, exclusive of turnings, then doubled to give the total measurement.

THE SHIRT SLEEVE measurement is taken across the pattern from C.B. neck to yoke level at armhole, then from top of sleeve to cuff edge plus depth of cuff.

LEG AND CROTCH measures are checked as given for trousers. Diagrams 132, 139. Compare the body measures plus ease with the pattern measures. The amounts for ease are about the same as for women's clothes, but be more generous. It is easier to take in at fitting than to let out. Alterations to the patterns are made in exactly the same way as given in Chapters 3 and 19.

Making up menswear

Strength in construction is a special consideration in regard to seam widths, turnings and stitching. Double stitched

CLOTHES FOR HIM 231

seams for shirts are often preferable to open seams which would be appropriate for shirts and blouses for girls. A double row of machining at stress points which take most strain will help in prolonging wear, as suggested for crotch seams (p. 224) and at underarms. Stretch fabrics need elastic seams and stitching which will not split. This applies to all joins and seams, e.g. roll collars to neck-lines, arm-hole seams, as well as edges which need to stretch when the clothing is put on. Elasticity is simplified with the use of swing needle machines, using a zigzag or special stretch stitch, but it can be achieved with straight stitching (see p. 200).

Yokes are frequently used on clothing for strength as well as style. They are designed on both mens' and womens' wear on shoulders, across the upper part of tops and shirts and at the waist of skirts and trousers. A yoke is a close-fitting section, small in proportion to the rest of the garment and is cut with the strong warp threads across the yoke. This gives maximum strength in wear—the back yoke on a shirt takes the strain of the shoulders and arms. Yokes may be lined or unlined, p. 68. On thick fabrics the lining (often referred to as 'the facing' in pattern instructions) may be cut from thinner fabric. The following is a useful method for attaching a double (that is, a lined) yoke on a shirt.

140. Fixing a yoke

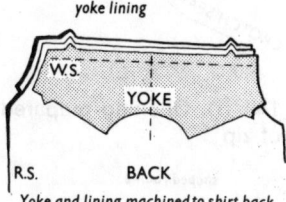

Yoke and lining machined to shirt back

140 (i).

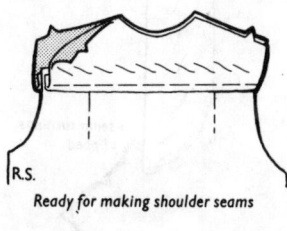

Ready for making shoulder seams

140 (ii).

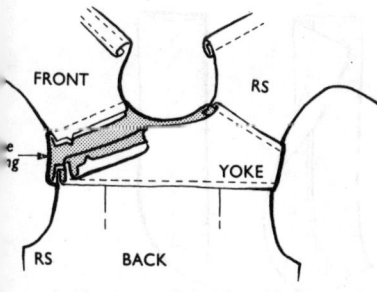

ering shoulder seams with the yoke and final top stitching

(iii).

Shirt yokes Diagram 140 (i), (ii), (iii).
1. Arrange any fullness in the main part such as pleats.
2. Pin R.S. of *yoke* over R.S. back shirt with edges level and centres matching. Tack them together on the P.L.
3. Pin R.S. of *yoke lining* to W.S. shirt back with edges level and tack in place. The shirt is now sandwiched between the two yoke sections, yoke and lining. Machine on the P.L. through the three thicknesses of fabric and trim the turnings to 6 mm.
4. Lift up both yoke and lining from the main part and tack them together just above the seam. Baste through the centre to hold the yoke and lining in place.
5. Now seam the shoulders of the *yoke lining* to the shirt front shoulders with plain seams (R.S. yoke lining to W.S. front shoulders). Trim and press turnings towards the yoke.
6. Place work flat on table with R.S. up. Fold turning allowance on *yoke* shoulder edges to W.S. and pin them over the turnings of the shoulder seams to cover the machining. Tack in place and top-stitch on the R.S. along the two shoulder seams and across the back. A second row can be stitched 0.5 cm away from the first.

Openings and fastenings

Openings on casual clothes have been simplified on menswear and are often similar to those used on girls' clothes. On trousers, however, a zipped fly-front opening will be needed. This is put in after the crotch seam is made and before the waist finish is attached. See p. 224.

Fly-front opening for trousers

There are special zips for these openings which are curved towards the base. These are not necessary for light weight fabrics but the zip chosen must be a strong type and a skirt weight.

The opening is not difficult to make if, before the attempt, the methods of making a shaped facing and putting in zips by the concealed method (Method C, p. 127) are clearly understood. The reason will be apparent in studying the construction of the opening.

Outline of construction

The upper edge has a shaped facing. The stitching holding it in place shows on the right side and this line is marked on the pattern. One zip tape is machined to the facing only and this stitching does not show on the right side. Diagram 141 (vii).

The under edge has the zip attached by the concealed method, and a fly-flap, shaped like the facing on the upper edge, is attached underneath the zip tape. One row of machining holds zip and fly-flap to the trousers. This stitching is covered by the upper edge when the opening is fastened and the zip is completely hidden. Diagram 141 (vii).

Directions for making a fly-front opening

1. PREPARE THE TROUSERS

Mark the stitching line on the upper edge of opening on the left-hand side for men and the right-hand side for women. The line will be about 3 cm away from the edge for adult sizes and curves to the centre front at the base of the opening.

Seam trouser fronts together from crotch to opening.

Fold and tack the under edge of the opening 3 mm outside the C.F. line in the turning allowance. (See Method C, p. 127) Diagram 141 (i).

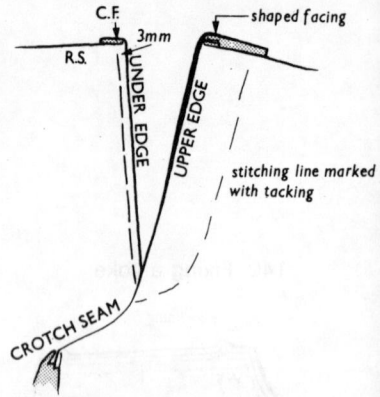

141 (i). Opening prepared for insertion of zip

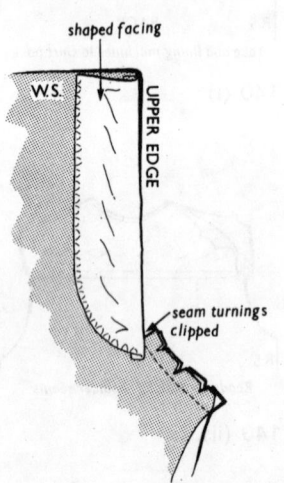

141 (ii). Upper edge on W.S.

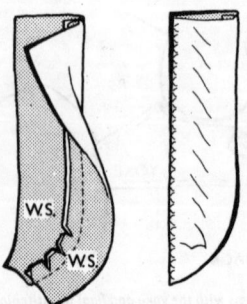

141 (iii). Making fly-flap

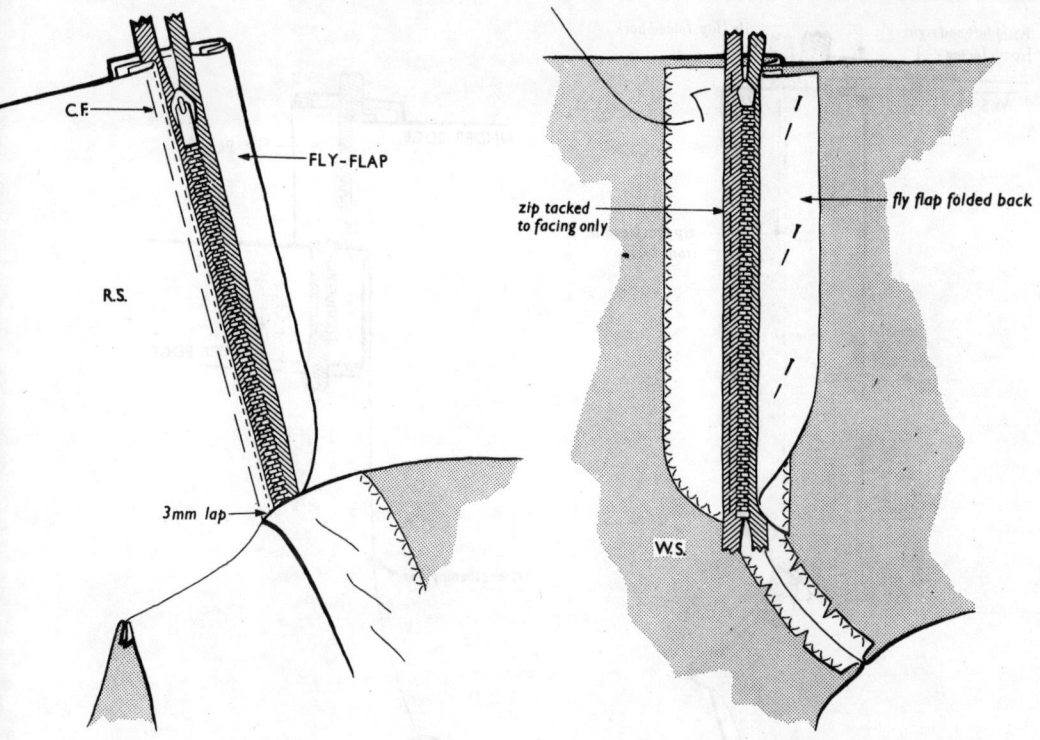

(iv). Zip and fly-flap machined in on under edge

141 (v). Zip tacked to upper edge

2. FACE UPPER EDGE

Make a shaped facing on to the wrong side of upper edge in the usual way (see p. 97). Be sure that the first stitching finishes in line with the centre front seam. Clip seam at base so that facing strip can be turned on to wrong side. Neaten free edge suitably and baste facing flat. Diagram 141 (ii).

3. MAKE A FLY-FLAP

Cut two pieces for the fly-flap from the shaped facing pattern.

Place pieces with right sides facing and machine the longer edges on the P.L. Trim, clip and turn so that right sides are outside. Baste layers together and neaten the cut edges. Diagram 141 (iii). Press each piece of work done so far.

4. FIX ZIP TO UNDER EDGE OF OPENING

Place the under edge on to right side of zip tape with the fold almost up to the teeth. See that top and bottom of zip are correctly placed and tack trousers to zip tape.

234 CONSTRUCTING CLOTHES

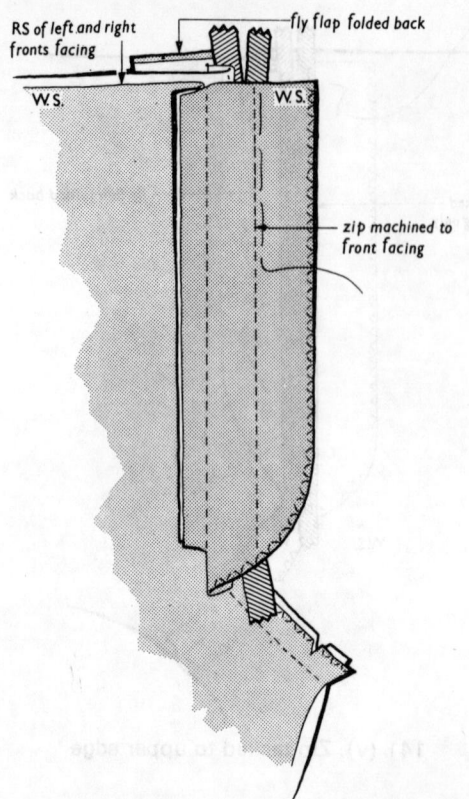

141 (vi). How to place work to machine zip to front facing

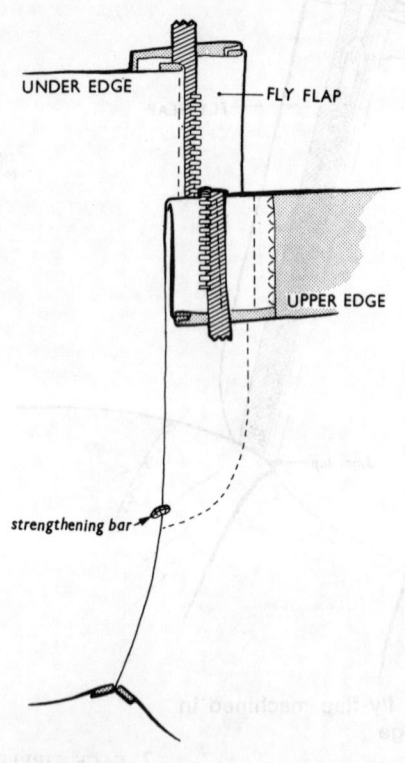

141 (vii). Completed fly opening on right side

Lap fly-flap behind the under edge and the zip so that it extends about 3 cm. Tack firmly through all layers—trousers, zip tape and fly-flap. Machine close to the fold (using a zipper foot) from top to bottom of the opening. Diagram 141 (iv).

5. FIX ZIP TO UPPER EDGE OF OPENING
Lay upper edge over the closed zip so that the edge is on the centre front and covers the machining. Tack firmly in place.
   Now work from the wrong side. Fold and pin the fly-flap away from zip to keep it out of the way. Diagram 141 (v).
   Remove basting tacks in the facing on upper edge.
   Pin free tape of zip to the facing and tack it carefully to this one layer of fabric.

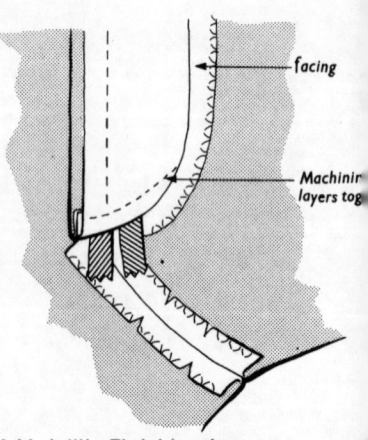

141 (viii). Finishing base on wrong

Now open out the facing and bring the two trouser fronts to one side with right sides facing, so that the zip can be machined to the single layer of fabric, Diagram 141 (vi). This stitching will not show on the right side of the trousers. Baste the facing back into position.

TO FINISH THE OPENING

Turn work to right side and machine through trousers and facing on the stitching line which was marked at the very beginning. Diagram 141 (vii).

Back-stitch or machine through all the free edges at the bottom of the opening on the wrong side and neaten cut edges. Diagram 141 (viii).

Strengthen opening with a worked bar across upper edge on R.S. just above the base of opening.

Special Notes

When trousers are made in thick fabrics the shaped facing and the backing to the fly-flap can be cut from strong lining fabric.

Sometimes it is more convenient to buy a longer zip than is required because variations in sizes and styles cause difficulty in buying the exact length needed. The surplus length of zip is taken into the seam at waist line when the band or facing is stitched on and trimmed off level with the turnings. It is vital that the zip is OPEN when the surplus is trimmed off with strong scissors, so that the SLIDE is not chopped off.

For some styles of women's trousers the pattern provides for a hem instead of a shaped facing on the upper edge (right-hand side for women). An extension "cut on" the C.F. allows for the hem.

Fastenings

Very strong fastenings are necessary for menswear. Heavy metal hooks, bars and snap fasteners can be bought with teeth to pierce through a band and stiffening. Press studs ready fixed on tapes only need machining in place. Other heavy weight fasteners and buttons must be sewn with strong button or heavy duty thread.

Machine made buttonholes always give a professional look. These can be made on fully automatic machines by simply selecting the controls; by moving a control at each stage of the work on semi-automatic machines or with manual control on zigzag models. It always helps in making a good and strong buttonhole if the area is interfaced with a strip of thin interfacing.

Buttonholes by machine (with manual control using a zigzag machine).
Two widths of stitch are used, a narrow one for the sides and a wider one for the bars, e.g. 2 and 4.
PREPARATION. Use a fine machine thread, e.g. 50 sylko. Attach a buttonhole foot on the machine, change the throat plate if necessary and select a zigzag stitch.

Set the stitch width to the narrow bight (2) and to a very short stitch. Test the stitch on double fabric for a good close stitch. Mark buttonhole as for worked ones. See p. 131.
FIRST SIDE. 1. Lower needle into mark at one end and stitch down the length of the mark towards the left. Leave needle down in the centre.
2. Raise foot, pivot work round so that the stitched side is now on the right. Lower foot and take one stitch towards the left.
FIRST BAR. 3. Raise needle, alter stitch width to the wider bight (4) and work 4–6 stitches across the buttonhole. To keep the bar narrow, hold the work steady so that it does not move under the foot.
SECOND SIDE. 4. With the needle up alter stitch back to narrow width and work the second side. Keep stitches just a thread away from those on the first side.
SECOND BAR. 5. Stop on the left hand side and make a second bar as 3 above. End off by hand on W.S.
FINISHING. 6. Press and cut very carefully between the stitches on W.S., from centre towards each end. See p. 61.

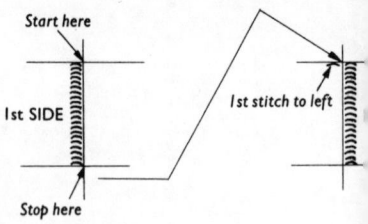

142. Buttonholes by machine manual control of swing needle

142 (i). Working on first side
142 (ii). Work turned ready to wo[rk]

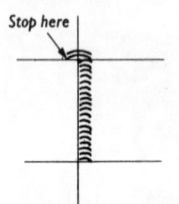

142 (iii). Working first bar rea[dy] second side

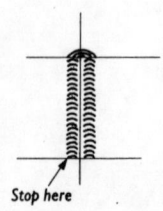

142 (iv). Working second side

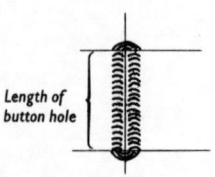

142 (v). Second bar

Pockets
Welt, patch and pockets in seams are the most usual. It is possible to buy ready-made pocket bags in very strong twill for trousers. These are useful for replacements, particularly when it would be cheaper than buying a length of specially strong fabric to make them.

Waist finishes. See Trousers p. 226.
Elastic casings are only suitable for beach and sportswear, and for juvenile clothing. Elasticized waistbands sold by the metre are useful, especially with knits. Zigzag stitching or stretch stitches are best for attaching them. See method for attaching elastic p. 303. Bands and facings need strong interfacings. Specially made band stiffening can be bought, usually of the iron-on variety. The width should equal the width of the finished band. Bands are always made with an extension on the left-hand front and fastened with a heavy hook and bar or a button and buttonhole. Facings are used

on trousers which are cut to finish below the waist. Belt carriers must be substantial and strongly stitched.

Adhesive bonding webs. Diagrams 143 (i)–(iii)

Another time saver which gives a slick finish is the use of bonding webs. Use them on pocket hems or facings and to fix motifs of your own design.

These nylon webs (e.g. Bondaweb) are a quick way of holding layers of fabric together instead of sewing—straight hems, facings, motifs—and for strengthening and repair work. The bonding web is sold in strips or pieces about 1 m square, adhering to a transfer paper. It can be washed and dry-cleaned. The usual method of applying is as follows:

1. Turn and press the hem and then open it.
2. Cut the paper to size required and place it with web-side down, *paper side up* on the garment. Iron with a cool iron, just as for transfers and leave to cool.
3. Peel off the transfer paper; re-fold the hem and press firmly with a damp cloth or use a steam iron. Leave for ten minutes and the hem will be bonded in place.

(i). Adhesive bonding web

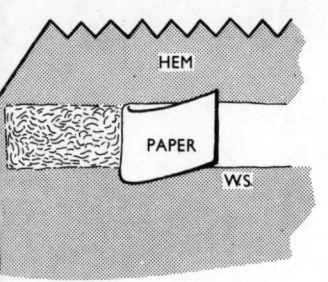

Wed bonded to one layer of fabric

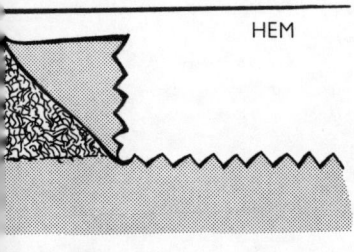

Hem bonded to web
(ii).

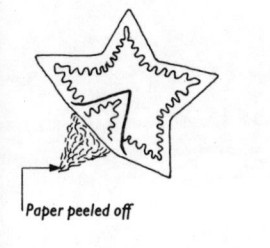

Paper peeled off

Motif bonded to web
(iii).

Fitting mens and boys clothes

To fit men is much easier than fitting women because there is less shaping to affect the hang. The general preparation of the garment and method of fitting is similar to womens but special note should be taken of the following:

1. Even if fashions are tight fitting do not fit too closely. Some fabrics shrink, so leave room for movement.
2. Note the fit at the neck: if too large the collar will not set well; if too tight it will be uncomfortable.
3. Be sure that the width across the back allows the arms to come forward without strain. See that there is plenty of room in a loosely fitting armhole.
4. Notice waist and hip fit of trousers. Check when the wearer is sitting down that there is enough length from crotch to waist at front and back. See p. 260.

21 Pattern design, cutting and fitting

A flair for pattern design and cutting is one which few people are fortunate enough to possess. However, it is not necessary to have such a gift in order to do some very useful, interesting and original work with patterns. While some may use their knowledge of pattern cutting to make complete patterns, the majority of people will confine it to the adaptation and alteration of commercial patterns. It is the simple things which make the difference between good and bad cut; e.g. a smoothly curved neckline; a pocket made just the correct size for the garment and the figure, and fixed in the right position; the right amount of fullness for the gathers in a skirt. The best way to improve judgment of this kind is to take special notice of the shape, design and details of good clothing, and to experiment with pattern work.

A block pattern

The foundation of pattern cutting is a block pattern. This is a plain pattern for a bodice, sleeve, skirt or knickers which can be used as a foundation shape. Alterations and adaptations are made to produce the final pattern. A block pattern may be specially made to individual measures, or a suitable trade paper pattern may be used instead. Directions for making block patterns to individual measures will be found in Chapter 22. but the method is given here for using a trade pattern as a block. It is rarely worth while for young people to make a personal block, because they grow so quickly that it soon becomes useless.

Directions for making a bodice and sleeve block from a trade pattern

Use the bodice and sleeve pattern from a dress in a very plain style, having a round neck, easy fitting bodice and plain long sleeve. There should be a dart on the shoulder or under the arm for all sizes of 82 cm bust and over. Select a style which has an inconspicuous opening at the neck such as a hem or faced slit opening. Adjust the pattern to fit the figure (Chapter 3). Pattern firms supply these basic patterns.

Cut off the turning allowances from all edges, and if the sleeve has a cuff, discard it and lengthen the sleeve to make the inside arm measurement correct. Outline the pattern on stiff paper or card and cut it out. Draw a line across the block back and front at underarm level; at the level where the measurement of the chest and back width is taken (Chapter 3, p. 35) and through the centre of the sleeve from crown to wrist. These lines will be a help in judging the position of style lines. Diagram 144. Bear in mind that there are no turning allowances on block patterns; that the pattern represents only half the garment and that the blocks must be outlined accurately on paper before starting to shape the pattern lines.

How to use a bodice block

To alter necklines
1. Outline the back and front bodice blocks.
2. Draw in the shape of the neck required on the front, considering the depth (the chest line will be a guide to this) and the width. If the neck is made too wide, the shoulder may become too narrow. When a satisfactory line has been drawn, alter the back neck. Obviously, the same amount must be taken off the back shoulder as the front, so that they will still fit together.

ROUND NECKLINES
Draw a good circular line rather straight from the shoulder and well curved at the front. Diagram 144.

SQUARE NECKLINES
Slant the side line slightly towards the centre front, otherwise the square will be a poor shape when the bodice is on the figure. Diagram 145 (i).

V-NECKLINES
Draw a straight line from the shoulder to where the point of the V is required. If liked, the line may be slightly curved out towards the centre, to improve the effect on the figure. Diagram 144.

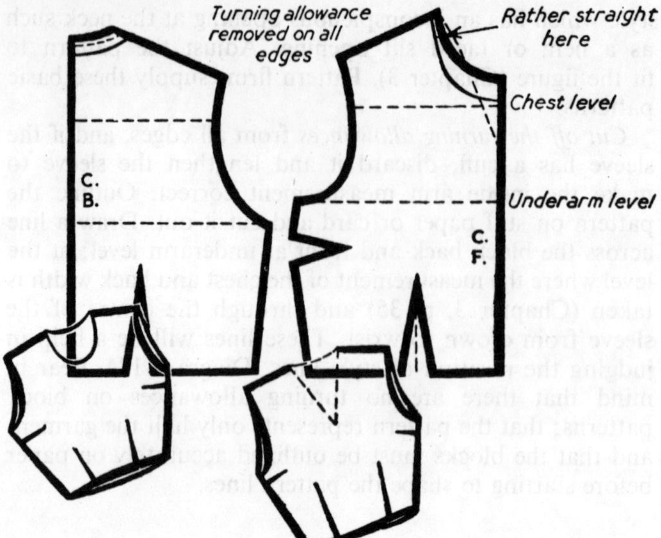

144. A bodice block made from a pattern and used to cut a round a V-neckline

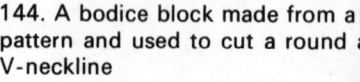

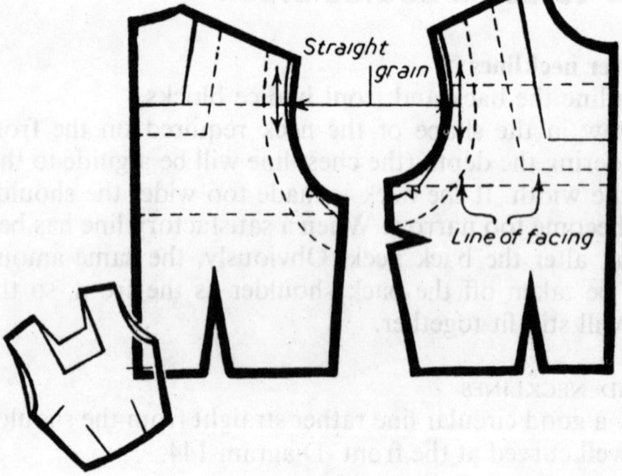

145 (i). Bodice pattern with low s neckline and lowered armholes. design is ready for tracing of patterns for the facings

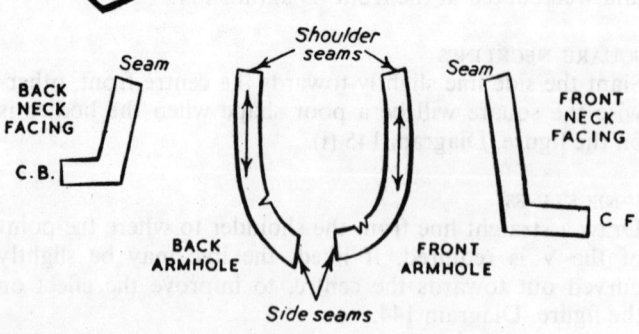

145 (ii). Patterns for facings tr from Diagram 145 (i) and cut out

To alter armholes

An armhole is never altered if a plain sleeve is to be set in, because it should already be a comfortable fit. The armhole may be slightly deepened for a sleeveless garment, or cut quite deep for pinafore dresses.

For slight alterations, lower the underarm 6 mm to 1 cm; make the shoulder a little narrower if required and re-draw the armhole curve. Keep the chest and back width as wide as possible, however deep the armhole, but keep the line a smooth curve. Diagram 145 (i).

TO CUT A SHAPED FACING
(a) Neck and armholes

Decide how wide the facing is to be and measure this distance from the neck or armhole lines, taking the measurement at right angles, and draw it on the pattern. Trace off the facings; mark in the straight grain; make notches to show where the pattern pieces join; label the facings and cut out. Diagrams 145 (i), (ii).

(b) Neck opening

Mark the depth of the opening on an outlined block. Draw in the lines for a facing so that the facing extends at least 4 cm below and all round the opening. If the opening is at the centre front and the neck has a turnover collar which is to be worn open, draw the facing so that it is 4 cm wide on the shoulders and tapers towards the bottom of the opening. Diagram 146. Label and cut out the back and front neck facings. Mark edges to be placed to a fold.

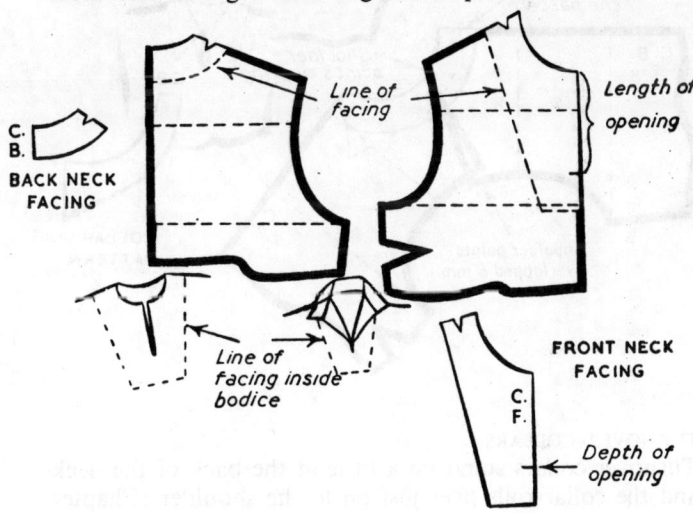

6. To cut a faced opening

To cut collars

THE PETER PAN TYPE

Any collar which lies flat on the shoulders falls into this class, whether the ends meet at the centre front or back, and whether the collar is narrow or wide, or like a bib. The shape of the ends may be rounded, pointed or designed in any shape suitable to the size of the collar. Diagram 147. As the neck of a collar will be the same shape as the bodice, it should be noted that the neckline of the bodice is satisfactory before beginning to make a collar pattern. See Chapter 14 for further information.

1. Outline the upper parts of the front and back bodice blocks, with the shoulders meeting at the neck and overlapping 6 mm at the armhole.
2. Decide how wide the collar is to be at the centre back, front and on the shoulder. Measure and mark these distances from the neck on the outline. Using these points as a guide in drawing curves, draw the shape of the collar, rounding or pointing it where the collar meets. If the collar is to be the same depth all round, measure at right angles to the neckline. Label the centre back; indicate which edge is to be placed to a fold in cutting out and cut out the pattern. Diagram 147.

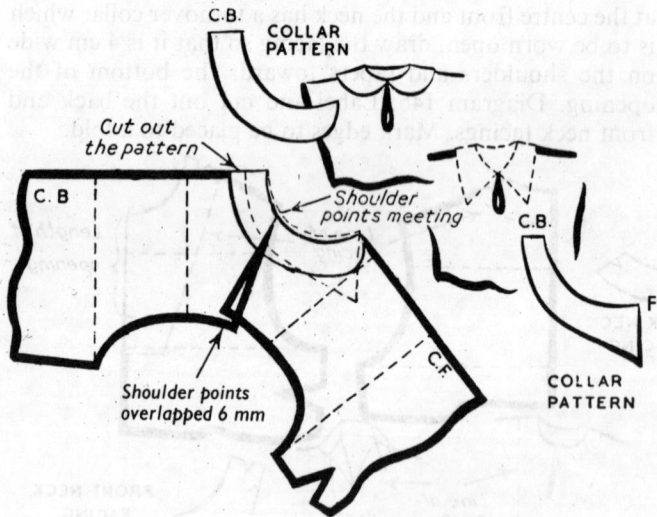

147. To cut patterns for Peter Pan collars

TURNOVER COLLARS

Turnover collars stand up a little at the back of the neck and the collar rolls over just on to the shoulder (Chapter

14). The part which stands up is called the stand and is wider on some collars than others. On dresses and blouses the collar and stand are made of one straight piece of material which is shaped at the ends. Diagram 148.

1. Measure the length of the neckline of the front and back bodice block. Decide how wide the collar is to be from the roll at the centre back and allow half as much again for the stand.

2. Draw a rectangle which is the measurement of the neck by the width of the collar plus stand, e.g. neck measure 36 cm; collar 4 cm deep; stand 2 cm. The rectangle will be 36 cm by 6 cm. Mark the centre of the rectangle, which will become the centre back of the collar. Mark the top line as a folded edge because the collar is cut double. Diagram 148. Cut out the collar pattern.

To make pointed ends, extend the two ends, e.g. 2.5 cm along the top, and join in a slanting line to the neck edge. If the collar is to be worn open, a shaped facing will be required for the faced opening. See p. 241.

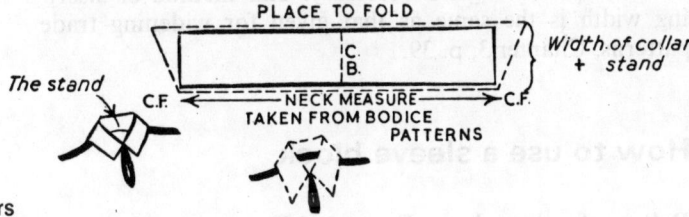

To cut patterns for turnover collars

To plan fullness in a pattern

DARTS

Darts are used to shape a garment to the figure, and are made from the width already in the garment. Therefore no extra material is needed. Darts set best if they are not more than 2.5 cm at the widest part. Several small darts set better than one large one. The distance of darts at the waist from the centre front should not be less than 6 cm or more than 10 cm according to the size of the person for whom the pattern is being made. Darts on each side of the centre back waist should be 2.5 cm closer together than the front ones. The length of darts above the waist should be such that the point of a dart is not above the level of an underarm dart. The length of darts below the waist should be planned so that the points do not reach below the level of the hip.

Method of making a dart at the waist of a bodice. Diagram 144.
1. Draw a straight line from the waist level, making it the length of the dart, and parallel with the centre front.
2. Measure half the width of the dart at each side of the straight line at the waist level, because this is the narrowest part of the figure and therefore the garment must be narrower at this level. Join these points in a straight line to the end of the first line. Further information in Chapter 7 and Chapter 22.

GATHERS

1. Mark with notches where the gathers are to be on the pattern. Diagram 149 (i). Between the notches, draw a line through the length of the pattern parallel with the centre front. Cut along this line and insert a strip of paper as wide as the extra fullness required for the gathers. Diagram 149 (ii). Amount of fullness for gathering. Chapter 7, p. 64.
2. Re-shape the edges if necessary. This method of inserting width is the same as that given for widening trade patterns. Chapter 3, p. 39.

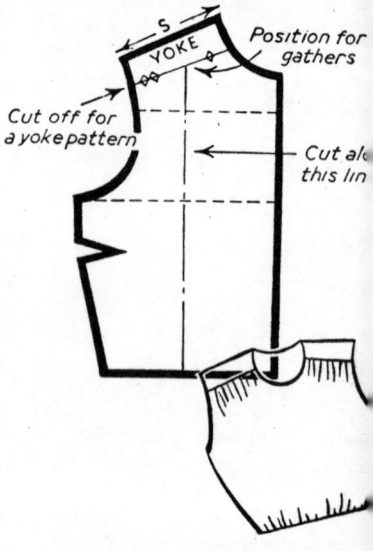

How to use a sleeve block

Pattern of a short sleeve. Diagram 150.
Outline a sleeve block and decide how long the sleeve is to be from the underarm. Measure this length from the armhole of the block along the seam line and draw a straight line across the sleeve. The width of a sleeve can be reduced to fit the arm by taking in the underarm seam and putting in tucks or pleats at the centre. The total width should, however, be at least 2.5 cm larger than the arm measure.

A short puffed sleeve
This type of sleeve is gathered at the shoulder and above the elbow, where it is set into a band or bind. It is a suitable sleeve for children's clothing.
  Use the pattern of a plain short sleeve and mark the position of the gathers with notches. Cut through the sleeve pattern on the central line. Insert a strip of paper equal in width to the extra amount required for gathers. Raise the crown, e.g. 1 to 2.5 cm, and re-shape the head to make it a well-rounded shape.

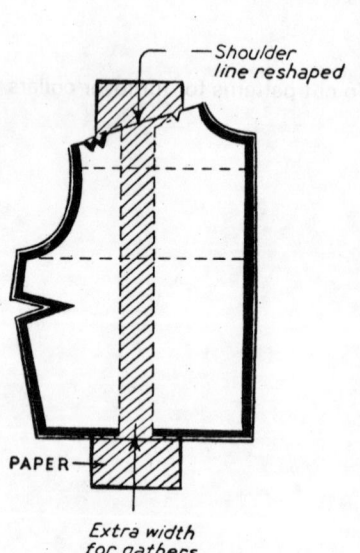

149 (i) and (ii). Method of introducing fullness into a pattern

A PATTERN OF A TURNED BACK CUFF

This type of cuff is used on short sleeves or fairly close-fitting long sleeves.

Plan the width of the cuff and draw it on the sleeve pattern, as it will be when turned back on the sleeve. Trace off the cuff, and if it is a style which is open in the middle, place it down on to another piece of paper with the side seams together and draw round the outline. Label the pattern 'Cut 2' and cut it out twice on double material, if a double cuff is required. Diagram 150.

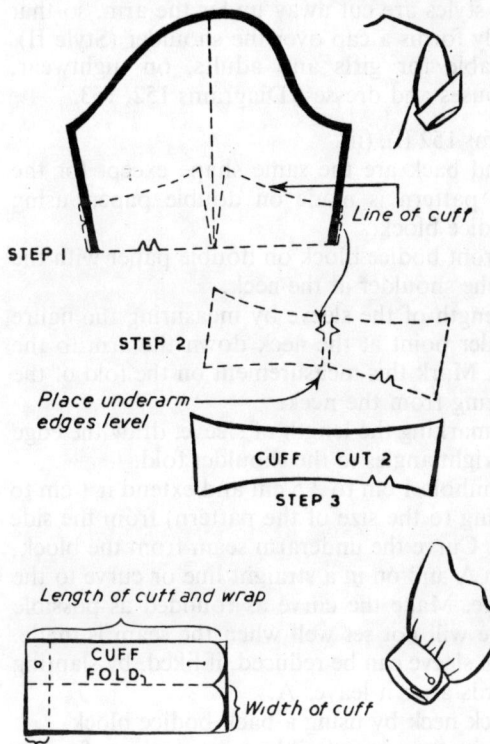

The pattern for a turned back cuff

The pattern for a straight cuff

PATTERN OF A STRAIGHT CUFF OF THE BAND TYPE

The sleeve is set into this type of cuff, which is made circular on a short sleeve, but has an opening on a long sleeve.

Decide the width the cuff is to be when finished and shorten the sleeve by that measure. Plan the length of the cuff allowing 2.5 cm for a wrap if it has an opening. Make a rectangle which is twice the width of the cuff by the length of the cuff plus wrap. If a round or pointed end is required, shape one end. Mark the position of the fastening, label the pattern and cut it out. Notice that the whole of the pattern of the cuff is made because it has to be placed on double material as two cuffs are required. Diagram 151.

Pattern of a magyar sleeve and bodice
A magyar sleeve is one which is cut in one with the bodice. A typical magyar style has a curved seam under the arm and no seam on the shoulder (Style I). The sleeve may be long or short, and is popular on children's and babies' clothing. Some styles are cut away under the arm, so that the sleeve merely forms a cap over the shoulder (Style II). Styles are suitable for girls and adults, on nightwear, housecoats, blouses and dresses. Diagrams 152, 153.

Style I. Diagrams 152 (i), (ii).
As the front and back are the same shape except for the back neck, the pattern is made on double paper, using only a front bodice block.
1. Outline the front bodice block on double paper with the fold level with the shoulder at the neck.
2. Decide the length of the sleeve by measuring the figure from the shoulder point at the neck down the arm to the length required. Mark this measurement on the fold of the pattern, measuring from the neck.
3. At the point marking the length of sleeve, draw the edge of the sleeve at right angles to the shoulder fold.
4. Lower the armhole 1 cm to 2.5 cm and extend it 1 cm to 2.5 cm (according to the size of the pattern) from the side seam (Point A). Curve the underarm seam from the block, passing through A and on in a straight line or curve to the end of the sleeve. Make the curve as rounded as possible as a sharp curve will not set well when the seam is made. The width of the sleeve can be reduced, if liked, by slanting the seam upwards after it leaves A.
5. Draw the back neck by using a back bodice block.
6. Cut out the pattern on double paper except for the neck lines which must be cut singly.

For economy or when a patterned material is used which has an 'up and down', a seam can be made on the shoulder.

Style II. Diagram 153.
This style is cut with a seam on the shoulder and both a back and front pattern are made.
1. Decide the length of the sleeve and outline the bodice blocks. Draw a line of indefinite length from the shoulder

points at the armhole, keeping them parallel with the waist level. Mark the length of the sleeve on this line, measuring from the shoulder point at the neck. Join it in a straight line to the neck ignoring the original shoulder line. Use this straight line as a guide and curve the new shoulder line slightly up from it as shown in Diagram 153. Draft a back pattern to match the front.

2. Lower the underarm 6 mm or 1 cm. Join this point in a slight curve to the new shoulder point at the armhole.

Both these magyar bodice patterns can be themselves used as blocks to make other patterns with a magyar foundation.

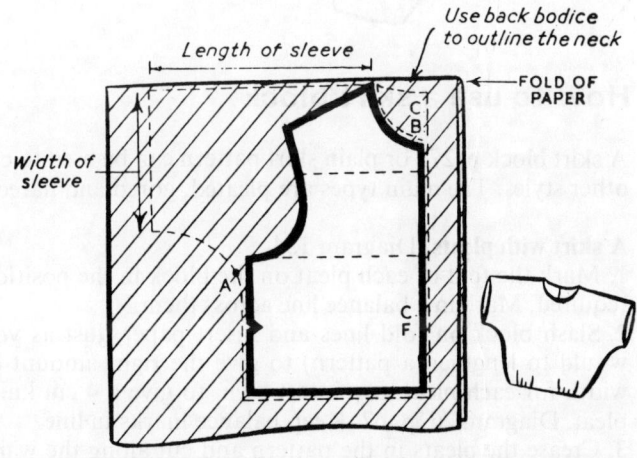

HOW TO DRAFT THE PATTERN

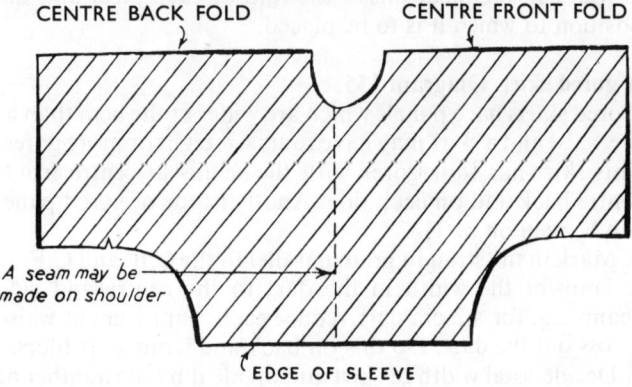

(i) and (ii). Magyar bodice pattern child (Style 1)

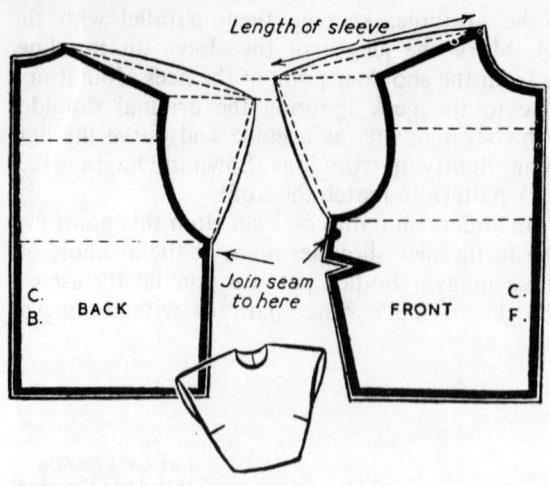

153. Magyar bodice pattern (Styl

How to use a skirt block

A skirt block p. 273 or plain skirt pattern can be used to cut other styles. The main types are pleated, gored and flared.

A skirt with pleats. Diagram 154.
1. Mark the fold of each pleat on the block in the position required. Mark in a balance line across them.
2. Slash block on fold lines and insert paper (just as you would to lengthen a pattern) to give the right amount of width for each pleat, e.g. insert 8 cm to give a 4 cm knife pleat. Diagram 26, p. 67. Keep balance marks in line.
3. Crease the pleats in the pattern and cut along the waist and hem lines.
4. Mark in the pleat lines—the fold of each pleat and the position to which it is to be placed.

A gored skirt. Diagram 155.
Gored skirts have panels which are wider at the hem than at the waist and a skirt may have four, six, eight or more gores. This skirt has four gores with the seams at centre front, centre back and on each side. Another type of gored panel can be seen on p. 38.
1. Mark in the straight grain parallel to the C.B. and C.F.
2. Transfer the width in the dart to the centre and side seams e.g. for a 2 cm dart reduce each seam 1 cm at waist. Cross out the dart. Do this on back and front skirt blocks.
3. Decide total width of skirt and divide it by the number of

PATTERN DESIGN, CUTTING AND FITTING 249

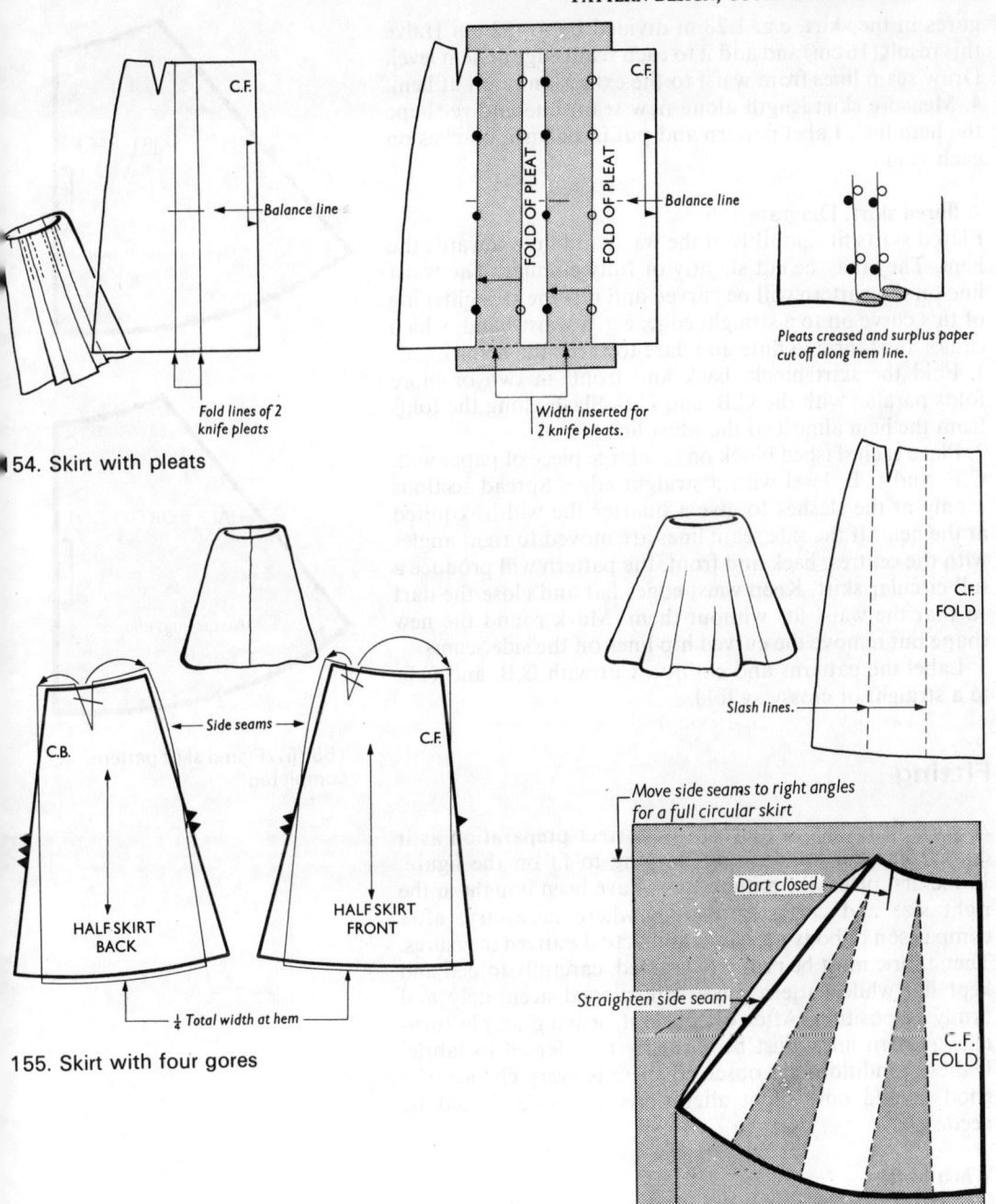

154. Skirt with pleats

155. Skirt with four gores

156 (i). A semi-circular flared skirt

gores in the skirt, e.g. 1.28 m divided by 4 = 32 cm. Halve this result (16 cm) and add it to each seam edge at hem level. Draw seam lines from waist to the extension point at hem.
4. Measure skirt length along new seam line and re-shape the hem line. Label pattern and put in balance notches on each seam.

A flared skirt. Diagram 156.
Flared skirts fit smoothly at the waist and flute towards the hem. They may be cut slightly or fully circular. The waist line on the pattern will be curved and it is the straightening of this curve on to a straight edge, e.g. a waist-band, which causes the fabric to flute and flare towards the hem.
1. Fold the skirt block, back and front, in two or more folds parallel with the C.B. and C.F. Slash along the folds from the hem almost to the waist line.
2. Place each slashed block on to a large piece of paper with C.F. and C.B. level with a straight edge. Spread sections evenly at the slashes to give a quarter the width required at the hem. If the side seam lines are moved to right angles with the centres, back and front, the pattern will produce a full circular skirt. Keep waist edges flat and close the dart so that the waist fits without them. Mark round the new shape but remove the curved hip lines on the side seams.
3. Label the patterns and cut out. Cut with C.B. and C.F. to a straight or crossway fold.

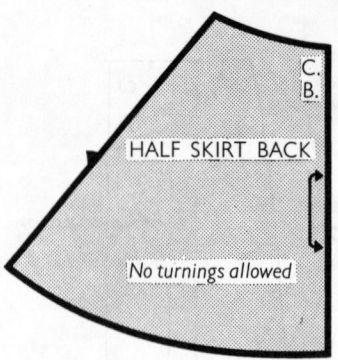

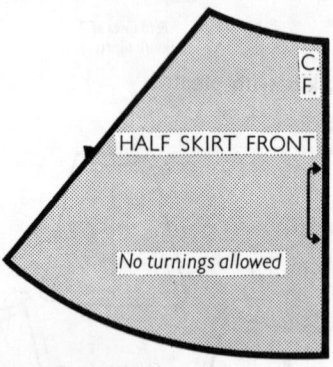

156 (ii). Flared skirt pattern completed

Fitting

A good fit results as much from correct preparation as it does from skill in adjusting clothing to fit on the figure. In the first place, the pattern must have been bought in the right size and correctly altered, where necessary, after comparison of body measures and actual pattern measures. Then fabric must be properly grained, carefully folded and kept flat while pattern pieces are pinned accurately and firmly in position. After cutting out, leaving ample turnings, pattern lines must be correctly transferred to fabric. If these conditions are observed there is every chance of a good fit and only slight alterations at fitting should be needed.

When to fit
Generally, clothing requires fitting twice with work at following stages as far as styles permit.

First fitting
Interfacings in place.
Garment tacked together without collar, facings or sleeves.
Waist band tacked to skirt.
Hems and cut-on front facings tacked in place.
Right sleeve tacked up for trying on.

Second fitting
Main stitching completed (e.g. darts, pleats, seams).
Collar tacked on.
Sleeves tacked in—wrist or elbow finish tacked in position.
Waist seam tacked.

To prepare for fitting
Usually a certain amount of final stitching and pressing can be done on units before assembling them for fitting, e.g. centre seams of back and front, gathers, pleats.

Assemble the garment with seam turnings inside ready for stitching (unless to be french-seamed). Fitting is done with the garment R.S. out. Of course, the correct order of work must be followed for tacking up, see p. 49. This saves time and avoids confusion. Make tacking stitches rather small with strong beginnings and endings so that they do not rip when they take the weight of the garment.

General points concerning fitting
1. Wear suitable shoes for the type of clothing. Have on the foundation garments which are likely to be worn, e.g. pantie girdles under trousers.
2. Fit dresses over a slip so that the fabric will fall smoothly. Fit jackets and coats over skirts and tops so that they are not fitted too tightly. Fit skirts and pants over a blouse.
3. Put the garment on properly, right side out. Pin up openings and be sure that central tacks on back or front opening are in line. Put on a belt if there is to be one or pin a strip of fabric round the waist.
4. Get a friend to help with the fitting. If this is not possible, put on the garment, decide alterations, remove garment to alter and put back on to see the result.
5. *Fit mainly on right-hand side of garment.* A few pins may be put on left-hand side to get the general effect and prevent the central tacks swinging out of position.
6. *Fit mainly at the fitting seams,* that is, the shoulder and side seams. Although it is permissible to make *very slight* alterations at other seams and on darts, there is a danger of upsetting the cut and style if much alteration is made.

7. *Take in or let out an even amount on back and front* on the fitting seams so that the proportion of front to back is not upset. The pattern designer has allowed extra on the front and an inexperienced fitter should not attempt to alter one side edge more than the other.

8. *Do not fit too tightly.* Make slight, rather than large alterations and re-fit. Probably amounts pinned in or let out will not be more than 6 mm to 1 cm from seam lines. Remember to allow for sitting, walking and moving arms and aim for an easy comfortable fit.

9. *Note that an alteration will nearly always affect another section of the garment,* e.g. if the side seam is taken in, the sleeve will have to be altered to fit the armhole; if neck shape is altered the facing will have to be altered also; shoulder alterations affect size and shape of neck line and armhole.

10. WATCH FABRIC GRAIN ALL THE TIME. The warp should hang plumb straight at centre front and back (unless garment is cut on the bias). The weft grain should be horizontal across the body and parallel to floor at bust and hip levels.

The first fitting

Take a good look, front, back and sides at the overall appearance before attempting to make any alteration. Note the following:

1. The hang of the fabric, see 10 above.
2. Position of main lines, e.g. darts, waist level, neckline and armhole line.
3. Position of style features, e.g. yokes, style seaming, pockets, trims.
4. Width of garment at bust, waist, hip and hem.

Then make necessary alterations. The following directions show how to recognise faults and how to put them right:

1. THE HANG OF THE FABRIC

If the grain is in the wrong position it will have certain results on the way various parts of the garment hang.

(a) When the weft grain is drawn up across the front bodice, wrinkles appear from bust down towards side seam and from shoulder towards armhole, waist seam curves upwards across centre, and, in one-piece garments, the centre front hem edge pokes out. Diagram 157 (i).

Possible causes—prominent bust, very sloping shoulders or a plump neck.

(b) When the weft grain drops down across front bodice wrinkles appear from the side seam under the arm down towards front and from shoulder towards bust. Waist and hem-lines will drop across the front. Diagram 157 (i).

Possible causes—flat chested figure, square shoulders, very thin neck.

Put these faults right at the SHOULDER SEAM.

Clip tacking and let out or take in the shoulder seam turnings at neck edge until weft grain hangs correctly

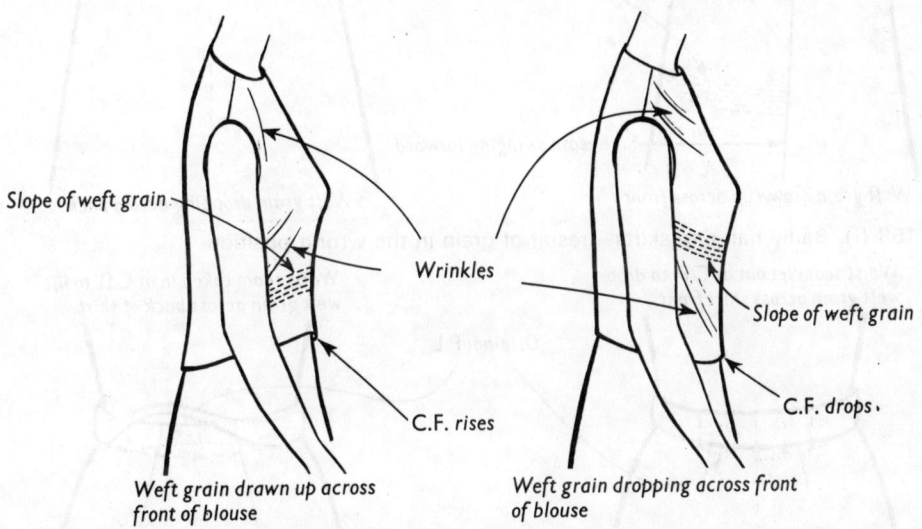

157 (i). Badly hanging blouses and tops—the result of grain in the wrong position

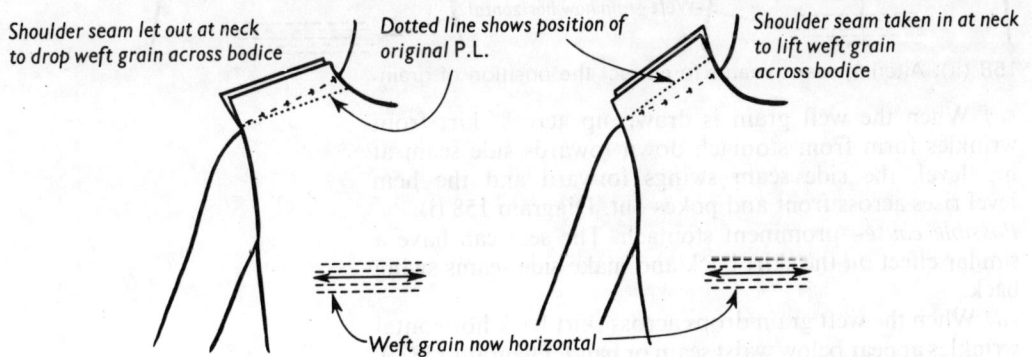

157 (ii). Altering shoulder seams to correct the position of grain across the front. Taper the pinning on the seam to the original seam at armhole. Diagram 157 (ii).

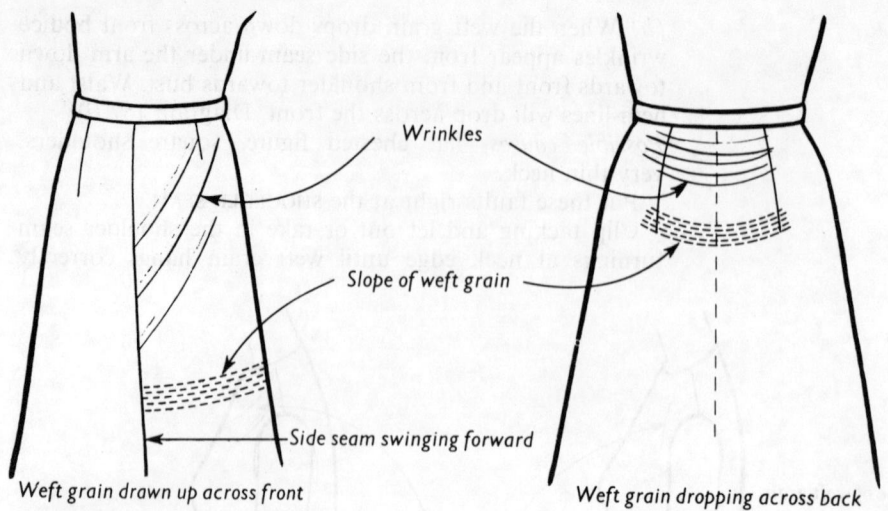

158 (i). Badly hanging skirts—result of grain in the wrong position

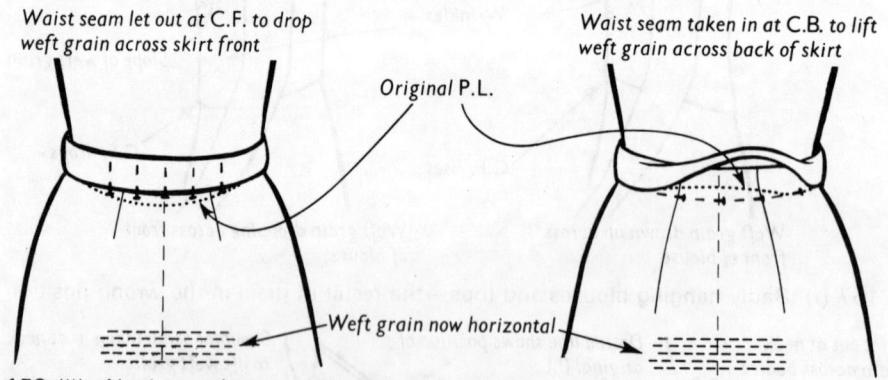

158 (ii). Altering waist seams to correct the position of grain

(c) When the weft grain is drawn up across skirt front wrinkles form from stomach down towards side seam at hip level, the side seam swings forward and the hem level rises across front and pokes out. Diagram 158 (i).
Possible cause—prominent stomach. The seat can have a similar effect on the skirt back and make side seams swing back.
(d) When the weft grain drops across skirt back horizontal wrinkles appear below waist seam or band. Diagram 158 (i).
Possible causes—a very hollow curved back.
Put these faults right at WAIST SEAM or BAND.
Clip tacking for about 12 to 20 cm across front or back. Either pull skirt down gently until the weft grain

is horizontal at hip level and the side seams hang straight, for alteration *(c)*, *or* smooth fabric upwards until wrinkles disappear for alteration *(d)*. Diagram 158 (ii).

Re-pin the waist seam tapering new line to join original one in a good shape.

2. POSITION OF MAIN LINES

Darts

Check that position and length of darts are right for shape.
To alter length—put a pin to mark where dart should end.

Re-shape on W.S. when garment is taken off. Draw a line with tailors' chalk from the wide end of dart to new point. Mark left-hand dart to match.

To alter position—put a row of pins in position required and measure this distance, e.g. 2 cm above the bust dart. Diagram 160. When garment is taken off, unpick portion of side seams and darts. Use the paper pattern to mark darts in new position, e.g. 2 cm away from old dart.

Waist level

It is essential that the waist level should be in the right position on the body. When there is no waist seam, the widest part of darts and the deepest curve of seams should be at waist level. Tie a string round waist to see if an alteration is necessary.

If waist seam is too high, note measurement between string round waist and the waist seam. Let out the turning on the bodice to match this amount.

If waist seam is too low, pin a tuck in the bodice above the waist to bring the seam to the correct position. Diagram 160. A 0.5 cm tuck would show that bodice is 1 cm too long. Mark a new waist seam line on the bodice when the garment has been taken off.

If waist level is wrong on a one-piece garment decide by how much the waist level should be raised or lowered. Unpick darts and seams and use the paper pattern to re-mark darts and seams in the new position.

Neck line

Note whether the neck sets flat and if it is the right depth and width. Sometimes the turning allowance on the neck is too wide to allow the neck to set properly. In this case make *short* clips in the turning at right angles to the cut edge until the fabric settles on the figure.

If the neck line is loose across front or back, Diagram 159 (i), unpick the shoulder seam and move the shoulder

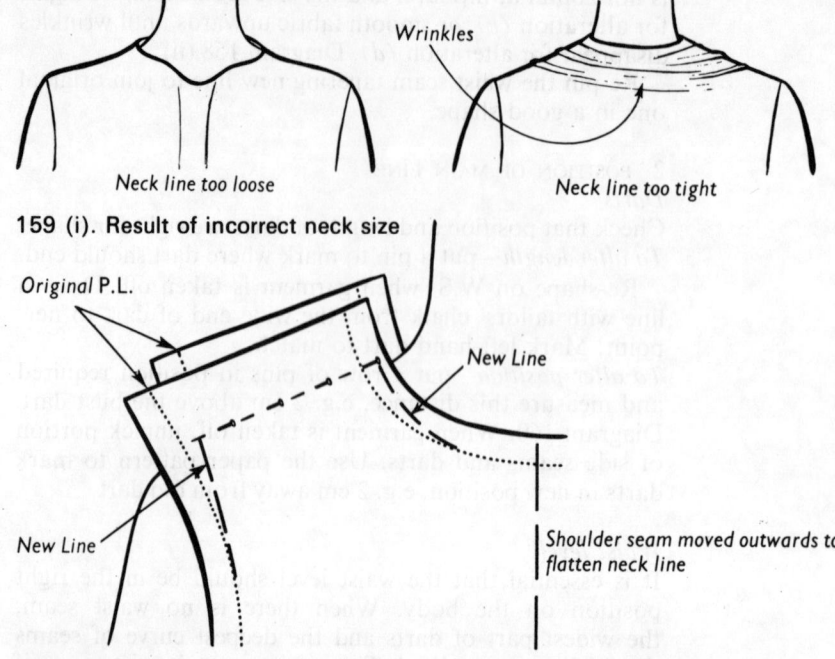

159 (i). Result of incorrect neck size

159 (ii). Altering a shoulder seam to correct the set of a neckline

edge out towards armhole to flatten the neck.

This alteration will throw out the seam lines at both neck and armhole. Re-mark these in a good line to join up with the original line. Diagram 159 (ii).

If the neck line is tight across front or back, horizontal wrinkles appear across the garment below the neck line. Diagram 159 (i).

Unpick the shoulder seams and move the shoulder edge towards neck-line until wrinkles disappear.

If the neck line is too low, or high, mark a new line with pins and when the garment has been taken off, use the paper pattern to mark neck line at level of pins.

Armhole line
This line must be in such a position that the seam will not drop below the shoulder when the sleeve is inserted and so that width at back and chest levels are in the correct places (see p. 35). If seam turnings are too wide to allow fabric to settle on the arm make *short* clips in the turnings

PATTERN DESIGN, CUTTING AND FITTING

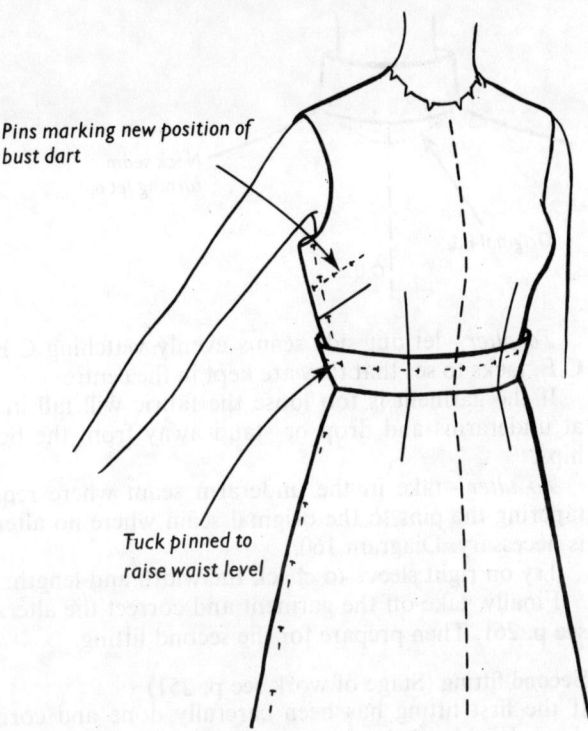

Pins marking new position of bust dart

Tuck pinned to raise waist level

Marking new position of dart and ~~ing waist level and width

at right angles to the cut edge until this edge lies comfortably round the arm.

Note size and shape of the armhole line. Indicate alterations required with a line of pins or tailors' chalk on right armhole. Be careful not to make the back width too narrow and to keep the line well out on the shoulder.

3. POSITION OF STYLE FEATURES

Notice positions of yokes, style seams, pockets, tabs and other trims and decide if they look well on the figure and are convenient to wear.

Fit either by pinning sections in a new position or by indicating a new position with a line of pins. Make alterations after garment is taken off.

Decide if skirt hem is the right distance from the ground. Correct level will be checked at second fitting.

4. WIDTH OF GARMENT

If the garment is too tight the fabric will strain across body causing horizontal wrinkles.

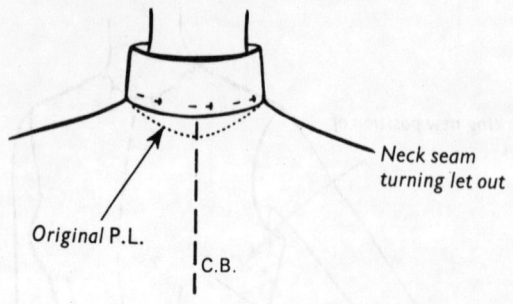

161. Altering the set of a collar

To alter—let out side seams evenly watching C.B. and C.F. tacks to see that they are kept in the centre.

If the garment is too loose the fabric will fall in loops at underarms and drop or stand away from the body at hips.

To alter—take in the underarm seam where required, tapering the pins to the original seam where no alteration is necessary. Diagram 160.

Try on right sleeve to check the width and length.

Finally, take off the garment and correct the alterations see p. 261. Then prepare for the second fitting.

Second fitting (Stage of work see p. 251)
If the first fitting has been carefully done and corrected there should only be minor alterations at this stage. Notice particularly the set of collar (or neckline if no collar), the appearance of sleeves, line of waist seam and hem level.

COLLAR
If a flat collar does not lie properly, clip tackings and arrange the collar on garment until the set is satisfactory. Pin collar to bodice and tack together on pattern line of collar.

If a turnover collar stands away from neck or does not roll over sufficiently, the neckline on bodice may be too deep at C.B. or at the sides.

Clip tackings at section of seam where the fault occurs and let out the seam turning until the collar fits correctly. Taper the turning allowance to join up to the original seam line on each side Diagram 161.

If the collar pulls to one side of centre, check accuracy of neck line. The collar cannot set properly if the neckline on one side is longer than the other.

SLEEVE
Note correct hang of sleeve (see p. 182, 183, para 4.)

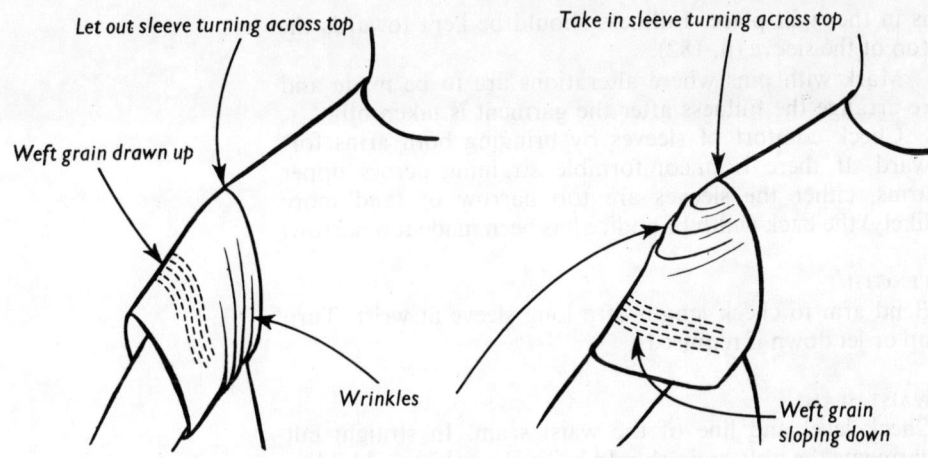

162. Badly hanging sleeves—result of grain in the wrong position

See that the armhole seam is in the right place; that fullness at head of sleeve is properly arranged in the right place and that the sleeve is comfortable.

Hang of sleeve. Diagram 162.
If the weft grain is drawn upwards across the arm wrinkles will form from crown towards armhole and short sleeves will poke up at the hem edge.

If the weft grain drops across the sleeve horizontal wrinkles loop across the arm and the hem edge drops on a short sleeve.

Put these faults right by altering the *sleeve line* at armhole.

Clip turnings across head of sleeve and either, let out the turning until the weft grain drops to horizontal position or take in the seam until weft grain rises to horizontal position.

Taper the seam turning to meet original seam line.

If the warp grain hangs forward or backwards note by how much the centre of the sleeve must be moved forward or back.

Take out sleeves and reset, so that the warp grain hangs straight.

Fullness at sleeve head
See that fullness is eased smoothly across head and that it

is in the right place. Fullness should be kept towards the top of the sleeve (p. 182).

Mark with pins where alterations are to be made and re-arrange the fullness after the garment is taken off.

Check comfort of sleeves by bringing both arms forward. If there is uncomfortable straining across upper arms, either the sleeves are too narrow or (and more likely) the back width of bodice has been made too narrow.

LENGTH

Bend arm to check length of a long sleeve at wrist. Turn up or let down if required.

WAIST SEAM

Check level and line of the waist seam. In straight cut garments the weft grain should be level on skirt and bodice (or band) for about 12 to 14 cm across centres front and back.

HEM LEVEL

See that openings and belts are fastened and check that hem edge is level. It is best not to keep turning round while this is being checked. Take a steady look at front, back and sides. If necessary alter the level. (See p. 94.)

Fitting trousers

Fit trousers with seams prepared for stitching, with waistband tacked in place or waist turning folded and tacked to W.S. on P.L. Wear the type of underclothes and shoes which would normally be worn with trousers. The aim in fitting is for comfort in wear and a smart good line. Test the fit with wearer sitting, striding and bending as well as standing still. Do not fit too tightly. Look at the general effect first and then note and deal with the following points in the order given.

1. HANG OF TROUSER LEGS AND POSITION OF SIDE SEAMS

The seams should hang straight down the sides. The direction of the seams can be adjusted at C.B. or C.F. waist level as for skirt side seams, see p. 254, the hang of the fabric.

2. WAIST AND HIPS

The fit should be smooth, snug and comfortable just as for skirts. Adjust width as far as possible at side seams first, see p. 257 and if necessary in small amounts at C.B. and C.F. seams. Be careful of making alterations in darts because the shaping is affected. Only slight amounts should be reduced or added.

3. POSITION OF CROTCH SEAM AND SEAT

If the crotch is too long the seat will be baggy and the fork too low down. Remove waist band, tie a string tightly round the waist and pull up the waist edge above the string until the seat is in the correct position. Let the wearer sit and bend and then mark the resulting position of the string with pins or chalk. This line will need correcting to make a good line. Method of correcting fitting lines (see below).

If the crotch is too short the waist edge will pull down at C.B. and C.F. Remove the tacking across the front and back of the trousers for about 12 to 20 cm and let out the turning. Repin the waist band tapering the turning to the original P.L. see diagram 158 (ii), p. 254. Test fit with wearer sitting down.

4. WIDTH AND LENGTH OF LEGS

If the thigh width is too narrow the trousers will crease on the inside leg, look tight and will be uncomfortable. Take the trousers off and let out the inside leg seams first from thigh to fork and tapering down to knee level. Be careful in reducing or increasing width at the fork because this would alter the length of the crotch seam. Re-fit and if still more width is required let out the side seams as well.

If the thigh width is too wide the trousers will look shapeless and baggy. Decide by how much the width must be reduced, divide by four and take in the seams equally.

Check that shaping, such as a flare, starts in the right place and note that the bottom of the trousers is at the correct length for style and fashion. See that narrow trousers can be pulled easily over the instep.

Correcting after fitting

Slight alterations can be done by measuring and making new lines on which to tack, with tailors' chalk on left and right hand sides of garment. Time is saved if the new tacking is put in before the old one is taken out to save placing and pinning the seams again.

Big or many alterations are best done in the professional manner known as 'correcting'.

Method of correcting. Diagram 163.

1. Mark every line of pins put in by the fitter on the right-

hand side of the garment with coloured tacking or tailors' chalk.

2. Put a tack or a chalk mark, at some point on all seams which have been altered to act as a notch or balance point so that seams can be placed together correctly again.

3. Unpick seams and darts where necessary and fold the garment in half through centre back and centre front with the wrong sides facing and the original pattern lines together.

4. Now pin through on the fitter's marks improving the line if necessary. A ruler can be used to make straight seams. Pin through on the balance tacks.

5. Check that the new lines will fit together properly, e.g. side seam of *front* to match side seam of *back* in length; armhole of sleeve the right measurement for armhole of bodice.

6. Mark new lines and balance marks with tailors' tacking through the two layers of fabric.

7. Remove original tacking where a new line has been made.

8. Trim turnings where necessary and tack up the garment again.

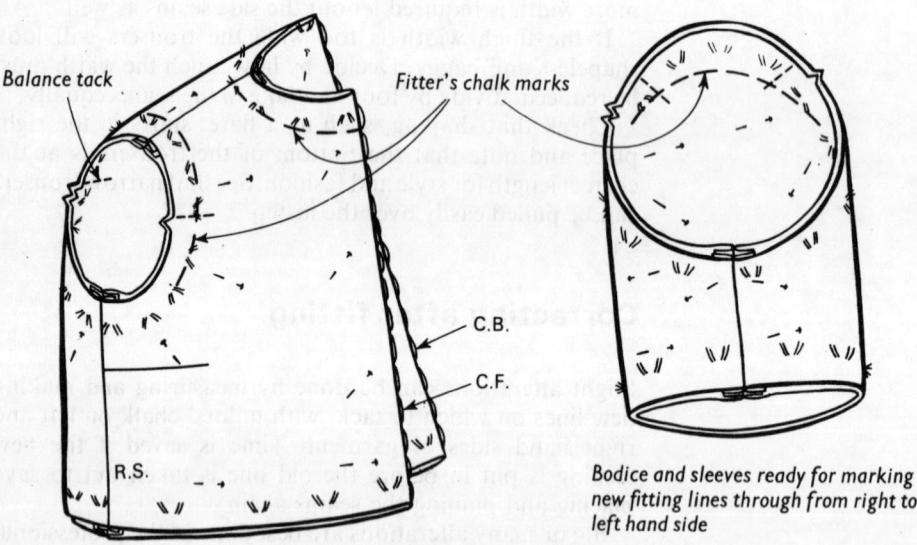

Bodice and sleeves ready for marking new fitting lines through from right to left hand side

163. Preparation for correcting the pattern lines after fitting

22 Block patterns to individual measures

Measurements required for making patterns must be taken with great care and clearly listed. The method of taking measurements will be found in Chapter 3, p. 34.

A bodice block for girls and women

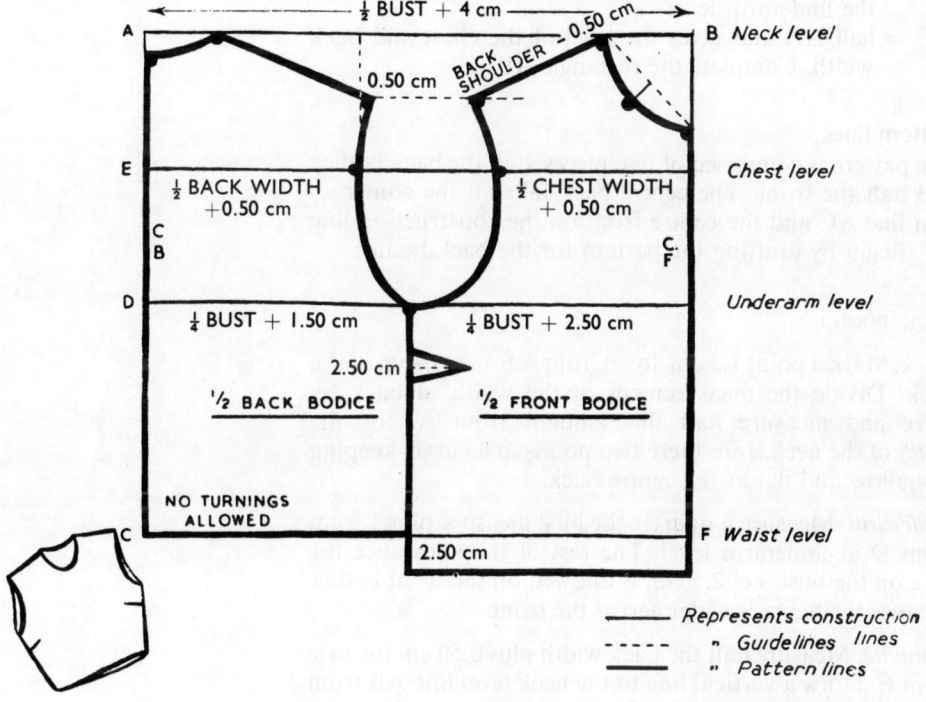

1.64. Bodice block pattern

The pattern is for a plain bodice with a high round neck and an underarm dart at bust level. It fits easily at the bust, but is not fitted to the waist. The armhole is a comfortable fit to take a 'set in' sleeve. Darts and shaping at the side seams can be put in to reduce waist to a fitted shape. p. 243.

Measures required

Nape to waist   Width across back
Bust   Width across chest

Construction lines

These are planned from certain of the figure measures and are used as a foundation on which to build the block pattern. They ensure that each pattern is in good proportion, even though the individual lines vary in size.

AB = half bust measure plus 4 cm for ease
AC = nape to waist plus 1 cm for ease
AD = a quarter the measurement of the bust. This gives the underarm level
AE = half AD and gives the level of the chest and back width. Complete the rectangle ABFC.

Pattern lines

The pattern is composed of two pieces, half the back bodice and half the front. The centre back falls on the construction line AC and the centre front on the construction line BF. Begin by drafting the pattern for the back bodice.

BACK BODICE

Neck. Mark a point 1.5 cm down from A for the *depth* of the neck. Divide the measurement of the width of back by three and measure half this amount from A, for the *width* of the neck. Join these two points in a curve, keeping it shallow and flat at the centre back.

Underarm. Measure a quarter the bust measure plus 1.5 cm from D at underarm level. The rest of the allowance for ease on the bust, i.e. 2.5 cm, is allowed on the front bodice because the figure is wider across the front.

Armhole. Measure half the back width plus 0.50 cm for ease from E. Draw a vertical line to the neck level line AB from this point. Then measure down 5 cm and move the point 0.5 cm out to give the position for the shoulder point at armhole. Draw the armhole curve from this point to the underarm point, passing through the back width mark. Notice that the curve is shallow and do not allow it, at any point, to slope in further than the back width mark.

Shoulder. Join the shoulder point at the armhole to the neck, in a straight line.

Underarm seam. Draw a vertical line from the underarm point to the waist level.

Outline and label the block in coloured pencil.

FRONT BODICE

The front bodice is drafted so that the lines will fit those of the back pattern, therefore constant reference will be made to the back.

Neck. The depth is equal to the width of the back neck plus 2 cm.
The width is equal to the width of the back neck plus 1.5 cm.

Notice that reference is made to the width of the back neck in both cases. Draw the neck curve between AB and the centre front. To help in drawing a good shape, draw a straight guide line first; divide it in half and from this point draw a line 2 cm long at right angles. Draw the neckline so that it passes through this point. (Shape of round necklines, Chapter 21, Diagram 144.)

Underarm point is a quarter of the bust measure plus 2.5 cm from the centre front.

Armhole and shoulder. Draw a guide line parallel to AB at the back shoulder point level, between the two patterns. Place the ruler at the highest point of the front neck where it touches AB and draw a straight line to end on the guide line, making it equal in length to the measurement of the back shoulder line minus 0.5 cm. The back shoulder will have to be eased into the front when the bodice is made up, and this provides for the natural roundness of the shoulder.

Mark a point at half the chest width plus 0.5 cm along the chest level line from the centre front. Draw the armhole curve from the shoulder point, passing through the chest width point, and making a deep curve to the underarm point.

Underarm dart. A dart is essential in a bodice for an adult figure, though not necessarily at bust level. It is just as frequently used at the shoulder or the waist. A dart gives the necessary extra length or width at the point where it is required, and controls the hang of the bodice at the waist. Without it, the level of the waist would drop at the sides and be lifted up in the centre. Draw a dart 2.5 cm wide and 6.5 cm long at 5 cm below the underarm point.

Waist. Drop the waistline 2.5 cm below the waist level line to allow for the 2.5 cm dart.

Label the pattern, cut it out and place the shoulder and underarm seam lines together to see that they make a good continuous line at the neck and armhole.

A sleeve block

A sleeve is always drafted after the bodice because the measurement of the bodice armhole is needed for reference for the sleeve pattern.

This pattern is for a one-piece, plain long loose sleeve which is fixed into the bodice so that the seams of bodice and sleeve are opposite.

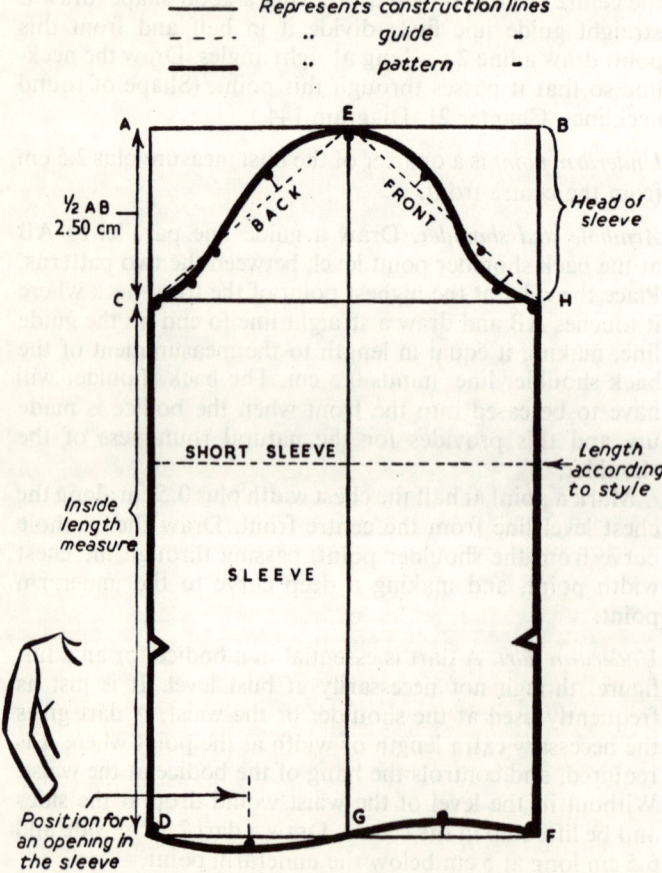

165. Sleeve block pattern

Measures required
Inside length of sleeve
Round arm
Armhole of garment (taken from bodice patterns)

Construction lines
AB = round arm measure plus 7.5 cm
AC = half AB minus 2.5 cm
CD = inside length measure
  Complete the rectangle ABFD
AE = half AB
DG = half DF

Guide lines. Join CE, EH and divide each into thirds. At the first third from E. measure 2 cm out at right angles to CE and EH.

Half-way between C and the next third, mark a point 0.5 cm down from CE. Half-way between H and the next third. mark a point 1.5 cm down from EH. These measurements must be altered slightly for smaller or larger sizes.

Pattern lines
HEAD OF THE SLEEVE

Draw a curve from C through E to H passing through the 0.5 cm point. the two 2 cm points and the 1.5 cm point. It does not matter where the curve cuts the guide lines elsewhere, as long as it is a good line. The curve should be smooth, shallow at the back and more deeply curved at the front. The head should be well rounded and symmetrical on both sides of the centre. With practice, the curve can be drawn with only the lines CE, EH as a guide.

Measure the armhole curve of the sleeve, i.e. the head, and compare it with the measurement of the armhole of the bodice. The armhole of the sleeve must measure at least 2.5 cm and not more than 4 cm. more than the armhole of the bodice, to allow for ease in setting in. (Read Chapter 15.) When the difference is not correct, alter the size of the sleeve head in one of the following ways:

(a) Increase or decrease the depth of the back and front curves.
(b) Raise or lower the curve at the crown of the head.
(c) Raise or lower the underarm points at C and H.
(d) Reduce or extend the width of the sleeve.

UNDERARM SEAM

The line CD and HF. The width of a sleeve can be narrowed at wrist level if required.

WRIST LINE
The curve at the wrist is lower at the back than the front to allow for the bend of the arm.

Mark a point 1.5 cm down at half DG and 0.5 cm up at half GF. Draw the curve from D to F to pass through these points.

Alterations to bodice and sleeve blocks for children's sizes

BACK
Neck. Depth = 0.5 or 1 cm from centre back.

Armhole. The shoulder point at the armhole must not be further from AB than half the distance between A and E.

FRONT
Neck. Depth = back neck plus 1 cm.
Width = back neck plus 0.5 cm.

Waist. For sizes under 81 cm bust, the figure does not need a dart, therefore there is no reason for lowering the waist level at the side seam.

For sizes up to eight years, lower the waist level at the centre front from 1 cm to 2.5 cm to allow for high stomachs. Slope the line to meet the side seam at the original waist level.

SLEEVE
Construction lines:
AB = round arm measure plus 5 cm for sizes up to eight years and 6.5 cm up to 12 years.
AC = half AB minus 4 cm.

Guide line. Measurements from CE and EH are less according to size, e.g. 0.5 to 1 cm at the crown and 3 mm and 0.5 cm for the back and front curves at the underarm.

Measurements from the wrist level are 0.5 cm at the back and 3 mm at the front curves.

A knicker block for children and girls

This knicker block pattern is for a standard knicker having a seam at the centre front and centre back. The back is cut higher than the front, and the waist and legs are made with a casing to take elastic. The pattern is composed of one piece which represents half the front and half the back. When the pattern is placed on double material the two halves or legs of the knickers are cut out. There are only slight differences between the back and front of the knickers, therefore the paper for the pattern is used double, and the front and back are drafted on top of each other. The block can be used for shorts, pants and pyjamas. Diagram 166.

Measures required
WAIST TO KNEE
This measure does not represent the final length of the knickers, but is required for the construction lines.

FINAL LENGTH FROM THE WAIST
Take both these measures down the side of the figure.

Size of paper to make the pattern
The size of the sheet of paper is based on the length of the knickers from waist to knee. The proportion varies with the size and allows extra length to provide for the necessary length on the back of the knickers.

DIMENSIONS OF PAPER

For sizes	Length of paper	Width of paper
Up to 7 years	Waist to knee	$1\frac{1}{3}$ times the length
8 to 12 years	Waist to knee plus 2.5 cm	$1\frac{1}{3}$ times the length
13 to 16 years	Waist to knee plus 5 cm	$1\frac{1}{4}$ times the length
Over 16 years	Waist to knee plus 8 cm	$1\frac{1}{4}$ times the length

Fold the paper in half through the short way of the paper.

Construction lines or folds
Construction lines can be pencilled but it is simpler to fold the paper in four each way and crease well.

Pattern lines
Place the paper on a table with the first fold made towards the left-hand side. Diagram 165. Spaces between the

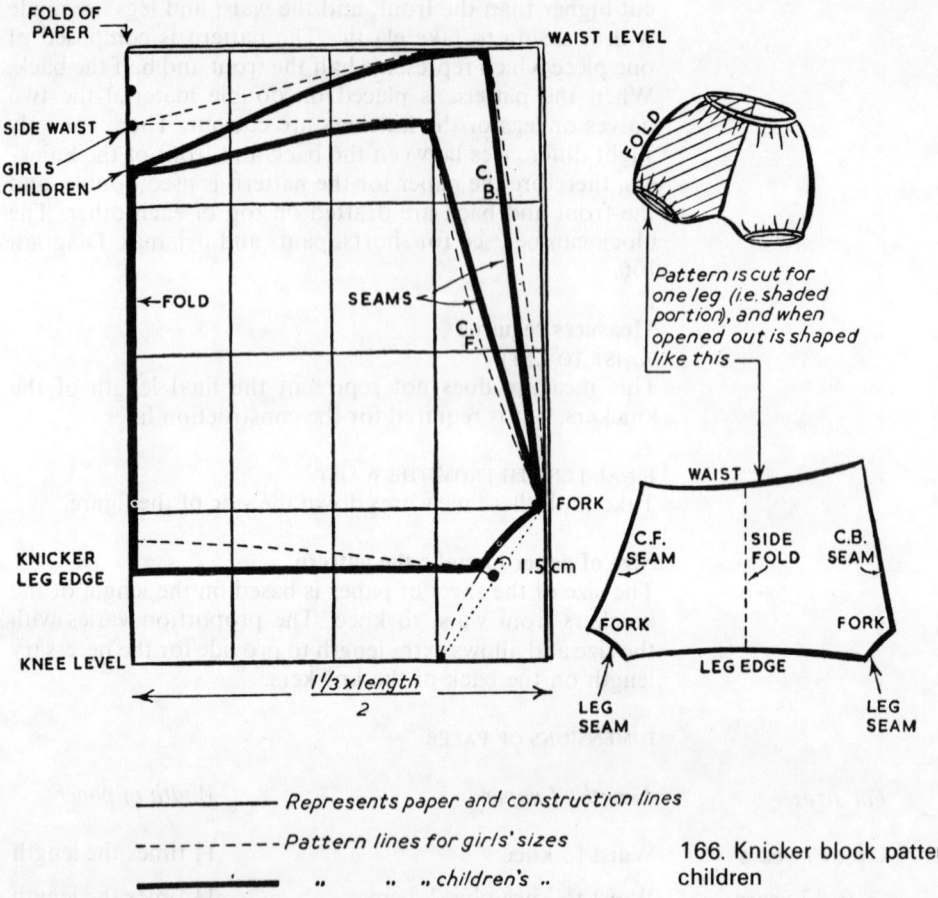

166. Knicker block pattern for girls children

creases representing construction lines will be referred to as divisions.

FORK
Mark a point one division up and a point one division along from the right-hand bottom corner. Join these two points in a straight line. Divide the line in half and draw a line at right angles to it measuring 1.5 cm. Curve the *leg seam* from the fork, through this point to knee level.

WAIST
Divide the top division on the left-hand side into four, along the fold. Mark the waist level half-way down for girls' sizes and three-quarters down for children's.

Mark a point one division in, and half a division down from the right-hand top corner to mark the centre front, and half a division along the top edge to mark the centre back. Draw the back waist from the fold at the side, curving up to the centre back. Keep the curve rather flat near the side and the centre back. Draw the front waist from the fold at the side, to the centre front. It will be seen that in the children's sizes the pattern line rises at the centre front waist, to allow for plumpness of the figure.

CENTRE FRONT AND BACK SEAMS
Join the centre front and back points at the waist to the fork. For girls' sizes curve the centre back seam slightly out and the centre front seam slightly inwards.

LEG EDGE
Measure the length the knicker is required to be from the side waist. Shorten leg by drawing a straight line parallel with the edge of the paper, or, if the garment is too short to do this, curve it towards the leg seam.

Cutting the pattern from the paper
Cut along the leg seam and leg edge, the centre back seam and waist in double paper. Cut along the centre front seam and waist in single paper. Label the pattern.

A dress block

This one-piece block produces the pattern for a plain, easy fitting sleeveless garment, e.g. a straight dress lining. It can be used to cut any garment which is longer than blouse length, e.g. tunics, dresses, slips, housecoats, overalls, jackets. Both closely or loosely fitting styles can be produced.

Measures required for dress block
Full length of garment from nape.
Waist.
Hip.

Construction lines
Outline bodice blocks keeping waist lines level. Measure full length of garment from the C.B. neck and draw the hem level line parallel to waist level. Extend C.B. and C.F. lines from waist to hem level. Draw a line parallel to the waist at hip level, i.e. 18, 20 or 22 cm below the waist.

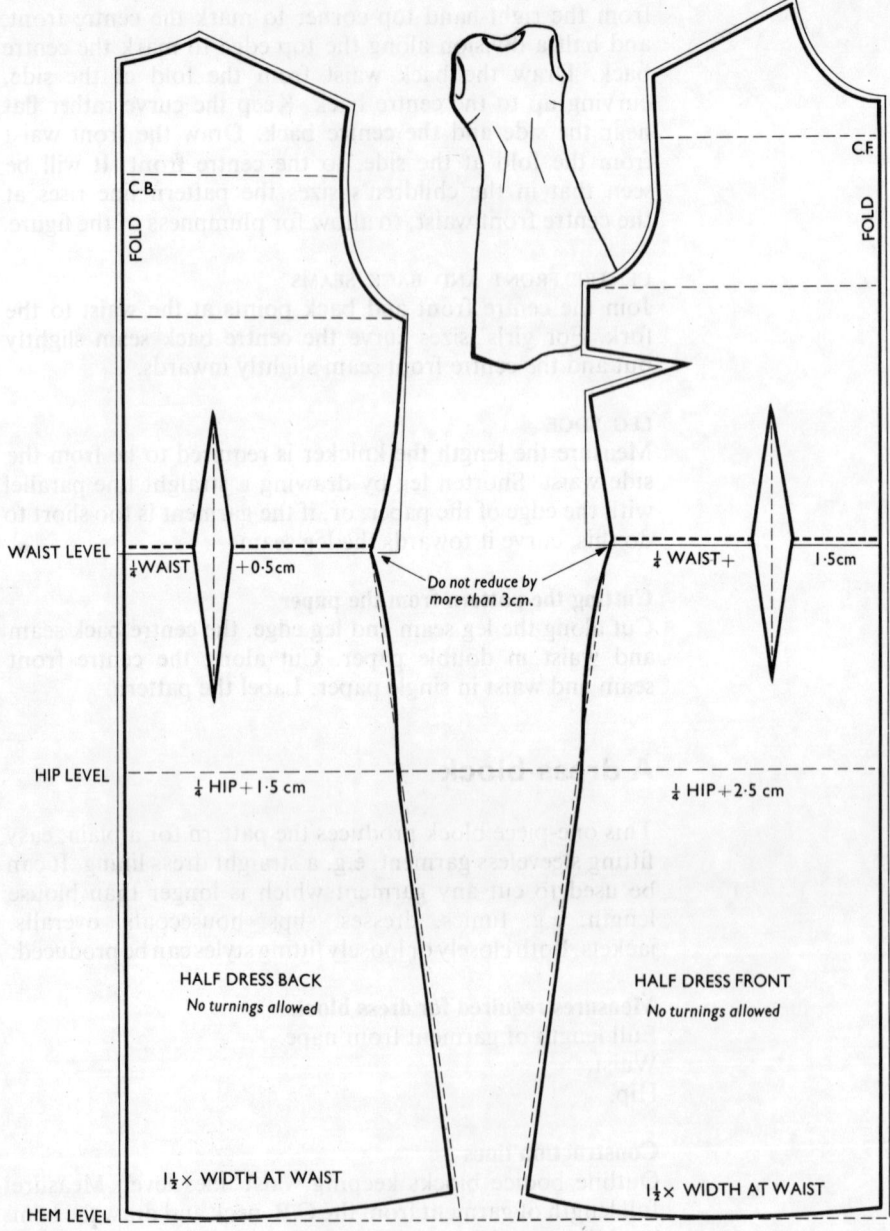

167. Dress block

Pattern lines

WAIST SHAPING

Reduce the waist with shaping at the side seam and darts so that the back waist measures a quarter of the waist measure +0.5 cm and the front waist measures a quarter of the waist measure +1.5 cm. This allows 4 cm ease all round. Planning darts see pp. 243, 244.

HIP WIDTH

Measure a quarter of the hip measure +1.5 cm from C.B. and a quarter of the hip measure +2.5 cm from C.F. along the hip level line. This allows 8 cm ease all round.

HEM WIDTH

From C.B. and C.F. at hem level measure $1\frac{1}{2}$ times the width of the pattern at the waist. e.g. if waist measures 18 cm across the back pattern, the width at hem would be 27 cm.

SIDE SEAMS

Draw a line from the underarm point to the hem passing through waist and hip points. Draw a straight line from waist to hem as a guide line. Curve out about 0.5 cm for the hip curve.

HEM LINE

Measure length from C.B. waist to hem level. Take this measure along side seam lines between the waist and hem level and shorten it 0.5 cm. Join this point in a smooth curve to the hem level line.

Label the pattern and cut it out.

Skirt block*

The lower part of the dress block can be used as a skirt block or to make a straight two-piece skirt.
1. Cut through the dress block at waist level.
2. Check the waist measure and decide if it needs reduction to make it a snugger fit. If so, the side seams can be taken in 1 to 3 cm at the waist and/or the darts increased in size.
3. Rearrange the darts if required, e.g. make two smaller shorter darts instead of the one large one.
4. Mark an opening in the side seam 22 cm long.
5. Label the pattern.

* Simple skirt patterns are given in *Introduction to Needlework*, pp. 82, 83, 86.

Part III
Planning and maintenance of clothes and household articles

The International Textile Care Labelling Code

Correct cleaning and laundering are essential to preserve fibres so that fabrics give good wear and keep a fresh appearance.

You need to know whether to wash or dry clean; how hot to have the water for washing and rinsing; how to handle fabric, e.g. gently, and if ironed, what heat to use.

You will often find this information on labels fixed to clothes and merchandise. The above named code has been worked out based on standard methods of treating different groups of fabrics. Some information is printed and some given in symbols. See p. 166.

Learn to recognise the symbols

 FABRIC CAN BE WASHED. Sometimes the temperature of the water in degrees centigrade is marked on the washtub and the code number of the washing process e.g. hand wash only.

 CAN BE BLEACHED.

 CAN BE IRONED. Dots indicate heat of iron ··· hot, ·· medium, · cool, e.g.

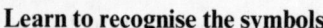 CAN BE DRY CLEANED. A letter inside the circle refers to the kind of cleaning spirit advised, e.g. (A) all solvents.

 PROCESS MUST NOT BE USED if it has this cross over it,

e.g.  do not bleach.

Code numbers on wash tub symbols
These refer to nine groups of fabrics which are given below.

 White cotton and linen without special finishes.

 Cotton, linen or viscose articles without special finishes where colours are fast at 60°C.

 White nylon; white polyester/cotton mixtures.

 Coloured nylon; polyester; cotton and viscose articles with special finishes; acrylic/cotton mixtures.

 Cotton linen or viscose articles where colours are fast at 40°C but not at 60°C.

 Acrylics; acetate and triacetate, including mixtures with wool; polyester/wool blends.

 Wool, including blankets and wool mixtures with cotton or viscose; silk.

 Silk and printed acetate fabrics with colours not fast at 40°C.

 Cotton articles with special finishes capable of being boiled but requiring drip-drying.

(Taken from 'Summary of Washing Symbols', *The International Textile Care Labelling Code*.)

23 Planning clothes

Choosing clothes

This is something which most girls do for themselves at quite an early age, and before many years have passed after leaving school will be doing so for their families. There are several aspects of choosing clothes which may be usefully considered.

How much to spend
The amount to be spent on a particular item depends on what is reasonable for it and what the buyer has to spend. If she wants enough money to go round for all her needs, she will find it best to allocate a proportion of her income to clothing. People's needs vary considerably—a housewife at home uses fewer clothes than a teacher; students often require fewer than girls in business houses. Young women, between leaving school and getting married, will spend a higher proportion of their income on clothes than young married women. People living in the country find clothes last longer so can spend less. Therefore, it is difficult to estimate how much should be allowed for clothes—some say 10 to 15 per cent of the total income but many people find they have to do with far less.

How to stretch the money spent on clothes
1. Make lists of clothes already in the wardrobe and requirements for self or members of the family so that the real necessities are clear. Include under and outer clothes, footwear, stockings and accessories.
2. Decide where money can be saved by dressmaking at home. This knotty point only applies if a housewife has the time and ability to make at home. Even if it is cheaper it may not be worthwhile making if it would mean too much loss of time for leisure and other things. On the other hand quality of fabric can be better on home-made clothes and smartness depends on the skill of the dressmaker. Consider where sales would help and ready cut-out garments sold packaged with haberdashery.

3. Watch the spending and try to keep within the budget.
4. Spread out the buying of expensive items over several years so that one member of the family does not require, say, both a new summer and winter coat in one year.
5. See that every new buy is wearable with something already in the wardrobe, so that clothes can be used to give varied outfits.
6. Make plans on paper—this saves buying on impulse, often extravagantly.
7. Buy rather plain basic clothes if money is short, so that clothes do not date quickly.

Getting value for money
While girls are at school and at first when earning money this aspect of spending may not seem important because many like to buy smart modern clothes fairly cheaply and renew them frequently. But the time will surely come when to get good value for money will mean that money is saved for other, more important things. A housewife can improve the standard of living for her family generally, if she knows how to spend and buy sensibly. Extravagance in the home can upset relationships between members of the family and cause trouble in the home. So one should know what to look for when buying or making clothes, to see that judgment is backed by knowledge.

POINTS TO LOOK FOR
Comparative prices
Before buying, notice prices of similar clothing advertised in papers and do some 'window shopping' so that an idea is gained of a reasonable price for the kind of clothing in mind. Become money conscious now by costing everything made at school and comparing it with the price of a comparable garment in the shops. Plan and cost ready-made items needed to complete an outfit for a dress or suit which has been made at school.

Quality, finish and fit
Try to assess the quality of the fabric and the properties which will affect the wear and comfort, e.g. a tricel foulard blouse would not be hardwearing for constant every day wear; a brushed nylon dress for a baby would be uncomfortable in hot weather. In both cases, cotton would be a much better choice.

The quality of the finish is quickly judged by looking for accuracy of work—the way designs are matched at seams;

even lengths of lapels; flat facings and openings; straight and evenly spaced top stitching and fastenings; smooth lines to seams at armholes and so on. Inside, there should be sufficient seam turnings for letting out if there is likelihood of alteration.

If clothes pass the test for quality and finish the next thing is to try them on and to have a good look at the whole effect, front, back and sideways on. Note if the seams hang straight, whether there is enough room for movement or too much. Look at the set of a collar, position of armhole seams, waist seam, how the sleeves hang and whether they are comfortable when arms are brought forward. It is obvious how your knowledge of dressmaking is going to help in buying ready-mades. Make quite sure that you like the colour or design and style. See the clothes in daylight and do not buy if there is any doubt. Better to try somewhere else before making up your mind.

Choosing clothes to make the best of appearance and personality

Fashions of to-day are exciting, original and particularly suited to youth. Never before have they been such fun, so free, relaxed and practical. Some styles may not be flattering to the not-so-slim. Fortunately the wide choice and versatility of fashion give everyone a chance to select something right up to date which also disguises figure faults. Most girls want to make the best of themselves and express their personalities by being inventive with fashion. This can be done more effectively by understanding basic fashion facts and some fundamental rules for dressing.

Colour, texture and style of clothing are all concerned in choosing becoming clothes, and the first consideration will be:

COLOUR

Hard and fast rules cannot be made about becoming colours, because every person presents an individual problem. Apart from natural colouring, vitality and personality make a difference too. Some people can carry off a colour which would overwhelm the individuality of another. The following advice may be helpful:
1. Make a study of colour. Attend art classes and learn which are the warm and which the cold colours, and why there are warm and cold shades and tints of both, such as cool and warm yellows, greys. Consider why certain

colours suit (or the reverse) the people one meets. Drape fabrics over shoulders and study the effect in a mirror.

2. Notice that to match or tone a colour with a particular feature draws attention to it. While this is excellent to show off lovely hair or eyes, in the same way it makes the worst of these features if they are not the owner's strong points. For example, a dark brown dress accentuates the beauty of brunette or chestnut hair, but fawn and greyish-brown shades against mouse-coloured hair increase the dull tones. To contrast colours with hair and skin is also effective. This accounts for the fact that dark shades are so generally becoming, particularly to fair people, and vivid colours to dark people and those with olive skins. Hair tinting widens the choice of colour.

3. Notice the effect of a colour on the complexion when considering whether it is becoming. There is no point in wearing black to stress the beauty of black hair, if it shows up a sallow skin. A clever introduction of another colour in this case will be kind to the complexion, as well as emphasising the dark hair.

People with blue eyes are fond of matching materials to them and while this is always successful in improving the most important feature in the face, the tone of blue does not always suit the complexion.

Watch the general tone of the skin against colours. Girls with rosy complexions may look hot and florid wearing warm tones of red, orange and wine, but look fresh and cool in cold blues and greens. Skins which are pale and colourless need the reflection of warm tones. Cold shades, e.g. cold green or grey, increase the general cold effect. Cosmetics can help in wearing colours.

4. Notice that light colours make a figure look larger than dark colours.

TEXTURE

1. The colour of material is altered considerably in tone by its quality or texture. Richness and depth is given to a shade if the fabric has a pile, so that a colour, too crude in satin, may suit well in velvet because it is softened and deepened.

A colour in transparent material may be lightened or subtly altered. Black, which many girls love to wear, suits them admirably in a diaphanous material, such as net or nylon, but is far too sombre for them in crêpe, even though

black does set off a pink and white skin and blonde hair.
2. Materials with shiny surfaces, such as satin, appear to increase size, whereas matt surfaces, such as crêpes and woollens, have the reverse effect.
3. Stiff materials, which stand away from the body, will obviously enlarge the outline and are to be avoided by very plump people to whom the softer textured materials are more becoming. Bulky fabrics, too, add to size.

STYLE

After the colour and material of an outfit have been decided, the next question will be the style in which it is to be made. The general shape will be guided by fashion and within these boundaries it is for each one to choose the lines which suit her best.

Vertical lines

Long vertical lines increase height (Diagram 168) and make the figure appear slimmer, because the eye is directed up and down the lines and diverted from the width. Lines may be interpreted in a variety of ways, e.g. seaming, pleating, panels, according to the ingenuity of the cutter. Sometimes the lines are indefinite and do not add to or detract appreciably from the size of the figure, or they may be accentuated by contrasting colours or conspicuous stitching. The material itself may be printed in lines.

Horizontal lines

Horizontal lines decrease height (Diagram 168) and consequently make the figure look wider, because the eye is carried across the figure and distracted from the height. Such lines are usually designed as seams, yokes, bands, inset panels, frills, etc., or a patterned material may be cut so that the stripes go across the figure.

With these facts in mind, styles can be chosen which improve the figure.

Tall thin girls will wear clothing designed with lines going across the figure, and a very tall girl can take several of them used boldly, e.g. wide contrasting waist belt, deep yoke, pockets on bodice and skirt. Full skirts and soft drapery hide the angularity of the figure. Boldly patterned materials and horizontal stripes are all becoming.

Tall plump girls will choose vertical lines to break up the width. They will avoid wide areas unbroken with any line or detail of style, e.g. skirts with six or eight panels will reduce width better than skirts with two or four. Well-

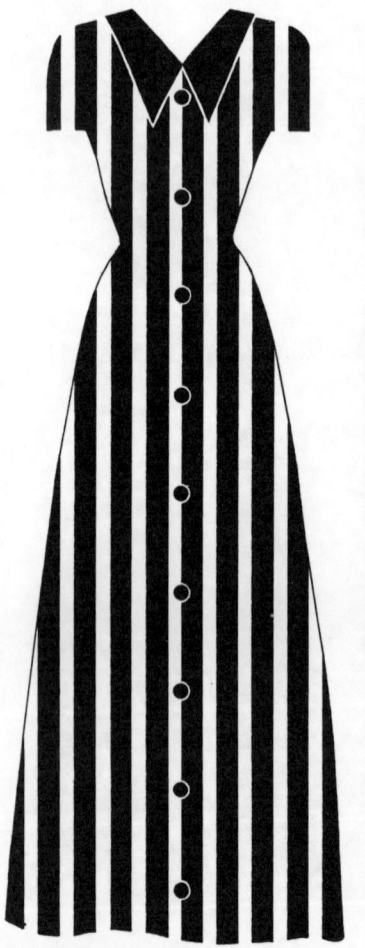

168. Two shapes to show the effect of VERTICAL and HORIZONTAL lines

PLANNING CLOTHES 281

placed pockets on a plain bodice and skirt can break up the width and will not add to the height. Spreading, gathered styles add width, but well-placed fullness can hide pronounced curves, e.g. bodice fullness can lessen the apparent size of a full bust. On the whole, rather straight styles, easy fitting and not very full, are best for plump girls.

Short thin girls will choose mainly long vertical lines to add to the height, and will counteract the slimming effect with fullness. Plainly cut clothes without much detail are best. There is not room for several pockets, plus yokes and a belt, for instance, as there is on a large figure. Immature figures are not improved in pencil line skirts and tightly fitting jackets. Skirts with a swing, bodices with fullness, are much more becoming to this type of figure.

Short plump girls will choose long vertical lines, particularly rejecting any conspicuous horizontal line which would make them look both shorter and fatter, e.g. a plain belt in material to match the dress may define the waistline without constituting a line across the figure, but a contrasting belt or conspicuously designed belt draws attention to the belt and in 'cutting the figure in half considerably reduces height. When patterned materials are chosen, the pattern should be small. Straight, but not skimpy styles suit these figures best.

Test your knowledge of basic fashion facts
See if you really understand these principles by doing the following pieces of work:
1. Paste six fashion cuttings in your notebook to illustrate styles which have mainly vertical lines.
2. Choose six which have mainly horizontal lines.
3. Choose a style which would be right for a tall slim girl. Make a sketch to show how it could be adapted for a short plump girl. Select two suitable materials for each design.
4. Choose six good styles for a slight, short thirteen-year-old.
5. Select pants and a top which would suit a tall and a short girl; suggest colours and fabrics.

How to team clothes and what to wear
Some girls are clever at choosing clothes which flatter them but often they do not have the fashion sense for teaming clothes together or knowing what clothes to wear for different occasions. Apart from underwear, leisure clothes, clothes for particular sports and games, clothes are

needed for the following activities:

CLOTHES FOR WORK

These should be right for the job being done. Sometimes special clothing is needed. For example, easily washable overalls or uniform are worn when food is handled or hygiene is particularly important—assistants in food shops, waitresses, dentists, chiropodists.

When such clothing is not required the choice of dress should generally be workmanlike and suitable for business. Glamorous styles are out of place and just as unsuitable as track suits and sun clothes would be. Naturally girls want to have fun choosing their clothes and enjoy wearing them at work. For some jobs there is often great freedom of choice and so long as a smart appearance is maintained girls may be allowed to wear quite extreme fashions. An important point is that the clothing must not impede the worker in any way from doing the job properly.

Co-ordinates are particularly useful for work because they allow maximum change and variety. A selection from skirts, trousers, pinafore dresses, smocks, blouses, tunics, pullovers, waistcoats, jackets (with and without sleeves), dresses, can be chosen to mix and match. Tops should be washable so that they can be changed frequently. Choice of style and fabric is legion—plain and prints, stretch knits and woven fabrics, wools, man-mades, mixtures and blends, all in light weight ranges.

A full length coat which co-ordinates in style and colour is a necessity. A good raincoat, a skin coat (or imitation skin) can be a wonderful investment for any season and occasion. Before buying suede or leather coats it is as well to find out what the cleaning costs are likely to be. Fur fabrics and piled fabrics made from man-made fibres bring the glamour of fur within reach of all. Fun furs, such as these, are used for coats, jackets and boleros.

In general fabrics for daily wear need to be sturdy and hardwearing, such as tweeds, worsteds, jersey, denim, corduroy, Crimplene, Courtelle and mixtures. Vibrant colour combinations can be planned, but light colours, unless in washable fabrics are not practical for constant use in towns.

Clothes for interviews in connection with work should be very carefully chosen because an applicant is judged by the impression she makes. Immaculate grooming is essential and a neat, clean-cut appearance presented. It is best not to wear anything too striking in which you might feel self-conscious and to avoid giving a fussy or overdressed appearance. Wear new clothes a few times beforehand. Tights or stockings should always be worn but a hat is a matter of preference. Go steadily on jewellery just as you should for work—not much of it and not jingly.

CLOTHES FOR SOCIAL AFFAIRS
There used to be accepted rules for these occasions and one knew exactly what to wear to a party or a theatre. These traditions have died and one is no longer tied by convention or restricted in choice. People wear mostly what they like according to their age and the custom of their circle of friends. It also depends on the transport being used. Travelling on a motor bike is more restricting for choice of outfit than travelling in a bus or car. Whatever the gathering or meeting—date, club social, party—it increases poise and confidence to have a change of outfit and therefore helps in making happy social contacts.

On really formal occasions when people dress to emphasize the importance, solemnity or special festivity of an occasion—guests should help create the required atmosphere by their dress.

CLOTHES FOR LEISURE TIME
Most people change out of their working clothes in the evenings and slip into something easy and comfortable for relaxing—trousers or skirt and top or perhaps a housecoat. It is important for the development of fashion sense that these clothes are not worn when they are grubby or torn. Bedroom dressing gowns and slippers should be kept for bedroom use, otherwise slovenly habits develop.

Clothes for outdoor activities must be comfortable and easily cleaned. For example. for walking one needs pants made of strong fabric with enough room for bending easily, or skirts with room to stride—for tennis, short dresses or shorts and top in easily washed drip-dry fabric. Stretch fabrics. both woven and knits. are ideal for active sports. Many kinds of gay and useful tops can be chosen for outdoor wear—heavy knits, anoraks, ski-jackets, boleros made in fluffy yarns. fur fabrics. bonded and quilted fabrics. which are warm and light.

ACCESSORIES
These are a very important part of a wardrobe and often the smart effect of an outfit depends on them. Fashion decides the shape and size of handbags, the colours and

style of shoes, gloves and hats and how many of them should match, contrast or tone with the outfit. They should always be chosen so that they can be worn with several main items in the wardrobe.

In choosing colours of accessories remember—
If all accessories match or tone with an outfit an effect of height is given.

If a bright colour or strong contrast is wanted it should be confined to one or two. More than this can spoil the dramatic effect.

It is generally safe to choose light to dark shades in the same colour family as the outfit plus a high light or splash of colour contrast with one accessory.

In choosing style of accessories remember—
Shoes or boots should be the right weight both for the clothing and the amount of wear they will get. For example, with trousers, comfortable, sturdy shoes are needed out of doors. For wear in wet weather the cut of the footwear should give protection.
Gloves, worn mainly for warmth, look best in plain colours and styles.
Handbags, shoulder and tote bags. Large ones are needed for everyday to hold all requirements without bulging. Leather lasts well but there are beautiful leather-look vinyls to be bought. The use of tapestry, upholstery fabrics, canvas and velveteen give scope for exciting decoration with beads, sequins, braids, textured yarns and raffias.
Hats or other head coverings are often essential in cold and wet weather. Simple pull-ons, turbans and berets look better than head scarves.
Belts give tremendous scope to the fashion planner. They can complete a colour scheme or make the focal point of an outfit. A great variety of fabrics, braids, ribbons and trimmings can be used to make them individual and unusual.
Scarves, plain or patterned should tone or contrast with an outfit. There are clever ways of wearing them.

Test your fashion flair by planning the following with cuttings from papers and/or sketches and cuttings of fabrics:
1. Outfit for working in a town office. Include one set of accessories.
2. Show how you would use *one* item from the above (1) to wear to an informal party in the evening after work.
3. Clothes to wear at a friend's eighteenth birthday party.

4. Clothes for your first big formal dinner and dance.
5. Outfit for a school holiday abroad, keeping costs as low as possible.
6. Clothes for any sport in which you are particularly interested. Include footwear.

Clothes for children

Many needlewomen particularly enjoy making clothes for babies and children. They are quick to make, money is saved and there is often scope for decorative handwork. There are, however, a number of other factors to be considered in the choice and construction of little clothes, if they are to be useful as well as pretty garments.

Fabrics for children's clothes

WARMTH is the first consideration because the tendency to cut down the number of garments worn makes it all the more necessary for clothes, especially underclothes, to keep in the body heat and keep out the cold. Wool, and mixtures with other fibres make the warmest fabrics, but brushed or quilted rayons and synthetics are warm, comfortable and inexpensive. Weave affects the warmth of fabrics so that a loosely constructed fabric such as cellular cotton is warmer than a plain woven cotton. Piled fabrics are warm, e.g. stretch towelling used for all-in-one night and day suits.

FLAMMABILITY is a very important consideration. Certain fabrics are highly flammable and should not be used unless they have been treated to reduce this quality—see p. 13. For further information on Fabrics see Chapter 2.

WASHABILITY AND STRENGTH. Any clothing in regular use must be made in a fabric which washes and wears well. Often these qualities go together. Cotton is splendid in both respects so denims, poplins, ginghams, seersuckers, towelling, corduroy, velveteen and knitted cottons are popular for play clothes, and lightweight and finer cottons for baby clothes, e.g. cotton prints for angel tops. Synthetics and man-mades and mixtures are much used because of their easy washing, quick drying and non-iron qualities. Some are much stronger than others so choose a strong one for garments which have hard wear. Wool and woollen mixtures wash well if correctly handled so it is important to learn the best way to launder fabrics.

DESIGNS. Simple designs are best which allow for growth in width and length. Deep hems, tucks, loosely fitting easy styles, are ways of dealing with the growth problem. Quickly done hand or machine decoration is effective or stick-on applique motifs give a smart, lively finish.

COLOUR is subject to fashion but an advantage of light colours is that they show when they need washing. This should be remembered when children are put into dark coloured dungarees and dresses. Printed fabrics should have small designs so that they are in proportion to small figures.

Choosing fabrics for making clothes at home

Success in dressmaking depends initially on fabric. Knowledge and experience play their part in helping to make the right choice, both for the style of the clothing and the skill of the home dressmaker. Much help is given in modern stores which display suitable paper patterns with their fabrics and drape them to simulate styles. Dress shows in the same departments are stimulating and helpful in showing how the fabrics look when made up. The following are considerations when choosing fabrics.

1. Weight and weave

The weight and weave of the fabric must be right for the style in mind.

STRAIGHT, TAILORED STYLES require firmly and closely woven weaves so that they will keep their shape. For example, for straight dresses, skirts and trousers a heavy cotton such as denim or needlecord would be a good choice where a cotton or Terylene lawn would not hang well and would cling to the body. When choosing wool for such styles worsteds are generally more satisfactory than woollens unless the woollens, e.g. flannel, tweeds, are very firmly woven. A common fault is to choose too thick a material for wool dresses and suits. One should ask whether the fabric is dress, suit or coat weight. Pleats are often designed on plain tailored clothes. Firm, rather thin materials pleat better than thick soft ones.

FULL AND DRAPED STYLES need fabrics which are light in

weight, have a soft handle and are not bulky when gathered or arranged in soft, unpressed pleats. Thin fabrics made with fine yarns are best, such as soft woollen crêpes, lawn, brushed rayon and nylon, silk and tricel foulards, tricots, Crimplene, jersey, to name a few.

Whatever thickness of yarn has been chosen by the manufacturer for the material, the weave to be used has much effect on the weight and drape of the fabric. Closely woven *plain weaves* result in firm, rather hard feeling fabrics which keep their shape. Loose, lacy weaves or knitted constructions make softer materials which stretch more easily. In some cases this kind of material must be backed with a firm one such as taffeta or poplin if it is to keep its shape.

Sometimes *diagonal weaves, such as twills,* are not suitable for styles with seams in certain directions, e.g. diagonal seaming. Paper patterns always give information in regard to this.

Many *fancy weaves* make a self pattern in the design which is not always immediately apparent when on the roll in the shop. It is as well to look out for this because the design would have to be properly placed for matching when planning the layout.

Pile or looped weaves give bulk to the fabric, so they are best for plain styles. Extra material is required in order to cut out all pattern pieces with the pile in one direction. The pile on fur fabrics should run down the garment and on velvets either up, to give a darker shade, or down to give a lighter shade.

Materials known as 'heavily textured' are chosen for the interesting surface which has been created by the yarn and weave. They should be used for simple styles which do not detract from the decorative appearance of the fabric.

2. Design

Plain materials and all-over prints with no 'up' or 'down' present no problems in making up. Designs which must be cut in one direction with each piece of pattern, take more material and the position of striking parts of the design must be considered in relation to their position on the body. The effect of large designs will be spoilt if the style has much seaming. Stripes and plaids are not suitable for such styles and need special treatment in cutting out (see PLAIDS, pp. 202–207). On the whole designed materials are better for styles with few seams, but on plain materials seaming shows up and is often accentuated with stitching or piping.

3. Washability
Clothing which is in daily use and is washed regularly must be made of fabrics which are not harmed by washing. This is an obvious point when buying fabrics for children's clothes and summer dresses but is sometimes forgotten when buying lightweight wool in light colours for tops and dresses. Washable wool should be bought for such clothing unless it is intended to send it to be dry-cleaned.

4. Price per metre
As a rough guide better quality fabrics cost more money and give better wear. It is wiser to buy a good quality of a cheaper type of fabric than a poor quality of a more expensive type. For example, a good quality wool and cotton mixture, such as Viyella, is preferable to a cheap woollen dress crêpe which may be the same price per metre; an Egyptian cotton for a shirt blouse is far better than a cheap spun silk. In both cases the clothing will look smarter and give much better wear. The width of the material must be noted in relation to the price per metre. Some woollens are only 90 cm wide for instance, instead of 140 cm, so they may not be as inexpensive as the price tag suggests at first glance.

5. Ease of handling in making up the fabric
Some materials are very much easier than others to cut out, stitch and press. Beginners are wise if they choose easy materials to work on and more advanced workers should know which are difficult so that they can choose styles suitable both to the fabric and their own skill. It may be sensible to choose a simpler style if it is known that the material will be difficult to work on in some respect.

A. EASY TO WORK ON
Fabrics which are easy to work on fall into two groups with the following qualities:
1. Those which are firm, neither heavy and coarse nor thin and limp, with plain even weaves where a thread can be pulled out easily. Fabrics which do not fray and will take and hold a crease when a turning is folded over. Plain coloured or small all-over designs which present no difficulties when cutting out.

Fabrics which fulfil these demands are cottons and linens

such as poplin, cotton with a linen finish, cotton prints, gingham, linen.

2. Those which are either softer or more stiffly textured than those in group 1, making them a little limp to handle such as cotton lawns, plissé, cambric, voile, spun or brushed rayons, or rather stiff, such as organdie, denim, sailcloth, glazed cottons. These materials are still quite firm to work on, do not fray but only take a light crease when folded by hand. Included in this group is any fabric from group 1, which has a one-way design or a weave which may make it more difficult to sew, e.g. a seerloop gingham.

B. SPECIAL CARE FABRICS

Fabrics which require special care in at least one respect are for those who have done some work on fabrics taken from 1 and 2, otherwise very simple styles must be chosen.

Fabrics which fray quickly at cut edges must be handled quickly and lightly. Extra turning allowance is needed when cutting out. When buying fabric, the condition of the cut edge on the roll will show whether the fraying is likely to be troublesome.

Fabrics which slip because the yarn is shiny causing a slippery surface. Unless care is taken the fabric moves out of position after it is placed flat for pinning on patterns and shifts during cutting and machining. Many materials fall into this group, such as spun silk, silk and rayon surahs, foulards, jerseys and tricots, satin and nylons.

Fabrics which require special stitching. On these fabrics it is not as easy to get a good machine stitch as it is on others. This applies especially to pure silk fabrics where the tension needs fine adjustment and stretch fabrics made wholly or partly from man-made fibres where special sewing threads and machine adjustment is necessary (see p. 31).

Fabrics which require special pressing. This applies particularly to woollens which must be damp pressed, and springy fabrics, often crease resistant, where it is difficult to press a sharp edge or flat seam, such as Terylene lawn, linen and Terylene, Courtelle, Crimplene. Velvet also requires special pressing so that the nap is not flattened or marked. Either the wrong side of the work must be pulled across an upturned iron as for pressing pin tucks (see p. 160) or with pile side down, pressed on a needle board.

C. FOR EXPERIENCED WORKERS

Fabrics which require skill and some experience to handle

them successfully, would be any which have more than one quality requiring special care such as tricel foulards, nylon chiffon, which both fray badly and are slippery to handle. Other fabrics which fall into this group are those requiring special knowledge or techniques such as heavy woollens and worsteds, fur, leather, stretch fabrics, laminates and foam backs. Certain designs can make a fabric, easy in itself to sew on, difficult because of the design, such as unbalanced plaids (see p. 202).

This rough classification should help in making a sensible choice to suit fabric to style and skill of the worker. Any new material can be tried out and classified into one of the groups and it would be useful to prepare a notebook into which is listed each material as it is used into one of the four groups, A1 or 2, B or C.

Tests of sewing quality

With quite a small amount of material experimental work can be done in the sewing room to see into which group to place it for ease of handling.

All or some of the following tests can be done and information recorded:

DETAILS OF FABRIC

Name, width, price, weave, general appearance and amount of fraying at edges.

1. *Crease resistance*

Hold some material crushed in the hand for a few moments. Release it and note amount of creasing and how long it takes to shed the creases.

2. *Washability and shrinkage*

Place a scrap of material (approximately 10 cm square) on a piece of paper and mark round it very accurately. Note weft and warp directions. Wash, dry and press the sample in the normal manner for its type. Replace on paper and note the amount of shrinkage both ways and the effect of washing on colour and texture.

3. *Slippage*

This quality affects style and fit.

Hold fabric as though to find the direction of the warp threads. Then pull and strain it over the fingers by drawing the elbows downwards. The amount of shifting of the threads will show whether there is likely to be much slippage in wear. Test the fabric both ways.

4. *Machine stitching*
Select suitable thread and needle for the fabric. Fold a rectangular piece of fabric in half and work rows of machining, trying out various stitch lengths. Decide the best length and note if any alteration in tension is required.

5. *Pressing*
Make two short open seams, one on the straight and another on the bias. Make a dart in another piece of fabric.

Press all these pieces of work on the wrong side experimenting with different heat settings both without and, where suitable, with, a damp cloth. Note results and whether seams show any signs of puckering. If they do then the machine stitch may not be quite right. Perhaps a finer needle or thread is needed.

6. *Fullness*
Gather a piece of the fabric with two rows of gathering along the weft, by hand or machine. Draw up and notice hang and bulkiness.

Make several pleats and press them on the wrong side. Note sharpness of crease and how long crease is retained.

GENERAL OBSERVATIONS ON THE FABRIC
Comment on ease of handling, springiness, bulkiness, whether material slips, whether any special difficulty was found.

RESULTS
Consider results and decide for what purposes the material is particularly suitable and into which group the fabric could be placed for ease of handling, groups A1 or 2, B or C.

24 Maintenance of clothing and household articles

Good grooming depends not only on keeping the hair, skin and nails clean and in good condition, but also in keeping all the clothes in the wardrobe fresh, neat, well pressed and in good repair. It is the frequent washing, mending and pressing which result in that certain finish which a well-groomed girl possesses. Therefore, clothes should be cared for regularly. Time spent in servicing clothes is well repaid too, because they last longer and keep something of their original smartness to the end.

To save wear on clothing

There are many things which can be done to clothing when it is new or lightly worn, which will improve the wear.

1. *Make fastenings secure* before they become loose and if they are not already sewn to double material, place a piece of tape behind a fastening on the wrong side, and sew through it, when stitching the fastening.

2. *Strengthen openings* at the base so that they cannot tear readily, e.g. work a bar just above the bottom of an opening.

3. *Neaten raw edges* of seams which are likely to fray. Some ready-made dresses are roughly finished inside and seam turnings are not neatened satisfactorily. In time, the turning may fray right down to the seam until it splits. Use a suitable method to neaten the edges.

4. *Sew hanging loops* on to jackets, coats and skirts (Chapter 17, p. 198) so they can be hung up properly if they are not put on to coat hangers.

5. *Keep clothing clean and free from dust* by regular washing or brushing. Remove spots and marks as soon as possible after they are noticed. Distilled water, cold or warm, will often remove marks without leaving a ring, if the fabric is one which will not be harmed with water. Alternatively, one of the commercial spot-removers can be used. Have

non-washable clothing cleaned regularly and press occasionally to keep edges crisp. Bagginess in the seat of skirts can usually be removed by damp pressing on the wrong side.

6. *Do not put off doing small repairs.* Loose fastenings, unstitched hems, split seams and trimmings which have parted from edges give a shabby appearance and can be quickly put right.

Mending

The general use of strong man-made fibre fabrics for clothing and household use has reduced the need for mending because these fabrics do not wear into thin and ragged places. There are, however, items which are sometimes preferred in less strong fabrics, such as children's and men's underwear and nightwear. Not everyone likes wearing nylon next to the skin and many people prefer cotton or linen sheets and pillowcases. Towels are made of cotton or linen. Housewives will find it saves money to do a certain amount of mending to delay the time for buying replacements and in order to keep members of the family well groomed and the home comfortable. Mending has become an occasional job, done as required and the aim is to do the mend quickly, strongly and neatly.

Methods of repair

As far as possible repair work is done by machine, and handwork only used when a machine is not available. Sewing machines can be employed in various ways—using straight stitching, zigzag machining or machine darning.

Machine darning or free motion machining used for darning and applying patches on any fabric, woven or knitted, is also used for modern machine embroidery. See p. 60.

General points for machine darning
1. Use mercerised thread No. 50 cotton for medium weight fabrics such as sheeting, and No. 80 to 90 for fine fabrics. Use a fine machine needle.
2. Stretch the work in an embroidery hoop so that the W.S. is on top where the R.S. would be normally for hand

embroidery. Stretch the fabric evenly to keep the grain straight and pull it very tight and taut.
3. Make the necessary adjustments to the machine. Sometimes a screw is turned to lower the feed, or there is a special cover to fit over it. Remove the machine foot. Some machines have a special machine darning foot.
4. Place the hoop under the needle with the flat side of the hoop down on the machine. Darns are worked on the inside of the hoop on the R.S.
5. Lower the presser bar; hold the top thread loosely and bring up the under thread so that both threads are on the surface and towards the back. Lower the needle into the work.
6. Hold work with fingers resting on the fabric inside the hoop and with thumbs and little fingers outside. Lean the arms, below the elbows, on the table edge in front of the machine to leave free movement for the wrists. Start machining and move the work steadily at an even pace, backwards and forwards or from side to side. Quick movement results in large stitches, slow movement in small ones. Diagram 169.

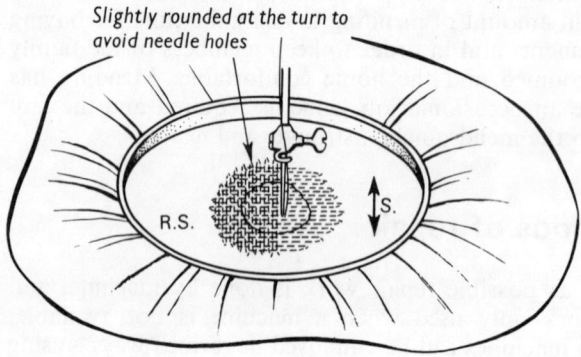

169. The arrangement of fabric in embroidery hoop for machine darning and the method of darning a hole

Hand darning
This consists of weaving strong threads into material to replace or strengthen worn threads. In order to obtain a satisfactory result, the following general points must be observed, whatever type of darn is being used.

General points for darning
(Read this before working each type of darn for the first time.)
1. Work all darns on the wrong side of the material if possible.

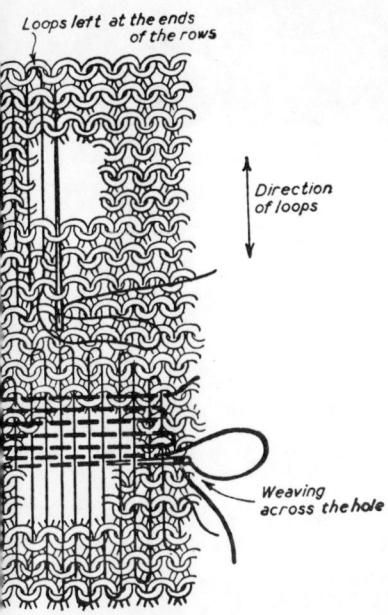

Stocking darn

2. Use a thread which matches the fabric in colour; is approximately the same thickness as the threads of the fabric and is the same kind of thread; e.g. fine wool for woollen underwear; soft cotton for knitted cotton jerseys. When it is practicable, draw a thread of the material from a seam turning or belt, to use for darning.

3. Use a darning needle, because its length makes it easier to handle for weaving. Choose a size to suit the thickness of the thread.

4. Spread the part to be darned over the front of the fingers, or if it is preferred, use a mushroom darner or a matchbox. Be careful, though, not to stretch jersey or hand-knitted fabric out of shape.

5. Hold the needle at the end, pointing it away from you as a poker is held. Move the wrist up and down in order to weave the needle over and under threads.

6. Shape the darn so that the stitches do not strain on any one set of threads in the fabric. The most usual shapes are round, diagonal, hexagonal or zigzag. Be sure that the darn covers the thin part near the hole, and is taken well into the strong part of the fabric.

7. Leave loops at the ends of the rows of stitches to allow for shrinkage and to prevent the darn drawing up at the edges.

DARNING A HOLE BY HAND. Diagram 170

Used for holes and thin places on all types of fabrics, garments and articles, e.g. socks, underwear, dresses, table-linen.

1. Begin darning at the left-hand side of a hole in the strong fabric and pass the needle over and under the loops or threads in the fabric. Work first in the direction of the loops in knitted fabrics and in the selvedge direction in woven fabrics. When the hole is reached, take the threads across the hole, putting the needle over and under the edge in alternate rows.

2. When darning and stranding are completed in one direction, turn the work and begin darning across the hole. Weave the needle over and under the strands, alternating the order in each row, so that an evenly woven piece of fabric is made to replace the worn part. Finish the darning a little above the edge of the hole and cut the thread close to the fabric. Notice how the arrangement of the darn thins out the stitching towards the edges so that it merges gradually into the strong material.

A THIN-PLACE DARN

Used when fabric has worn thin, but not worn into a hole, or in order to reinforce an area to prevent wear.

Work exactly as directed for a stocking darn except that:
1. there is no weaving to be done because there is no hole, and
2. the darning is done in one direction only across the thin area.

DARNING A HOLE BY MACHINE

1. Trim off ragged edges.
2. Work across the hole in the weft direction first spacing the rows a bare 3 mm apart and making the rows long enough to cover the worn part.
3. Turn the work and darn in the warp direction keeping the rows close together. Cover the first stitching, the hole and the whole of the worn part, making the completed darn a round shape. Diagram 169.

A thin piece of fabric can be placed behind the hole first for extra strength on large holes.

A HEDGE-TEAR DARN BY HAND. Diagram 171

Used on rents and tears caused by accidents. These tears are usually triangular, on the straight threads, and there is no worn area surrounding them. Consequently, the darn can be confined more closely to the rent, and can be kept a regular shape without straining the fabric. If the rent is large or stretched, draw the edges together with fishbone tacking, before beginning to darn.

1. Plan the darn to extend 6 mm to 1 cm beyond the rent, according to the type of fabric and the size of the rent; e.g. 6 mm on a small rent in a silk frock. 1 cm on a boy's trousers. Mark the position of the darn with pencil dots or pins. It is a great advantage to use a thread of the same material for this type of darn.
2. Begin darning beyond the end of the rent in the direction of the selvedge threads, so that when the slit is reached, the darning will cross the edges. See that the needle alternately picks up and passes over the edges, so that they are neatly woven into the darn. Continue darning until within 6 mm or 1 cm of the vertical rent and leave the end of the thread hanging.
3. Darn in a similar way from the other end of the rent and continue darning across the corner until the stitches are level with the first set of darning.
4. Re-thread the needle with the first thread and finish

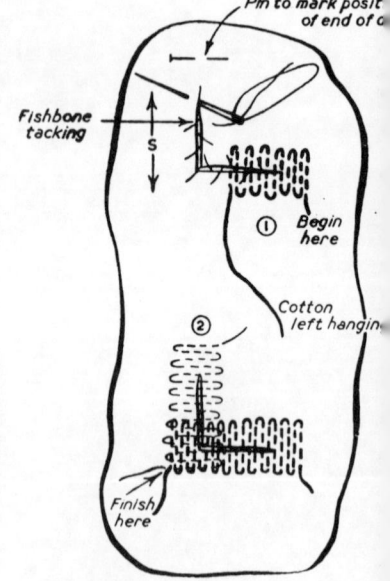

171. Hedge-tear darn

darning across the corner until the stitches are level with the second darn. This method of darning gives extra strength at the corner and helps to keep the fabric in shape.

HEDGE-TEAR DARN BY MACHINE

Follow directions for darning by hand but draw the edges together first with zigzag stitching. Shape the darn in the same way but do not make the corner double.

A CROSS-CUT DARN

Used as its name suggests, for cuts in material which are not with the straight grain. The mend is needed more frequently on table and house linen than on clothing. Darning by hand or machine must be done in the direction of the straight selvedge and weft threads, and this results in a shape which has caused the darn to be known as a 'fish-tail darn'.

A STRAIGHT-CUT DARN. Diagram 172

Used for any small cut or rent which falls along the straight threads and has no worn area surrounding the cut. It is particularly useful on table linen. The darn by hand or machine is worked on the right side.

1. Begin with a few rows of darning stitches beyond the end of the cut.
2. When the cut is reached, put the needle under the opposite edge and bring it out a few threads above the edge. Return the needle to the cut and put it under the lower edge and bring it out close to the first stitch. Continue working stitches alternately on each side of the cut until the slit is mended. Work a few darning stitches and end off.

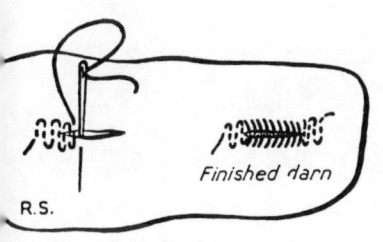

2. Straight-cut darn

To make an extra strong machined mend with straight or zigzag stitching the following method may be used:

Place a piece of material beneath the hole or thin place on the wrong side of the garment. The strengthening piece may be the same material as garment fabric or similar in weight. Take stitches right through the two layers of material. The darn will have to be done from the right side of the work in this case, and can be done *by hand*, or stitched to and fro with *a machine*. The machine method has great general use for such repairs as torn openings, gussets of knickers, tears from the corners of pockets on boys' trousers, split seams on rayon clothing, thin places on sheets and towels. Machine in rows 3 to 6 mm apart

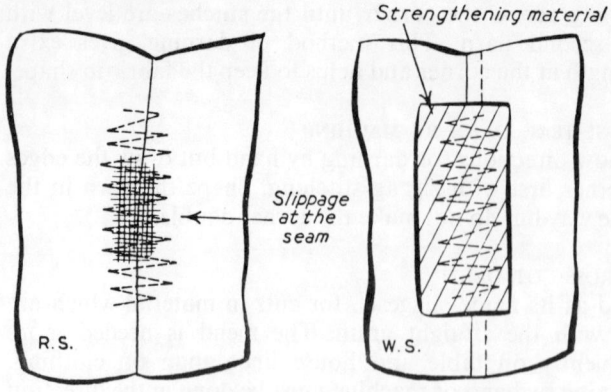

173. A strong machined darn

across the hole and worn part. Diagram 173. Cut the strengthening material away at the back, close to the machining. If necessary, rows of machining can be done across the first set, but usually one way is sufficient. When this method is used on jersey or elastic materials, e.g. on elastic suspender belts, stretch the material under the machine as it is stitched so that the stretch of the garment is not impaired unless a zigzag or stretch stitch is used.

Repairs by patching
When large areas are worn thin or are in holes the quickest way to mend is to replace the worn part with a strong piece of fabric. Patches must be flat, neat and strong. They can be done best by machine.

General points for patching
(Read these through before working each type of patch for the first time.)
1. Use material for patching which matches as nearly as possible in texture and colour the article to be patched. Make use of pockets, belts or cuttings from wide facings if there are no scraps of the same material available. If new material is used for patching, wash it first to prevent shrinkage after it is inserted into a garment.
2. Mark the size of the patch on the article with pins and plan it large enough to take in all the worn area around the hole, and so that it is fixed on to the strong part. Shape the patch to a square or rectangle because these edges are easier to handle than circular shapes.

3. Unpick seams or hems if they are near the hole, so that the patch can be taken into the seam or hem.
4. Place the patch on the article so that the selvedge threads of both are running in the same direction, and so that any pattern on the fabric matches. Always fix the patch on the article before cutting away the worn part.

MACHINE-DARNED PATCHES

Patches put in with machine darning are suitable for any fabric.
1. Cut patch the size required on the straight grain. Round off the corners.
2. Place patch flat in position on the R.S. and machine (straight stitch or zigzag) near the raw edge.
3. Cut away the worn part on the W.S. close to the machining.
4. Darn across the edge all round the patch taking the stitches a little deeper into the patch than into the main part to make sure that all raw edges are caught in.

STRAIGHT STITCH MACHINED PATCHES

Patches put in with straight machining or, if necessary, by hand are suitable for fine or medium weight fabrics.

(a) Household or calico patch used on sheets, pillow cases, towels, boys' pyjamas, shirts, overalls.
1. Cut the patch the size required on the straight grain, allowing 6 mm turnings on all edges. Fold the turnings on to the right side creasing the selvedge edges first.
2. Place the patch on to the wrong side, quite flat and so that grain lines are straight with those of the article. Tack near the fold and machine (or hem) it in position.
3. Cut away the worn part on the right side to within 1 cm of the machining. Snip a further 6 mm into each corner, turn under the raw edge and tack the fold flat. Machine (or oversew) in position. Diagrams 174 (i), (ii), (iii), (iv).

(b) Outergarment or print patch used on light and medium weight fabrics, e.g. cotton skirts, dresses, loose covers.
1. Cut patch to required size allowing 1 cm turnings. Fold turnings on to the W.S. Thickness can be cut away at corners if necessary.
2. Pin and tack patch on to R.S. of the garment, matching the grain and design, if any. Machine or oversew the patch in place.
3. Cut away the worn part on the W.S. leaving 1 cm turnings.

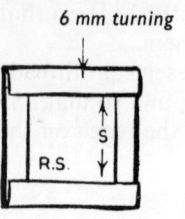

174 (i). Square of material prepared for a household patch

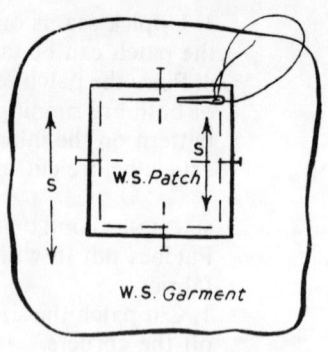

174 (ii). Patch fixed over the hole on W.S. garment ready for hemming or machining

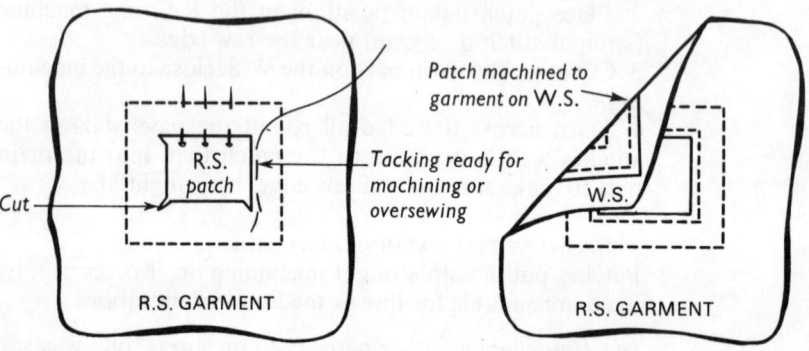

174 (iii). Preparing for the final stitching

174 (iv). A household patch

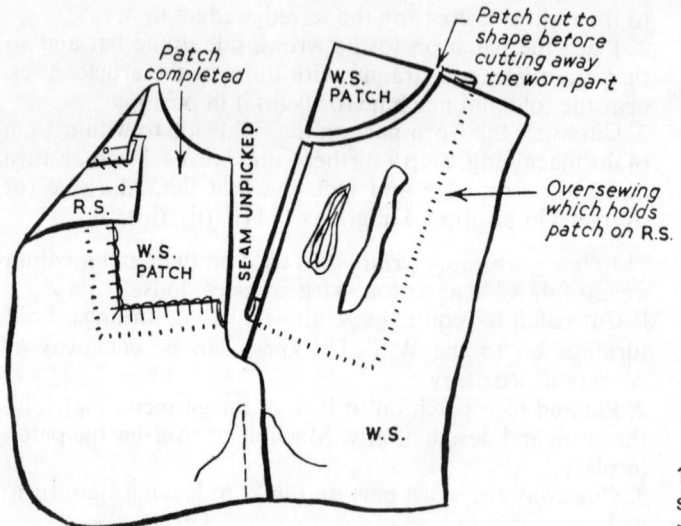

175. To show an outergarment patch stitched by hand and the treatment of patches which occur in seams

4. Loop stitch or overcast the raw edges together. Diagram 175.

TO INSERT A PATCH INTO A SEAM
Unpick the seam to well below where the patch will be fixed.

Prepare a rectangular or square patch. The shaping of the patch to the seam edge is done *after* the patch is stitched to the garment.

Fix and stitch the patch in position on the right or wrong side of the garment, according to the type of patch. Before cutting away the worn part on the garment, cut the patch the correct shape at the seam edges. Finish the patch (or patches if there is one on each side of the seam) and re-make the seam. Diagram 175.

GENERAL UTILITY PATCH
To be applied using 3-step or multiple zigzag machine stitching.

This patch is quickly done and can be used on many different fabrics. It is particularly useful on blankets, towels and machine knitted underclothes.

1. Cut the patch to the required size without turnings and round off the corners.
2. Place patch on to the R.S. of the article and tack it in place.
3. Work a full width multiple zigzag stitch (one with several stitches across the width) across the raw edge of the patch. Space stitches about 3 mm apart.
4. Cut away the worn part on the W.S. 1 cm away from the stitching.
5. Work a second row of stitching 3 to 6 mm away from the first row to cover the raw edges on the W.S.

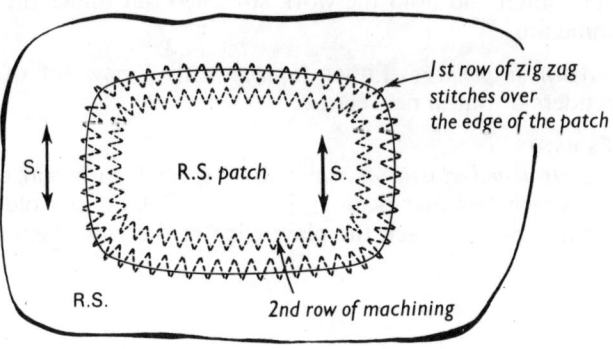

176. General utility patch

When a machine is not available fix the patch *by hand* with the following differences:

Place the patch on to the W.S. of the article and hold it in position with herringboning. On the right side, cut away the worn part leaving 1 cm turning and herringbone it down.

Quick invisible mending

Holes and tears caused by accident to outer clothing need to be mended as invisibly as possible. Sometimes careful darning with a thread of the fabric can be done or the rents can be closed or holes patched with commercial adhesive mending fabrics or tapes. Instructions given with the pack must be followed exactly. Generally, a piece of fabric is cut to the exact size of the hole and placed into it on the W.S. of the garment. This is covered with a piece of adhesive mending fabric which is ironed in place. This type of mending is not always suitable for washable fabrics.

Bonding web can be used for strengthening and holding small patches in place, see p. 237.

Quick methods for some essential repairs to clothing

BRAS

Worn fastenings and straps. Buy new parts to replace the hook and eye sections at the back. Unpick the old fastening strips and replace with new ones of the correct width. Replace the worn straps with new strong ribbon or buy a new set of straps with adjusters to replace the old ones.

GIRDLES AND PANTIE GIRDLES

(a) Worn elastic at edges and crotch. Tidy up and strengthen worn elastic with a strong machined mend, p. 297. Use a piece of thin, crosscut fabric on the W.S. and machine it with zigzag stitch to preserve the stretch. Otherwise use a straight stitch and hold the work stretched out under the machine foot.

(b) Worn suspenders. Either replace with a new set of suspenders or put in new elastic.

MEN'S PANTS

Worn, stretched elastic at waist. Buy special pant waist elastic which has one plain frilled edge. Cut off the old elastic and pin and tack the plain edge of the new elastic

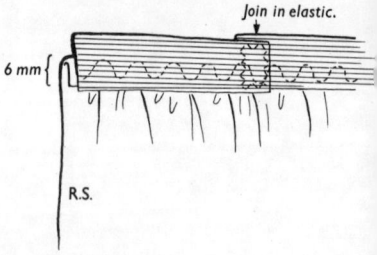

177. Elastic attached with a stretch stitch

evenly to the waist of the pants on the R.S. Machine with a zigzag stitch, if possible, holding the elastic stretched out under the machine foot, or use a stretch stitch. Diagram 177 shows how to stitch plain elastic.

Other repairs with elastic

Shirelastic yarn sold on spools is useful for repairing worn out elasticity on sections of a garment as well as in the construction of new clothing. If several rows are worked the effect will be as shown on p. 65 – shirring – except that as elastic thread is used it will stretch. It is best done on single fabric, e.g. at sleeve edges, waist edges of peasant skirts, frilled neck edges, ruffles. Whole sections of clothing can be shirred – swim suits, close fitting tops, yokes. *There are two ways of using elastic yarn*, one with a straight machine stitch and one with a zigzag stitch.

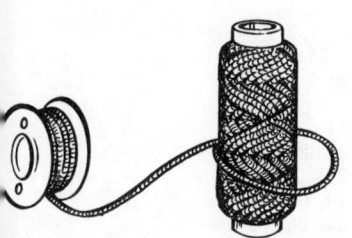

ELASTIC YARN FIXED WITH A STRAIGHT MACHINE STITCH
1. Wind elastic on bobbin by hand stretching elastic firmly and evenly. On some machines the elastic can be wound on the machine in the usual way.
2. Thread needle with sewing thread, matching colour to fabric. Set a long stitch and try out on fabric to be used. Tensions may need adjustment.
3. Machine with R.S. up on line to be gathered. If more than one row is to be worked, pull fabric flat in front of needle as stitching progresses. To finish, tie threads firmly together on W.S. and end off securely.

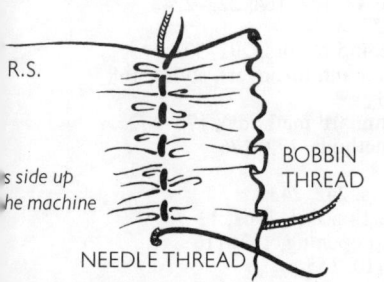

(i). Gathering with a straight stitch and elastic yarn   Wind elastic yarn by hand stretching it firmly and evenly

ELASTIC YARN, OR NARROW FLAT ELASTIC FIXED WITH A ZIGZAG STITCH
1. Set width of zigzag stitch so that it will cross elastic without piercing it, and length about 2 or 3.
2. Wind bobbin and thread up the machine with ordinary sewing thread in the usual way.
3. Sew or pin elastic firmly in place on W.S. at one end on line to be gathered. Lay elastic along this line and zigzag stitch across the elastic, stretching it in front of the needle. Adjust elastic to length required and sew end firmly in position. On circular parts e.g. wrists, join the two ends together.

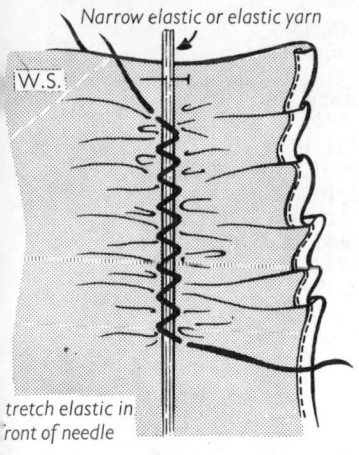

(ii). Gathering with a zigzag stitch and flat elastic

Index

Abbreviations, xii
Accessories, 283, 284
—, dress, 283, 284
—, machine, 59–61
Accordian pleats, 66
Acetate, 7, 21, 30, 156, 158
Acrilan, 8, 26, 156, 157, 158
Acrylic fibres, 8, 25
Alcozip, 224
Anoraks, 163
Anti-stat fabric, 24
Arnel, 22
Assembling garments, 49, 50, 224
Automatic machines, 51–53, 55, 56

Balance points (*see* Notches)
Ball point needles, 30, 31, 61, 200
Bands, to cut pattern, 245
—, to interline, 187
—, to make, 176, 187, 188
—, to attach, 178, 187–189
Banlon, 8
Bar tacks, 220
Bars, worked, 118, 143, 180
—, metal, 143
Belts, buckled, 196
—, tie, 196
—, carriers 197, 198
Binding, general information, 103
—, bias, (*see also* Crossway), 6
—, straight, 95, 107, 117, 118
—, seams, 74
—, hems, 95
Blanket stitch (loop stitch), 147, 149, 150
Blended yarns, 9
Block patterns, bodice, 238–250, 263–273
— —, dress, 271–273
— —, skirt, 273
— —, sleeve, 266–268
— —, magyar styles, 246–248
— —, knickers, 268–271
Bonding, 9, 12, 13
Bonding web, 237
Bonded interfacing, 208
Bound opening, 121–123
Box pleats, 66, 219
Bri-nylon, 8, 22, 24
Brushed fabrics, 26, 31, 158, 285
Budgeting, 276, 277
Bulked yarn, 8
Buttonhole threads, 6, 132
Buttonholes, 129–137
—, bound, 135–137

—, buttonhole stitch, 147
—, dressmakers', 134
—, machine made, 235–236
—, worked, 130–134
Buttons, 137, 138
—, and loops, 138, 139

Cardigans, 163
Casings, 68, 190
Cellular cotton, 16, 285
Cellulose fibres, 7, 20
Celon, 8, 23, 24
Chain stitch, 150, 151
Checks, (*see* Plaids), 202, 207
Children's clothes, 285–286
— —, construction of, 162–164
—, —, block patterns, 268–271
Circular knits, 12
Circular skirts, 249, 250
Clothes, choice, 276–285
—, construction, 49, 162–164, 223–224
—, quality of, 277
—, maintenance and repairs, 292–303
Collars (Peter Pan and turnover), styles, 168
—, to make, 168
—, to attach (standard methods), 170–172
—, alternative methods, 172–176
—, fitting, 258
—, to cut patterns, 242, 243
Consumer Protection Act, 1961, 13
Continuous wrap opening, 113–116
Cording stitch, 110, 155
Corduroy, 158
Correcting after fitting, 261, 262
Cotton fabric, 15, 16, 156, 285, 288
—, thread, 5, 6, 30
Courtelle, 8, 26, 31
Crease resistant finish, 13
Crimplene, 8, 25, 156, 157
Crimped yarn, 9
Crossway strips, cutting, 45
— —, joining, 103, 104
— — for binding, 103–107
— — for facings, 98, 102–104, 190
— — for piping, 82, 107
— — for collars and cuffs, 170, 171, 177
Cuffs (turned back and band), to make, 176
—, to attach, 176–178
—, to cut patterns, 245
Cutting out, 41–44, 200–207
— —, to grain material, 12, 41
— — crossway strips, 45

Dacron, 8, 25
Darelle, 20
Darning, by hand and machine, 293–298

304

Darts, to make, 62, 63
—, to press, 159
—, in patterns, 243, 244, 265
—, fitting, 255
Decorative stitches, 149–155
— edges, 107–110
Denier, 7
Dior pleat (flap), 219
Dicel, 21
Double stitched seams, 79–82
Dralon, 8, 26
Drawstring casing, (*see* Casings)
Dress stand, 220
Dresses, construction, 164
—, choice, 278–282, 286–288
Dressing gowns, 162
Dressmakers' carbon paper, 57, 58
Durable press, 14
Durafil, 20
Dynel, 27

Easing, 65, 102, 181, 217
Easy-Care finish, 13
Edge finishes, general points, 88
— —, hems, 88–96
— —, facings, 96–103
— —, bindings, 103–107
— —, pipings, 107, 108
— —, decorative finishes, 108–110, 152–155
Edge-stitched hems, 92, 154
— — seams, 73, 74
Elastic yarn, 303
Elasticized edges, 68, 303
Elastofibres, 8, 27
Embroidery stitches, 160–166
Enkalon, 18, 23
Equipment for sewing, 3–6
— for pressing, 2
Evlan, 20
Eyelet holes, 140, 197

Fabrics, general information, 6–31, 200–202, 286–291
—, patterned fabric, 14
—, non-woven, 12, 28, 207, 208
—, weaves, 9–11
—, mixtures, 11
—, true cross of, 45
—, kinds and qualities, 6–28, 30, 31, 200–202
—, quantities for clothing, 162–164
—, slippage of, 30, 290
—, fraying edges of, 45, 74
—, requiring special handling, 30, 31, 200–207
—, choice for dressmaking, 286–290
—, tests for sewing qualities, 290, 291
—, choice for children's clothing, 285, 286
—, choice for men, 229

—, finishes, 13, 14
—, to press, 156, 157, 158, 289
Fabric care labelling, 274
Faced slit opening, 119–121
Facings, general information, 96, 97
—, to cut patterns for, 97, 240, 241
—, shaped, 100, 101, 173–174, 227
—, straight, 97, 99
—, on corners and curves, 100, 101, 103
Faggotting stitch, 154
False hems (*see* Facings), 97, 180
Fashion tests, 281, 284
Fastenings, choice, 129, 162–164, 235
—, to strengthen, 118, 292
—, worked buttonholes, 130–134
—, bound buttonholes, 135–137
—, machine made, 236
—, loops, 138, 212–214
—, eyelet holes, 139, 140, 197
—, tie strings, 139–141
—, hooks, eyes and bars, 141, 142, 143
—, Velcro, 143
—, press studs, 141
Fibre content labelling, 166
Fibres, natural vegetable, 7, 15, 16, 17
—, natural animal, 7, 17–19
—, man-made from vegetable sources, 7, 20–22
—, man-made from mineral sources, 7, 8, 22–28
—, staple, 8, 23
—, filament, 8, 9, 12, 23
Figure, to measure, 34–36, 222, 229, 230
—, types and sizes, 165
—, styles to suit, 280, 281
Fishbone tacking, 145, 296
Fitting, general points, 250–252
—, first, 251, 252
—, second, 251, 258
—, preparation for, 49, 50, 250, 260
—, faults and alterations, 252–260
—, trousers, 260
—, men and boys' 237
—, corrections, 261, 262
Fitting lines, 32, 33
Flammability of clothing, 13, 285
Flares, 250
Flat method of construction, 49, 50
Flax, 7, 16
Fly-flaps, 124, 128, 131, 232
Foam backed fabrics, 28, 201, 290
Fullness, arrangement in, darts, 62, 63, 159, 243, 244, 265, 266
—, — —, tucks, 63, 64, 160
—, — —, gathers, 64, 65
—, — —, easing, 65, 102, 181, 217
—, — —, pleats, 66–68, 159, 248
—, setting in, 65, 68, 177, 178, 182
—, in patterns, 36, 37, 243, 244, 248, 249
—, shrinking, 161

305

—, to fit, 255, 256
Gathers, to work, 64, 65
—, setting in to seams, 68, 76, 86
—, setting in to bands, 176, 177, 187, 188, 189
—, in pattern cutting, 244
Glassfibre fabrics, 27, 202
Gores, 88, 248, 249
Grain of material, 12, 33, 41
— indicators, 33, 42, 205
— in fitting, 252–254, 259–260
Gussets, 184–186

Haberdashery, 5, 6, 29, 30
Hanging loops, 198
Helanca, 9
Hem openings, choice, 112, 162–164
— —, to make, 112, 180
Hemming, plain, 147, 148
—, slip or invisible, 96, 148
Hemp, 17
Hems, 88–96
—, levelling, 93, 94, 260
—, curved, 92, 94, 95, 96
—, corners in, 90, 91
—, methods of finishing, 89, 93, 95, 96, 109
Hemstitching, 152, 153
—, mock, 153, 154
Herringbone stitch, 148, 149
Hessian, 17
Hooks, eyes and bars, 142, 143
Housecoats, 162

Interfacing (Interlining), 207
—, kinds, 207
—, choice, 208
—, cutting and using, 209–212
—, joining, 209
Inverted pleats, 66
Invisible hemming (slip), 96, 148
Iron-on interfacings (fusible), 208, 211

Jackets, 163, 216, 217
Jerkins, 163
Jersey, 12, 200, 289
Joins in lace, 110
— in crossway strips, 103, 104
— in stitches, 114, 146, 148, 150, 151
Jute, 17

Knickers, to alter patterns, 38, 39
—, to cut patterns, 268–271
—, construction, 50, 162
—, waist and leg finishes, 190
—, mending, 293, 294, 298, 301–303
Knife pleats, 66
Knitted fabric, 12

Lace, choice, 108, 109
—, edgings, 109, 110
—, joins, 110
Laminates, 28, 201, 290
Lansil, 22
Lancola, 22
Lay-out of patterns, 42–44, 205–207
Linen fabric, 16, 150
Linings, 24
—, fabrics, 214
—, cutting and making, 215
—, inserting 215, 216
—, for jackets, 216, 217
—, for dresses, 218
—, for skirts, 218, 219, 220
—, for yokes, 231
Lirelle, 25
Loops, worked, 138–140
—, fabric, 197, 198
—, tape, 198
—, rouleau, 74, 212, 213, 214
Loop stitch (blanket stitch), 74, 147, 148, 149
Lurex, 27
Lycra, 8, 27

Machine attachments, 59, 60, 61
—, manual control, 52, 236
—, to machine over pins, 59
—, outline machining, 199
—, to machine straight, 57
Machine darning, 296
Magyar and Raglan styles, 193, 194, 232–234
Measurements, to take, 34–36, 222, 229, 230
Mending, to delay, 292, 293
—, darning by hand and machine, 293–298
—, patching, 298–302
—, quick and invisible methods, 301–302
Menswear, 221–224, 229–237
—, choosing, 229
—, making, 230
—, fitting, 237, 260, 261
Mercerised fabric, 16
Milium, 14
Mitin, 13
Mitred corner, 91
Mixture fabrics, 11
Modified rayons, 20
Moth-proofing, 13
Mock hemstitch, 153, 154
Modacrylic fibres, 26, 27
Mounting a skirt, on a band, 187–189
—, to a top, 188–190
Multiple zigzag, 110, 301

Napped fabrics, 158
Necklines, to cut patterns for, 239, 240, 241
—, neck finishes (*see* Edge finishes and Collars)

Needles, kinds, 4, 29
—, selection of, 29, 30, 31, 200–202, 291
Nightdresses, 172
Non-woven fabrics, 12, 28, 207, 208
Notches, 33, 47, 48, 205, 249
Nylin, 17
Nylon, 8, 22, 23, 156, 157

Open seams, 70–74, 159
Openings, general points, 111–112
—, choice for garments, 162–164
—, hem openings, 111–112
—, continuous wrap, 113–116
—, skirt placket, 116–119
—, faced slit, 119–121, 241
—, bound, 121–123
—, with loops, 212–214
—, fly-front, 232
—, to strengthen, 115, 118, 234, 292
Order of making garments, 49, 50, 224
Orlon, 8, 26, 156, 157
Overlaid seam, 74–77
Overlap and underlap, 112
Overcasting stitch, 146
— edges, 72, 96
—, machining and, 73
Oversewing, 146

Paper fabrics, 12, 28
Paris binding, 6, 95, 118
Patterns, to select, 32, 40, 165, 229
—, symbols, 32, 33
—, to prepare for use, 33
—, to measure, 36, 222, 230
—, alterations to, 34
—, to pin up, 40
—, pattern lines, 32, 39, 46, 262
—, lay-outs for, 43, 44, 205
Pattern cutting, block patterns, 238, 246–254, 263–273
— —, bodices, 239–244, 246–248
— —, facings, 240, 241
— —, collars, 242, 243
— —, cuffs, 245
— —, sleeves, 232–234, 244, 246–248
— —, skirts, 249, 250
— —, fullness in patterns, 243, 244
Patterned fabric, 14
Permanent Sheen finish, 13
Permanent Stiffening finish, 14
Permanent Pleating, 14, 23, 66
Perforation marks, 47, 48
Perlon, 24
Pile, 11, 43, 158, 287
Pin stitch or single punch stitch, 153
Pin tucks, 63, 160

Pinking shears, 4, 45
—, edges, 72, 175, 227
Piping, flat and corded, 82
—, seams, 83, 84
—, edges, 108
—, joins, 85, 86
—, angles, 84, 85
—, curves, 84
Plackets (*see* Openings)
Plaids, even and uneven, 202–204
—, planning pattern lays, 205–207
Plain seam, 70, 178, 182, 189
Pleats, kinds, 66, 67
—, to make, 67, 68
—, to press, 159
—, seams in, 68
—, to cut, 248
Ply-yarns, 9
Pockets, patch, 191
—, bound, 193, 194
—, in seam, 192
—, welt, 194, 195
Polyester fibres, 8, 24–27
Polymers, 22, 24, 25
Polymide fibres, 8, 22–24
Press studs, 141, 142, 235
Pressing equipment, 3
—, general points, 156
—, to damp press, 157
—, types of fabrics, 157, 158, 289, 291
—, to remove shine, 161
—, directions for, 159, 161
—, to shrink, 161
Proban, 13
Prussian binding, (*see* Paris)
Puffed sleeves, 244
P.V.C., 27, 201
Pyjamas, construction, 162
—, to alter patterns, 38, 39, 40, 222

Rayon, *See* Viscose
—, to press.
Regenerated fibres, 7, 20
Rever necks, to cut patterns for, 241, 243
— —, to make, 169, 170, 172–175
Ribbon binding, (*see* Straight binding)
Roller presser foot, 61, 201
Rouleau, to make, 212
—, for edges, 154
—, for openings, 213, 214
Round method of construction, 49
Running stitch, 145
Rhonel, 22

Sarille, 20
Seams, choice, 30, 31, 69, 162–164, 200, 201

Seams (continued)
—, general points, 69, 70, 86, 87
—, open or plain, 70–74
—, overlaid, 74–77, 186
—, french, 31, 77–79
—, double stitched, 31, 79–82
—, piped, 82–86
—, imitation machined fell, 162, 163
—, preparation for inserting openings, 114, 117, 180
—, strengthening angled, 76, 184, 185
—, strengthening curved, 184, 224
—, at waist, 188, 189
—, in pleats, 68
—, curves and angles in, 71, 75, 76, 77, 184, 185
—, grading (layering), 87, 212
—, junctions in, 87
—, neatening, 72–74
—, to press, 159
Selvedge or warp, 9, 10, 11
Sequence of work, 49, 50, 223
Sewing machines, 51–61
— —, choice, 51
— —, use, 55–57
— —, needles, 29, 30, 54, 200–203
— —, tensions, 31, 54, 55
— —, stitch, 30, 54, 55
— —, swing needle, 51–53
— —, stretch stitches, 200
Sewing threads, 5, 29, 30, 31, 132, 145, 201, 202
Shaped facings (*see* Facings)
Shears and scissors, 4, 44
Shirring, 65, 303
Shorts (*see* Skirts)
Shrink resistant finish, 13
Side openings, 113–119, 123, 126, 127, 224
Silk, 7, 19, 156
Skirts and shorts, to alter patterns, 38, 39
— — —, construction, 163
— — —, casings, 190
— — —, waist bands, 187–189
— — —, hem edges, 94–96, 227
Skirt linings, 218–220
Sleeves, to alter patterns, 38, 39, 40
—, openings for, 163, 179, 180
—, pairing, 179
—, to make, 179–181
—, setting in, 181–183
—, to fit, 258, 259, 260
—, to press, 160
—, to cut patterns for, 244–248
—, block patterns, 238, 266–268
Slippage, 30, 290
Slips, 163
Slip tucking, 145, 207
Spanzelle, 8, 27
Static electricity, 24

Stay, 118, 184, 207
Stay-stitching, 77
Stitches, general points, 144
—, tacking, 144, 145
—, basting, 68, 145
—, catch stitch, 210
—, thread marking, 47, 48
—, running, 63, 145
—, backstitch, 145
—, oversewing, 91, 101, 146
—, overcasting, 72, 146
—, loop stitch or blanket stitch, 147, 149
—, buttonhole stitch, 147
—, hemming, 112, 147
—, hand-picking, 155
—, slip-hemming, 148
—, slip-stitch, 96, 148
—, saddle, 155
—, invisible hemming, 148
—, herringbone, 148, 149
—, chain, 150, 151
—, stem, 151, 152
—, hemstitching, 152, 153
—, pin stitch, 163
—, faggotting, 154
—, cording, 155
Stitch ripper, 61
Straight facings, (*see* Facings)
Straps, 197, 198, 212
Strengthening corners, 77, 184, 185
—, seams, 184, 224
Stretch fabrics, 12, 288, 290
Stripes, 202, 207
Styles, 280–284, 286–287
Sunray pleats, 66
Swing needle machines, 51, 53
Synthetic fabrics, 23–28, 31, 201, 289
Synthetic fibres, 7, 8, 22, 24, 25, 26, 27

Tacking, even tacking, 70, 145
—, long and short, 90, 145
—, basting, 68, 145
—, tailors' tacks, 47, 48, 262
—, slip tacking, 145, 207
—, fish bone, 171, 296
—, tracing, 48
—, order of tacking up, 49, 50, 223
Tailored corner, 90
Tailors' hem, 96
Tape, 6
—, loops, 198, 199
Taslan, 8
Tebilized fabric, 13
Teflon presser foot, 31, 61, 200
Teklan, 27
Tests for sewing qualities, 290, 291

Terylene, 8, 24, 31, 156, 157, 289
Textured fabrics, 14, 279, 287
Thread for tacking, 6, 144
—, for sewing, 5, 29, 145
—, for machining, 5, 29, 30, 31, 200–202
—, for mending, 6, 293
—, for buttonholes, 6, 132
Thread marking, 47, 48
Trevira, 8, 12, 24
Trousers, 163, 221
—, style and fabric, 221
—, patterns, 38, 222
—, construction, 163, 223, 224, 226, 227
—, fitting, 260, 261
Tie-strings, 141, 196
Tools, 3–5, 159, and back endpaper
Triacetate fibres, 22, 30
Tricel, 22, 30, 156, 157
Tricelon, 9
True cross of fabric, 45
Tucks, to make, 63, 64
—, to press, 160
Turn-ups, 227
Turned back cuffs (see Cuffs)
Turning allowances, 31, 33, 44, 70
— —, grading, 212
— —, to crease, 89
— —, stitched to facings, 101
Turnover collars (see Collars)

Ultron, 22
Underarm gussets, 184, 185, 186
Underlining, 211, 212
Understitching, 101, 102
Unit method of construction, 49

Velcro, 6, 143
Velvet, 11, 158, 289
Velveteen, 11, 158
Vilene, 12, 208
Vincel, 20
Vinyls, 27

Viscose, 7, 20, 30, 156, 157, 158
Vyrene, 27

Waist band, 44, 187–189
Waist seam, 188, 189, 255
Waist facing, 227
Warp, 9, 10, 11
Waterproofing, 13
Water repellent finish, 13
Weaves, 9–11, 286, 287
Weft or woof, 10, 11
Wool, 7, 17–19
Woollens and worsted, qualities, 17–19
— — —, to press, 156, 157
Woolmark, 18
Worked bar, 118, 143, 190
Wrap, openings with, 112–119
—, openings without, 119–123
—, at neckline, 169, 170
Wrist band, 176, 178, 245

Yarns, kinds of, 8
—, staple, 8, 31, 36
—, stretch, 9
—, filament, 8, 9, 12, 35, 37
—, treatment in manufacture, 8, 9
Yokes, to cut pattern, 244
—, single, 68
—, lined, 231
—, placing for cutting out, 44
—, making, 231

Zigzag machines, 51–53
Zigzag machining, 52, 53, 72, 301
Zip fasteners, 123–128, 224–226, 232–235
— —, inserted into a slit, 124, 125
— —, inserted into a seam, 126–129
— —, semi-concealed, 126, 127
— —, concealed, 127, 128
— —, invisible, 224–226
— —, fly-front, 232–235
Zipper (piping) foot, 59, 95